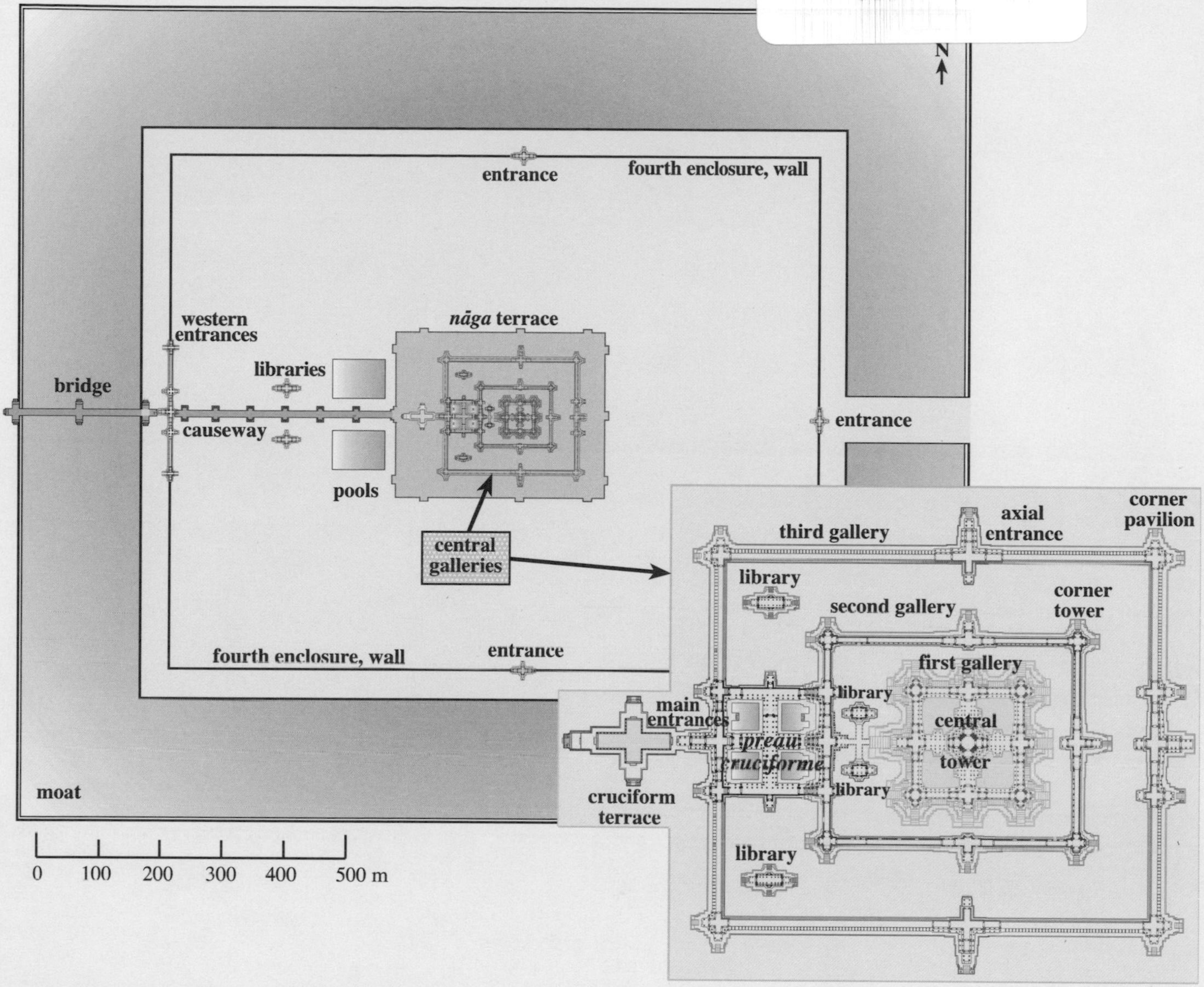

Angkor Wat

Approaches and Central Galleries

ANGKOR WAT

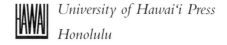

ANGKOR WAT

Time, Space, and Kingship

Eleanor Mannikka

University of Hawai'i Press
Honolulu

Printed in the United States of America

01 00 99 98 97 96 5 4 3 2 1

Library of Congress Cataloging-in-Publication Data
Mannikka, Eleanor.
Angkor Wat : time, space, and kingship / Eleanor Mannikka.
p. cm.
Includes bibliographical references and index.
ISBN 0–8248–1720–6 (alk. paper)
1. Angkor Wat (Angkor) 2. Temples, Buddhist—Cambodia—Angkor (Extinct city) 3. Astronomy, Khmer. 4. Angkor (Extinct city)—Buildings, structures, etc. I. Title.
DS554.98.A5M36 1996
959.6—dc20 96–4368
CIP

University of Hawai'i Press books are printed on acid-free paper and meet the guidelines for permanence and durability of the Council on Library Resources

Frontispiece photo by Yves Coffin

Book design by Paula Newcomb

CONTENTS

PREFACE

When I first saw the precise measurements of Angkor Wat's central galleries in print in 1972, I was astonished to find that the north and south sides of the third gallery were exactly 202.14 m each. That discovery set off a search for the meaning behind the extraordinary accuracy, not only in that measurement, but in similar measurements along the circumferences and axes. At the time I had no idea this research would take me to documents in Paris and elsewhere in France, to the National Museum in Phnom Penh, and, finally, to Angkor itself.

During the genocidal Khmer Rouge regime (April 1975–January 1979), as well as the subsequent U.S.-led trade (and diplomatic) embargo throughout the 1980s and early 1990s, Americans were officially discouraged from travel to Cambodia. But Cambodia's situation was to improve. U.S. recognition, as well as that of most other countries, came after the first U.N.-supervised elections in 1993. Long before that, however, I was encouraged to visit Angkor through discussions at a UNESCO meeting held in Bangkok in June 1990. I made my first visit in late December of that year. Eighteen years had gone by since my curiosity was aroused by the uncanny accuracy of Angkor Wat's measurements.

By this time I had deciphered all of the measurement systems explained in this book, except for the circumference of the upper elevation. That was the last major pattern to be unraveled. But to investigate the two solstice alignments on the western entrance bridge, the solstice phenomena at the center of the *preau cruciforme,* and all of the solstice interactions with the bas-reliefs, I had to be at the site on the solstice days. Those opportunities arose between 1991 and 1994.

It had taken me two years to find the key to several measurements on the western entrance bridge, and two years also to decode and ascertain the planetary sequence in the northwest corner pavilion. A timely suggestion of the late Albert Le Bonheur, who was the curator of Southeast Asian art at the Musée Guimet in Paris, completed the correct identification of the planetary deities. After more than a year of research I finally realized there was a unique module in the second gallery. Trying to decipher the logic behind the measurement systems of the temple was like chopping through dense jungle growth. Preconceived assumptions were fairly thick and pernicious. But when pathways were revealed, they were clear, straight, and well defined. It simply was hard to reach them.

When I began this work, no one in the scholarly world had suggested a temple could be constructed based on measurements that conveyed any particular meaning, much less solar, lunar, and historical meaning—at least not in Asia. No one had explored the role of astronomy in the narrative reliefs of an Asian temple. No one had discovered solar and lunar alignments within a temple compound. There may have been interest, but scholars were engaged in other pursuits. Astronomers had researched Native American remains, but those cultures were very different from the Brahmanical, Buddhist, and ancestral focus of the Khmers. In other words, there was no precedent to hint at what lay ahead in this cultural context. Worse yet, in 1972 my knowledge of astronomy was limited to the shape of the Big Dipper.

When I started to investigate Angkor Wat I was surprised at how little we knew about it. There was debate, for example, as to why it faced west. There was uncertainty about its main deity. And although the bas-reliefs in the third gallery were identified long ago, no one seemed to know whether they were sequential or had any particular organization at all. Other than what was visible to the naked eye or obtained from inscriptions, the temple was a blank. It seemed unthinkable that one of the world's greatest monuments could be so anonymous. I set forth to remedy the situation somewhat in the manner of Don Quixote, not stopping to consider that if 75 years of professional French efforts had not yielded better results, what could I hope to achieve as an obvious neophyte—a neophyte, moreover, without any hope of traveling to Angkor? If I had known any better, I would have put my lance away.

In the early 1960s, Guy Nafilyan, then of the École française d'Extrême-Orient, and a team of surveyors spent two years recording the measurements of Angkor Wat. When the subsequent drawings were published, the measurements of the temple were made available to the public. But it was not until I changed the measurements from meters to cubits that the unusual numerical totals appeared. The reasons for the astounding accuracy were soon clear: the measurements of the temple recorded data, fixed solar and lunar alignments, defined pathways into and out of sanctuaries, and put segments of the temple in precise association with rays of sunlight during the equinox and solstice days. Years of work were rewarded with some of the most fascinating discoveries one could hope to make.

I found that the temple is composed of thematic sets that were revealed number by number, measurement by measurement, but were not apparent before all of the individual parts came to light. For example, each pair of libraries at Angkor Wat has a different theme as the focus of its set of measurements. It turned out that the measurements of each gallery focused on its own themes as well. Based on the coincidence of identical themes, each set of libraries seemed to be joined to only one gallery.

Continuing with the example of the libraries, all six are a unique architectural group. Thus it was not surprising to find that one particular measurement tied the libraries together as a nondifferentiated whole. Finally, the measurements of each library complemented those of its twin counterpart. A pair is divided to the north and south of the main axis of Angkor Wat, and inscriptions indicated that each pair may have alternated in use between the waxing and waning moon. Their complementary or reciprocal measurements agreed with their physical placement and possible alternation in use. Indeed, three different thematic sets applied to the libraries: their shared iconography with one gallery alone, their meaning as one group, and their lunar-related alternating use. Such thematic sets are found throughout the temple. In fact, they define how the temple functioned and what each level or architectural grouping meant.

Measurements, too, occur in systems. They are divided (in a broad overview) between axes and circumference lengths, on the one hand, and ritual pathways into the temple on the other. There are outer axes, which measure the full length and breadth of a structure, and inner axes that measure sanctuary spaces. Circumference measurements define the meaning of the six successive rectangles in the ground plan of the temple, from the outer border of the moat to the topmost gallery. Moreover, the same comprehensive ritual circuit was repeated systematically in each gallery, and essentially the same entrance pathway was repeated in the four sequential western entrances that lead up to the central tower.

The content of the measurement systems and thematic sets is not only coherent and logical, it reinforces everything we know about Brahmanical temple architecture, whether in India or Southeast Asia. In the end, the measurements' corroboration of Hindu concepts demands a great deal of respect—both for the coding of these concepts and for the priests who developed this system of temple construction. The architects of Angkor Wat were brilliant and well educated—true sages whose knowledge ranged from architecture to Sanskrit poetry to astronomy to religious rituals. They were extraordinary human beings for any society, in any era.

Many years would elapse before I understood the rules, before I knew for sure where numerically meaningful measurements began and ended, before I knew which measurements were meant to convey meaning and which were not. The architects left no texts in stone, and manuscripts did not survive centuries of depredation from monsoons and scorching heat. There was no continuing oral architectural tradition, and nothing in extant Indian architectural texts hinted at the systems employed at Angkor Wat. It is no wonder that when I first brought forward my discoveries in conferences, lectures, or articles, people were taken by surprise.

Edifying material on Cambodia and its history, architecture, culture, and the Khmer language is rare to find in one place in English. Therefore, Chapter 1 provides some background on that material, twelfth-century Angkor, and methods of measurement analysis. The introductory chapter is not simply general information, however. My views on the *devarāja* cult, for example, carry current scholarship a bit further. Since there were ancestral and regional gods throughout Cambodia, one such god was needed for the capital and for the ancestors of the king. But the capital changed location with each king, and kings were often overthrown. Thus the set of royal ancestors might radically change. If each king were to install his own ancestral god, or regional god at the capital, how did that distinguish him from any other feudal lord? How could his regional deity preside over the capital as well? These problems were resolved with the creation of the *devarāja*. This god obviously remained the same. He was taken over by each new monarch, and he always resided at the capital, wherever it was located. The purpose of this cult object was to independently hold sway over all the other regional and ancestral gods. More important, perhaps, the need for a *devarāja* reveals the depth and breadth of the power of the ancestral and regional deities. They were almost a political elite unto themselves, for without the *devarāja* the king could not rule. The cult began, in fact, with the first king to declare himself ruler over other, heretofore independent, regional lords. Among many other topics, Chapter 1 explains this unique *devarāja* cult and suggests how it must have functioned.

More than anywhere else in the book, the discussion of the western entrance bridge in Chapter 2 illustrates how five or six different concepts can be pinned onto one architectural-numerical symbol. The bridge connects much more than two opposite sides of the moat. It connects the king to Viṣṇu, the gods to the antigods, the axis of the earth to the spring equinox, the coronation of the king to the beginning of Angkor Wat, and the oscillation of the sun each year to the temple itself. And having accomplished that, it also shows how these apparently separate elements are quite interdependent and overlapping in time and space.

Chapter 3 continues our journey into the temple. But first it presents the meaning behind many of the calendrical or cosmological numbers at Angkor Wat and suggests how they may have originated and where. The cross-cultural transmission of constellations and standards for measuring time is not only fascinating but lies at the base of Angkor Wat's symbolism. Chapters 4, 7, and 8 explore the measurement systems in the temple from the long causeway to the central galleries and up to the central tower itself. This progression is interrupted in Chapters 5 and 6 to consider the captivating series of bas-reliefs in the third gallery.

Chapter 9, the concluding chapter, puts the temple in perspective from several points of view, including that of the god Viṣṇu and the king. These two figures sit at the top of the pyramid, above all others. Their defining characteristics are identical in certain respects. There is something of the divine essence in the king and something of the king's essence in Viṣṇu. Indeed, the ancient Khmer association of king and supreme deity constituted one of the most subtle and abstract facets of kingship. Just how much that association encompassed and how clearly defined it was in the architecture of Angkor Wat will, page by page, become apparent.

Throughout the book there are drawings to illustrate measurement patterns. To underscore the intent of the architects, the measurements in these drawings are rounded off to whole numbers. The exact measurements in decimals are listed in Appendix A. Since it would have been impossible to coordinate so many systems without compromise, the priests were not beyond accepting an approximation when pinpoint accuracy was not feasible. Finally, numbers such as 32/33 or 27/28 in the drawings mean that the priests set the distance at 32 and a fraction or 27 and a fraction—on purpose. This was the only way to indicate that *both* 27 and 28, or 32 and 33, were intended. Therefore, the drawings give two numbers with a slash whenever *both* numbers were the objective.

For anyone interested in more data on the bas-reliefs in the third gallery, the tables in Appendix B record such details as the numbers of parasols over various dignitaries, the names of the 32 hells, and the sequence of figures in each relief. This information is given with a schematic representation of the pillars across from each relief, so the reader can see exactly where a particular segment occurs. The tables are there to address issues raised by others in the past, issues that may or may not be of interest to the general reader.

The book proceeds by stages from the entrance to Angkor Wat, on the west, up to the central tower. Indeed, the design of the temple itself offers the best means of organizing the conceptual, cosmological, and historical references that come to bear on the meaning of the temple's measurements. By the time our journey through Angkor Wat and the book has reached its end, the measurement systems should seem less complex, clearer, and, I think, eminently logical.

My objective was not only to explore the architectural splendor of Angkor Wat, however, but to offer new methods of architectural analysis in the process. If researchers are armed with the knowledge that astronomy, history, cosmology, and politics might partially, jointly, or wholly determine a structure's format and dimensions, then new possibilities open up for the study of other temples as well.

ACKNOWLEDGMENTS

Even though the process of deciphering Angkor Wat and then putting it on paper was a solitary endeavor, preparing the final manuscript and its illustrations involved the help of many people and organizations. Among several benefactors, the generosity and friendship of Sandra and Tim Collins stand out as constant and dependable from the beginning. The same is true for John and Silvie Thierry and the Southeast Asia Art Foundation. These kind people bestowed not only funding but enthusiasm, warmth, and hospitality on many occasions over the long years of research and writing.

At the University of Michigan, the Office of the Vice-President for Research, the Rackham School of Graduate Studies, the Center for South and Southeast Asian Studies (CSSEAS), and the Department of the History of Art have all funded research travel as well. At the same time, the CSSEAS staff have been exemplary in their moral support. Of particular note are the former directors of CSSEAS, Karl Hutterer and Vic Lieberman, who never flagged in their interest or encouragement. Former CSSEAS editors Jan Opdike and Catherine Arnott were infinitely helpful in making my English intelligible to someone other than myself. In a similar vein, the untiring staff at the university computing center in the North University Building rescued me from electronic oblivion more than once, as I grappled with graphics for the first time in my life. And Wendy Holden of the Asian Art Archives helped to push through the processing of photographs with an expediency that deserves recognition.

Thanks to a grant from the Asian Cultural Council in New York I was finally able to make a visit to Angkor Wat during the summer solstice and record the effects of sunlight on the bas-reliefs and other sectors of the temple. Without their financial backing, there would be no summer solstice information or images in this book. I was always struck by the fact that this agency, and the others noted above, were far from impersonal funding sources. In each instance, there was real human contact by visits, telephone, fax, or letter which made it clear that real people were taking note of the project. At no point were the grants I received impersonal.

Hiram Woodward, Jr., was my dissertation adviser, and it was in one of his classes that I first started to work on Angkor Wat. His intellectual challenges, good ideas, and pertinent questions gave impetus to the research. Walter Spink, who was pivotal in encouraging me to continue at the Ph.D. level, provided a broad and sometimes humorous perspective on the subject. More recently, the students in several of my seminars on Angkor have also injected vigor into the work. Of note is Jenifer Levin, who went far beyond the call of duty in helping to organize our first major student trip to Angkor, and whose kind heart found a kindred resonance in the Cambodian people.

In France, Guy and Jacqueline Nafilyan took me into their home on two separate occasions. I was feted, given grand tours of the wonderful regions of Le Puy and Toulon, and treated to both gourmet food and engaging conversation. Without Guy Nafilyan's written records of the measurements of Angkor Wat, I would have had no means of verifying the measurements I obtained from his drawings. I should not have worried, though. Angkor Wat and his drawings are equally accurate.

René Dumont and his family also made me welcome during several visits to their home. René went far out of his way to take me to Le Puy on that first research visit to Paris and made sure I met all the scholars who could be helpful. Conversations with Claude Jacques, Albert Le Bonheur, Jacques Dumarçay, and Madeleine Giteau provided special insights and ideas. These few words cannot adequately express my gratitude for their friendship and help.

Janos Jelen introduced me to the world of U.N. committees and UNESCO activities in Cambodia. His energetic enthusiasm for projects related to Angkor—whether my own, his own, or any others—has been a continuing source of inspiration.

Although all of us are moved and sometimes overcome by the power of Angkor, the monuments are that much more deeply rooted and emotional an experience for Cambodian visitors. It was the profound Khmer empathy and identification with Angkor Wat that made me resolve to give back to those who survived the 1975–1979 holocaust something of the full grandeur of their heritage. I am indebted most to my Cambodian acquaintances and friends for the motivation that overcame all difficulties.

The Khmers who have helped me in countless ways are too many to list, but they include Vann Moulyvann, Minister of State in the Council of Ministries, Pich Keo, director of the National Museum in Phnom Penh, Ouk Chea, in charge of the Conservation of Monuments and Museums, and Uong Von, curator of the Conservation d'Angkor. Cambodian members of UNESCO committees on Angkor and now in the National Assembly or heading government departments, officials such as Ing Kieth, Penn Thol, and Son Soubert, have given me valuable assistance and fascinating information. From tour guides and friends like Kit Sothea Rith and his sister, Kham Lay Orn and his wife, and Kousum Bun Soeuth, to name just a few, I learned much more than data on the monuments. Their sincere friendship, unfailing courtesy, and enjoyable companionship helped me to come to a better—living—understanding of Cambodian culture and morés. I deeply appreciate their practical on-site assistance as well. Also, I am grateful to Kousoum Saroeuth and his family for giving me a place in their home during my stays at Angkor.

Throughout the long years of research, my two daughters Natalia and Analis always listened sympathetically. Their early grasp of the topic ("Where are the bathrooms at Angkor Wat?") was eventually supplanted by encouragement to finish. With unspoken understanding, my late father and my brother and his family openly accepted the many times I could not visit due to work on the book. There was never any reproach. Last in chronological sequence in this 20-year endeavor, the staff and editors at the University of Hawai'i Press worked diligently, and consistently answered my novice questions with patience. Whatever misconceptions or mistakes occur in the pages of this book are not due to the editors and staff, and the others who have generously given their time and thoughts, but to my own pernicious ability to err.

1

Introduction

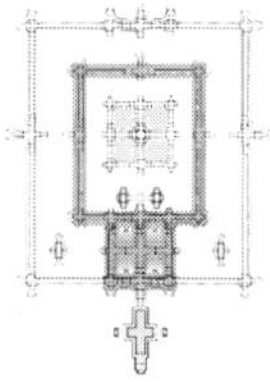

"INDOCHINA" became a European designation for mainland Southeast Asia in the mid-nineteenth century.[1] This term homogenizes the distinct cultural and ethnic groups of the region under a half-Indian, half-Chinese rubric. In its bias toward the two Asian giants to the west and north of Southeast Asia, it reflects a general predisposition that continues today.

Although everything of value in ancient Cambodia cannot be explained in terms of Indian or Chinese religions and texts, it is still obvious that India—and China to a lesser degree—contributed to Khmer culture. There are many references in stone inscriptions to things Indian: Brahman priests and sacred texts, gods and goddesses, constellations and planets, and the Sanskrit written language. These references reveal the role of India in the growth of Cambodia's politico-religious infrastructure.[2] Confucius was no competitor in that arena. The Chinese may have settled in Cambodia in numbers far beyond any Indian immigration, their language may be related to Khmer, and the Khmer may have obtained many Chinese goods from junks that came up the Tonle Sap River to Angkor, but the Chinese lost out where it mattered most: in government and religion.[3] The Khmer kings do not trace their ancestry to a Chinese master, but to an Indian named Kauṇḍiṇya and to Somā, a Khmer *nāginī* (snake) princess. Taoism and Confucianism were not exported to Cambodia, but the Brahmanical and

Buddhist gods were introduced and Buddhism is still practiced throughout Cambodia today.

When the capital was moved from Angkor to Phnom Penh in the mid-fifteenth century, none of the Brahmanical systems that built Angkor's temples remained in effect. In fact, Cambodia became Buddhist and abandoned the Brahmanical gods before it abandoned Angkor, so not even an oral tradition survived. The challenge in reconstructing Cambodia's historical and architectural past, then, lies in an expanded literacy: the ability to "read" architecture and sculpture for meaning and stylistic development; the ability to "read" the remnants of canals, foundations, earthen levees, moats, and ancient walls to reconstruct the past from the ruins and debris it left behind. But the Cambodians also wrote their history and named their gods on temple door frames, window frames, foundation steles, bas-reliefs, and pedestals. Generations of French epigraphists have translated this vast body of material, making volumes of information accessible to others. They brought Cambodia's past out of obscurity and into the realm of scholarship and general knowledge.

In that legend defining the origins of kingship, Kauṇḍiṇya arrived on the coast one long-ago day in prehistory and married Somā, daughter of the king of the *nāga*s.[4] Kauṇḍiṇya and Somā were the revered founders of the *somavaṃśa* line of kings (*soma* = moon, *vaṃśa* = lineage), associated by inscriptions with the state of Funan and also with the states of Aninditapura and Bhavapura, founded in the early sixth century.[5] Funan is a Chinese name for Cambodia and the only name we have for the region before the sixth century. Some think it might be an attempt at recording "Phnom," or mountain.[6] So far as we know, Funan covered most of the territory in southern Cambodia and the Mekong Delta region, but it did not extend into the north. Bhavapura was probably located north of the Tonle Sap Lake,[7] and Aninditapura included the area of Angkor.[8] In other words, these two states were in northern Cambodia.

As for *nāga*s, or snakes, they are found throughout Khmer architecture, sometimes actually sleeping on a ledge, but most often as the safer, stone-cut variety. The stone *nāga*s come down the roofs of temples to rear their multiheaded hoods as antefixes at the corners. They support the meditating Buddha. Their long bodies extend over balustrades to form sacred railings alongside causeways. A snake is held in the right hand of King Sūryavarman in a bas-relief of homage and allegiance from the third gallery of Angkor Wat. Local legend says a snake—or, more accurately, a *nāga* god—asked King Jayavarman VII to build the great temple of the Bayon. From the scene of the Churning of the Sea of Milk, in which the snake Vāsuki is used as a rope, to the creation of the universe in which Viṣṇu lies on a sacred snake on that same Sea of Milk, *nāga*s are everywhere in the sculpture and bas-reliefs of Angkor.

Snake gods can be depicted as anthropomorphs with reptilian heads for a face, as beings with human heads and reptilian bodies, or simply as multiheaded snakes. Since snake gods can assume human form whenever they choose, the *nāga* princess is envisioned quite like any other woman. She symbolizes a matrilineal society in which women have some control over the land, water, and power structures. In Cambodia, rulers generally claimed ascendancy through a mother, sister, or aunt. Somā's marriage to the Brahman Kauṇḍiṇya begins this matrilineal system and at the same time mythologizes the marriage of indigenous beliefs and territorial sovereignty with Indian religions. The *somavaṃśa* lineage of kings, then, emphasizes the Khmer and female half of the marriage: the *vaṃśa* is determined by female ancestry, and the moon *(soma)* is associated with female principles of darkness, water, softness, fertility, and so forth.

Zhou Daguan, a late-thirteenth-century Chinese traveler to Angkor, recounts the belief that the king climbed to the top of the Golden Tower at the palace and united with a *nāginī,* or snake goddess, every night, 365 nights a year.[9] This account resuscitates the marriage of Kauṇḍiṇya and Somā, with the king in the role of the Brahman father of Cambodia. Clearly the legend was no idle story in the thirteenth century but a living belief.

An emphasis on lunar and female characteristics in the *somavaṃśa* coincides with the popularity of Śiva worship. Śiva wears the crescent moon in his hair, has several consorts, and is known for his yogic powers. Nevertheless, once this lunar-related god was transplanted on Cambodian soil he became something of a dual personality. Like all other images of gods and goddesses, an image of Śiva was also identified as an ancestral or regional god, or both in one. This was formally accomplished by giving Śiva a name that combined a suffix indicating Śiva ("*-īśvara*"), for instance, with a root that spelled out the name of the ancestor in question. Rājendreśvara, then, combines the name Rājendra with *īśvara,* making the Rājendreśvara image a combination of Rājendra and Śiva.

Images could also look like great-grandfather or grandmother, father or mother. One eleventh-century inscription says: "By his homage he made manifest the Śambhu (Śiva) that resided at Dviradapura. . . . He created an image of Devī in the likeness of his mother."[10] The "Śambhu that resided at Dviradapura" is a reference to a Śiva image that functioned as the local god for Dviradapura, literally understood as living there. The image of Devī in the likeness of the donor's mother is clear in itself. Although no name other than Devī is given here, it is common for an inscription to refer to an image in one breath as "Devī" and in another by a name such as "Rājendreśvarī," to continue our example.

This union of a goddess and an ancestor is not Indian, it is Khmer. If we were to walk through a museum and see this statue of Devī today, we would recognize it as a representation of Devī and nothing more. Almost no attention has been paid to the fact that these statues were once understood as ancestors or regional gods: there are no labels to that effect in the museums. Once again, due to a bias in favor of the better-known classical Indian gods and goddesses, versus the unknown ancestor titles, the Khmer meaning of the images has been buried under classical iconography.

Other facets of Khmer culture are rich in their own fertile, conceptual, and abstract meanings. The numerical systems at Angkor Wat, for example, illustrate a curious way of thinking. Boundaries, axes, and other architectural parameters have measurements based on their physical extent and their internal divisions. That is nothing new. All architecture can be considered as subdivided into logical parts, each part measurable against a whole. At Angkor Wat, however, the measurements of both parts and whole contain calendrically and cosmologically significant totals.

As an illustration of the part/whole relationship, the circumference of the fourth (outer) enclosure at Angkor Wat measures 1 lunar year expressed as 354.36 units. (There are 354.36 days in 12 lunar months.)[11] The circumference also includes a 28-unit ritual path through the triad of eastern, northern, and southern entrances. One lunar month is often expressed as 28 days in length and is a subdivision of the lunar year.[12] In other words, the 28-unit path is contained within the 354.36-unit circumference, and the 28-day month is contained within the 354-day year. The part/whole relationship in architecture parallels the part/whole relationship in the calendar.

In astronomy, the yearly cycles of the sun and moon, as well as the cycles of the planets, have their own subcycles and interrelationships. The architectural components of Angkor Wat also have sets and subsets. The circumferences of the temple are made up of axial and corner entrances connected by corridors or walls. Circumferences also lie within other circumferences and are crossed not only by the axes of the temple, but by various routes into Angkor Wat as well. The measurement systems are part of these associations and relationships.

Similarly, the paths of the planets may seem to cross each other at random, but in fact they behave according to very precise rules. These associations and relationships formed the basis of Khmer astrology/astronomy. The process of deriving calendrical and cosmological data from Angkor Wat and deriving data in Khmer astronomy is also the same: one starts with a set measurement total; then, following clear rules, one adds, subtracts, multiplies, and divides to arrive at a conclusion.[13]

The concept of cycles and subcycles (astronomy) and systems and subsystems (architecture), the interrelationships between various cycles (astronomy) or various systems (architecture), and the arithmetic calculations that result in time-related data, either time eras, time cycles, or dates, were shared in the methodology and practice of Khmer astronomers and architects.

These procedures may or may not have involved geometry and trigonometry. In Khmer astronomy, the positions of planets and stars can be determined without using trigonometry. Nevertheless, at some point between the second and fifth centuries A.D., Indian astronomy adopted the trigonometric calculations of the Greeks and Romans.[14] These methods may have been introduced into Cambodia by the fifth or sixth centuries. When solar and lunar alignments were found at Angkor Wat in 1976, it was clear that the angles between the towers, the moon or sun, and the observation points were very carefully calculated, further suggesting that a knowledge of trigonometry was current when the temple was constructed.[15]

HISTORY

At the beginning of the ninth century, when King Jayavarman II (r. 802–ca. 834) established a new capital near Angkor,[16] the country's borders extended from the Mekong Delta up the Mekong River into parts of Laos and Thailand. By the twelfth century, when the vast pyramid-temple of Angkor Wat was constructed, Khmer hegemony had been strengthened in the northwest around Phimai, Phnom Rung, and in Lopburi, areas now part of Thailand. Wars were continually waged, and brief alliances maintained, with the Chams in central Vietnam, then known as Champa, and with the Dai Viet in northern Vietnam.

Aside from the destructive effects of recurrent wars, Khmer kings constructively made it a priority to build reservoirs and canals, all necessary for collective irrigation. Some kings built rest houses along roads; others built hospitals. Irrigation systems to enhance rice production were complemented by the natural abundance of fish in the Tonle Sap Lake, or Great Lake. Even the West Baray (Western Reservoir), built in the early eleventh century, is filled with fish. Between fish, chicken, rice, and a wealth of oranges, mangoes, coconuts, and other tropical fruit, the Khmers of Angkor never wanted for food.

The Khmer language has been extensively studied over the last several decades, and theorists at odds with each other link Khmer to ancient Chinese, to the Austro-Asiatic languages, or to both.[17] Khmer and Mon are related. Pockets of Mon-speaking people are still found in the hills and mountains of mainland Southeast Asia. These isolated units originally covered much larger areas. They testify to an early Mon presence before being "engulfed, partially assimilated, and pushed into the hills by succeeding migrations of Vietnamese, Thai, and Burmese."[18] Unlike the

Mon, the Khmer maintained a tenacious foothold in Cambodia and were never engulfed or fragmented by the Thai or Vietnamese.

In the seventh century, another legendary couple, Kambu and Merā, appear on the scene and establish the *sūryavamśa,* or solar lineage of kings.[19] One inscription, dated February 23, 948, refers to Kambu and Merā. It says: "Honor to Kambu Svāyambhuva [self-created], endowed with the preeminent glory of his lineage, who obtained the alliance of the solar and lunar races [and] clarified all the sacred texts (*śāstras*), shining with sweet rays, and who is accomplished in all the arts."[20] His consort, Merā, is the counterpart of the *nāginī* Somâ. She is "the most glorious of celestial maidens (*apsarases*), she was given as a consort to the Great Sage by Śiva, guru of the three worlds, who wanted a perfect creation for his three eyes to gaze upon."[21] As indicated by these legends, the Cambodians tended to mythologize or deify the founders of dynasties and lineages as directly descending from gods or demigods, like Kambu and Merā or Kauṇḍiṇya and Somā.

During the sixth to eighth centuries, Cambodia was divided into separate feudal kingdoms that were not at peace with each other. Then, in 802, King Jayavarman II declared himself a "universal ruler" *(cakravartin)* in a ceremony on Mount Kulen, about 30 km northeast of Angkor. That moment in history is counted as the date when Cambodia began to coalesce into one nation ruled by one sovereign.

At the turn of the tenth century, King Yaśovarman (r. 889–ca. 910) moved into Angkor from nearby Hariharalaya. One of his first acts was to build the royal pyramid temple known today as the Bakheng. Located on top of a mountain right at the heart of Angkor and the new capital, the Bakheng was the beginning of a historic series of construction projects. Yaśovarman also excavated the great Eastern Reservoir and set down irrigation canals. Future kings would continue to expand and improve the irrigation system and to build their own distinctive royal temples (see map). In 952, King Rājendravarman (r. 944–968) built the East Mebon temple on an island at the center of the Eastern Reservoir. He followed this in 961 with Pre Rup, an equally impressive temple due south of the East Mebon, and a few hundred meters south of the reservoir itself. Rājendravarman's son followed him in succession and built Ta Keo (ca. A.D. 1000) near the western border of the reservoir. Ta Keo remains one of the most massive temples at Angkor. Although many other temples were built during the tenth and eleventh centuries, the culminating achievement was Angkor Wat in the first half of the twelfth century. After Angkor Wat there was a hiatus in construction for 30 years. But at the close of the twelfth century, three centuries of building ended in a blaze of architectural expansion. This feverish, unparalleled activity created the multifaced towers and labyrinthian corridors of the Bayon (ca. 1200), the long axial stretch of Preah Khan (1191) and the multitowered Ta Prohm (1186). These architectural paeans to the gods were all constructed under the great Buddhist king Jayavarman VII (r. 1181–ca. 1220).

After 1220, no major monuments were constructed at the site and the architectural history of Angkor was a closed chapter 200 years before a final Thai invasion drove the Khmers south to Phnom Penh. Angkor then turned in upon itself. Balanced precariously between the encroaching jungle and the pull of gravity, the temples succumbed to age and isolation until Henri Mouhot rediscovered the site in 1860. Mouhot brought Angkor out of the jungle and into the European consciousness.[22] From that point onward, Angkor was no longer alone. By 1901, the École française d'Extrême-Orient had sent its first mission to record and photograph the bas-reliefs of the

Bayon, and Angkor slowly emerged into the twentieth century.

THE DEVARĀJA CULT

King Jayavarman II, then, was inaugurated as a *cakravartin* or "universal ruler" on Mount Kulen in 802 A.D. Sometime after that date, he moved his capital to the present-day Roluos, about 15 km southeast of Angkor. We know that he brought a *devarāja* with him when he moved.[23] Because this term has been translated as "god-king," popular belief today assumes it refers to the king himself. But inscriptions clearly describe the *devarāja* as a sacred object—perhaps a lingam (a sacred phallic symbol representative of the god Śiva) or a statue—that traveled to each successive capital with each successive king. The *devarāja* had to reside in the capital, in fact, and nowhere else.

The word *"deva"* in Sanskrit can be translated as "god," but it can also be a kind of honorific title that is not meant to be translated. *"Rāja,"* of course, means king. *Devarāja* is the Sanskritic translation of the original Khmer phrase *"kamrateng jagat ta rāja,"* and "god-king" is a translation of *devarāja*. This is yet one more example of a bias toward Indian sources at the expense of the original Khmer. The Khmer says, "the *kamrateng jagat* who is king"; it does not say "god-king."

The title *kamrateng jagat* is an honorific for images of gods associated with a particular site. *Kamrateng jagat Chok Gargyar*, for example, would roughly translate as "Universal Lord, Chok Gargyar." (Chok Gargyar, the modern Koh Ker, was once an interim capital and is about 95 km east-northeast of Angkor.) The fact that the cult object was called the "*kamrateng jagat* who is king" suggests that the object itself occupied a place of supremacy among all the territorial and ancestral gods. Ancestral gods also had titles of *kamrateng*, *kamrateng añ*, or other variations including *kamrateng jagat* plus modifiers such as *śrī*, *añ*, and so forth.

If *kamrateng* and all its variations were more correctly translated as "Lord" or the French "Seigneur," there would be no misunderstanding. The *kamrateng jagat,* or "Lord" who is king, can only mean the "Lord" who rules supreme over all others of his class. It would make sense, then, that this image should be kept in the capital. Not only is the capital associated with the Khmer king but, in its own way, it is also the highest-ranking geographical locus in the nation.

At the same time, since the kings (and therefore sets of ancestors), as well as the capital itself, changed continually, the *devarāja* could not be bound by the same rules as the other *kamrateng* deities. The *devarāja* cult, therefore, was needed to distinguish the "local" god of the capital as a deity who remained constant despite changes in the location of the capital. The *devarāja* also had to rank above each king's own ancestral deity. From another perspective, one might say that as the king stood to his subjects, as the capital stood to the other cities, so the *devarāja* stood to the local and ancestral gods.

While "god-king" was a mistranslation of *kamrateng jagat ta rāja*, it may not have been far off the mark as a description of how people felt about the king of Cambodia. An eleventh-century inscription describes the king as possessing a "subtle inner self" that actually resided in a lingam found in the king's royal pyramid-temple.[24] This "subtle inner self" implies that whatever essence is shared by the king and the lingam derives from Śiva. As a verification, inscriptions also refer to the king as having within himself a portion (*āṃśa*) of Śiva. An inscription praising King Udayādityavarman (r. 1050–1066), the same king of the "subtle inner self," states that "the most minor details of the ritual of Śiva prescribed in the texts . . . were known in their totality... by this king who was a portion of Śiva (*Śivāṃśa*)."[25] If these statements do not exactly make the king Śiva incarnate, he at least embodied some indefinable segment of the divine Śiva.

The issue of the royal assimilation of the essence of Śiva is not necessarily straightforward, nevertheless. Another inscription says: "Homage to the propitious Śiva, a portion (*āṃśa*) of whom, consisting of Brahmā and other gods, has appeared on earth. . . . [These appearances] are not different from his own substance, like the sun reflected in water."[26] If Brahmā and other gods can represent a portion of Śiva, this would seem to imply that kings could be joined to Brahmā or other gods and still contain a segment of Śiva's divinity. A similar inscription states that a certain King Jayavarman was "an incarnate portion of Brahmā and Kṣatra *(brahmākṣatrāṃśathave)*."[27] This has traditionally been interpreted as meaning "from a family of Brahmans and Kṣatriyas," but this reading does not rule out the suggestion that a portion of two specific deities would symbolize the special qualities of the king.

Whatever the word *āṃśa* or "portion" might mean, its use in inscriptions certainly indicates that some aspect of the divine nature of Śiva, construed as a supreme deity, was shared by the king. In the end, one must concede that the mistaken translation of *devarāja* was, for totally different reasons, not so mistaken after all.

POLITICS AND COSMOLOGY COMBINED

The *devarāja* had to be at the capital, the king had to reside at the capital, and the royal pyramid-temple was centered at the heart of the capital. No wonder scholars thought for a long time that the *devarāja* image was in the central sanctuary of the king's temple. It was not. And yet the "portion" of Śiva that was both in the king and in the lingam in the central sanctuary of the king's pyramid-temple created an especially sacred and venerated image—and a king who was worshiped as part deity.

At Angkor Wat, the floor of the central sanctuary was raised 23 m above ground level. The tower that symbolized the union of king and divinity could be seen for miles around. Whether or not the city extended physically outward from the axes of the temple, as it did from the Bakheng (ca. A.D. 900) or from the Bayon (ca. 1200), the central pyramid-temple dominated the city like Kafka's mysterious castle.[28] Exactly how much the heart of the temple would have shared in the castle's inaccessibility is unknown, but it is highly doubtful that people unconnected with the worship and maintenance of the images were allowed into the sanctuaries.[29]

Thanks to dozens of inscriptions at the Bayon, we do know that the outlying chambers of the central temple may have been given over to the worship of images that came from all parts of Cambodia.[30] Although it is unlikely that an original stone image from any region was installed at the Bayon, it is possible that bronze or stone replicas were created for consecration at the capital. Rather than focusing only on the king's immediate predecessors or ancestors, the central temple was thus more nationally oriented, bringing the provinces of the nation closely under the king's control.

In the examples of the Bakheng and the Bayon just noted, the temple's north–south and east–west axes extended outward, through the city, to the boundaries of the city moat. This axial arrangement fixed the temple in a spatial hierarchy, placing it at the hub of the city and, symbolically, the nation as well. It was at the generative center of royal and religious power, and in this guise it can be more readily understood in its relation to the universe as a whole.

On equinox days (March 21 and September

23), the sun rises due east and sets due west everywhere on the planet. The sun's east–west trajectory defines one of the earth's two major geophysical axes; the other axis, the north–south axis, is perpendicular to the first and, in some locations, equivalent to the magnetic poles. Khmer architects aligned their temples to accord with both these axes. Numerous ancient texts as well as the present living tradition stipulate that temple architecture must be in harmony with the universe and thus conform to the dictates of religious standards. This is true all over Asia. Khmer temple architecture was no exception.

The importance of geophysical location in temple construction has been cited by Alice Boner. She quotes Rāmacandra Kaulācāra, an eleventh-century Orissan architect:

> He, the Creator (Viśvakarman), . . . lays out the plan of the universe according to measure and number. . . . He is the prototype and model of the temple builder, who also unites in his single person, the

Fig. 1.1. Aerial view of Angkor Wat from the southwest.

The moat around Angkor Wat is 200 m wide but very shallow. It forms a sacred periphery of water that separates the temple from the secular world. At the heart of the enclosed, tree-filled confines, sandstone galleries and towers rise skyward. They are reached by a long western causeway that almost seems to be a continuation of the east–west road leading to the front of the temple.

> architect, the priest, and the sculptor. . . . This small universe (the temple) has to be situated with respect to the vaster universe, of which it forms a part. . . . It has to fall into line with the position of the earth in relation to the course of the sun, and also the movements of the planets.[31] . . . Far from being a simple arithmetical operation to be achieved by applying the measuring rod, the layout of a temple is based on fundamental cosmic and metaphysical conceptions that govern the whole structure. . . . The situation of the temple must, in its space directions, be established in relation to the motion of the heavenly bodies. But inasmuch as it incorporates in a single synthesis the unequal courses of the sun, the moon, and the planets, it also symbolizes all recurrent time sequences: the day, the month, the year.[32]

Thus the axes that joined the temple to the city also joined it to the planets and the sky above. The gods that were gathered in the chambers of the temple not only represented regions of Cambodia: they also represented deities connected to the stars and planets, sun and moon, who controlled the various seasons of the earth. The temples of Angkor were therefore spiritual, political, cosmological, and astronomical or geophysical centers. They embodied and encapsulated the world spheres through which Khmer culture and power structures moved, lived, and breathed. In their scope and conception alone, they are among the most spectacular of human achievements.

ANGKOR WAT

The temple of Angkor Wat was built at the height of Cambodian political power, during the reign of King Sūryavarman II (r. 1113–ca. 1150). Like the kings before him, Sūryavarman decided to build his own royal sanctuary at a place distinct from those of his predecessors.[33] He chose a site in the southern sector of Angkor and faced the temple toward the west because it was dedicated to Viṣṇu, the great Brahmanical god who rules over the western quarter of the compass. With its 1300-m north–south axis and 1500-m west–east axis—since the entrance is on the west, that axis runs west–east—no other temple at Angkor is as spacious and open as Angkor Wat. Today tourists still request to be taken to watch the sun rise over the temple, for it is a view that cannot be obtained anywhere else at Angkor.

The design of Angkor Wat (see front endpaper) is focused on three rising, concentric galleries at the heart of the temple and a vast amount of space circling the galleries. Around it all is a rectangular moat, a water-filled border that isolates the grounds of the monument (Fig. 1.1).

About 40 m in from the rectangular moat is a laterite wall, 4.5 m high, an imposing and effective barrier. The wall is cut into by large single entrances on the east, north, and south and by a total of five entrances on the west (Fig. 1.2). Of these western entrances, the two gateways at each end were built for the ground-level passage of elephants and horse-drawn chariots. The central three gateways are the main entrance tower and its two flanking towers (Fig. 1.3).

A visitor crosses the moat by means of a bridge that now fronts onto a paved road leading to Angkor Thom. This bridge (Fig. 1.4) is the only way into the temple except for an earthen road across the moat on the east.

On the east side, the dirt road over the moat allows one to approach the central area of the temple by motorcycle or car. A part of the eastern enclosing wall has been demolished to allow for the passage of vehicles. No bridges or roads cross the moat on the north or south.

Once past the western entrance in the fourth (outer) enclosure, the visitor sees the towers of

Fig. 1.2. Main western entrances and connecting corridors, view from the west end of the bridge.

With the sky reflected in the moat, the bridge heads right to the main entrance of Angkor Wat like some sort of celestial runway. The right (south) side of the bridge was restored in the 1960s.

Fig. 1.3. Main western entrances, west facade.

The central triad of main tower and two flanking towers conveys a sense of hierarchy and axial authority that sets the theme for the rest of the temple.

Angkor Wat at the far end of an elevated sandstone promenade that shoots arrow-straight for nearly 350 m across the open courtyard (Fig. 1.5). Two libraries flank this stone walkway at its midpoint; at its end, two reflecting pools just in front of the galleries mirror temple and sky (Fig. 1.6). These pools were renovated in the spring of 1993, and the northern pool is filled with water once again. The southern pool is partially filled with water and, unlike its companion, is complemented by water plants and an evening chorus of frogs.

The three central galleries, numbered from first to third from the center outward, rest on a raised terrace bordered by a *nāga* balustrade, which can be seen in the background of Fig. 1.6. Three sets of staircases lead to ground level on each side of this terrace (Fig. 1.7), and a ramp on the east allows access for conservation vehicles (Fig. 1.8).[34]

On top of the *nāga* terrace on the west, a large cruciform platform leads up to the central galleries (Fig. 1.9). It is commonly thought that this cruciform structure might have been the setting for special ceremonies or ritual dances watched by hundreds or even thousands of people in the temple

Fig. 1.4. Western entrance bridge, north (unrestored) side, from the northeast.

The steps in the central staircase have crumbled, and most of the columns and balustrades are missing, yet the strong laterite sides of the bridge are still in place. In the dry season, the moat has little or no water, allowing one to see that a raised border runs along the base of the bridge. Due to the effect of a zoom lens, the 200-m span of the moat is deceptively foreshortened.

Fig. 1.5. Central galleries and courtyard libraries from the west.

Although this classic view of the causeway and central galleries of Angkor Wat seems to repeat the pattern of the long bridge reaching to three entrances, this setting is more enclosed, the distant towers rise much higher on the horizon, and the causeway stretches 140 m farther than the bridge. At the halfway point, two libraries guard each side of the causeway.

Fig. 1.6. Three central galleries from the northwest.

This spectacular view of Angkor Wat is as much a view of the space above, below, and around the temple as of the volumetric stone itself. Space not only frames the temple but integrates the sweep from the vertical towers down to the horizontal corridors.

courtyard. If dances or rituals were indeed performed in this space, a good view could be obtained only from the western causeway or the facade of the third gallery.

The three rectangular galleries at the heart of Angkor Wat are covered by vaulted corridors and decorated with elaborate foliated and figural reliefs (Fig. 1.10). Sandstone vines climb sandstone pilasters, and twelfth-century sandstone celestial maidens (*apsarases*) have been smiling for 800 years now.

Each of the three central levels of Angkor Wat is higher, steeper, and narrower than the preceding one, until the surrounding architecture closes in around the central tower. Whereas the plains of Angkor may be intermittently visible through balustered windows or entrance doors from the

Fig. 1.7. Nāga *terrace, north side, westernmost staircase.*

Stairways descend three to a side on the *nāga* terrace that supports the central galleries at the level of the western causeway. The multiheaded *nāgas* with their long, balustrade bodies give the terrace its name.

Fig. 1.8. Nāga *terrace, east side, central axial ramp.*

Instead of a normal staircase, a ramp leads up to the *nāga* terrace along its eastern axis. The long ramp was necessary for wheeled chariots, horses, and elephants.

upper levels, the sandstone city of the gods is immediate and all-encompassing. Towers, courtyards, and vaulted corridors create a dense environment comparable to a modern apartment complex.

The architectural focus of Angkor Wat is the central tower. Indeed, it looms over the upper elevation like a giant god itself (Fig. 1.11). The tower is connected to the gallery around it by roofed and pillared corridors on the east, north, and south. But on the west side, the corridor that leads directly into the tower has been crudely walled up (Fig. 1.12). The effect of these corridors is to fracture the surrounding courtyard into segments that ultimately may not be quite as spatially satisfying as a large open area. Nevertheless, these connecting passageways must have had major ritual functions, and they would have protected priests and visitors during the monsoon season.

Two small anterooms on each side of the central tower lead to the main sanctuary. The sanctuary is now walled up on three sides and adorned with a standing Buddha image in front of each former entrance. A gaping hole takes up most of the floor in the sanctuary, a remnant of the 1935 excavation of the shaft under the tower. The hole, the bats, and sometimes the cockroaches dissuade one from lin-

Fig. 1.9. Cruciform terrace in front of the third gallery, view to the west.
From the east side of the cruciform terrace, the main western entrance of the temple can be seen in the distance. The flat surface of the platform is carefully laid and is framed by a miniature *nāga* balustrade. To the right and left the north–south cross-arm is aligned with the lateral staircases of the *nāga* terrace, about 50 m away.

Fig. 1.10. Main western entrances, north lateral entrance, east facade: pillar and wall reliefs.

Celestial maidens called *apsarases* (in Khmer usage the plural is *apsaras*) stand decorously near the entrances of the temple, along the walls of the upper elevation, and on the central tower. Their smooth forms are enhanced by the textured foliated patterns surrounding them. They are inhabitants of Indra's heaven of the gods.

Fig. 1.11. Central tower, northwest facade.

The sheer tonnage of this graceful structure is not only successfully supported by weight-bearing walls and pillars, but visually lightened with delicate carvings of *nāgas*, sages, *apsarases*, *garuḍas*, narrative scenes, and foliage. The tower can be seen from the main floor of the Grand Hotel, 6 km away.

gering in the sanctum sanctorum. Moreover, an exceedingly tall threshold in front of the sanctuary, in conjunction with the narrow space between the standing Buddha and the door frame, is a challenge to negotiate. The Buddha hides the sanctuary well: most people do not know it is there. Lingering in the sanctuary, then, is rarely an issue.

Originally, a wooden ceiling placed over the square sanctuary would have separated it from the round tower that rises far above it. The ceiling has not survived the passage of time, however, nor have the four wooden doors that would have closed off the sanctuary if necessary. Both of these wooden dividers—doors and ceiling—were also boundary markers for architectural units that were distinct from each other in terms of their measurements and meaning. That function first became apparent when the measurements of Angkor Wat were changed from meters to cubits. It was then that the temple began to demonstrate the ways in which the history of the king, cosmology, astronomy, the calendar, and the realm of the gods were all interrelated (Fig. 1.13). All the information gleaned from inscriptions about the culture and architecture of Angkor was suddenly manifest in the temple itself.

In the early 1960s, Angkor Wat was completely surveyed for the first time by Guy Nafilyan, a French architect, one of several who has worked for years at Angkor, and his team of Khmer and French assistants. Their results, incorporating 113 plans and drawings, were published in France in 1969 as *Angkor Vat: description graphique du temple.* On close inspection, I noticed that the temple's measurements were extraordinarily precise along certain sectors.[35] As an example of this precision, both the northern and southern corridors of the third gallery are 202.14 m long.[36] The eastern and western corridors are 114.22 and 114.24 m, respectively. Why—and how—would anyone construct the circumference in such a remarkably accurate manner?

To find out why Angkor Wat was constructed so precisely, I started to search for the unit of mea-

Fig. 1.12. Upper elevation, western axial corridor, north facade.

A central porch breaks up the already short length of each corridor connecting the central tower (on the left) with the surrounding gallery (right). This corridor was walled up at a later date; its embedded pillars are still visible on each side of the windows.

sure used to build the temple. That unit had to be a cubit length—the distance between the elbow and outstretched fingertips—since no viable alternative existed in Khmer inscriptions. Cubits and related units of measure were inherited from India. Although there was no standard cubit at Angkor, or anywhere else in Asia for that matter, we can be fairly certain that King Sūryavarman's cubit was used to build his temple. In the end, the cubit length would have to be deduced from the temple itself. Aside from the cubit length, another common measurement was equal to 4 cubits, called a *phyeam* in Khmer. As it turned out, the builders of Angkor Wat used various cubit "blocks" as modules: 10 cubits, 27/28 cubits, 32 cubits, 108 cubits, and similar groupings.

A standard cubit in Cambodia would range roughly between .40 and .50 m. I used this range to divide axes and circumferences at Angkor Wat until finally, after 4 months of trial and error, a very precise unit of .43545 m yielded the most consistent results. Originally this figure was derived from the north–south axis of the central sanctuary. I estimated that, between steps, the axis should be 12 cubits long.[37] In other words, 11 cubits would make the cubit length too long and 13 would

Fig. 1.13. Three central galleries, west facade.

As one approaches the cruciform terrace and begins to climb to the level of the third gallery, space slowly changes from horizontal (causeway) to vertical (central tower) and from wide-open to enclosed. And the number of calendrically and cosmologically significant measurements increases as well.

make it too short. Whether or not this turned out to be a valid procedure—since the distance between steps was later discarded as not always relevant—it gave a fortunate result. Since then, experimentation with other central sanctuaries at Angkor has indicated that the number 12 might be present in their axial measurements too.

The number 12 is highly significant at Angkor Wat. There are 12 staircases leading up to the central sanctuary at this level. They face the four cardinal directions, three staircases in each direction. The Khmer astronomers described the sun as traveling in a counterclockwise direction, from south to east to north to west, with 3 months between the equinox and solstice days. The 12 stairways are thus excellent symbols for the yearly solar calendar. Viṣṇu is a supreme solar deity, one of the 12 *ādityas* or gods of the solar months. His solar aspect and the solar interpretation of the 12 staircases leading up to the main central sanctuary are in agreement.

When I measured the same north–south axis in the sanctuary, door to door, it came to 13.41 cubits. Angkor is at 13.43 degrees north latitude, expressed by the fact that the north celestial pole is 13.43 degrees above the northern horizon at Angkor (Fig. 1.14).[38] As it turned out, 13.41 cubits is a basic module in the second gallery, devoted to Brahmā who is "situated" at the north celestial pole. When all of this information began to be assimilated, I started to wonder where it would lead me. I did not suspect that it would take 20 years of research to answer that question fully.

The difficulty at first was to determine what the architects considered to be significant in terms of measurement. Given the design of Angkor Wat, it was obvious that the axes and circumferences were primary, repetitive elements in the temple's basic format. But how were they measured? Once again, it was several years before the following parameters emerged as the system for rules of measurement:

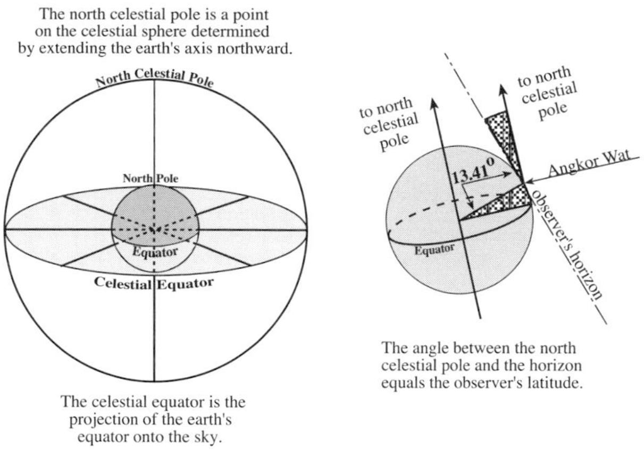
The north celestial pole is a point on the celestial sphere determined by extending the earth's axis northward.
North Celestial Pole
North Pole
Equator
Celestial Equator
The celestial equator is the projection of the earth's equator onto the sky.
to north celestial pole
to north celestial pole
13.41°
Angkor Wat
observer's horizon
Equator
The angle between the north celestial pole and the horizon equals the observer's latitude.

Fig. 1.14. Diagram of the north celestial pole, celestial equator, and latitude of Angkor Wat.

1. The outer axial measurements of any segment of the temple, whether a gallery, library, or entranceway, extend to the *farthest physical point of the structure* and include the last step in a staircase. When a half-moon step *(candraśilā)* extends past the staircase, it is included too. When the base of a structure or gallery extends past the staircase, the axial measurement includes the base.

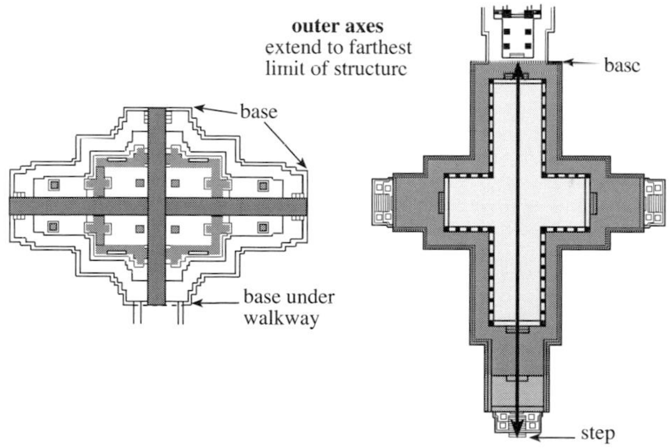
outer axes
extend to farthest limit of structure
base
base
base under walkway
step

2. Inner axes—that is, the interior axial dimensions of chambers at Angkor Wat—extend from doorway to doorway inside the chamber. They do not cross over thresholds.

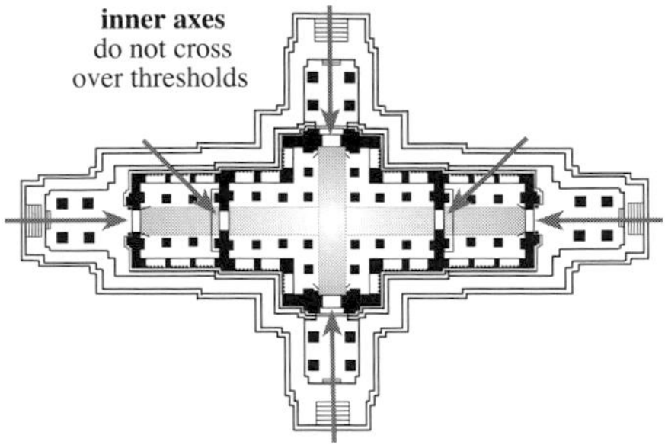

3. Aside from its obvious outer axial measurements, which follow rule 1 above, the western entrance bridge has significant measurements between raised ledges around the perimeter of its flat surface. The same applies to the cruciform terrace that precedes the third gallery, the only other structure with raised surface ledges at Angkor Wat. This is a unique trait exclusive to these two structures.

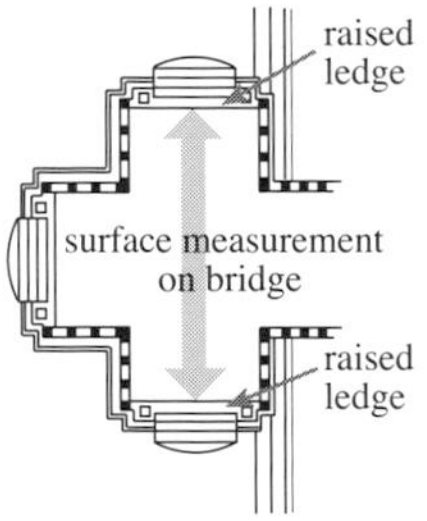

4. For the western entrance bridge and the causeway leading to the heart of Angkor Wat, measurements can be taken between projecting staircases, from one wall of the projection to the other, or between the center of each successive projecting staircase. The bridge and the causeway are also unique in this respect.

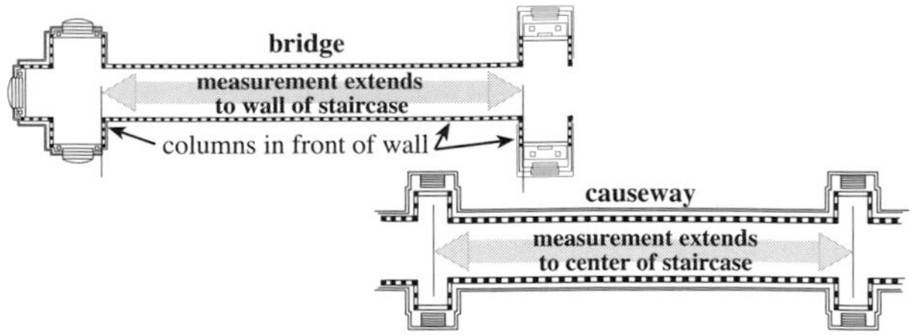

5. There is a balustrade around the central three galleries of Angkor Wat that meets the long western causeway as it approaches these galleries. This balustrade, on the west, is a boundary for several axial lines between itself and the western entrances to Angkor Wat's enclosing galleries. It is also a boundary for measurements along the causeway. This is the only such reference point at the temple.

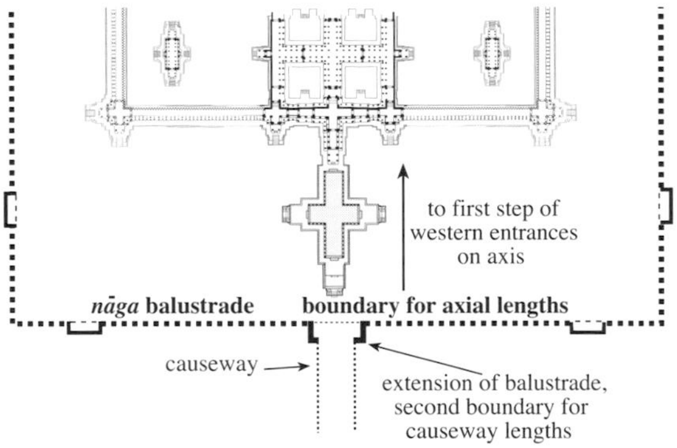

6. Paths of circumambulation are routes that ritually circle an image or sacred structure, usually in a clockwise direction. At Angkor Wat, these paths include three circuits of a central image and one or three circuits of flanking images. These paths begin from and end at the outermost steps of a chamber. The most common path enters a chamber from an outer perime-

ter, circles the central image three times, and exits in the same direction as entry—*except on the west.* The central western entrance in every enclosure of Angkor Wat has the same type of circuit through its chambers to the inside of the temple. This route involves walking around the central image three times, and also around any flanking images, before returning to the central chamber and passing on through to the inside of the temple. This western entrant path and the in-and-out circuit through the other entrances in a gallery are the two standard patterns in the temple. Together they indicate that one was to circle the gallery first and then enter on the west.

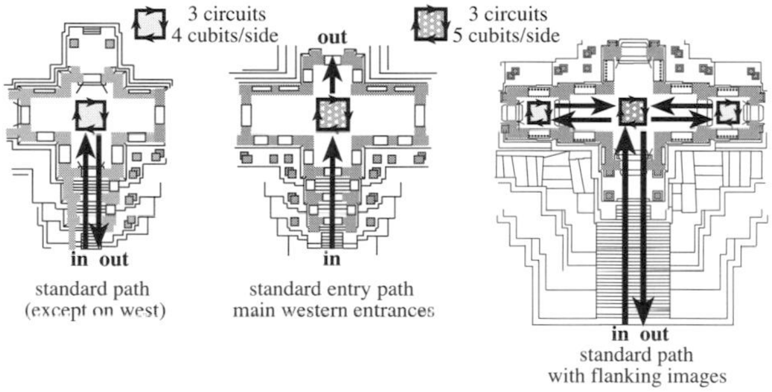

7. Axial measurements, whether interior or exterior, may exclude the circumambulation space around the main image in a chamber or even the central space of the chamber itself, usually marked by columns or reentrant corners.

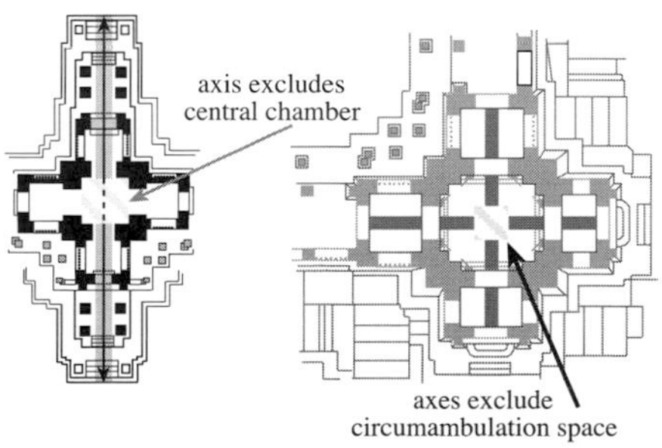

8. The circumference of each of the four enclosures of Angkor Wat is determined by a line along the center of the circumference corridors—*in combination with the distance between the entrance and exit doors of the main western entrance chamber of the enclosure.*

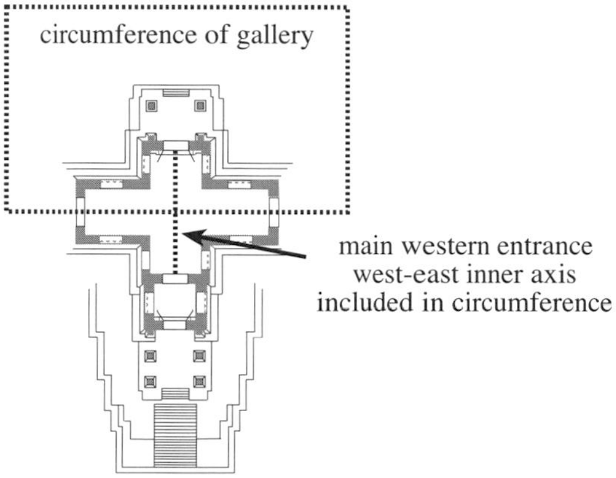

In summary, most measurements at Angkor Wat fall into three categories: axes (interior or exterior), circumferences, and circumambulatory paths. In some cases, the architects would find it necessary to adjust a distance to fit within a larger total or to give priority to another measurement. Circumference measurements of a gallery, for example, seem to have been established in conjunction with the gallery's axes. Neither of these measurements was compromised or altered to accommodate lesser measurements. They seem to have been primary units. Working within a system of priorities, the architects were still able to provide all of the chambers, axes, and galleries of Angkor Wat with measurements that were cosmologically or calendrically significant. These distances were accurate down to a few centimeters, in the case of top-priority measurements, or to 30 to 40 cm in the case of low-priority or "compromised" measurements.

KING SŪRYAVARMAN II

King Sūryavarman II is justifiably known to history because he built the temple of Angkor Wat (Fig. 1.15). After this king, Khmer monuments would never again reach the standards of precise construction and detailed low relief found here.

Sūryavarman's lineage began with his great-grandfather Hiraṇyavarman ("Protected by Brahmā"), who founded the dynasty that took control of Cambodia in 1080 and produced two of the most famous rulers in Khmer history: Sūryavarman II and Jayavarman VII. It is not clear where Hiraṇyavarman originally lived. An inscription detailing his dynastic line through King Sūryavarman II was found in northeastern Thailand, at Phnom Rung, and so it has been assumed that the family was from that region. This inscription praises Hiraṇyavarman as a descendant of Āditya, the sun, and Lakṣmī, the consort of Viṣṇu.[39] Because of these divine origins, the suffixes of *-āditya* and *-lakṣmī* were used to characterize members of this family, although not exclusively.

The father of Sūryavarman II was Kṣitīndr*āditya* and his mother, Narendra*lakṣmī*. As their names indicate, both were descendants of Hiraṇyavarman; he was their mutual grandfather. According to the Phnom Rung inscription, the queen of Hiraṇyavarman, Hiraṇyalakṣmī, bore him three sons and a daughter. The youngest son, Śrī Yuvarāja ("Royal Heir"), died before he could ascend the throne. His wife, Śrī Vijayendralakṣmī, was then married to the middle of the three brothers, the first reigning king of the family, Jayavarman VI (r. 1080–1107).[40] When Jayavarman died nearly three decades later in 1107, his elder brother Dharanīndravarman I (r. 1107–1113) assumed the throne with reluctance: "Without wanting the royalty, when his younger brother returned to heaven, out of simple compassion and ceding to the supplication of the multitudes without a protector, [he] governed the land with prudence."[41]

Dharanīndravarman's reluctance may have stemmed from an unstable political situation in Cambodia. An inscription on a stone stele from Wat Phu, across Cambodia's northern frontier, says that King Sūryavarman II united two opposing factions when he succeeded his great-uncle, Dharanīndravarman, in 1113.[42] This statement implies political disunity during Dharanīndravarman's rule, if not before.

Dharanīndravarman's two younger brothers were dead in 1107, and his sister, as a female, could not reign. According to extant inscriptions, neither Dharanīndravarman nor his brothers had any children. One assumes, then, that Sūryavarman's parents were not descended from this line of the family. Thus in order for this branch of the family to retain control of Cambodia, Dharanīndravarman had to assume the throne, reluctantly or not. When he became king he married Śrī Vijayendralakṣmī and reigned for 6 years.

When Dharanīndravarman came to power, only two known men stood to inherit the throne after him. The first was Kṣitīndrāditya, Sūryavarman's father. Like Dharanīndravarman he was a descendant of Hiraṇyavarman, but by another (unnamed) queen. The second man was Mahīdharāditya, Dharanīndravarman's uncle on his mother's side.[43]

For reasons unknown—perhaps out of deference in the one case and old age in the other—neither of these men contested Dharanīndravarman himself for the throne. Instead, after 6 years, it was the young Sūryavarman, Kṣitīndrāditya's son, who challenged his aged great-uncle in battle and "jumped on the enemy king's elephant and killed him . . . like Garuḍa, landing on the peak of a mountain, kills a serpent."[44] Or as an inscription written during the reign of Jayavarman VII has it: "After a battle that lasted for only one day, Śrī

Fig. 1.15. Third gallery, south side, west half, procession scene, King Sūryavarman.

King Sūryavarman is shown in audience with his ministers. He reaches out to them with an object held in his left hand, while his right inexplicably holds a dead snake. The Angkor Wat figural style is defined by his square jaw, somewhat flattened face, narrow or small features, strong eyebrows that tend to connect at the center, and a panel of animated drapery at each hip.

Sūryavarman stripped the defenseless royalty from Śrī Dharanīndravarman."[45] The sympathies in this statement lie with Dharanīndravarman, which is logical since Jayavarman's grandfather, Mahīdharāditya, was Dharanīndravarman's uncle. In fact, the antipathy toward King Sūryavarman in the inscriptions of Jayavarman VII implies a definite split between these two branches of the dynasty.

Another inscription dated to 1128 partially recounts the story of Sūryavarman's rise to power and other aspects of his reign.[46] He is described as fighting the battle for the throne and killing Dharanīndravarman while he was "still very young, at the end of his studies." The inscription goes on to say that "he fulfilled the desire of the royal dignity of his family while still under the dependence of two masters, like the nectar in Rāhu."[47] As Khmer inscriptions rarely refer to a king's age in any context, the reference to Sūryavarman's youth in this 1128 inscription is highly unusual. The "end of his studies" could have come as early as the age of 16. His youth would explain why he had not challenged Dharanīndravarman for the throne when the latter assumed power 6 years earlier.

There is no written evidence that King Sūryavarman had any children, nor do we know if he had any brothers or sisters or if his parents were alive during his reign. He did take a second queen when the first apparently died. When Sūryavarman himself died, sometime around 1150, he was succeeded not by a son or a sibling but by Yaśovarman II, someone from another family and lineage.[48]

The years during which Sūryavarman built Angkor Wat (ca. 1116–1150) and other monuments were by no means peaceful ones. Although Angkor itself was not invaded during this time, the king fought many battles with the Dai Viet in the northern part of Vietnam during the early years of his reign, and in the later years he fought the Chams in central Vietnam.[49] These latter battles were generally unsuccessful, due to the growing strength of the Chams, who would finally invade Angkor in 1177 to pillage and sack the city.

Toward the end of his reign, after two defeats on the battlefield, Sūryavarman tried to establish Prince Harideva, younger brother of his first queen, on the throne of Champa. There was a battle on the plains of Mahiṣa and Harideva was killed, together with all the Khmer troops, in 1149.[50] Since there remain no inscriptions referring to the king or his activities after this battle, it can be assumed that Sūryavarman died in 1149 or 1150.

Angkor Wat was not the only temple constructed during the reign of King Sūryavarman. Either the king or high-ranking officials or priests were responsible for beginning work on the temple of Banteay Samré, located at the east-southeast corner of the East Baray (Eastern Reservoir), and for constructing the smaller temples of Thommanon and Chau Say Tevoda. This paired set of temples is located between the East Baray and Angkor Thom, along the east–west axis of the Porte de la Victoire, 500 m west of the gateway to Angkor Thom.[51] The temple of Beng Mealea, about 50 km east of Angkor, was also begun during the first half of the twelfth century.[52] This latter temple was at an east–west and north–south crossroads between major settlement areas during the Angkor period.

THE ARCHITECT OF ANGKOR WAT

Angkor Wat has remained a historical enigma for one good reason: no inscriptions bear any known reference to the monument. Why one of the most imposing temples in Khmer history did not merit more notice in stone steles is indeed a mystery. Perhaps inscriptions that mentioned Angkor Wat simply did not survive. Whatever the reason, we know neither the original name of the temple nor the identity of its principal architect.

Although the architects of Angkor Wat are unknown, one can still use extant inscriptions to divine who they might have been. In that regard, no single royal priest is so praised in surviving inscriptions as Divākarapaṇḍita, and no priest outranked him in status. In effect, Divākarapaṇḍita was the chief spiritual adviser and most venerable and senior priest at the onset of Sūryavarman's reign. Because of his status, it is highly probable that he was the guiding genius behind the temple's construction.

Divākara served as the Vraḥ Guru, or main priest, during the reigns of Sūryavarman's two royal predecessors and had therefore consecrated the first three kings in this family.[53] We know that he was born in Vnur Dan in the district of Sakya—both locations presently unidentified. We do not know when he was born, but he was old enough to assist at the rites for the main image in the Baphuon, the architectural precursor of Angkor Wat built during the reign of Udayādityavarman I (r. 1050–1066). Thus Divākara was probably born by 1050 or so.[54] He received the special title *dhuli jen kamrateng añ* in 1119 or 1120, and hence was still active at that time,[55] but in 1136 an image of Divākara was set up at Wat Phu, a clear indication that he was no longer living.[56] These scanty references to events and dates give evidence that his life must have spanned at least 80 years.

It is likely that Divākara was the grandson of Śrī Kavīśvarapaṇḍita, one of the major priests of King Sūryavarman I (r. ca. 1002–1050).[57] His priestly ancestry could then be traced to Angkor's very beginnings in the early ninth century, making him one of a long family line of priests with a well-established reputation and standing. During the reign of Harṣavarman II (r. 1066–1080) Divākara was given the title of *ācārya pradhāna,* or "chief spiritual teacher."[58] In 1080, when he officiated at the coronation of Jayavarman VI, he was promoted to the rank of *bhagavat pāda kamrateng añ ta guru,* or "Lord Master Guru." Since the accession of Jayavarman VI was not in line with the preceding king—he came from another family—Divākara seems to have chosen to remain with the new Khmer ruler rather than continuing with the family that had lost power. It is also possible that he may have been allowed to continue in his official position regardless of the identity of the new ruler, as the priestly castes tended to have a great deal of autonomy. Whatever the case, Divākara traveled with Jayavarman VI when the king made pilgrimages to sacred sites, and he donated considerable wealth to a variety of temples during the reign of all three kings of this royal line. He was awarded honors and possessions, the most spectacular of which was the temple of Banteay Srei. We also know that he presided over yearly ritual sacrifices during the reign of King Sūryavarman II and that at one point he persuaded the king to reinstate lost territories to a group of priests.

We do not really know what role Divākara played in the building of the temple; nor do we know who succeeded him at his death. In the scarce information available there is no mention of his overseeing any construction. We can surmise, however, that he was closely associated with the building of Angkor Wat because of his elevated rank: no priest would have held a higher position.

Whoever may have been the creative force behind the monument of Angkor Wat, the temple exemplifies the shared expertise of its builders and the mastery they achieved through centuries of architectural tradition. It is the culminating achievement in a long architectural history of stone temple construction, a history that would end less than 100 years after Angkor Wat was completed.

2

The Western Entrance Bridge: Transitions in Time, Space, and History

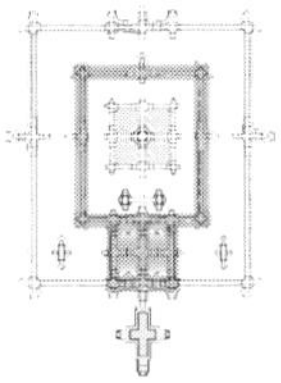

ONE of the many attractions of Angkor Wat is that it is set apart from our world—apart from the daily routines, the work demands, the sometimes heavy burden of social and business interactions. From our side of the moat, the temple appears dignified and majestic, a safe haven on a grandiose scale. Offset by the vast space around it, the heart of Angkor Wat does indeed rise like a mountain of the gods. For one thing, it is prominent. The Khmers believed that the longer the approach to a sanctuary, the more hallowed the image. At Angkor Wat, the approach is open and spacious and there for all to see. It does, in fact, add presence and stature to the monument.

The bridge on the west is the first part of this approach to the elegant ensemble of stone galleries and towers in the distance. By means of the bridge—actually a solid structure with an earthen core, laterite facing, and sandstone surface—the transition between the ordinary world and the sacred realm of the temple can be realized. Transition, as it turns out, characterizes the nature and function of the bridge on many levels.

The 200-m horizontal span of the bridge would have been monotonous if it had been unbroken and plain. Instead, it has a set of opposite staircases at the center that lead down to the water of the moat (Fig. 2.1). Two lions flank the top of the stairs, looking outward, as though watching the horizon for uninvited guests. There is also a pair of north–south stairs at each end of the bridge, equally adorned with lions about to rise up and walk away.

A *nāga* balustrade or railing, almost shoulder height, originally ran along each side of the span. Parts of the balustrade still remain, with the multi-headed hoods of the *nāgas* rearing skyward behind each lion and at each juncture with a staircase (Figs. 2.2 and 2.3). The balustrade body of each *nāga* was once supported by 54 pedestals on each half of the span. These 54 balustrade supports, in turn, were set above 54 sandstone columns that decorated the laterite sides of the bridge (Fig. 2.4). Several of these columns are still in place. Their sandstone texture and color stand out elegantly against the coarse, yellow surface of the laterite.

The original 54 sandstone columns and 54 balustrade supports on each half of the span are the first visible sign of numerically significant subdivisions at Angkor Wat. Their meaning is related to the measurements of the bridge itself (Fig. 2.5), which include other 54/54 pairs (see Appendix A, Table 2.1).[1]

The 54/54 unit pairing occurs in only four parts of the temple: the bridge, the western entrances, the central tower, and the third or historical gallery. The bridge and the western entrances introduce the general meaning of a 54/54 pairing, while the central tower and the third gallery further define 54/54 in very specific terms.

Fig. 2.1. Western bridge, south central staircase and main western entrances, south half.

The staircase and bridge columns (foreground) once echoed the design of the pillars along the corridors of the western entrances. The staircase divides the bridge in half, just as the central tower seen at the end of the bridge divides the western entrances in half. In fact, the length of the western entrances is the same as the length of the bridge, and they share the same symbolism.

Fig. 2.2. Western entrance bridge, west side, main staircase.

Mythical lions (left) flank the top of stairways, while *nāga*s (right) lift their multi-headed hoods at the end of the balustrades along walkways and causeways. When the balustrade ends at a stairway, as here, the two divinities function like an honor guard into the temple grounds.

Fig. 2.3. Western entrance bridge, west side, north staircase.

Here the solar lion and lunar *nāga* appear to be watching activities along the moat. Although the ravages of time and vandals have taken their toll on the lion and *nāga* statuary, their presence transforms the bridge and causeway from flat surfaces into processional pathways.

Fig. 2.4. Western entrance bridge, southwest corner at border of moat.

The balustrade supports for the *nāga* railing on the bridge rested over sandstone columns, rather than on the bridge itself. The sandstone entablature was unstable and, with time, the columns collapsed and were undoubtedly carried off for use elsewhere.

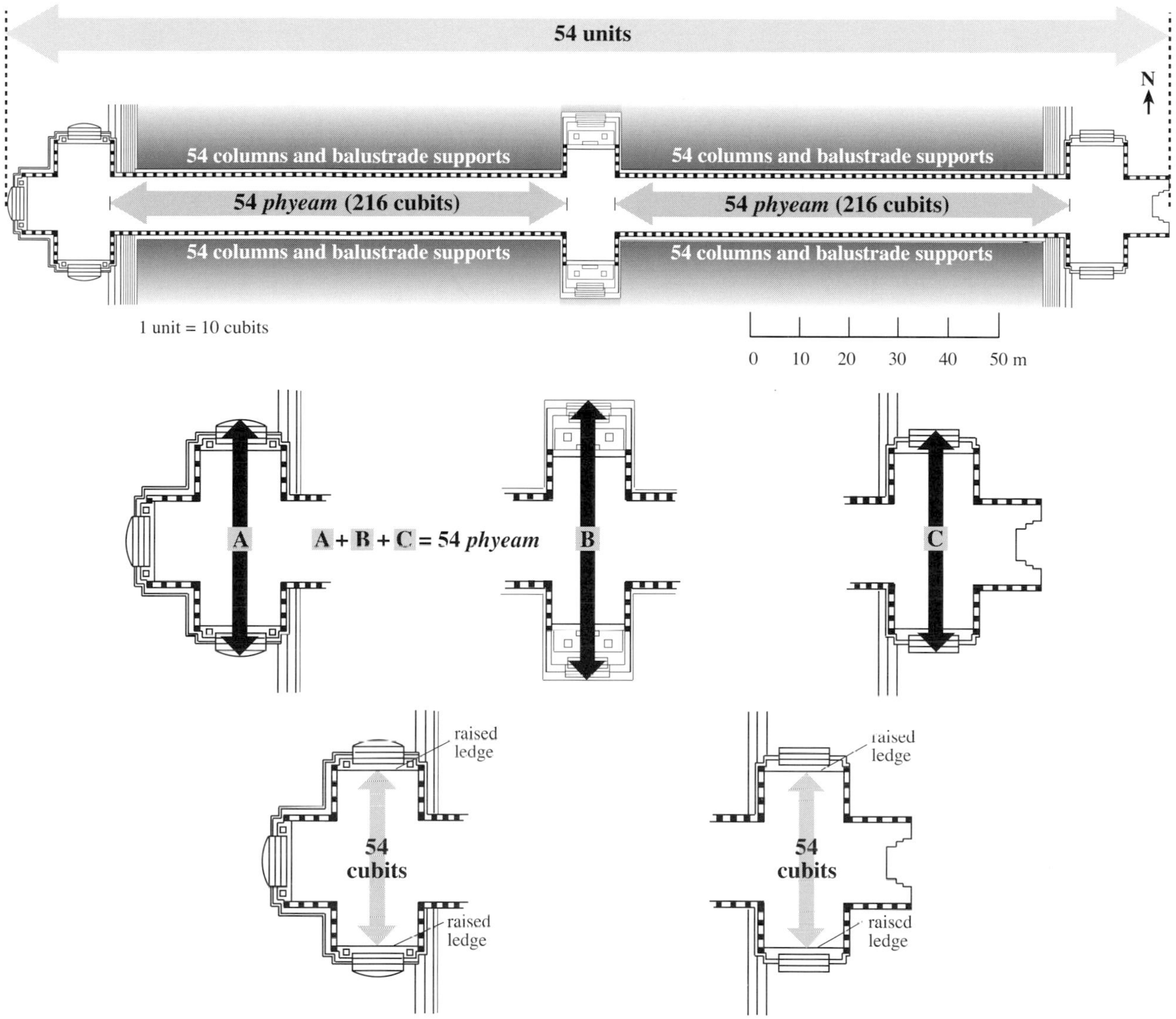

Fig. 2.5. Plan of western entrance bridge and 54-unit lengths.

The 54/54 pairs on the bridge define it several times over as a symbol of the 54 gods and 54 antigods holding the body of a *nāga* and pulling against each other. Their cosmic tug-of-war was believed to cause the sun and moon to oscillate across the sky between the northern and southern solstices. The two 216-cubit lengths symbolize one total: 432 cubits and the 432,000 years in our current *kali yuga*. (See Appendix A, Table 2.1.)

Fig. 2.6. Western entrance bridge, west side, north staircase, view north.

Surface measurements on the bridge are taken between ledges 10–12 cm high, seen here running underneath the *nāga* railing and in back of the lion. The ledges mark the top of a staircase just as a threshold marks a doorway into a sanctuary.

There are five bridges over the moat to Angkor Thom, the capital of Jayavarman VII, one in each cardinal direction plus an additional bridge on the east. Each has 54 *asura*s or antigods on one side and 54 *deva*s or gods on the other (Fig. 2.7). The *deva*s and *asura*s are all "pulling" on a *nāga* balustrade that begins with a multiheaded *nāga,* whose body forms the balustrade, and ends with an upraised tail.

The pairs of 54/54 on the western bridge to Angkor Wat numerically echo the pair of 54/54 *deva*s and *asura*s on the bridges to Angkor Thom. And the total of 540 *deva*s and *asura*s on all five bridges to Angkor Thom numerically mirrors the approximately 540-cubit length of the bridge and the western entrances into Angkor Wat.

This pairing of gods and antigods began in Indian mythology with the Churning of the Sea of Milk, but the number 54 is Khmer in origin. By combining the legend with the 54/54 pairing, a surprising twist to the mythology appears, a twist that brings in the sun and moon and cosmology.

THE CHURNING OF THE SEA OF MILK

The churning myth begins with the *deva*s losing battles against the *asura*s and continues in several variations. To defeat their classic *asura* enemies, the *deva*s (or Viṣṇu, depending on the text) devised an ingenious scheme.[2] They asked Bali, the king of the *asuras,* to call a truce and command the *asura*s to help them churn up (and share in) the elixir of immortality from the Sea of Milk. If the gods could gain immortality, the *asura*s, finally, could be defeated for good. If the *asura*s drank the elixir, too, the plan would fail, of course, but that possibility was ruled out from the start.

The *deva*s persuaded the *asura*s to cooperate and then asked the great Lord Viṣṇu to help them. First the king of mountains, Mount Mandara, was uprooted from its place to the east of Mount Meru, the home of the gods, to be used as the churning pivot. Next the king of snakes, Vāsuki, was roused from the bottom of the Sea of Milk to serve as the churning rope. Viṣṇu supported the churning pivot in his incarnation as the tortoise Kūrma ("half a globe"). With Vāsuki wrapped around the pivot, the gods stationed at the multi-headed side of the snake, and the antigods aligned along the tail, the great churning began.

Eventually the elixir emerged, but neither the gods nor antigods had a chance to drink it. The *asuras*, piqued that they were never intended to share in the benefits of immortality, attacked the *devas*, which led to another great battle. Viṣṇu intervened, helped the *devas* to win, and left with the elixir to keep it out of harm's way. Once the battle had ended, Indra was crowned king of the gods: "Indra, after slaying the *asuras*, became king of the *devas* and with the help of the sages began to rule with joy."[3] This last detail, which seems at first irrelevant to the main thrust of the story, is in fact a key to the significance of the Churning of the Sea of Milk at Angkor.

A bas-relief of the churning event is sculpted across 49 m of the eastern wall in the third gallery of Angkor Wat (Figs. 2.8 and 2.9). This relief measures 54 cubits on the side of the *devas* and 54 on the side of the *asuras*, repeating the numerology found on the western entrance bridge and on the bridges to Angkor Thom.[4]

The Khmers were the only people in South and Southeast Asia to depict precisely 54 *asuras* and 54 *devas* in the illustration of the churning scene.

Fig. 2.7. Angkor Thom, south bridge across moat, view to southwest.

Over the five bridges into the site of Angkor Thom (ca. 1200), 54 *devas* and 54 *asuras* pull on a *nāga* railing. If the road in this view is followed southward and out, it passes just a few feet in front of the bridge into Angkor Wat.

This might be because 108 is the most auspicious number in all of Asia. It occurs in Buddhist and Hindu texts in many guises and forms. Viṣṇu, for example, has 108 names; Buddhist and Hindu "prayer beads" number 108. Therefore mantras are often chanted with these beads 108 times (or multiples thereof). The recurrences of 108 seem endless. The number 108 is important in astrology and astronomy, as well. In this specific instance, the deliberate pairing of units of 54 may have a connection to the relationship of Mount Mandara (the churning pivot), Mount Meru (the home of the gods), and the earth's axis.

A bas-relief of the churning scene in the southwest corner pavilion at Angkor Wat, like many Asian depictions of the Churning of the Sea of Milk, has the sun and moon on each side of the central mountain (Fig. 2.10). Sūrya and Candra, the solar and lunar gods, are usually shown inside large disks (their "orbs") on each side of the central pivot. As it happens, Sūrya and Candra, the sun and moon, move approximately 54 degrees north and south during the year.

On the day of the winter solstice, around December 22, the sun is at its southernmost position in the sky. The sun starts to move northward

Fig. 2.8. Third gallery, east side, south half, churning scene.

An epic Churning of the Sea of Milk is paid homage by an epic size—49 m. This view covers about one-third of the scene. Viṣṇu is at the center holding onto the churning pivot. Beneath him is Kūrma, his tortoise incarnation. Above, a *deva* who may be the god Indra flies down to hold the top of the churning pivot. The many *asuras* can be seen pulling to the south (left), and the *devas* to the north (right).

Fig. 2.9. Third gallery, east side, south half, view north through corridor.

The telescoping perspective down the corridors of Angkor Wat is a characteristic architectural motif. The roof over the corridor, and over the bare walls of the northeast pavilion in the foreground, is now back in place. This segment of the gallery was dismantled at the end of the 1960s and has only recently been restored.

with each successive sunrise until, on June 21, the summer solstice day, it is at its northernmost point in the sky (Fig. 2.11). After that, it starts to rise farther south each day. This north–south and south–north solar oscillation ranges between 49°12′ and 43°58′, depending on the year in question.[5] Could the venerated numbers 49 and 44 (see Fig. 2.27) derive from the limits of the sun's yearly oscillation? The moon oscillates between north–south extremes across the celestial equator in an arc that can reach a maximum of 59°28′.[6] Could the 54/54 pairing at Angkor also trace its origins to solar and lunar movement? Although there is no precise and unvarying figure for the amount of north–south arc crossed by the sun and moon, the average degree of *maximum* oscillation is 54°20′ for both the sun and moon combined, or 108 degrees for the annual north–south, back and forth, movement. At present the sun oscillates at 46°54′ and the arc is decreasing. The 54° maximum average arc may have inspired the 54/54 pairing of gods and antigods in Cambodia.

The bas-relief of the Churning of the Sea of Milk has several other aspects that refer to a north–south oscillation. Brahmanical astronomy, for example, locates the *deva*s on Mount Meru, the axis of the earth:

> The round ball of the earth, composed of the five elements, abides in the midst of the starry sphere, like a piece of iron suspended between magnets. . . . In its middle there is Sumeru, the abode of the gods. Below [at the pole opposite

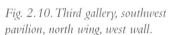

Fig. 2.10. Third gallery, southwest pavilion, north wing, west wall.

As one enters the pavilion from the front (west side) of the gallery, there is a scene of the Churning of the Sea of Milk to the right. A small image of Candra (shown here) circled by the disk of the moon is still visible to the left of Mount Mandara. Nothing remains of the companion image of Sūrya on the right of the churning stick, although over half of the figure can still be seen in old photographs.

> Meru] there are placed the Asuras. . . . Straight above Meru in space one pole is seen; the other pole is seen below, placed in space. . . . For those who dwell on the back of Meru the sun once risen remains visible for six months, while he moves in the six signs beginning with Aries; for the Asuras he is visible as long as he is in the latter [half of the ecliptic].[7]

One of the more unusual revelations in this paragraph is that the Indians knew the earth was round in the sixth century A.D. In addition, these stanzas and others like them describe Mount Meru as the north–south axis of the earth, with the *devas* at the north celestial pole and the *asuras* at the south. This is why the bas-reliefs of the Churning of the Sea of Milk at Angkor Wat and at the Bayon (ca. 1200) put the *asuras* on the south side of the scene and the *devas* on the north. And this may be why 54/54 is associated with the gods and antigods.

Their "pulling" on the snake Vāsuki causes the sun and moon to move back and forth, north and south, each year, covering a 54-degree maximum arc every 6 months.[8]

In the bas-relief at Angkor Wat, the position of the churning pivot would correspond to the position of the spring equinox (Fig. 2.12). The 91 *asuras* in the south represent the 91 days from equinox to winter solstice (Fig. 2.13), and the 88 northern *devas* represent the 88 days from equinox to summer solstice (Fig. 2.14). In fact, there are either 88 or 89 *devas* in the scene, 89 if the *deva* atop Mount Mandara is counted with the others. There are 88 or 89 days from the spring equinox, counted from the first day of the new year, to the summer solstice.

In Cambodia, the spring equinox (beginning of the sun's yearly journey) lasted for 3 or 4 days: Thngai Chaul, "day of entry," Vone Bat, "day(s) of the middle," and the last day, the Langsak.[9] The

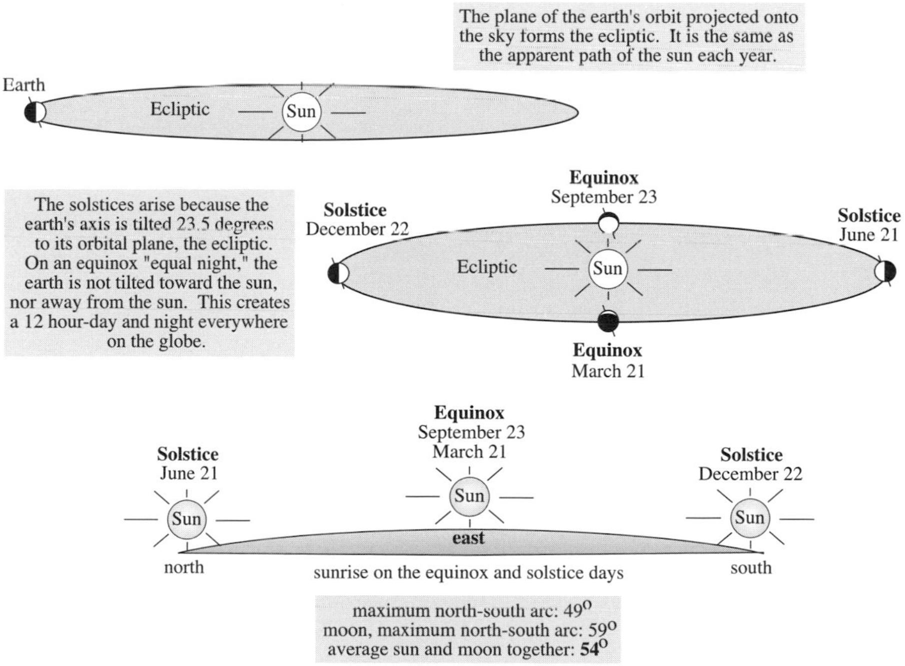

Fig. 2.11. Diagram of the ecliptic and the solstice and equinox days.

The ecliptic—or the apparent path of the sun each year—is actually the earth's orbit around the sun. Due to the inclination of the earth's axis the north and south poles will alternately have 24 hours of sunlight on June 21 and December 22, respectively.

Fig. 2.12. Third gallery, east side, south half, churning scene, center.

Viṣṇu, Mount Mandara, Kūrma, and a flying *deva* who is most likely Indra mark the equinox center of the churning scene. Scholars believe the Khmers worked from the ends of a corridor to the center, but there is no logical explanation why the center of this relief is unfinished. It might have been only a matter of hours to smooth over the rough surfaces here, yet it was never done.

Langsak, the first day of the new year, occurred 3 or 4 days after the spring equinox, depending on the year. (In some years, there were two Vone Bat, or middle days.) Mount Mandara as the churning pivot would symbolize the 3 or 4 days of the equinox period, the northernmost *deva* would represent the summer solstice day, and the southernmost *asura* would correspond to the winter solstice day. In other words, this scene is a calendar. It positions the two solstice days at the extreme north and south, counts the days between them, and measures 54 units for the north- and south-bound arcs of the sun and moon in its own 54/54-*phyeam* halves. In all of these aspects, it emulates the symbolism on the bridge or in the western entrances, which repeat the 54/54-unit pairs several times.

Three oversize figures depicted on each side of Mount Mandara divide the churning scene into six segments representing the 6 months between December 22 and June 21. One large figure holds the snake Vāsuki at his head, another holds the tail.

Fig. 2.13. Third gallery, east side, south half, churning scene, asuras.

A total of 91 *asuras* pull southward on the body of the *nāga* Vāsuki in a neat chorus line of rhythmic legs, feet, and arms that bend with the effort. Their headdress, bulging eyes, frown mark between their joined brows, and fangs over the lower lip are clear identifying traits.

Fig. 2.14. Third gallery, east side, south half, churning scene, devas.

The 88 *deva*s are less corpulent and more passive or gentle than the *asura*s, hardly exerting themselves in the tug-of-war. They are distinguished by their conical headdress, the fine line of their downward-turning eyes, and, in this case, their lack of a beard.

These are the figures representing the solstice days. There are two large, equidistant *devas* on the north and two large, equidistant *asuras* on the south that further divide the space between the end solstice figures and the central pivot into three segments on each side.

The period between the solstices is also expressed in terms of days: the total of 180 *devas* and *asuras* in the relief, plus the 3 days symbolized by the churning pivot at the spring equinox center of the relief, add up to the 183 days between solstices (182 if the flying *deva* on top of Mandara is excluded). Both numbers, 183 and 182, are correct, depending on the year (183 + 183 = 366, one leap year; 183 + 182 = 365, a normal year).

Every aspect of this relief—the number of figures it contains; the distances the figures cover (54 *phyeam* on each side); the way the figures are divided; the composition's use of a central axis, equally symbolic of the vernal equinox and Mount Mandara; the cardinal directions occupied by the figures on each side of the axis—all work together to define the lunisolar calendar.

There is another connection between the

Fig. 2.15. Main western entrances, south solstitial gateway at sunrise, winter solstice.

When seen from the center of the western end of the bridge, the sun appears to crown the pediment over this gateway on December 22. For a week or so before and after this date, the effect will remain the same. The same conjunction occurs with the northern gateway on June 21.

Fig. 2.16. Western entrance bridge, west end, center point between three end staircases.

Even if it is simply coincidental, the sunken rectangular stone on the west end of the bridge is a good marker for solstice observation with the gateways.

solstice and 54/54, and that is on the bridge to Angkor Wat. If one stands at the center point between all three end staircases on the west side of the bridge on December 21, the sun rises exactly over the center of the southern gateway of the western entrances (Fig. 2.15).[10] On June 21, the summer solstice, the sun rises over the center of the northern gateway. It is convenient, but probably coincidental, that the point of observation on the bridge is marked by a sunken, rectangular space (Fig. 2.16). The north and south end gateways in the western entrances thus correspond to the north and south end figures in the churning scene: both are defined by the movement of the sun and the calendar dates of June 21 and December 22, respectively. The central tower of the western entrances is equivalent, in this regard, to the churning pivot. Both are positioned at the spring equinox center, both are central to the north and south arms that extend outward from them, and both have 54/54 divisions in measurements on each side of them. The bas-relief of the Churning of the Sea of Milk and the main entrance to Angkor Wat therefore convey exactly the same calendrical information in the same type of solstice-equinox pattern.

The two solstice alignments at the very beginning of the bridge are an extraordinary component of the architecture of Angkor Wat. They bracket the western entrances just as the solstices themselves bracket the north–south journey of the sun each year. They are the first alignments to occur on entering the temple and are highly significant in defining the function and meaning of the western entrances. The pattern, or conceptual set, that created this solstice bracketing could be expressed as the principle of using the solstice sun to flank an equinox center, based on the fact that the equinox point is at the center in time and in space between the two solstices. The bas-relief and the western entrances mirror this formation. At the same time, the king is like the equinox: he is at the center of

AITAREYA BRĀHMANA (RIG VEDA)

his realm. The central sanctuary of Angkor Wat is at the conceptual center of the capital and the nation. As it turns out, the king himself is, in fact, directly tied to the symbolism of the solstice-equinox movement and to the Churning of the Sea of Milk. There is no need to postulate. The relationship is spelled out.

THE *INDRĀBHIṢEKA*

Even though the bas-relief of the Churning of the Sea of Milk has a seemingly endless line of identical *deva*s pulling against the chorus of *asura*s, the delicate carving and detail of each piece of jewelry, each eyebrow and mustache, and the very rhythm of the repetitive figures create visually rich and opulent images (Fig. 2.17). From the fingertips of the gods and antigods to the tiny striations in the cloth of the *sampot*s, the sculptors have lavished microscopic attention on this panoramic scene.

The finesse of the master's chisel imparts a sense of luxury to the scene, and with good reason. A series of disparate literary and visual clues indicates that this graceful tug-of-war may allude to the coronation of King Sūryavarman II. Evidence for this occurs not only in the relief itself but in both Khmer and foreign sources ranging from India in the first centuries of our era to fifteenth-century Thailand.

The possible connection between an Indrābhiṣeka (coronation of a king) and the churning scene is not a new concept. An unsigned review that appeared in the *Journal of Indian History* states:

> An *Indrābhiṣeka* is a ceremony symbolizing the reinstallation of Indra in his position after having lost his wealth and position, as the result of the slaying of Vṛtra; and the recovering of it was after a long period of penance by the Churning of the Ocean of Milk.[11]

Aside from this reference, various texts and commentators have said that it was after the battle following the Churning of the Sea of Milk that Indra either became king for the first time or had his kingship over the *deva*s restored.[12]

The very name of the royal consecration throughout Indian literature always makes reference to the god Indra. The association is not accidental. The *Aitareya Brāhmaṇa* (one of two brāhmaṇas or commentaries on the Rig Veda) describes the coronation as an *abhiṣeka* of Indra, the principal features of which are repeated in the *mahābhiṣeka* of the king that follows it. Both of these *abhiṣeka*s take place around the new year, or the spring equinox period. Divinities of all four quarters of the compass are called upon to bless the king or Indra as they sit on the throne and are anointed. In both ceremonies, the royal figure is recognized for his "overlordship . . . paramount rule . . . supreme authority . . . and preeminence."[13] By word, gesture, and nuance, the consecration establishes the king as a sovereign ruler. The *Bṛhat Saṁhitā*, a sixth-century Indian text, describes the rite as "very salutary at the king's inauguration and also when he aspires to the rank of an emperor."[14]

From the earliest textual beginnings in India, then, Indra and the king were associated with the same *abhiṣeka,* a ceremony that came to bear the name of Indra alone (*Indrābhiṣeka,* or Indra's *abhiṣeka*). Since Indra was crowned king of the *devas* after the Churning of the Sea of Milk, the royal *abhiṣeka,* equated to Indra's, might logically take place around the time of the spring equinox, after an enactment of the churning scene.

In fact, the Churning of the Sea of Milk was dramatically enacted during the *Indrābhiṣeka* of at least one Thai king.[15] This ceremony lasted 21 days; the churning enactment took place on the fifth day and featured 100 men dressed as *asura*s and another 100 as *deva*s, churning a large replica of Mount Meru. The Thais understood Meru, rather

Fig. 2.17. Third gallery, east side, south half, churning scene, large deva *nearest tail.*

Six large figures punctuate the series of *deva*s and *asura*s in the churning scene at regular intervals. This multiheaded *deva* on the north is probably Viṣṇu in disguise. This image is flanked by solstice shafts of light in December and June and is fully illuminated at the equinoxes.

than Mandara, to be the churning pivot (as did the Khmers, quite often). At the conclusion of the churning scene, the king was given objects symbolic of those churned up from the Sea of Milk. Before the elixir emerged, Śrī Devī, the goddess of good fortune, emerged, along with Indra's three-headed elephant Airāvata, the horse Uccaiḥśravas, a wishing tree, and many other auspicious objects. Moreover, a poison came up that Śiva drank to protect others, leaving him with a blue throat. The Thai ritual did not use a 54/54 division, of course, but since the Thai Brahmanical rituals were adopted from Cambodia, there is every reason to believe that the *Indrābhiṣeka* was Khmer in origin.

At the Bayon there is a scene in which the future King Jayavarman VII is on elephantback heading into a wooded area. Below him and to the right is an inscription, the remains of which read:

> ... the peace of all the universe. Then the king retreats into the forest at the moment when he is about to celebrate the holy *Indrābhiṣeka*.[16]

This inscription makes three references: one to

Fig. 2.18. Third gallery, east side, south half, churning scene, flying deva.
In this rare break from a strict iconography, the four-headed Brahmā is not at the top of Mount Mandara. The *deva* that flies down to steady the churning pivot is most likely Indra before he was crowned king of the gods. Unlike the ordinary *devas* he wears a jeweled belt and flowered *sampot*. His headdress and flying drapery are unfinished.

JAYAVARMAN VII PEACE

"peace," one to a forest, and one to the king's *Indrābhiṣeka*. The first reference to peace, preceding as it does the ritual of the *abhiṣeka* or consecration, may be related to the Churning of the Sea of Milk. Only after peace was restored, following the battle for the elixir of immortality, was Indra crowned king of the gods. Second, the reference to the king going into a forest corresponds to a statement in the *Bṛhat Saṁhitā,* which specifies that the *Indrābhiṣeka* takes place in a forest setting and, further, describes the natural setting at length.[17] Third, the *Indrābhiṣeka* itself occurs only after the "peace of all the universe." Jayavarman VII had just brought peace (or at least the beginnings of peace) to Angkor, ending the effects of the sack of Angkor by the Chams. Angkor had been in a state of chaos between 1177 and 1181, the latter year being the date when the king was crowned. "Universal peace" may have been a flattering exaggeration, but at least the end of chaos was at hand in 1181.

Bernard-Philippe Groslier notes that the scene of the Churning of the Sea of Milk on the inner gallery of the Bayon is placed in exact correspondence to that of the *Indrābhiṣeka* on the outer gallery. Groslier suggests: "[It] seems to be something more than accidental when one realizes [the importance of] the role of the churning scene in Khmer symbolism, especially how much it is constantly utilized to evoke the beginning of a reign that brings prosperity to the universe."[18] The evidence of the bas-reliefs at the Bayon and the evidence at Angkor Wat are in agreement. Even the bas-relief at Angkor Wat reveals subtle indications that the relationship between Indra, kingship, and the Churning of the Sea of Milk was a reality in twelfth-century Cambodia.

The *deva* who flies down to steady the churning pivot in the Angkor Wat scene is not Brahmā, who is usually on top of Mandara. This is the only instance in Khmer art in which the figure atop Mount Mandara looks exactly like the other *deva*s, in clothing, facial features, headdress, and jewelry (Fig. 2.18). Since no ordinary *deva* would be so especially singled out in this honored position, various scholars have suggested that this god is quite likely Indra himself before his coronation.[19] In the Thai enactment of the churning scene, someone in the guise of Indra did sit on top of "Mount Meru." As Indra flies down to steady the churning pivot in the Angkor Wat relief, he is not yet king, since the churning event is not yet completed nor the subsequent battle won. Nevertheless, the presence of many other "kings" in this relief presages the imminent coronation of Indra.

Bali, the large *asura* holding onto the head of Vāsuki (Fig. 2.19), is the king of the *asura*s, and Sugrīva who holds the tail of Vāsuki is the king of the monkeys (Fig. 2.20).[20] Sugrīva's monkeys are equivalent to *deva*s at Angkor Wat, as their fathers were gods. Viṣṇu incarnates briefly as a king in the forms of Rāma and Kṛṣṇa. Kūrma is the king of tortoises and wears a crown (Fig. 2.21), Mandara is the king of mountains, and Vāsuki, each of his heads also crowned, is the king of *nāga*s. Indra will soon be the king of the gods. Certainly the coronation of a worldly king could not have a better peer group of royal protagonists.

The combined weight of this evidence would suggest that the 54/54-unit pairs on the bridge parallel the king and Indra by means of the sacred *Indrābhiṣeka* and the Churning of the Sea of Milk. This concept is repeated again in the third gallery, the gallery of historical bas-reliefs. On the western half of the gallery, the south panel depicts King Sūryavarman among his ministers. The panel is placed opposite another on the north that depicts Indra and 20 other gods. Both of these relief panels measure 54 *phyeam,* making another 54/54 set at Angkor Wat. This time, King Sūryavarman and Indra are paired explicitly since they are positioned directly opposite each other across the gallery.

Based on the preceding data, Sūryavarman's rise to power and his *Indrābhiṣeka* are underlying allusions in the 54/54-unit symbolism on the bridge. By combining the *Indrābhiṣeka*, or inauguration of the king, with the yearly solstices, the architects have brilliantly joined the celebration of the king's coronation (at the spring equinox?) with a celebration of the solstitial calendar and the never-ending oscillation of the sun and moon. Cosmology and kingship are therefore fused in an eternal architectural union. The inauguration at the beginning of King Sūryavarman's reign is appropriately represented in the bridge at the beginning of his temple. At the same time, the sun and moon rise first to the left and then to the right of the bridge throughout the year, moving from one solstice to the next like the swing of a pendulum. This movement refers indirectly to the second major numerical characteristic of the bridge: the passage of time cycles.

Fig. 2.19. Third gallery, east side, south half, churning scene, Bali and heads of Vāsuki.

Bali, the king of the *asuras*, holds the five heads of Vāsuki as he pulls with his legs and arms against the weight of the *nāga*. The crowned heads of Vāsuki are seen again on the left as they rise up from his position in the Sea of Milk. Thus the *nāga* king is shown twice in the relief.

Fig. 2.20. Third gallery, east side, south half, churning scene, Sugrīva at the tail of Vāsuki.

Just as Bali marks the southernmost, winter solstice position in the sequence of *asuras*, his counterpart Sugrīva holds up the *nāga*'s tail at the far north, a symbol for the summer solstice day. He has a human form except for his tail and his fierce animal face.

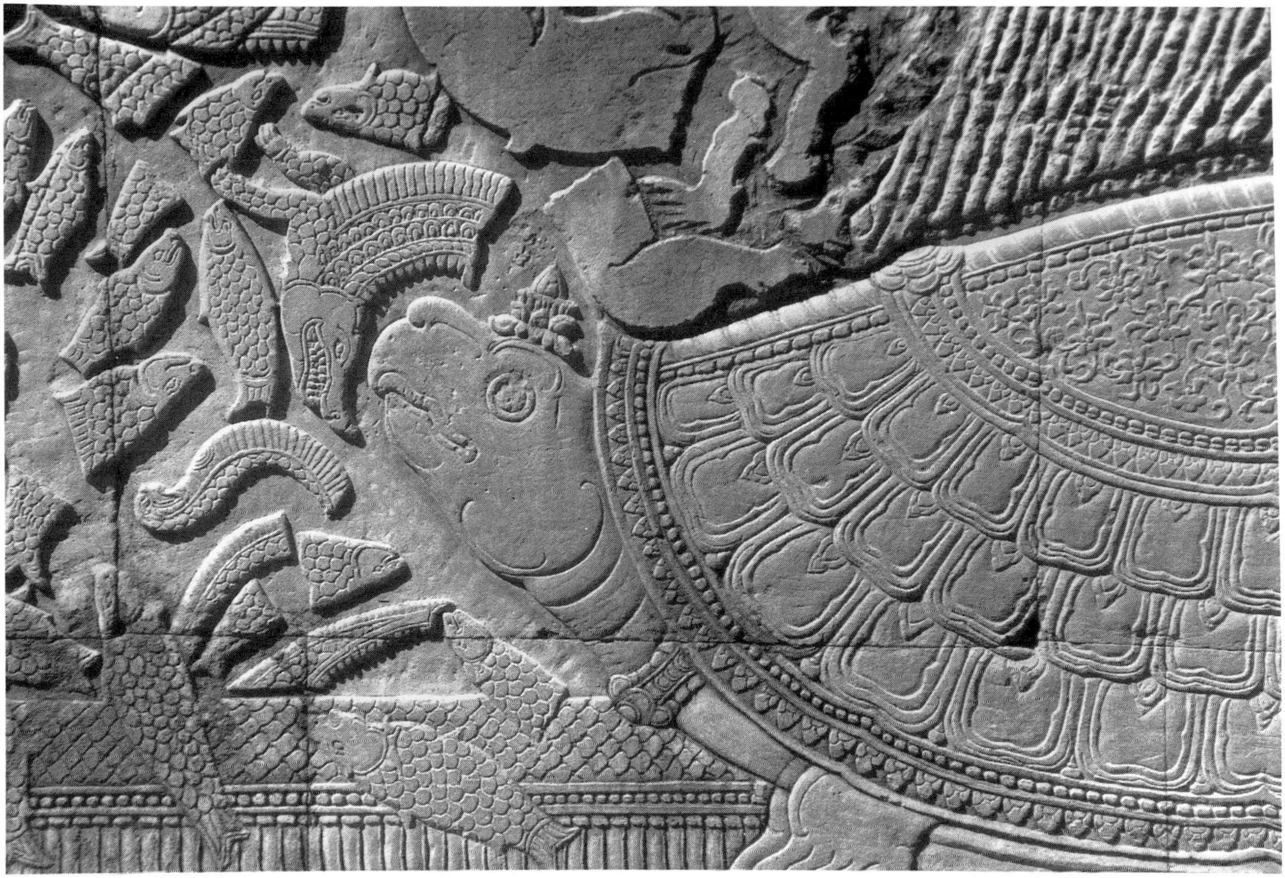

Fig. 2.21. Third gallery, east side, south half, churning scene, center, Kūrma.

Kūrma, the king of tortoises, is shown with his own crown in this scene. His enormous scale is implied by the size of the large fish and crocodiles that have been torn up by the force of the churning itself.

TIME CYCLES

In Brahmanical cosmology, our universe is transformed during four distinct and successive time periods, called yugas, repeated over and over again. Of these four cycles, the *kali yuga,* our own time period, is the worst of all. During the *kali yuga* the human life span is the shortest ever; wars and famine are common; morality and ethics are all but lost. This ill-fated time cycle lasts for 432,000 years and according to legend began a few thousand years ago (at an undetermined date) with a battle on the plains of Kuru in northwestern India. When the two halves of the span of the western entrance bridge are measured in cubits, together they equal 431.07 cubits,[21] or very close to a total that may symbolize the 432,000 years in a *kali yuga.* In this type of correspondence, each cubit would be a "module" for 1000 years. Space then becomes a symbol for time, and we would consequently leave our own era behind on the bridge before entering the temple.

As our era is clearly inauspicious—indeed, there is no worse time period—the architects kept this approximate 432-unit measurement the farthest possible distance from the central sanctuary. In fact, it lies outside the protective enclosing wall of the temple. Perhaps to ameliorate its aura of negativity, the *kali yuga* represented by the span of the bridge is overlapped by much better time periods. The *kṛta yuga* lasts for 1,728,000 years measured in terrestrial, or human, time; in celestial or divine time, the *kṛta yuga* is 4800 years long. It is the first, most perfect, and longest time cycle in the series of four.[22] After the *kṛta yuga* follow the *tretā*, the *dvāpara,* and the *kali yuga*s in a slow and inexorable degeneration:

Yuga	*Celestial years*	*Terrestrial years*
kṛta	4800	1,728,000
tretā	3600	1,296,000
dvāpara	2400	864,000
kali	1200	432,000

Time does not stop at the end of these four yugas. Cycles continue until a final and total dissolution:

4 yuga cycles = 1 *mahāyuga* (4,320,000 years)
14 *mahāyuga*s + 15 *kṛta yuga*s (between each *mahāyuga* and at the end) = 1 *kalpa* (4,320,000,000 years)
720 *kalpa*s (360 days and 360 nights for Brahmā) = 1 year
100 years for Brahmā = dissolution of universe at all levels; Brahmā merges again with the sleeping Viṣṇu

At some point when Viṣṇu was awake, the architects inserted the beginning of the three remaining yuga periods into the beginning, middle, and end of the bridge (Fig. 2.22):

kṛta yuga: from the first step up to the bridge to the last step out of the threshold of the second gallery, facing the upper elevation of the temple (1725.89 cubits)[23]
tretā yuga: from the center of the bridge to the doorway into the third gallery (1292.02 cubits)[24]
dvāpara yuga: from the end of the bridge on the east, at the point where the first step up to the

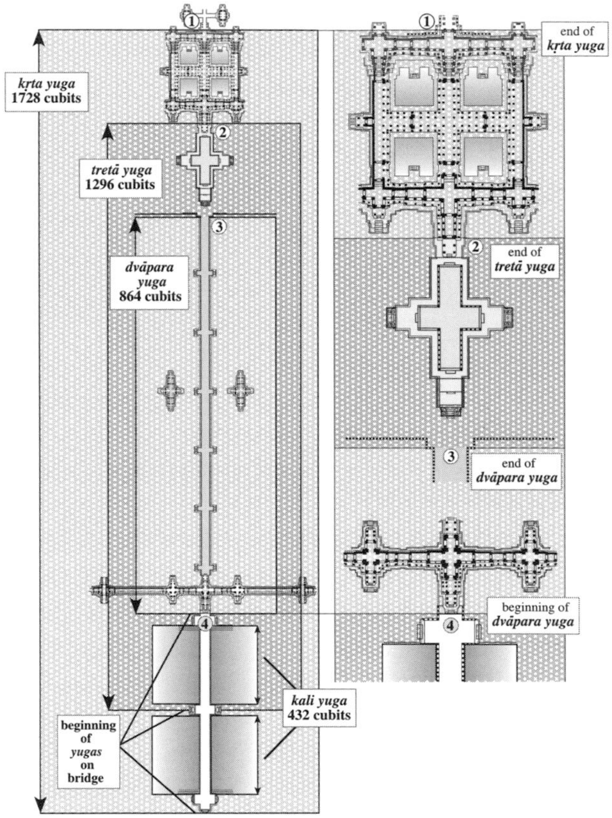

Fig. 2.22. Diagram of 4 yuga cycles on the western axis.

Three of the Hindu time cycles generated on the western entrance bridge are connected by measurements to specific architectural boundaries inside the temple. The longer the measurement, the purer and more perfect the time period. The worst period, the *kali yuga,* remains isolated on the two halves of the span of the bridge.

western entrance begins, to the point at which the *nāga* balustrade around the central galleries of Angkor Wat intersects the causeway (864.83 cubits)[25]

The golden era, the *kṛta* age, takes us all the way through the second gallery to face the upper elevation for the first time. It introduces the home of the gods at Angkor Wat. The *tretā yuga* introduces the third gallery of historical bas-reliefs, but does not cross into it. Only the golden age and most perfect time period coincides with Sūryavarman's gallery. The *dvāpara yuga* takes us up to the beginning of the central galleries and no farther. The *kali yuga* remains outside the temple's outer walls.

As we leave each negative yuga behind on a journey to the center of Angkor Wat, time becomes purer as a consequence. These changes indicate that time was not conceived as a neutral entity but had greater or lesser proportions of good qualities that could either enhance or undermine the temple and its rituals. Because time is not inert but dynamic, it is not surprising to discover that a good king had the power to change the qualities of his—and our—time period. What the architects "built" into Angkor Wat could be equally manufactured by a wise and benevolent king.

KING SŪRYAVARMAN AND THE *KṚTA YUGA*

Returning to the bridge and its dimensions, if there were no staircases in the middle, there could be no 54/54-unit pairs on the bridge. The architects could have created a 432-cubit distance with no division in it. And according to Brahmanical cosmology, the Churning of the Sea of Milk occurs only during a *kṛta yuga*. Why then divide the bridge in half and place the *kali yuga* and the Churning of the Sea of Milk in exactly the same space?

The answer is very straightforward. It lies in the belief that a good king can eradicate the *kali yuga* and install the *kṛta* age when he comes to power, that is, at the time of his *Indrābhiṣeka*. When a king is not quite that good, the era may change to the *tretā yuga*. A barely good king might manage the *dvāpara yuga*. The *Mahābhārata* says:

> When a king pursues strict government perfectly and completely, then the best of eras begins, the *kṛta* age. Have no doubt whether the time causes the king or the king causes the time: it is the king who is the cause of the times (eras). The king is the creator of the *kṛta* age.[26]

Other Khmer inscriptions describe the king as follows:

> This king, with the brilliance of fire, began the *kṛta yuga* . . . . Under the reign of this king, who has manifested the *kṛta yuga* and thrown away the evils of the *kali yuga* . . . . This king . . . by means of his politics, actualized the conditions of the *kṛta* age.[27]

Based on the measurements of the bridge, one could postulate that when the Churning of the Sea of Milk was enacted at King Sūryavarman's *Indrābhiṣeka,* the *kṛta yuga* was then in effect. The new king had thus banished the *kali* era. The Churning of the Sea of Milk and the *kali yuga* could be juxtaposed on the bridge to symbolize that change and a new beginning. If the 54/54 symbolism were not juxtaposed over the 432 cubits of the *kali yuga* measurement, there would be no clear association between that period and the *Indrābhiṣeka* of the king.

Angkor Wat starts here, on the bridge. The beginning of King Sūryavarman's reign (the churning event) starts on the bridge, as well, and so too does the *kṛta yuga*. The juxtaposition of all these elements is clear enough: the king inaugurates a new temple and a new era at his own inauguration.

YUGA CYCLES AROUND THE FOURTH ENCLOSURE

Time moves in transformation across the bridge and into the central galleries around the outer enclosure, as well, in a second series of yuga cycles (Fig. 2.23). As before, the *kali yuga* is represented by the two halves of the span of the bridge. As the journey continues through the triad of western sanctuaries at the end of the bridge, the yugas cease and a brief hiatus from worldly time transpires. The *dvāpara yuga* then begins—between the lateral entrances and the corners of the enclosing wall (862.81 cubits on the south and 865.68 on the north).[28] The *tretā yuga* covers the distance between the corner of the enclosing wall and the doorway of the axial entrance on the south (1293.56 cubits) or north (1296.60 cubits).[29] And the *kṛta yuga* lies in the distance between the northern and southern axial entrances, excluding the upper elevation (base to base). This comes to 1723.92 cubits.[30] Another *kṛta yuga* results if we turn around at the base of the upper elevation and go back to the axial entrance (1729.61 cubits on the north, 1718.22 on the south). Just as in the sequence along the western axis, space is transformed by the yuga cycles: it becomes more sacred as the upper elevation nears and less and less sacred as we exit the temple.

Significantly, there are no yuga sequences on the east side of the temple. But there are 1738.32 cubits (10 cubits longer than the ideal length) between the east end of the east causeway/bridge and the base of the main western staircase, hidden under the walkway (Fig. 2.24).[31] This approximate *kṛta yuga* length matches the *kṛta yuga* on the west side of the axis (Fig. 2.25). Between these two dis-

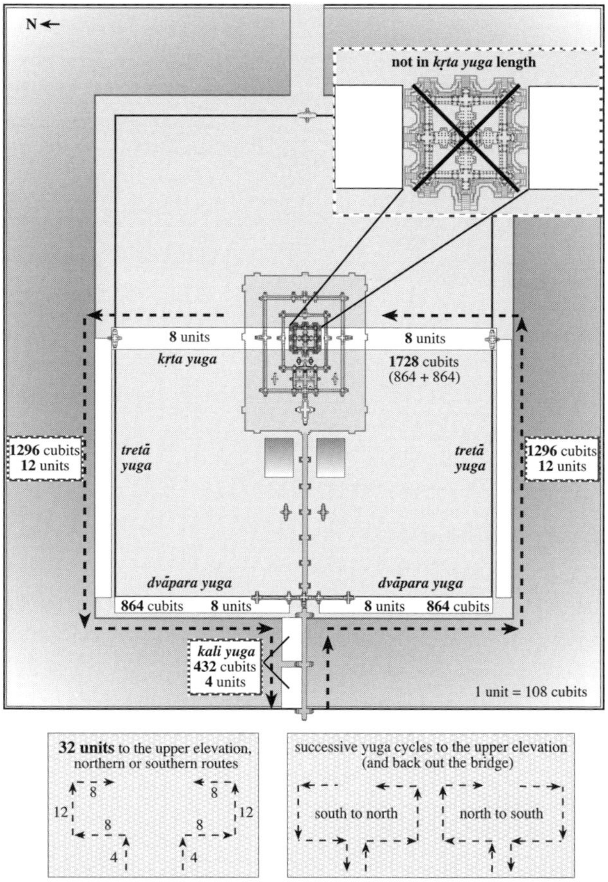

Fig. 2.23. Yuga cycles from the bridge to the base of the upper elevation.

After crossing the *kali yuga* on the bridge, we could walk north or south to the upper elevation of the temple, passing through a cubit distance equivalent to the *dvāpara* and *tretā yuga* in sequence. At the north or south entrance to the outer enclosure, a *kṛta yuga* length crosses the courtyard from end to end, omitting the distance across the upper elevation itself. If these time periods are expressed in units of 108 cubits, they trace a path of 32 units to the upper elevation.

tances is a length of 31.62 cubits (Fig. 2.26).[32] The entire west–east axis of Angkor Wat is therefore defined by the golden age, the era created by King Sūryavarman when he came to power. That golden era is centered on 32, the number of gods on the top of the cosmic mountain, Mount Meru.

Before considering the central role of 32 at Angkor Wat, we should note that Mount Meru has its own complex geography, with several different heavens of the gods in an ascending order.[33] At the very top of the mountain is Indra's heaven of 33 or Trayastriṁśā heaven (33 = 32 + a supreme divinity). The description of his palace and its location is reminiscent of the walled cities at Angkor with a temple in the center. Indra's city, Sudarśana, is walled in gold with the palace at its center. The summit of Meru has been flattened (as have the three mountain peaks at Angkor with temples on their summits) to accommodate the palace. Far outside and below the city are four subsidiary

Fig. 2.24. Main western staircase, upper elevation, juncture with walkway.

The cruciform walkway that leads to the great western staircase on the upper level covers the base and first step of the staircase. This gives the upper elevation two different end points for the axes on the west. One terminus is with the end of the walkway as it hits the second step; the other includes the base under the walkway.

mountain peaks marking the corners and boundaries of this heaven. These four peaks correspond to the four subsidiary towers we find on the upper level of Angkor Wat and on monuments such as the Bakheng (ca. 900) and Takeo (ca. 1000). As has often been stated, the surrounding galleries and towers at Angkor Wat, as well as the moat, can be understood as symbols for the seven concentric mountain ranges and seven oceans that circle the base of Meru.

The realm of the guardians of the four directions covers the lower reaches of Meru, which includes the mansions of the sun and moon (constellations), the summits of the concentric mountain ranges, and four ascending levels of minor deities on the lower half of Meru.[34] The fourth and highest level houses the directional gods themselves, each on their appropriate side of the mountain. Their expanded realm constitutes the first heaven of the gods. Above them is Indra's heaven,

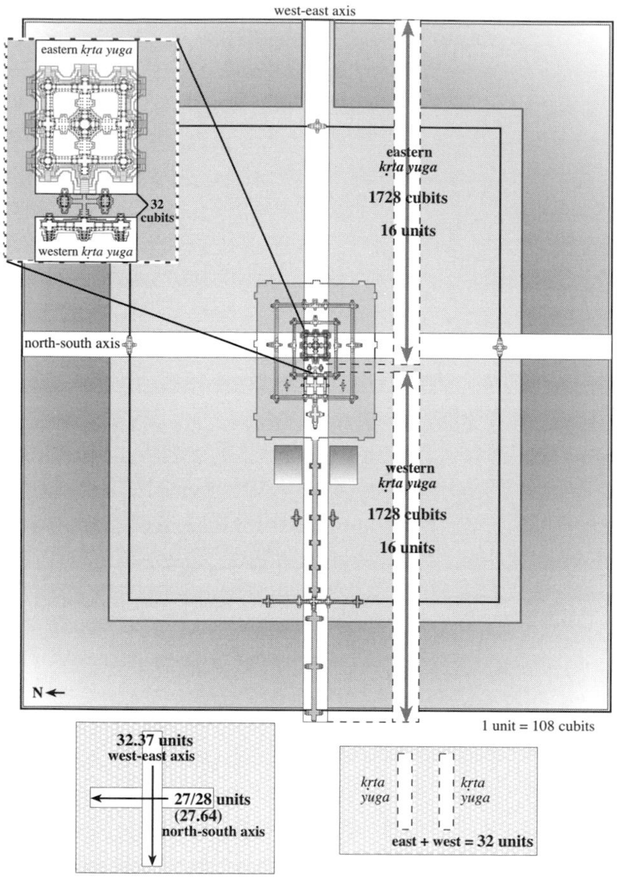

Fig. 2.25. Temple axes and west-east kṛṣta yuga *lengths.*

There are two *kṛta yuga* lengths on the west and east sides of the main axis of Angkor Wat. They start at the farthest border of the axis and end facing each other across the short, 32-cubit walkway that connects the second gallery to the upper level. If both axes of the temple are measured in 108-cubit modules they total slightly more than 32 west–east (the 32 *devas*) and between 27 and 28 units north–south (lunar constellations).

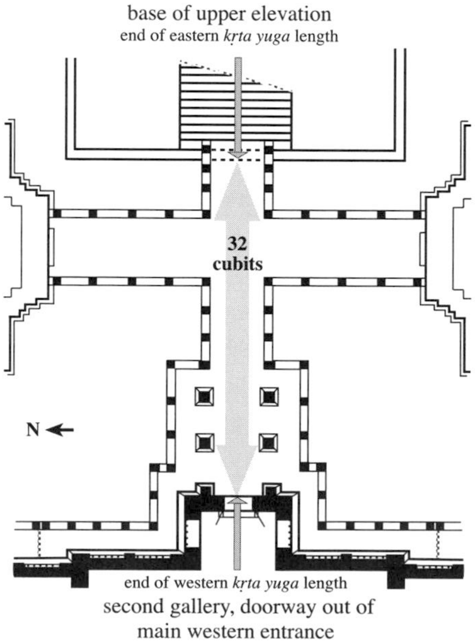

Fig. 2.26. Walkway between the second gallery and upper elevation, 32-cubit axis.

A length of 31.62, or approximately 32 cubits connects the end of the *kṛta yuga* on the west to the end of the *kṛta yuga* on the east, at the base of the upper elevation.

and above that there are 24 heavens of gods in which form is still manifest. The heaven of Brahmā himself is the seventh in this ascending list of 24. The central tower of Angkor Wat has seven levels, including the two telescoping axial roofs that lead to the upper five tiers. Perhaps these levels refer to the first seven heavens. Above the twenty-fourth heaven there are four "formless" heavens, perhaps a misnomer. The god realms on Mount Meru thus total 28. To recapitulate, the 28 heavens are: (1) the realm of the directional guardian kings; (2) Indra's heaven of 33; (3–6) four heavens in which desire is still a component, including Tuṣita heaven; (7–24) 18 "Brahmā" heavens with individual traits; and (25–28) four formless realms.

Both 28 and 24 are commonly found measurements at Angkor Wat, especially in regard to lunar symbolism. As for the 32 gods that live at the summit of Meru, they are sequentially dispersed in a mandala of time and space that is intimately related to our world. Their central role at Angkor Wat has a lot to do with their central position at the top of Mount Meru.

A MANDALA *OF DEVAS*

A certain genre of diagrams or mandalas for the foundation of a Brahmanical temple serves as one of the foremost sources of numerical symbolism in Khmer temples and merits detailed attention here. This diagram is called a *vāstupuruṣamaṇḍala: vāstu* means "architecture"; *puruṣa* means "Person," or the primordial, supreme principle, the cause and essence of existence; and mandala means "cosmic diagram" in this instance. Angkor Wat may derive a good portion of its symbolism from the *vāstupuruṣamaṇḍala*.

This well-known diagram depicts 32 *devas* and 12 *ādityas*, or solar gods, around a square perimeter at the center of which resides Brahmā (Fig. 2.27), *kalpa* after *kalpa*.[35] This type of mandala divides the 32 *devas* into 28 *nakṣatra* (constellations around the ecliptic) and 4 planetary gods: Yama, Soma (or Kubera), Indra, and Varuṇa, who are also associated with the cardinal points of the compass (south, north, east, and west, respectively).[36] The 32 deities that ring the mandala are also sometimes referred to as the 32 *nakṣatra;* while their individual names may vary, it is always the *nakṣatra* with which these deities are identified and associated.[37] Between these *devas* and the god Brahmā are the 12 *ādityas*, gods of the solar months. They are arranged in differing patterns depending on the mandala. Brahmā is at both the center and the apex; the other gods are below him as on Mount Meru.

Perhaps this diagram is so crucial to the meaning of Angkor Wat because it also represents the northern sky. Brahmā resides at the north celestial pole, just above Mount Meru. We have already seen that Meru is the axis of the earth. Thus, from Brahmā's perspective, the sun would circumambulate him every day, coming closer during the summer solstice and disappearing under the horizon during the winter solstice. As the sun (and moon) oscillate back and forth, the 28 *nakṣatra* would remain fixed around his outer border. The four planetary deities, in charge of the directions as well, would also be fixed in space. In this way, the 32 gods on Mount Meru are equated with the constellations and directions of space. Since Brahmā is the creator of time and space, these constellations were created by him. They are the backdrop against which the movements of the sun, moon, and planets are measured. They are essential to all astrologers. When seen from the perspective of the stellar night sky, the 32 *devas* are thus much more than gods on Mount Meru. The patterns of stars and the planets, the sun (Sūrya), and the moon (Candra) are all manifestations of deities. Through astrology, which gave character traits to the constellations and interpreted the positions of

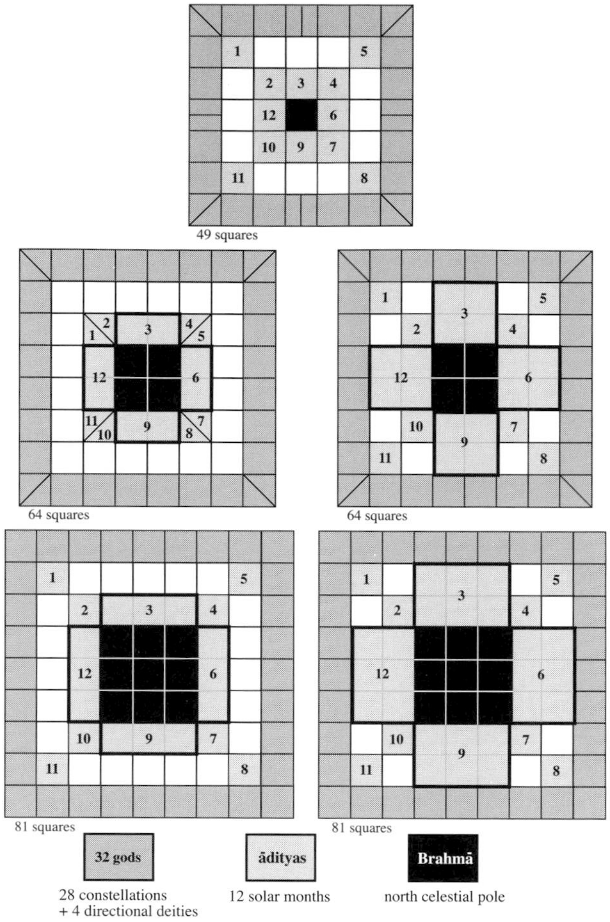

Fig. 2.27. Architectural mandalas.

Temple architecture has a wide variety of mandalas that are drawn on the ground before construction begins. At Angkor Wat, the mandala most in evidence is the *vāstupuruṣamaṇḍala* shown here. These mandalas have several different patterns and vary in the number of squares in their grid. The general location of the deities in each mandala is always the same, however. The central square area represents Brahmā; there are 12 lightly shaded squares between Brahmā and the perimeter that represent the solar gods of the zodiac, and 32 squares (bifurcated in mandalas of a smaller perimeter) that represent the lunar constellations and 4 planetary or directional deities. The number 49 is recurrent at Angkor Wat, whereas 64 and 81 are not a part of the temple's system of measurements. The 64- and 81-square designs are found in the literature on mandalas, the 49-square grid appears to be a Khmer invention. Therefore, I have suggested a possible arrangement for the deities in the 49-unit grid, based on logic but not on any known text. The numbering of the solar deities in the mandalas is meant to highlight their place, but is arbitrary in its starting and ending points.

the moving points of deified light (planets) in space, the gods were ultimately related to every aspect of life at Angkor.

MANIFESTATIONS OF 32

Earlier we noted that 108 was a particularly sacred number in Asia—probably the most universally sacred number of all. If the *kali yuga* on the bridge is measured in a 108-cubit module, it becomes 4 units long. The subsequent *dvāpara yuga, tretā yuga,* and one-half of the *kṛta yuga* distance, the actual distance up to the upper elevation on the south or north, comes to 28 large units. In this way, the 4 units on the bridge plus the remaining 28 units up to the upper elevation on the north or south not only define the 32 *deva*s: they divide the *deva*s into the 4 planetary or directional gods (bridge) and the 28 *nakṣatra.* If these north–south paths of 32 units each refer to the border of the *vāstupuruṣamaṇḍala,* then the 12 staircases around the upper elevation would symbolize the 12 months in the year, or the 12 *āditya*s in the mandala, and the central tower, the Mount Meru axis at Angkor Wat, would signal the position of Brahmā at the center of the mandala. In fact, there are 44 pillars around the central tower, making the tower itself a "forty-fifth" master pillar. Brahmā is surrounded by 44 deities in the mandala and represents the forty-fifth and supreme deity himself. The temple as a whole may be one vast mandala of the *devas* on Mount Meru.

When the two *kṛta yugas* that flank the central 32 cubits on the west–east axis are measured in 108-cubit units, they also total 32. If this axis is expressed in the larger 108-cubit unit, it is exactly 32.27 units long.[38] The north–south axis of Angkor Wat between the far borders of the moat is 1300 m, or 27.64 units of 108 cubits each.[39] It is possible that a combination of 27/28 and 32 was intended in these two axial lengths—which would then clearly join the 27/28 *nakṣatra* on the north–south axis to the 32 *devas* on the west–east axis (Fig. 2.25).

Axial lengths and perimeters or circumferences form clear-cut pairs at Angkor Wat, and the outermost boundaries of the temple are no exception. The perimeter around the moat is 120 units of 108 cubits each.[40] Once again, it would appear that the three most distinctive numerical components of the architectural mandala—12, 27/28, and 32—are intended in the axes and the perimeter of Angkor Wat's outermost border. Yet this may not have been the primary intent of the architects. Axial lengths are whole numbers in the rest of the temple, and so the total for these axes, (27.64 + 32.37, or 60.01 units), may have been the objective all along—especially since this number matches the exact 120.02-unit distance of the perimeter so well (Fig. 2.28).

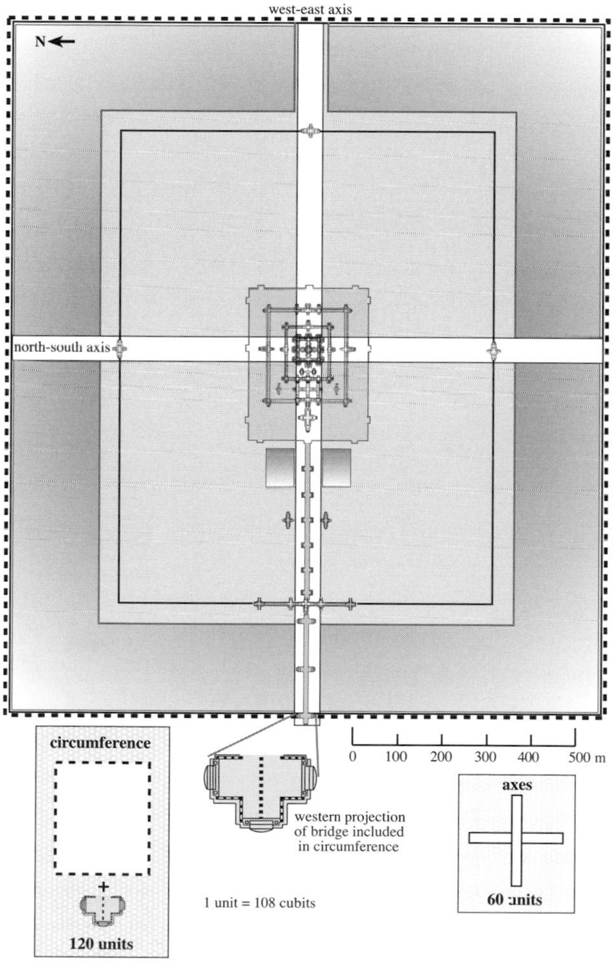

Fig. 2.28. Temple axes and circumference.
The largest axes at Angkor Wat come to 60.01 units when measured in modules of 108 cubits. That is a more precise total than the individual lengths of the axes shown in Fig. 2.25 and therefore may have been a primary goal of the architects. The circumference total is also a precise 120.02. Both of these numbers are related to the basic units for measuring time and space (60, 12, 10) developed in the Mesopotamian area several millennia before the creation of Angkor Wat. The circumference of the temple includes the western extension of the surface of the bridge because it follows the pattern for circumference calculation at the temple. A circumference includes the inner west–east axis of the main entrance chamber in its gallery, or an equivalent extension on the west when there is no entrance chamber. In this case, the flat surface of the bridge between raised ledges is equivalent to the interior space of an entrance chamber.

As we shall see in the next chapter, 60 and 120 (and also 12 as an arithmetic factor in each case) are the foundation stones on which all subsequent time cycles were constructed. Although there might be a subsidiary meaning in the individual axial lengths (27/28 and 32 here) that is satisfactory, it is ultimately not as ideal as the meaning of 60 units.

A PIVOT OF TIME AND PLACE

What began as an emphasis on 54/54-unit pairs on the bridge became a means of understanding many of the basic principles that guided the construction of Angkor Wat. One of these paramount concepts is that time, divinity, and the king are inextricably conjoined. First, the *Indrābhiṣeka* of the king joins Sūryavarman to the king of *deva*s, Indra. The design of Angkor Wat also seems to link the temple to Indra's city and Mount Meru. By placing *Indrābhiṣeka* measurements of 54/54 on the bridge over a 432-cubit distance, both covered by the beginning of a *kṛta yuga* length, the king is depicted as changing the contemporary *kali yuga* into the perfect golden age when he came to power.

The *Indrābhiṣeka* ceremonies described in the texts cluster around the spring equinox.[41] The fluctuating solstices marked by the end gateways through the movement of the sun also place the central western entrance tower at a spring equinox juncture. This coincidence is highly appropriate given the importance of the spring equinox to the *Indrābhiṣeka* and to the center of the Churning of the Sea of Milk, the thematic focus of the bridge and the central western entrances.

To finalize the merging of kingship, divinity, and time, the transformation of the yuga cycles into numbers representative of the 32 gods creates another link between king, time, and deity. Using this image, we can begin to see corollaries that recur throughout the temple. Neither time nor place, divinity nor humanity, celestial nor terrestrial realms, are independent of each other.

From the point of view of Brahmā, all of time and all of space, divine and human, revolve in unity around him, as he presides over everything in his place above Mount Meru and above the north celestial pole of the earth. King Sūryavarman is joined to Brahmā (who is equated with Viṣṇu in this guise) at the heart of Angkor Wat, in the central tower, which is itself a representation of Mount Meru.

A celestial and terrestrial pivot of time and place, generated by heavenly gods or earthly kings in a parallel conjunction, has an enormous philosophical scope. We thus find a kind of abstract fusion of King Sūryavarman, Indra, Viṣṇu, Brahmā, and an axis of place and time: a "Mount Meru" axis manifest at the center of the Churning of the Sea of Milk, the central tower of Angkor Wat, the planet earth, and the mandala of *deva*s. From the horizontal configuration of the bridge to the vertical configuration of the central tower of the temple, our journey through Angkor Wat is a continually changing experience of these facets of time and place. The bridge, as we soon shall find out, is only the beginning.

3

Measurement Patterns and the Outer Enclosure

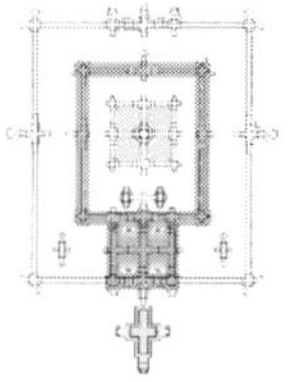

MANY measurements at Angkor Wat, as we have seen, function on several levels at once. Their multiple layers of meaning, moreover, are arranged in patterns throughout the temple. For the Khmers in twelfth-century Angkor, the realms of existence—human or divine—and their multiple facets on earth and in the sky were interrelated in a complex manner. These relationships were, nevertheless, systematized in a way that included certain numerical values. Both the systematization and its attendant numbers find their arena in astronomy and Brahmanical philosophy. Since the latter are not daily fare for most of us, some of the concepts and numbers that appear again and again at the temple are introduced here.

VIṢṆU, AQUILA AND LEO, AND THE SUN

In ways that will become apparent, one by one, astronomy has a bearing on the most hallowed image of the Supreme Viṣṇu in the central tower. To honor this image, the vast outer courtyard provides a long, introductory, horizontal approach to the pyramidal galleries that lead upward to the enclosed image. The floor of the main sanctuary raises Viṣṇu 23 m above ground level and all else at the temple. Combined with the architectural homage, the unsurpassed delicacy of the foliated relief and figural motifs further praise the deity with their exquisitely sculpted forms. The multitude of celestial maidens on the walls and corners add their own beauty and grace to the elegant home of the supreme deity. All the magnificence of Angkor Wat was dedicated to Viṣṇu.

It is clear that Viṣṇu entered Cambodia from India, where he first appeared in the ancient Vedas, the four books sacred to Hinduism. His main epic achievement was as his dwarf avatar when he took three steps encompassing the earth, air, and heavens. Other versions say the steps symbolized the sun's point of rising, its zenith, and its point of setting. Curious about the well-recorded connection between Viṣṇu and the star Altair, I found some information in a dusty astronomy book on the library shelf that corroborates the solar aspects of Viṣṇu described in the Vedas. But Viṣṇu's *stellar* origins surfaced in this book also. That aspect of the deity had remained undiscovered, though, because scholars were not likely to look into the history of constellations to find the birth of Viṣṇu and astronomers were not likely to recognize the birth when it occurred.

Viṣṇu, like many Brahmanical gods, rides a mount unique to himself. Many deities were provided with their own means of transportation, which in Viṣṇu's case is Garuḍa, a mythical, rapacious-looking bird whose physiognomy resembles an eagle (Fig. 3.1). At some unrecorded but very distant point in Indian history, Viṣṇu came to be associated with the star Altair in the constellation Aquila, the Eagle. As the constellation has a history much older than the worship of Viṣṇu, it is clear that Viṣṇu was connected to the constellation and given the eagle as his mount for reasons related to astronomy. Or, viewed from another perspective, could one say that Viṣṇu and Garuḍa were born from the constellation Aquila and its mythology? The history of this constellation goes back to ancient Mesopotamia and sheds solar light on why Viṣṇu and the eagle were joined together.

There are Sumer-Akkadian references to the Eagle constellation as Idkhu, so we do know where the constellation first emerged.[1] As stated by Robert Brown in that dusty book in 1899:

> The constellation of the Eagle is especially interesting both because in this case we can trace very clearly the pre-constellational history of the sign, and because the original Euphratean name has been preserved. The Sumer-Akkadian Eagle was Alala ("the Great Spirit". . .), "the symbol of the noontide sun.". . . Here we have the pre-constellational history of the sign, which is subsequently reduplicated in stellar form as *Kakkab Idkhu, ilu Zamama,* "the constellation the Eagle, i.e., the god Zamama." The principal star of this constellation is also called *Idkhu* (otherwise *Erigu,* i.e., "the Powerful Bird"), the Eagle, in Arabic, *Al Tair* ("the Great Bird"), the *Altair* of star maps.[2]

Thus the "Great Spirit" Alala was in the form of an eagle who also symbolized the afternoon sun—and this belief was current before the constellation Aquila was defined. The text clarifies that "Great Spirit" means the supreme spirit: the highest god. The cultures that followed in this region continued to worship both the eagle and the sun together, as the deities Zamama or Idkhu indicate. By that time, however, the constellation Aquila was created to give the eagle/sun/supreme deity a place in the nighttime sky among the other gods. Is it only coincidence that the solar deity Viṣṇu, certainly a "Great Spirit" in all respects, has a connection to the preconstellational mythology of Aquila? In fact, this mythology dictates the development of the constellation's iconography in later times. The name "eagle" was given both to the star Altair (Arabic for "Great Bird," as noted above) and to the constellation Aquila.[3] The word "Altair" made its way into Ptolemy's star lists, and from there into our modern nomenclature, and eventually it became Viṣṇu's star.

The constellation Aquila is a symbol of the eagle manifestation of Alala. It is also a form of the solar god Zamama, according to cuneiform tablets, and of the god Ninip, yet another solar deity. The word Zamama itself can be translated as "the Living Eye," or the sun. Ninip is described as manifesting as the noontime sun (as was Alala). Thus there is a correlation between the "eye" of the sun during the day and the "eye" of the constellation Aquila at night—the star Altair.

The solar connections of the constellation Aquila, the Eagle, are the same for the god Viṣṇu. In Brahmanical cosmology, Viṣṇu is definitely the highest of all solar gods. Chapter XI of Book II of the *Viṣṇu Purāṇa* is dedicated to the identification of the sun as Viṣṇu. In summary, then, the solar Viṣṇu and his eaglelike mount Garuḍa can be found in remote antiquity as the solar Alala, who appears as an eagle, and as the solar Zamama and Ninip, who appear as the constellation Aquila and

Fig. 3.1. Third gallery, northwest pavilion, east entrance, south wall, Kṛṣṇa on Garuḍa with Mount Maṇiparvata.
In this scene a powerful Garuḍa carries Kṛṣṇa (an avatar of Viṣṇu) on his shoulders and bears Mount Maṇiparvata and Kṛṣṇa's spouse Satyabhāmā in his upraised hands. This same configuration of Viṣṇu on Garuḍa is found in many bronzes and is repeated on the east and north walls of this gallery.

its main star, Altair. Whether Viṣṇu came into being as a transformation of Alala/Zamama/Ninip in Brahmanical guise, or whether the mythology of Aquila was naturally joined to the already existent Viṣṇu, is not a decision I would dare venture here. But the outcome is the same: the relationship is there.

Alala, Zamama, and Ninip, however, are very much connected to the meaning of Viṣṇu at the heart of Angkor Wat. In twelfth-century Cambodia, based on the analysis of Angkor Wat that is the focus of this book, Viṣṇu definitely inherited the role of the nighttime "Living Eye" of Altair, a symbol for the daytime "eye of the sun." The solar Viṣṇu therefore ruled supreme over the day and over the night as well. This belief is made thoroughly clear in the measurement systems at Angkor Wat. Nothing less would befit a supreme deity.

The constellation Aquila is called Śrāvaṇa in Indian and Khmer astronomy. Śrāvaṇa, or Aquila, is one of the 27/28 lunar mansions. Just as our zodiac signs are associated with specific months of the year, the lunar months are defined by these 27/28 constellations. Viṣṇu also manifests as one of the zodiac signs. The twelfth *āditya* is identified with Viṣṇu and would correspond to the month of Phālguna in the zodiac sequence, or the constellation Leo, the Lion. The month of Aquila or Śrāvaṇa encompasses late July/early August, and Leo, the Lion, covers the time between July 23 and August 22 in our Western astrological system. The lion is a solar symbol also. I have no expertise in either Asian or Western astrology, but the coincidence of Leo sharing the same time of year with Śrāvaṇa is striking.

Viṣṇu thus manifests in the solar system of zodiac signs as the constellation Leo and manifests in the lunar system of constellations as Aquila. These two systems, solar and lunar, share not only the space around the ecliptic but several other aspects as well. First of all, the solar months use the same names as the lunar months, in addition to their more commonly known names, such as Makara for January. Twelve names were chosen in sequence from the list of 24 lunar half-months to designate the solar months in sequence. This practice unifies the solar and lunar calendars, joining them under a common nomenclature to show that they are a parallel means of measuring the same time in two different ways. Viṣṇu is one god, the ultimate creator of time, who manifests in both the lunar and solar constellation systems. He is also the *same god,* whether seen as Aquila/Śrāvaṇa or as Leo.

Second, the lions that guard the staircases all over Angkor are accompanied by the great *nāga*s that form the balustrades of the walkways. Just as the lions are solar, the *nāga*s are manifestly lunar. Their inseparability as guardians of the stairways and walkways of the temple is yet another statement about the inherent unity of the solar (lion, eagle) and lunar *(nāga)* systems in the sky and on earth—and the inherent unity, too, of these facets of Viṣṇu himself. Parallel to Viṣṇu in some ways, the later kings of Cambodia, including Sūryavarman, are praised as unifying the solar and lunar races of kings. That tradition of associating a lineage with the sun or moon came from India originally.

Finally, the leonine head of a mythical creature at the center of many lintels and in the decorative temple reliefs at Angkor, not just at Angkor Wat, has two thick undulating vines that emerge from its mouth (Fig. 3.2). These *nāga*-like bodies/vines usually terminate in a foliated *makara* motif. The *makara* itself, with a fishlike torso and elephant's trunk, is aquatic. Its relationship to a *nāga* is clear because of this aquatic symbolism and the long undulating body emerging from the mouth of the central head. Besides, the *makara* motif is replaced by *nāga* heads at Angkor Wat.

This composition has many variants. In fact, it is sometimes shown as a *garuḍa* head at the center

Fig. 3.2. Main western entrances, east facade, figures over windows.

The lionlike *kāla* head over this gesticulating, mounted figure is shown holding two foliated branches that emerge from his mouth. *Garuḍa*s hold up the ends of the foliated frame around the guardian figure on horseback, as can be seen at the lower right. (Photograph courtesy of Yves Coffin.)

with claws holding two *nāgas*, one on each side. Could this lionlike central head, often called a *kāla* head in Indonesian and Cambodian art, have its origins in the mythical lion of the constellation Leo?[4] If so, this central head was meant to be a solar symbol and an indirect reference to Viṣṇu through his guise as Leo. This would explain why a *garuḍa*-like *kāla* head could function in this same role.

The *kāla-makara* motif has yet another interesting facet. *Makara* is the Sanskrit word for the constellation Capricorn, the Goat's Horn. The constellation Makara/Capricorn rules the time period between December 22 and January 20. This is why Makara is the name for January in the Sanskrit-based series of names for the solar months. January is still called Makara in Khmer today. But a glance at the dates shows that Makara marks the winter solstice. At that time of year, the sun turns around, in a sense, and begins its northward journey to the summer solstice.

Although the correspondences are not exact, in a very general manner we may have a design with a solar symbol in the center and a solstice symbol at two ends in the *kāla-makara* motif. Whatever the definitive interpretation of one of the most common themes in the decorative reliefs of Angkor may be, the *kāla-makara-nāga* motif seems to cast a lunisolar light over the doorways to Angkor Wat.

Given the calendrical associations of Leo and Aquila, the period from July 23 to August 22 is a logical interim for the worship of Viṣṇu. There is a bas-relief showing homage to Viṣṇu in the third gallery that may be a reference to this time of year. In that relief, discussed in detail later, a possible planetary sequence of deities is en route to Viṣṇu, encoding one particular date. When I first identified the relief as a series of planets and checked it against planetary tables, I found that the sequence it contained occurred precisely between July 24 and July 29, 1131. In other words, this unusual planetary procession was especially related to Viṣṇu's time of year. Beyond that, it actually started out that time of year with a rare sequence that was not to be found within 200 years before and after that date. (My enthusiasm for finding the sequence again waned as these 400 years went by and no repetition was in sight.) For additional reasons connected to the year 1131 and explained in the next chapter, King Sūryavarman may have been born during the month of Śrāvaṇa—under the tutelage, then, of Viṣṇu. This special connection to Viṣṇu is strengthened by evidence also presented in the next chapter. For now, it is worth mentioning because it indicates that Angkor Wat might exist today because of the incidental timing of Sūryavarman's birth.

27/28, 29.53, AND THE LUNAR MONTH

Although the number of days in a lunar month is not a matter of dispute, the number does vary. When the movement of the moon is measured against the stars, the moon returns to its point of origin in 27.3 days (27 days, 7 hours, and 43 minutes), completing one *sidereal* lunar month.[5] Moreover, the moon is visible between 27 and 28 days a month, no more, no less. And coincidentally or not, the "lunar mansions" or *nakṣatra* total 27 or 28, as noted earlier. The system of lunar constellations can also be traced to the third millennium B.C. in Assyro-Babylonian astronomy, from whence it disseminated to Persia, Sogdiana, the Arab world, China, and India.[6] In China and Japan, 28 constellations were always a set number. In India, and later in Cambodia and other Southeast Asian countries, there were sometimes 27 *nakṣatra,* perhaps because this made them easier to manipulate arithmetically. Each of the 27 *nakṣatra* equals exactly 800 minutes of arc, without the need for fractions.

Sometimes these 27 or 28 constellations were

handled as simple units of space, on the order of a grid pattern, independent of any stars within their boundaries. In that case, the movement of the stars was measured across "vacant" *nakṣatra.*[7] The moon travels through each of these constellations (or vacant arcs) in 27.3 days. In summary, then, by a remarkable overlapping of phenomena, which the Khmer astronomers would have celebrated, the moon travels through 27/28 *nakṣatra* in 27.3 days and is visible for 27/28 days each month.

The menstrual (literally "monthly") cycle of most women, related to the lunar cycle, falls between 27 and 28 days in length. The moon has always been associated with female principles in Cambodia and in most of Asia—in opposition to the sun and its male attributes. The *somavaṃśa* lineage of kings, as noted, is both lunar and female, tracing its beginnings back to the *nāginī* Somā. Therefore, when 27/28-unit alternations appear at Angkor Wat, the moon, female principles, snakes, dragons, clouds, fertility, night, dark, water, coolness, and related phenomena are certainly called to mind.

The god Śiva would embody much of the iconography found in the 27/28-unit measurements at Angkor Wat. His "sacred thread" is worn over his left shoulder and across his chest. He wears the crescent moon in his hair. The Ganges River was caught by his hair as it descended to earth, moderating the force of its cascade. Śiva is the Lord of Yogins whose symbol is the phallic lingam and who has several consorts. All of these traits might connote—but do not affirm—the presence of Śiva in the lunar-related numbers at Angkor Wat. Most of these 27/28-unit alternating measurements (or single measurements of either number) are ordinarily found in the circumference and not the axial lines of the temple. They "circle" the central tower just as the moon and the *nakṣatra* seem to circle Brahmā and the axis of the earth.

The synodic lunar month, as opposed to the sidereal month, is the moon's position measured against the sun and not the stars. It is 29.53 days long (29 days, 12 hours, and 44 minutes).[8] This extends the 27/28-day cycle of lunar visibility by nearly two nights of darkness. There are a few examples of this 29.53-unit measurement at Angkor Wat, but not nearly as many as the 27/28-unit measurements.

During the month, the new moon and full moon mark two turning points in the moon's behavior. For 14 or 15 days, depending on the month, the moon increases in size as it rises closer and closer to the eastern horizon each night. At the time of the full moon, the lunar disk rises in the east at sunset and for 14 or 15 days begins to rise further and further westward as it steadily wanes. Finally, it is no longer visible on the western horizon, and the cycle begins again. In Khmer, Indian, and other Asian texts, these two opposite patterns are called the light and dark halves of the lunar month, respectively. They are literally summed up by the number 24. Like the 12 *āditya*s, or solar months, the 24 lunar half-months are connected to specific deities and bear the names of constellations.[9]

When the two halves of the lunar month occur at Angkor Wat, they are most often found in architectural sets. Twin rooms, twin towers, twin libraries, and all similarly paired segments may have parallel, 12/12-unit measurements. The numbers 14/15 also appear once in the third gallery, defining a lunar month. In that case, they occur in two opposite sets of blind windows.

THE LUNAR AND SOLAR YEARS

The lunar year, 354.36 days long, defines both the circumference of the outer enclosure and the axes of the terrace under the central three galleries. In the outer enclosure, it is paired with a solar axial measurement; in the terrace, it ends a long series of lunar measurements along the western causeway. The 365.24-day solar year occurs in two of the most important axes of the temple: those of the upper elevation and the outermost enclosure. This measurement is also found in various axial entrances.

Based on the axes/circumference measurement patterns at Angkor Wat, lunar measurements in general predominate along the circumferences, as noted, as well as in the corner towers of the temple, while solar measurements predominate along the axes and axial entrances. Other solar numbers that form part of primarily the upper elevation are 12, for the solar *ādityas*, and 90/91 for the days between the equinox and solstice periods. The number 12, of course, refers to the 12 solar zodiac signs and the 12 solar months (*ādityas*) in the year. It is particularly connected to Viṣṇu and is "opposed" by the number 24, the symbol for the 24 lunar half-months in 1 year.[10] The opposition between solar elements—such as the sun itself, the number 12, heat, light, the male gender, dryness, the eagle, and Viṣṇu—and the lunar elements listed earlier is often symbolized at Angkor Wat by Garuḍa holding or fighting with two *nāgas*.

BRAHMĀ AND A MANDALA OF *DEVAS*

As described in the preceding chapter, the god Brahmā resides at the center of his cosmic mandala with 32 *devas* encircling the periphery and 12 solar gods (*ādityas*) between Brahmā and the *devas*. Brahmā is the creator: the originator of space and time. From his center over the north celestial pole, the stars of the night sky, as well as the sun and moon, spin around him endlessly. Representing these celestial phenomena are the 44 gods (12 solar gods plus 32 gods that symbolize the 28 constellations and 4 directions). Brahmā is the forty-fifth component in this mandala with 44 lesser gods, and he is a thirty-third component in relation to the 32 *devas* around the outer squares of the mandala. Sets of alternating numbers such as 32/33 and 44/45, then, refer to Brahmā in his position at the center of the universe, as well as to the gods that surround him in the mandala (Fig. 2.27).

The deities in a mandala are arranged in a grid of 49, 64, or 81 squares. The squares "house" the gods, the *ādityas*, and Brahmā. At Angkor Wat, only the 49-square mandala is consistently present; 64- or 81-unit measurements are not depicted.

SACRED MEASUREMENTS: 360, 60, 12, AND 10

A year of the gods is 360 days long, and a day of the gods is one of our years in length. As a reminder, the 6 months that the sun rises and sets to the south of due east is the night of the gods; the other 6 months is their day. Thus 360 years of our time equals 1 year for Indra and his retinue. When celestial years are multiplied by 360, the result is terrestrial time:

Yuga	*Celestial years × 360*	= *Terrestrial years*
kali	1200	432,000
dvāpara	2400	864,000
tretā	3600	1,296,000
kṛta	4800	1,728,000

This poses several profound questions whose answers may ultimately lie in prehistory. For example, the Indians used a 360-degree circle: was this related to the 360-day divine year or to the relationship between terrestrial and celestial time? Degrees in a circle are subdivided into 60' (60 minutes) and 60" (60 seconds). If we multiply 60 × 60 to get the number of seconds in 1 degree, the result is 3600 seconds. And if we multiply 3600 seconds by the 360 degrees in a circle, the result is 1,296,000 seconds in a circle. There are 1,296,000 years in a *tretā yuga.* Is this a coincidence? The explanation, once again, may lie in Assyro-Babylonian astronomy.

According to cuneiform records, Mesopotamian astronomers divided the sky into 10 degrees for each sign of the zodiac, which they invented and characterized, or 120 degrees for one circle. Cuneiform records state that the 10 antediluvian kings of Babylon ruled for 432,000 years.[11] This figure was interpreted by scholars as symbolizing a spatial division of the zodiac, rather than recording an actual period of time. Around 650 B.C. there was a set of 12 northern constellations above the zodiac, which were given a 60-degree circle, and a set of 12 constellations below the zodiac given a 240-degree circle.[12] Just the number 36 alone (12 above + 12 zodiac signs + 12 below) seems to be an intentional way of reinforcing the importance of 360, or 3600. Robert Brown argues for the existence of a 360-degree circle in ancient Babylon, which, as noted, is equal to 1,296,000 seconds.[13] Brown himself postulates a connection between the passage of time and the description of the circle in the celestial sphere, as well as a link to the celestial yugas in Indian astronomy.

The full system can be summarized as:

12 constellations north of the zodiac, a 60-degree circle
12 zodiac constellations, a 120-degree circle
12 constellations south of the zodiac, a 240-degree circle

Expressed in seconds, this system can be explained as:

60-degree circle: 60 × 60 × 60 = 216,000 seconds of arc
120-degree circle: 60 × 60 × 120 (12 signs × 10 degrees) = 432,000 seconds (*kali yuga* number)
240-degree circle: 60 × 60 × 240 [(12 + 12) × 10] = 864,000 seconds *(dvāpara yuga)*
360-degree circle: 60 × 60 × 360 [(12 + 12 + 12) × 10] = 1,296,000 seconds *(tretā yuga)*

Of course, time is measured by the movement of our planets, including the sun and moon, across the unchanging backdrop of the stars. Our system of 24 hours, with 60 minutes to the hour and 60 seconds to the minute, repeats the pattern of divisions in a circle (minutes and seconds) and also originates in ancient Mesopotamia.[14] Examining the Assyro-Babylonian system of recording the passage of time, we find the same 60-unit base repeated 60 times, plus a factor of 12: 60 × 60 × 24 (12 + 12) = 86,400 seconds in 1 day.

The Chinese divided the day into 12 segments of 2 hours each, each segment defined by one of the 12 animals in a well-known 12-year cycle. The Cambodians adopted the 12-year animal cycle from the Chinese, which combines with another cycle of 10 years to form a pattern that repeats every 60 years.[15] That is to say, the monkey, as an example of one of the 12 animals, might be combined with the first of the 10 years, and then the next animal would be combined with the next year. Finally, the tenth animal would be combined with the tenth year, and the eleventh animal with the first of the 10 years. The 10-year cycle is repeated again, this time with a different animal for each of the 10 years. After a total of 60 years, we are back to the monkey and the first of the 10 years again.

It may not be a coincidence that the most common and ancient yuga period was a 5-year cycle of 60 solar months.[16] Twelve 5-year cycles, of 60 months each, equal the number of months in one 60-year cycle of 12 animals and 10 years. Both the basis for the Chinese calendar and the basis for the Indian calendar come into perfect conjunction every 60 years. Both calendars could be used together. Both calendars were current in Cambodia.

There are only three or possibly four numbers in these systems that give rise to time and space measurements from seconds to aeons to degrees of arc: 60 (5 × 12), 12, and 10. These are the same three numbers that define the outermost axes of Angkor Wat (60 units) and the perimeter around the moat (120 units or 12 × 10, equivalent to the 120 degrees in the original zodiac circle). Thus the axes and perimeter of Angkor Wat provide a key to unlocking the basic units of our time and space measurements: minutes, hours, degrees of arc, and even the long yuga periods.

The outer axes and perimeter of the temple are the first and most crucial element in the measurement patterns because they provide the numerical basis for the calendrical systems we will find in the galleries and passages ahead. They also define one of the patterns that sets the tenor and meaning for each stage of Angkor Wat: the circumference and axial lengths as one complementary, conceptual whole.

SACRED MEASUREMENTS: 21 AND 108

The number 21, one of the most recurrent measurements at Angkor Wat, is connected to the gods but not to astronomy or time cycles. It dominates the second gallery where it helps to define the iconography of Brahmā. At Angkor Wat this number often appears as a combination of 19, which represents the gods, or 20, which includes their king Indra, plus a twenty-first encompassing or originating unit. A set of 20 gods with Indra as their king is a common iconographic element in Hindu mythology.[17]

As illustrated in the bas-reliefs of the third gallery, the number 19 also refers to the ministers under King Sūryavarman, and 20 therefore symbolizes the king himself. This group of three numbers (19, 20, 21) is essential in demonstrating a connection between the realm of Indra and the gods, the realm of King Sūryavarman and his ministers, and a supreme deity who rules over both realms. It appears that Sūryavarman not only patterned his temple on Indra's palace, but set up his ministers on Indra's model as well.

Unlike 21, the number 108 functions more in the mode of the preceding numbers 60, 12, and 10. In fact, the 60- and 120-unit outer measurements of Angkor Wat occur only because of a 108-cubit module. The number 108 has already been noted for changing the yuga cycles at the temple into the 32 gods on Mount Meru or vice versa. In this instance and others, 108 transforms time into divinity, or divinity into time. Moreover, the terrestrial yuga cycles are all divisible by 108, and there is a maximum 108 degrees of arc in the north–south lunisolar oscillation each year. Curiously, when the celestial yuga cycles *(kali* to *kṛta)* are divided by 108, they come to 11.1111, 22.2222, 33.3333, and 44.4444. The decimals could be continued indefinitely. *Kṛta* means "four." The Spanish "cuatro" or French "quatre" or English "quarter" all illustrate a linguistic connection to this Sanskrit word. Similarly, *tretā* means "three" and *dvāpara* means "two" (*dvā* = duo, two, and so on). *Kali,* however, has no numerical meaning. Aside from this interesting relationship, there may have been 1,080,000 years in each yuga, rather than a staggered amount, according to one ancient system of equal yuga cycles.[18] Since 108 = 27 × 4, the number also comes close to defining one-third of a lunar year.

None of these definitions, however, can convey the magical, spiritual, and profoundly sacred qualities of the number 108. It probably occurs in one guise or another (as 1008, or 1080, or 10,800, and so forth) in more Asian religious texts than any other number.[19] Moreover, Ptolemy lists exactly 108 stars as lying outside of constellation patterns, and Hipparchos listed 1080 stars in all, even though many more must have been observed at the time.[20] Since Mesopotamian astronomy was the basis for the later Greco-Roman systems, the roots of 108 may one day be found in Assyro-Babylonian astronomy.

If our current calendrical systems were destroyed in the future but Angkor Wat remained as it stands today, these systems could be derived from the temple once again. Angkor Wat needs only to be measured to retrieve numerical data. Solar and lunar alignments would soon become apparent in its obvious arrangement of towers and causeway. This research began with nothing to indicate that the temple was other than a breathtaking design of volume and space. It is not that difficult to ascertain the original Angkor Wat cubit, the monument is so precisely constructed along its axes and circumferences. Once that cubit length is determined and applied against the measurements taken in surveying, all else follows.

MEASUREMENTS IN THE OUTER ENCLOSURE

The two side towers that flank the central tower in the western entrances to Angkor Wat have several 54/54-unit measurements. This configuration not only situates the 54 gods and 54 antigods spatially on each side of the main western entrance but illustrates the architectural principle that twins such as these towers will have "twin" measurements as well.

Similarly, a triad of towers or a triad of entrances may have measurements that form a triad. In this instance, there is a primary/subsidiary relationship between a central tower (or chamber) and flanking towers. A triad with equal parts, such as the three identical entrances on the north, south, and east sides of the outer enclosure, can also be divided into measurements that are one-third, one-third, and one-third of a total. Each third is not cosmologically or calendrically meaningful in itself, but the total is.

The galleries and enclosures of Angkor Wat are formed by a set of crossing axes framed by a rectangle. The rectangle is the gallery or enclosure itself, and its axes extend to the base of its entrances on all four sides. Both the axes and the rectangle in every gallery have measurements that are two halves of one set. These two parts together define the gallery, and they depend on each other to create one whole meaning and, simultaneously, one whole architectural unit. In the former case, the meaning focuses on one conceptual set, such as a pairing of the lunar and solar years or the pairing of 60 and 120. Since the axes are usually solar in connotation and the circumference lunar, this characteristic set for each gallery is yet another way of joining the sun and moon in a mutually dependent fashion.

In relation to the rectangle of a gallery, the measurements of opposite facades at Angkor Wat are often related to directionality. This principle is particularly illustrated in the second gallery, where the east–west movement of the moon is emphasized on the east and west sides of the gallery.

One of the greatest revelations of the measurement systems at Angkor Wat is the existence of ritual paths that conducted visitors first around and then into a gallery. For the first time, we know how the temple might have been used in a formal, liturgical sense. The triad of western entrances in the outer enclosure has several patterns of circumambulation that allow a circuit of one or both images in a lateral chamber, followed by an entry into the temple from the central western entrance. That option must have been a welcome alternative. Otherwise a forced circuit around the 3700-m enclosing wall would have severely limited patronage.

Circumambulation paths begin at the edge of the first step up to a structure or an entrance, and they end at the last step out. These paths circle a main image three times and circle subsidiary images either not at all (rarely) or one or three times, a standard throughout the temple. The circuit of a main image covers 5 cubits on a side, and lateral images are circuited by a path 4 cubits on a side. I discovered that the length of all circumambulation routes has a cosmologically or calendrically meaningful total when measured in the *phyeam* unit. Cubits seem to be used as a measure in large totals (such as 365 or a yuga period) simply because they fit the distance allowed.

THE OUTER ENCLOSURE: AN OVERVIEW

The outer enclosure of Angkor Wat blocks off the mundane world— allowing passage only through single entrances on the east, north, and south and through five entrances on the west, for a total of eight. The single entrances are identical in plan, elevation, and cross section. The five western entrances are 540 cubits long divided between two distant "twin" end structures (the solstice gateways) and a triad of central entrances (Figs. 3.3–3.5). The main entrance to Angkor Wat is thus flanked by lateral towers 20 m distant on each side, a distance broached by connecting chambers (Fig. 3.6).

The lateral towers are like paired complementary units, both balanced against the central western tower. Their smaller interior sanctuary has a porch leading to it on the west and east, and there are side chambers on the north and south. In a north–south direction, one could leave the lateral entrances and step out to the pillared corridors or walk toward the main entrance through the three side chambers. Today, light shines through what remains of the tower above each of the three entrances.[21]

The long corridors that reach north and south from the central three entrances have a solid, windowless wall on the east and two rows of parallel pillars on the west that support a corbeled vaulting (Figs. 3.4 and 3.7). They are punctuated at the center by a small, roofed porch and stairway that face outward toward the moat. These stairways visually interrupt the north–south movement of the corridors without interfering with the regular progression of the pillars. The corridors stop at a false door marking the end of their length and the beginning of the large gateways, 100 m from the central western entrance. Because of the false door, the gateways are inaccessible from the corridors. Whatever image was held in the lateral chambers of the solstice gateways, therefore, could be approached only from inside each gateway.

In comparison to the central three entrances, the solstice gateways are rather unusual structures. They have neither a tower nor a central sanctuary but rather a 7-m-high west–east corridor with a flat floor, no steps, and laterite pavement (Fig. 3.4). Inside the gateways, two staircases meet the pavement at the center and lead up into large alcoves that are part of the north–south cross-arm of the corridor (Fig. 3.8). At the end of each of these alcoves, a doorway introduces a final, elongated, and rather solitary chamber, flooded with light by a window that faces the outside of the temple. Images were probably installed in these lateral end chambers on the north and south, at least according to measurement patterns that indicate auspicious circumambulation routes around the center of each chamber. Aside from a central image, these chambers have a false door sculpted on their back wall, the only such instance at Angkor Wat. The real doorway in each end chamber is devoid of any holes for door hinges or posts, which means that these sanctuaries were always open to the visitor. Perhaps on the special days that involved great processions, riders on elephantback or on chariots could pause and pay homage to the images in the gateways before exiting the temple or, likewise, on entering as well.

There is a delicate pattern of various geometric and floral designs in registers all across the interior west–east walls of the gateway, about 2 m or so in height (Fig. 3.9). This relief creates a masterfully textured surface that seems like embroidery in the raking light. The high quality of the sculpting

Fig. 3.3. Western bridge and main entrances into Angkor Wat from southwest.
The bridge meets the five western entrances across a dry moat until the rainy season starts in earnest. The towers on the upper elevation can be seen in the distance.

Fig. 3.4. Main western entrances, north half, and nāga *railing at center of bridge.*
A long corridor stretches between the central triad of entrances and the end (solstice) gateway. Where the corridor meets the gateway there is a false door or dead-end. In that regard, the corridor does not function as a link between the interior of the gateways and the central western entrances.

Fig. 3.5. Main western entrances, south gateway, east facade.

The end gateways have a high ceiling, flat floor, and a wide space to allow wheeled vehicles and work or processional animals such as horses and elephants, easy entry and egress. Their two interior chambers are small side sanctuaries, each reached by a staircase from the center of the passage.

Fig. 3.6. Main western entrances, central triad from southwest.

Based on circumambulation paths and measurements, these entrances functioned as a set comprised of a central axis and flanking, complementary halves.

Fig. 3.7. Main western entrances, south corridor, view south along outside edge.

The pillars on the outside row, now missing, would have sustained a demivault overhead. The bits of stone protruding from the upper segment of each pillar are the remains of a connecting "beam" between the inside and outside pillars.

Fig. 3.8. Main western entrances, south solstice gateway, central staircase and chamber on the north, view north.

On each side at the center of the gateway, a staircase with narrow and eroded steps (foreground) leads up to a landing with a window. The landing, in turn, opens onto a small, elevated sanctuary. The false door at the back of the chamber is visible here through the sanctuary doorway.

Fig. 3.9. Main western entrances, south solstice gateway, north wall.

The solstice gateways have lavish decorative carving in geometric bands along their walls, adding stature and considerable aesthetic presence to their interior space.

attests to the ritual and spiritual status of the gateway passages. It is not often that an interior space, meant as a passage from one area to the next, is so carefully carved and decorated.

54/54-UNIT PAIRS IN THE OUTER ENCLOSURE

One might say that the Churning of the Sea of Milk spills over into the western entrances. Both in its placement and in the sets of measurements, the central western entrance acts as a pivot, a focal point, for the 54/54-unit pairs on each side of it (Fig. 3.10). No other sector of Angkor Wat has so many 54/54-unit pairs, not even the bridge (Figs. 3.11–3.12).[22] (See Appendix A, Table 3.1.)

Based on these multiple occurrences of 54/54 pairs, one might guess, and correctly so, that the 54-unit measurements at Angkor Wat cluster around the central entrances and the bridge. It is as though the great churning event, with its rich, complex allusions to golden eras, perfect kings, immortality, and Viṣṇu, ushers the visitor into the temple's enclosed compound on clouds of auspicious symbolism.

The solar chariot, pulled by seven horses, makes a yearly round-trip, leaving the south end gateway on December 22 and arriving at the north gateway on June 21, to leave again immediately and arrive back at the south gateway on December 22. On the ground, inside the towers, the multiple 54/54 divisions on either side of the central axis represent the real reason for the sun's movement: the gods and antigods are pulling Mount Mandara first to the south and then to the north in an eternal oscillation.

Through a poetic and creative application of mythology, through the visual interpretation of a well-known myth, the Khmers fashioned the sunlight, the sandstone towers, and long, pillared corridors into an eloquent, aesthetic, moving picture of the churning event. To repeat a statement originally made in Orissa in the twelfth century: "This small universe (the temple) has to be situated with respect to the vaster universe, of which it forms a part. . . . It has to fall into line with the position of the earth in relation to the course of the sun."[23]

The elongated corridors out to the end gateways on the north and south, it should be noted, have an uneven split in a 108-pillar total (Fig. 3.11). The imbalance is due to the fact that the southern corridor is 2.75 m shorter than the

Fig. 3.10. Main western entrances, central entrance.

There are many parallels between the central western entrance into the temple and the distant tower over the main sanctuary. Both function as a kind of pivot, both are at the center of 54/54-unit divisions, and both are in alignment: one at the beginning of the temple grounds and one at the apex.

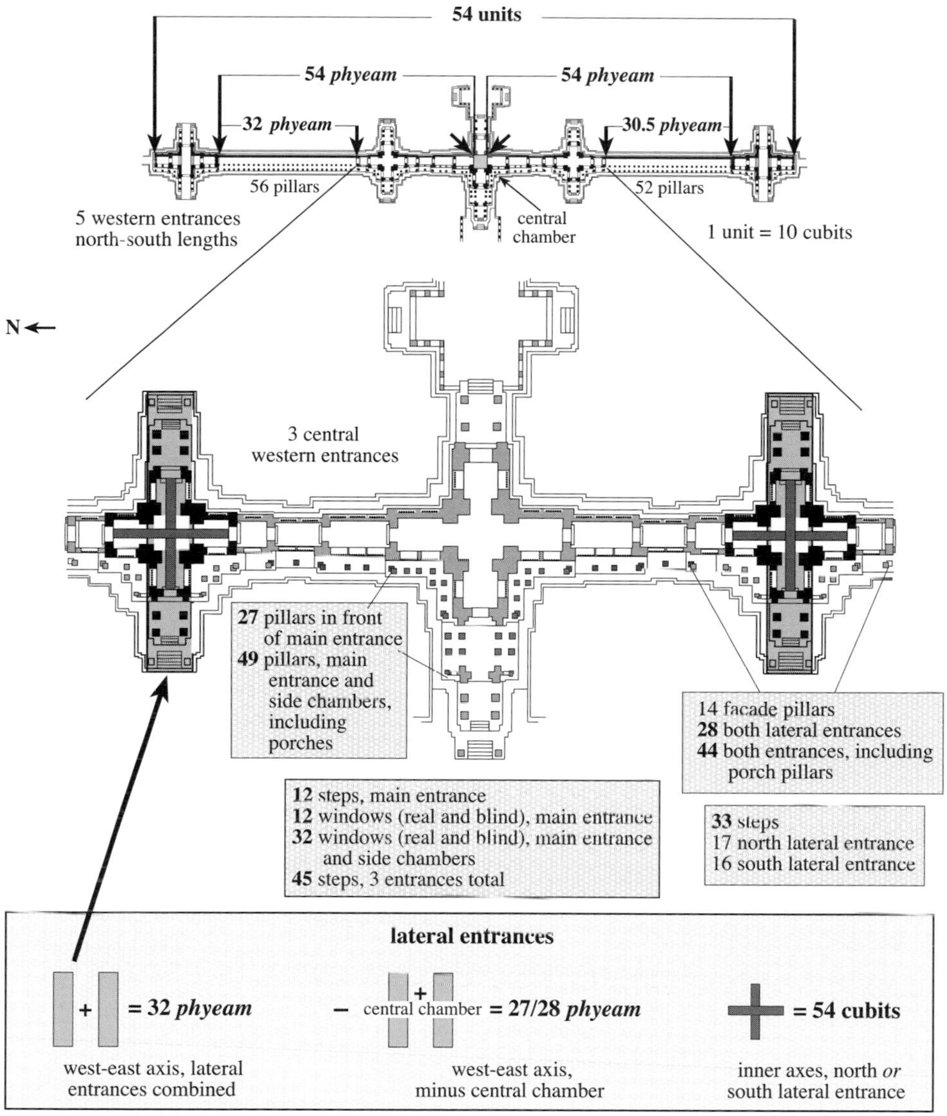

Fig. 3.11. Fourth (outer) enclosure, 5 western entrances, axes and distribution of pillars, windows, and steps.

Several 54-unit sets define the 5 western entrances together, including their full length—equal to the length of the western entrance bridge. Other than the 54-unit measurements, the windows, pillars, steps, and one set of axes focus on the deities found in the architectural mandala: 12, 28, 32, 33, 44, and 45. The two outer west–east axes of the lateral chamber total 31.87 *phyeam* exactly. If the central area is excluded the result is 27/28 (27 or 28 lunar mansions) indicated by 27 and a fraction, in this case, 27.44. In this alternate measurement a distinction is made between the 32 gods around the border of the mandala and the 27/28 lunar constellations that are included in the 32 gods. The 49 pillars in front of the main entrance and its side chambers, as well as the 49-*phyeam* length of all three entrances together (Fig. 3.12) refer to the Khmer grid of 49 squares in the architectural mandala. (See Appendix A, Tables 3.1, 3.2, 3.4, 3.6.)

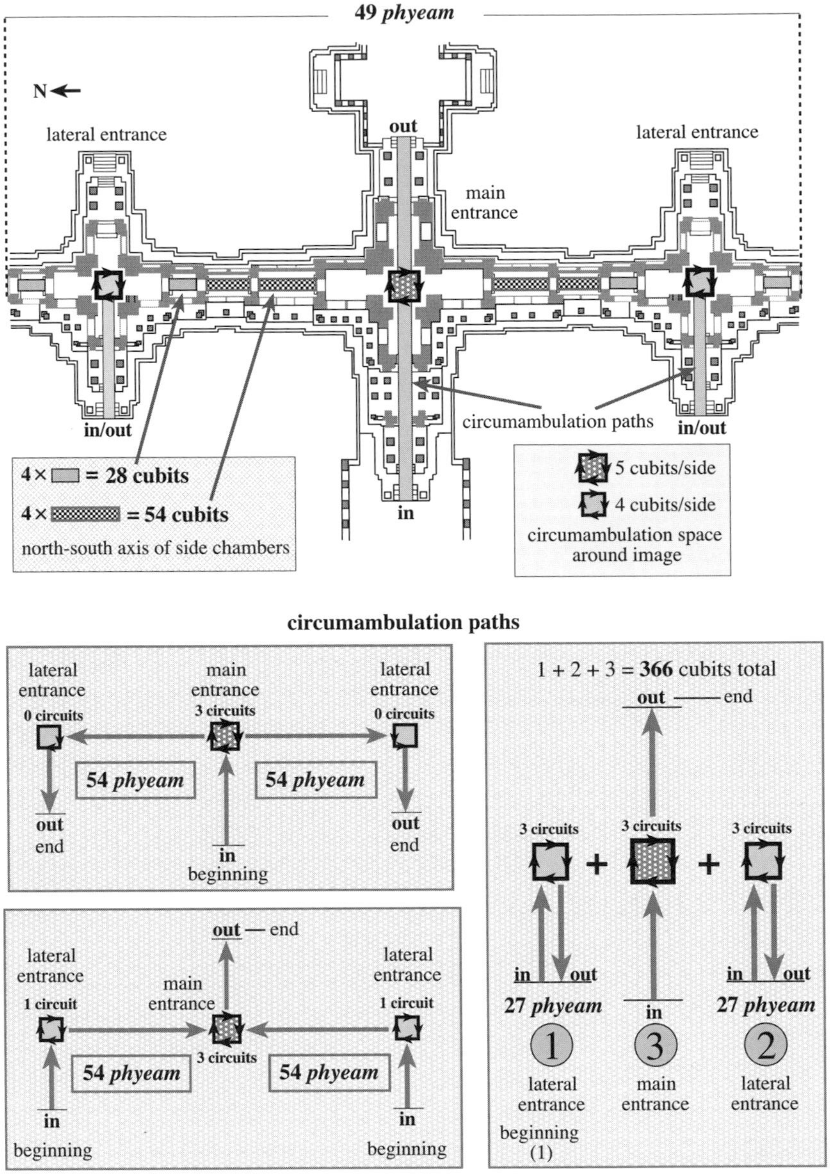

Fig. 3.12. Fourth (outer) enclosure, 3 central western entrances, ritual paths and axes.

The lateral chambers on the west side of the outer enclosure have 54-cubit axes (Fig. 3.11), two different 54-*phyeam* circumambulation paths each, and one joint 54-*phyeam* path. They are also included in the 54-*phyeam* length between the gateways and the central area of the main entrance (Fig. 3.11). Other than the emphasis on 54, there is one important 366-cubit circumambulation path through the main entrance that should be noted. In this path an in-and-out circuit of each lateral chamber (1 and 2) precedes an entry into the temple through the main entrance (3). (See Appendix A, Table 3.2)

northern, making an ideal 54/54 division impossible.[24] Given the special meaning of a 54/54-unit set, the reasons for altering the lengths of these two corridors might be worth exploring for a moment. It is possible that the southern corridor was shortened to create the winter solstice alignment between the south gateway and the bridge. But we also found more than a dozen lunar alignments at Angkor Wat in the mid-1970s, and three of these connect the western entrances to the towers of the first and second galleries (Fig. 4.3).[25] Perhaps a 54/54 symmetry in the pillars of the corridors was secondary to preserving both the lunar and the solstice alignments. The alignments and actual observation may have taken precedence—at least in this instance—over aesthetic or symbolic concerns of balance.

ANALOGIES TO THE CHURNING SCENE

The symbolism of the Churning of the Sea of Milk involves a central axis that usually supports a seated Brahmā on top. The axis rests on Kūrma and is steadied by Viṣṇu. This very same format is repeated in the lintels over the western and eastern doors of the central entrance, which hardly seems accidental. The lintel over the central doorway on the west illustrates cosmic Viṣṇu lying on the Sea of Milk (Fig. 3.13). His consort, Śrī Lakṣmī, is at his feet and, in an unusual gesture, holds his hand. A lotus stalk ascends from Viṣṇu's navel. The four-headed Brahmā crowns the top like a theomorphic blossom, surveying the universe he created, which now revolves around him. Although these central figures are somewhat crowded by the dense foliated decor, the format of a horizontal base (Viṣṇu), an axis (the lotus stalk), and Brahmā is still visible.

The lintel over the eastern doorway into the central entrance has a similar design. An axial stalk or pole rises from behind a royally dressed deity and his consort at its base (Fig. 3.14). It is surmounted by a posturing figure, parallel in position to Brahmā, though not in attitude. Viṣṇu and the *asura* on each side of this stalk call to mind the *deva*s and *asura*s on each side of Mount Mandara in the churning scene. The regal figure at the base is likewise in the position of Kūrma at the base of Mandara or Viṣṇu lying on the Sea of Milk.

Despite the clarity with which it is expressed, the story this scene depicts cannot be identified. Nevertheless, the unknown scene is another illustration of the Khmer tendency to read a multiplicity of meaning into the composition and design of the Churning of the Sea of Milk. In fact, an axis with an accompanying north–south oscillation or a north–south division is an underlying theme throughout the architecture of Angkor Wat. Ultimately, the motif must derive its origins from the movement of the sun, the axis of the earth, and the consequent legends that enhance and mythologize that format.

The generally accepted points of similarity between the Churning of the Sea of Milk and Viṣṇu lying on that same Sea of Milk (Viṣṇu Anantaśayin) are clear in themselves.[26] But these scenes also share their traits with the lintel on the east side of the main entrance. These three different scenes, it is suggested here, have four common features: (1) their *central axis* (Mandara, a lotus stalk, and possibly a pole). (2) The axis is *crowned either by Brahmā or by a figure similar to those in bronze carried on battle standards* seen in the bas-reliefs of Angkor Wat. (3) There is *another figure or group of figures at the base,* either Kūrma, Viṣṇu, or a seated deity, and (4) *consorts are nearby.* The consorts are Śrī Devī who rises up from the Sea of Milk near Kūrma in the churning scene, Śrī Lakṣmī who strokes Viṣṇu's lower legs, or the consort on the knees of the central, royally clad figure seated in the eastern lintel.

Other elements of these scenes are shared by

Fig. 3.13. Main western entrances, central entrance, lintel over western doorway.

As Viṣṇu lies on the Sea of Milk on his multiheaded *nāga* support, his consort reaches out to touch his hand, or vice versa, in a very informal gesture. Brahmā is shown seated on top of the lotus stalk.

Fig. 3.14. Main western entrances, central entrance, lintel over eastern doorway.

Opposite the lintel of the reclining Viṣṇu (Fig. 3.13) a royal figure sits with a consort while an axial pole with a dancing figure on top rises above the royal couple. This pole is a common battle standard. To the left and right of the pole, Viṣṇu stands on Garuḍa and an *asura* leader brandishes his weapons. At the bottom of the scene, two subsidiary royal couples are held up on a platform to the right and left of center. A lion sustains each platform that supports a seated couple.

two out of three—opposing forces on each side of the central axis, for example, or the *nāga* Vāsuki and the Sea of Milk. If the royal seated figure with his consort on the eastern lintel was meant as an allusion to kingship, then these lintels reiterate the associations we found earlier between the king *(Indrābhiṣeka)* and the Churning of the Sea of Milk.

The doorways beneath the two lintels lead into the central tower of the western entrance, which represents Mount Mandara or Mount Meru in several ways. First, it is flanked several times on both sides by the number 54, the *deva*s and *asura*s. Second, the tower is positioned like the churning pivot in relation to the sun as it oscillates between the northern and southern gateways of the western entrances. Third, the tower corresponds directly to the spring equinox point, symbolized by Mount Mandara in the churning scene at Angkor Wat.

Finally, if there was indeed an image of Viṣṇu inside the tower, as postulated here, it would have been located, like any other image, at the baseline of the tower—just as Kūrma is at the base of Mandara, or Viṣṇu at the base of the lotus stalk, or the royal figure at the base of the axial pole. And the stone lotus capping the top of the original tower would also have been parallel to the lotus seat of Brahmā over the central axis of Mandara or the top of the lotus stalk itself. This shared juxtaposition merges the architecture of the tower with the image inside the tower and the lintels over the tower's doorways. The measurements that surround the tower are also a part of that merging. In fact, these entrances inaugurate the beginning of Angkor Wat just as the churning scene once inaugurated the beginning of King Sūryavarman's reign and the *kṛta yuga*. These new, propitious beginnings are founded on the symbolism of the axial lotus stalk that rose from Viṣṇu's navel as he created the universe, and everything that evolved from that point onward.

THE *VĀSTUPURUṢAMAṆḌALA* IN THE OUTER ENCLOSURE

Mandala numerology is a means of bringing Viṣṇu's universe to the temple's precincts—a means of binding Angkor Wat to the heavens and to the powers that hold sway over the heavens and the earth. There are more than 20 examples of commonly recurring mandala measurements such as 28, 32/33, and 44 in the outer enclosure, primarily in the western entrances.[27] In fact, the mandala symbolism in the western entrances contrasts with the moon and its symbolism on the east, north, and south. At the same time, it should be kept in mind that the number 28 relates both to the mandala and to the moon as well (Figs. 3.11, 3.12, 3.15a, b, c).

The concentration of mandala symbolism is in the solstice gateways with their six examples of the numbers 32 and 33. Since these gateways are placed at the ends of the western entrances their position also corresponds to the farthest, 32-deity border of the mandala. As might be expected, the central three entrances complete the mandala with numbers referring to the 49-square grid, the 12 *āditya*s, the *nakṣatra* (28,32,33), and the totality of gods together, 44/45 (Figs. 3.11, 3.12). The remaining axial entrances in the outer enclosure have a meager representation of 28 and 32 (Fig. 3.16a, d). In their case, however, the context of the number 28 defines it as lunar-related. Without a doubt, these entrances are focused on the moon.

The central western triad of entrances not only contains a full complement of mandala symbolism, but that symbolism is well-integrated into the meaning of the central triad as an architectural group. The 49-*phyeam* length of the entrances, their total of 45 outside steps, and the 44 pillars in the flanking entrances place Brahmā at the center—on top of that lotus seat over the central western entrance tower. This joins the center of the

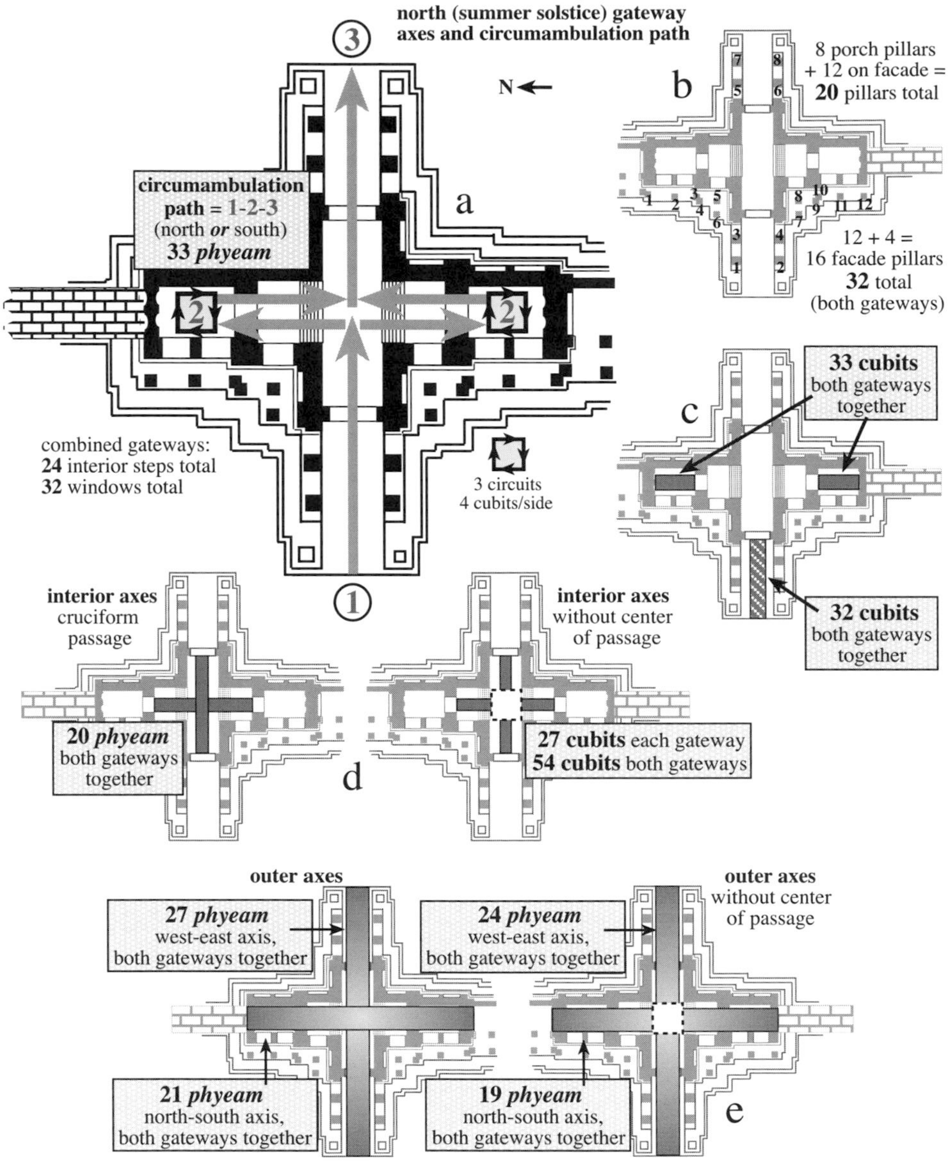

Fig. 3.15. Fourth (outer) enclosure, western end gateway, axes and ritual paths.

Whereas the axes in the solstice or end gateways have isolated references to the gods and their subdivisions (19/20/21 and 54) as well as the moon (24 and 27), the circumambulation paths, antechambers, and pillars almost exclusively pay homage to the 32/33 gods around the perimeter of the architectural mandala. (See Appendix A, Tables 3.3, 3.8.)

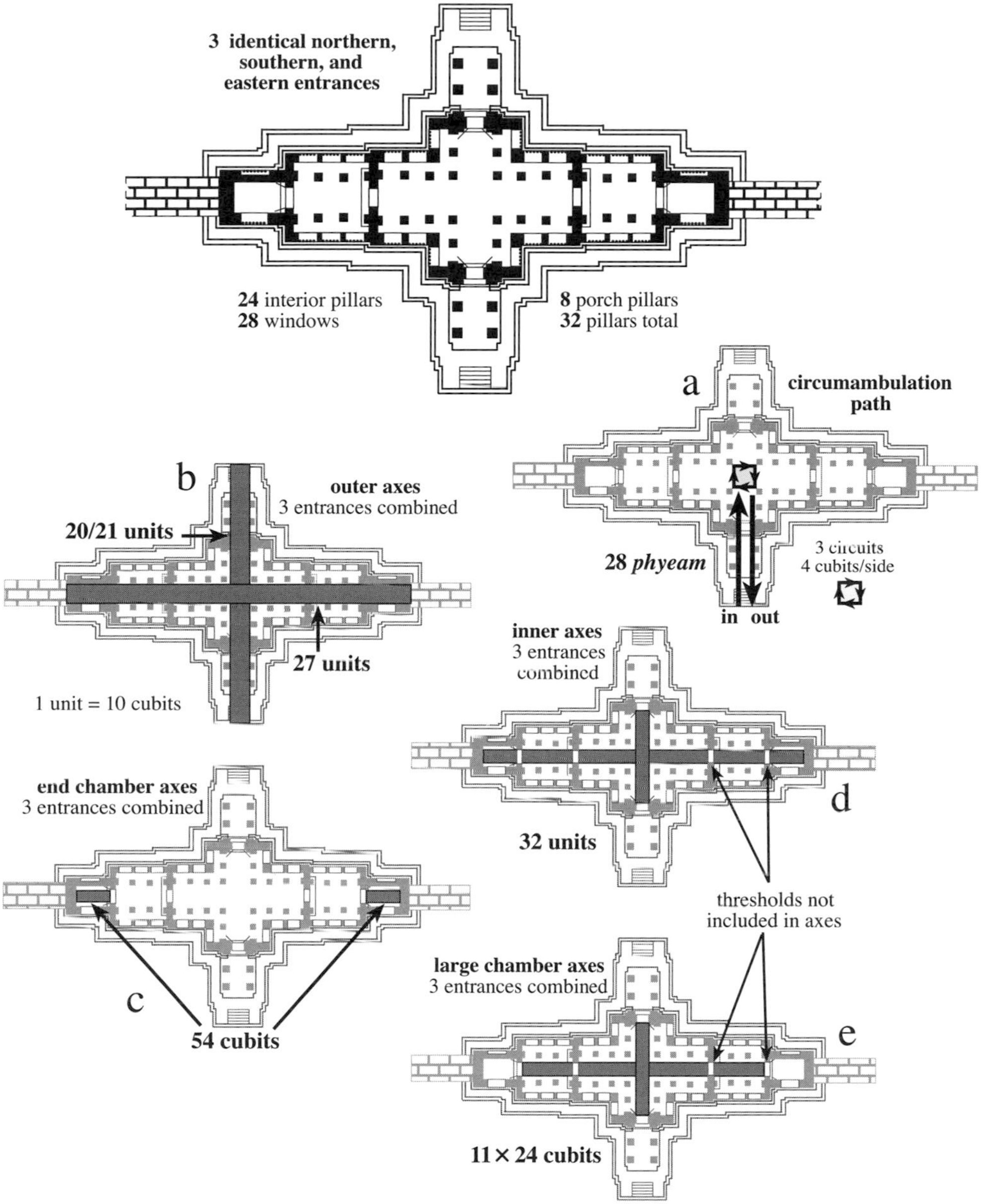

Fig. 3.16. Fourth (outer) enclosure, axial entrance (north, south, or east are identical), axes and circumambulation path.

In contrast to the 5 western entrances, there are only two references to the 32 gods in the axial entrances of the outer enclosure and one occurrence of 54. The majority of pillars, windows, steps, axes, and the circumambulation path refer to the lunar constellations or lunar periodicity in one way or another (24, 27, 28, and 11). All of the axial totals are based on the sum of the three entrances together. (See Appendix A, Tables 3.5, 3.7.)

vāstupuruṣamaṇḍala to Mount Mandara, Mount Meru, the churning pivot, and the lotus stalk that rises from Viṣṇu's navel. No one would dispute this overlay of images, but its specific combination is not usually noted. Although the iconography and the legends are old, the unique conjunction found here is original to the Khmers.

In the creation legend, both Viṣṇu and Brahmā are given the name of Nārāyaṇa, and the two are not always distinguished from one another. As Nārāyaṇa, Viṣṇu creates Brahmā; also as Nārāyaṇa, Brahmā creates time and space. Perhaps in reference to the interchangeable Nārāyaṇa, the mandala symbolism in the western entrances eloquently builds on the theme of Viṣṇu at the center of creation by placing Brahmā on the same axis. As Nārāyaṇa, both create the universe.

This unity underscores the nature of Viṣṇu as both a daytime and a nighttime god, since Brahmā at Angkor Wat is intimately connected to the night sky in the second gallery. This is not even to mention Brahmā's position at the north celestial pole, visible at night but not during the day. This day and night aspect of Viṣṇu is in agreement with his manifestation as the sun during the day and his manifestation as the constellation Aquila/Śrāvaṇa and the star Altair at night. The inseparability of Viṣṇu and Brahmā, and the diurnal and nocturnal worlds dominated by the sun and moon, are ultimately joined in the complex symbolism that defines the main western entrance of Angkor Wat.

LUNAR MEASUREMENTS ON THE NORTH, SOUTH, AND EAST

The northern, southern, and eastern entrances in the fourth enclosure, as noted earlier, are the same in all respects (Fig. 3.17). Although the three entrances are completely constructed, the southern entrance is the most finished in terms of smoothing away the chiseled stone surface and providing decorative reliefs. It also has a strange addition of a walled-up, partial Buddha image on one side of the main chamber (no illustration). Shapeless and odd, this inept and relatively recent form will probably be removed if these entrances are ever restored. As in other sectors of Angkor Wat, holes for door posts indicate that access to these entrances could have been blocked when the door was closed, so that entry into the temple from all four sides might have been restricted at any time.

At present, all three of these entrances are in very sorry condition, and there are no plans for their conservation. Off the beaten path of tourists, they are suffering from neglect. And because they are far removed from the rest of Angkor Wat, the feeling of isolation inside their chambers is sudden and palpable. It is as though one has walked off the planet and arrived at a strange, empty world of sandstone rooms surrounded by dense jungle and chirping birds or crickets. Perhaps nowhere else within the temple does one sense to this degree the presence of lost time, lost civilization, and the abandonment of Angkor.

At the center of each entrance, a broad cruciform chamber extends through a lateral doorway into two annexed chambers. A view from one end creates the classic telescoping effect found in every gallery at Angkor Wat, as doorway after doorway leads to a distant vista or a dead end.

The central set of three rooms is characterized by 24 large interior pillars that sustain a low, secondary half-vault that runs alongside the central ceiling. Pillars within a walled chamber are not unusual in Khmer architecture: they are found in the libraries, too, including those that architecturally duplicate these entrances, alongside the western causeway. The number of interior pillars commonly echoes the number of windows; these entrances prove no exception. They have 24 win-

Fig. 3.17. Fourth enclosure, southern entrance, south facade.

This is the first view of Angkor Wat, and of Angkor itself, as one approaches from the north-south road leading to the site. The entrance is duplicated on the north and east, and the doorway (center) marks the end of a *tretā yuga* distance from the southwest corner of the enclosing wall. At that point, a *kṛta yuga* distance to the upper elevation begins. All three of these entrances have predominantly lunar symbolism.

dows (both real and false) in the three chambers with 24 pillars (Fig. 3.14).

The entrances end on each side with a long and narrow chamber that once had a wooden door. There is only one window in each of these small rooms, and it is so large in proportion to the space inside that the effect is like being outside. The clever architects have evoked the feeling one would have if standing on the porch on either side of the causeway libraries. And with good reason: these small end chambers are equivalent to the porches in the plan of the causeway libraries.

There are several lunar measurements in the axial entrances: 11, 24, 27, and 28 (Fig. 3.16a, b, e). Just a note on one of the new lunar measurements is needed here for clarity. The number 11 will occur again in relation to the libraries between the first and second galleries. It is a numerical symbol for the 11 *kāraṇa,* or lunar deities, that preside over the lunar half-days in 1 month.[28] One *kāraṇa* presides over the first half-day; the next 7 *kāraṇa* succeed each other in turn for 56 half-days. The last 3 *kāraṇa*—Śakūni, Nāga, and Caturpāda—preside over the last 3 half-days. The *kāraṇa* determine when it is best to carry out specific actions and what the results might be for actions performed on specific days.

Other than the fact that these entrances pay homage to the moon in their measurements, another major attribute emerges in their scheme of significant numbers. Although these three entrances are the architectural twins or triplets, perhaps, of the causeway libraries, their numerically significant measurements do not correspond one-to-one with those of the libraries. Indeed, the interior and exterior axes of the entrances are numerically significant only when seen as a triad or set. The libraries form their own set, and their measurements are relevant within that framework. So although the measurement totals are similar, 27 or 28 primarily, they occur in differing patterns in the triad of entrances and the pair of causeway libraries.

Because the end gateways are not architecturally parallel to the north, south, or east axial entrances, they have only four instances of two lunar-related numbers (24 and 27), none of which are in circumambulation paths. The emphasis here, in contrast, is on the architectural mandala.

JUXTAPOSED SYMBOLS IN THE OUTER ENCLOSURE

In looking at the measurements, we can see that the circumference of the outer enclosure is reminiscent of the belt of 27/28 *nakṣatra* around the ecliptic because it has circumambulation paths that are 27 and 28 *phyeam* long. An in-and-out circumambulation of the main image in the triad of the northern, southern, and eastern entrances comes to 28 *phyeam* each (28–28–28, Fig. 3.14a). One would enter each main chamber from outside the temple, circuit the central image three times at 4 cubits on a side, and leave the temple again.

Once back at the western entrances, the same in-and-out circumambulation of each lateral chamber comes to 27 *phyeam* (Fig. 3.12). This makes a circuit of 28–28–28 on the east, north, and south and 27–27 on the west. The last sequence of two 27-unit circumambulation paths on the west, then, is joined to the preceding 28–28–28 sequence by virtue of both its meaning (27/28 *nakṣatra*) and the ritual in-and-out pattern.

The Creator Brahmā is the architect of time and therefore the lunar months. One might say that the Khmers translated Brahmā's lunar structures into sandstone buildings and placed them along the cardinal directions. These structures of sandstone and the lunar months were once joined together through ritual consecration. The foregoing measurements reflect their close association.

Having drawn a clear picture of a lunar circumference thus far, the architects completed this scenario with a stunning circumference measurement. The circumference measures, quite incredibly, a precise 354.3671 × 24.007 cubits—the length of one exact lunar year of 24 half-months (Fig. 3.18).[29]

It is not only the astounding accuracy of the 354.3671-unit measurement that makes the enclosing wall in modest laterite one of the most spectacular achievements at Angkor Wat. It is a combination of that accuracy and the choice of encircling the temple grounds with a 3700-m expression of the lunar calendar. If someone had set off fireworks to draw attention to the outer wall of the temple, the effect would not have been greater than the brilliant lunar symbolism that now suddenly illuminates this area.

The moon is predominant in this first and largest circuit around the temple grounds. It is given a position which almost rivals that of Viṣṇu in the central sanctuary, simply because of the enormous size of the enclosing wall and its place as the first major ritual circuit at Angkor Wat. Homage to the moon takes precedence over all else as one walks around the gallery, following the 27/28-*phyeam* circumambulation paths. At the end of this long journey, as we face the main western entrance into the temple grounds, orientation does a turnaround. The circumference disappears and we are immediately in alignment with the axis of the temple. That alignment places the circumference and its lunar meaning behind us in the path we have completed, and we are now facing the direction of the rising sun along the axis. In fact, one indication of the sun's increased importance at this juncture is the 366-unit circumambulation path into the temple through the central western entrance tower (Fig. 3.12).[30]

The exact 366.58-cubit measurement through the central entrance tower includes the in-and-out circuits of the images in the lateral chambers, which we just completed a moment ago as the last 27-*phyeam* sequence in the lunar route around the enclosure. The difference between a 27-*phyeam* circuit in and out of each flanking tower and the same circuit expressed as 108 cubits is not merely an academic conversion, as in meters to centimeters or yards to feet. By adding the two lateral entrances to the path through the central tower, we are looking at the triad of central western entrances as one group again. The lateral towers flank the axis and, in this circumambulation path, are seen only in relation to the axis—and no longer in relation to the circumference. The dual role of their ritual paths as either lunar or solar depends on which set is in operation. But more important, perhaps, is the parallel to the solar zodiac and lunar *nakṣatra*. How we look at the belt of stars around the ecliptic and what constellations we see depends on whether we are looking for lunar mansions or solar zodiac signs. How we choose to configure the lateral entrances—with the lunar circumference or the solar axis—depends on what rituals we wish to perform.

The first step up to the main western entrance is also a step into the western tip of a 365.24-cubit solar axis. To be precise, the axes of the outer enclosure are 365.24 × 12.02 cubits, or 1 solar year (in days) repeated 12 times (Fig. 3.18).[31] The axes match the format, the numerical pattern, and the accuracy of the lunar year in the circumference—over nearly a 2000-m distance. The precisely-crafted 365.24-cubit measurement is the foundation on which all the other axes inside the temple rest. In fact, there is a logical progression in this pyramid-like stack of axial measurements that helps put the remarkable solar axes of the temple into a much broader perspective (Fig. 3.19).

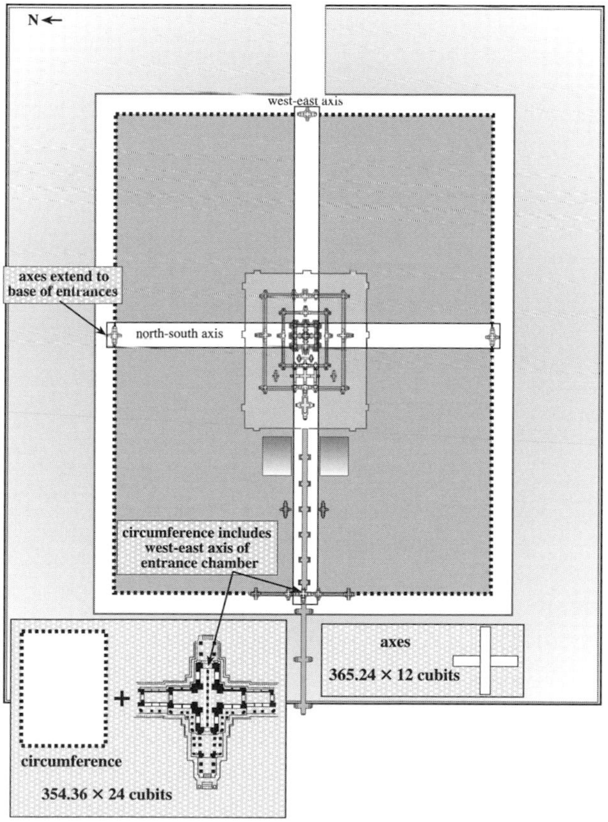

Fig. 3.18. Fourth (outer) enclosure, axes and circumference.
The circumference that encloses the grounds of Angkor Wat is equal to an exact lunar year measured in 24-cubit modules. The axes that reach through the grounds of the temple record the precise solar year in 12-cubit modules. The axes extend to the base of the entrances on the north, south, and east, and to the first step up the western staircase to the main entrance of the temple. The circumference follows the rule of including the west–east axis of the entrant chamber in its total. Astonishing for their accuracy, these measurements are among the most impressive accomplishments of the builders of Angkor Wat.

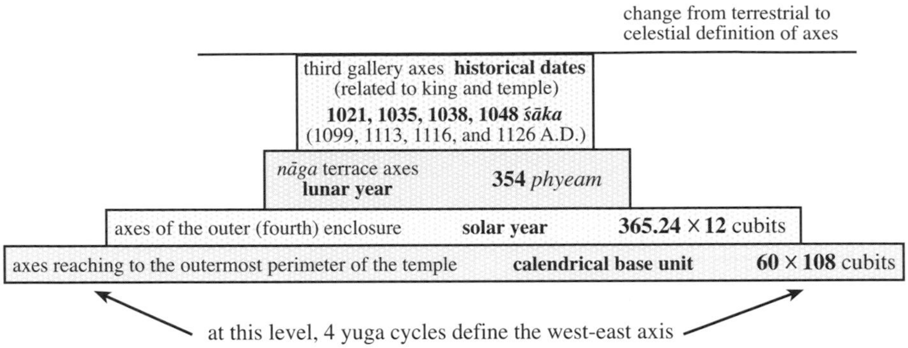

Fig. 3.19. Progression of temple's axes from outer perimeter through the third gallery.

The successive axes of Angkor Wat describe terrestrial time measurements from the largest (yugas) to the smallest and most specific (dates in the life of the king). Once the historically focused third gallery is left behind, time is viewed from the perspective of the gods on Mount Meru.

Angkor Wat rises from axes that symbolize the creation of time and its measurement boundaries: 108 (cubits), which function as a key to changing divinity to time and back again, and the number 60, the key to a shared system (minutes and seconds) of time and space measurement. Right at the beginning of the bridge, just as these axes are entered, the yuga cycles begin. They are the largest unitary time divisions, and their numerical years can be arithmetically derived from the 60-unit basis for measuring time and space.

Next in sequence is the solar year, the axes inside the grounds of Angkor Wat. The solar year, in turn, is the largest unitary element within the yuga cycles. It is used to measure our time, and the time of the gods as well. Quite logically, the next axes in this sequence define the lunar year of 354 days, and these axes lie under the central three galleries of Angkor Wat. The progression will continue in this pattern to reveal that Angkor Wat is organized to reach the world of King Sūryavarman and then, from there, continue into the realm of the gods. Sūryavarman's kingdom, in a sense, becomes a gateway to the stars and the gods that inhabit the universe above and around us. Angkor Wat itself provides the setting for this transition. The solar axes in the outer enclosure belong to this larger picture of a gradual progression and metamorphosis of time itself.

Returning to the main western entrance once more, we note that the moon and all its attributes are intimately tied to Somā, the *nāginī* mother of the Khmer people. She was the consort of Kauṇḍinya and together they started the lunar race of kings. The consort Śrī Lakṣmī strokes Viṣṇu's legs in the scene on the lintel over this entrance. Opposite this lunisolar pair of deities, a consort sits on the left knee of the god who is the focus of the lintel on the east. Consorts and celestial maidens are everywhere at Angkor Wat, and in this instance especially they symbolize the lunar aspects of the temple. Their importance to the meaning of Angkor Wat may have been underscored in this entrance. We know that King Sūryavarman had two successive queens. Could these two women have been honored as the goddess Śrī Lakṣmī on either side of a central Viṣṇu image in the main entrance chamber? This is not an unfounded flight of fantasy by any means. Consider that there is no ritual pathway into the central tower that does not involve one or both of the lateral images. Given the dominant symbolism of the Churning of the Sea of Milk, the *Indrābhiṣeka* of the king, and the beginning of Sūryavarman's reign in conjunction with these chambers and the bridge, his two queens would be logical companions for an image of Viṣṇu as a symbol for the king in this introductory triad of towers.

When we walk into the main entrance of Angkor Wat, we are entering a sacred space that symbolized Brahmā and the center of a mandala. From the 32 chambers around the enclosure to the 32-unit axes of the eastern, northern, and southern entrances, to the pillars in front of the lateral entrances, to the length of the pillared corridors out to the end gateways, the mandala surrounds this abode of Brahmā.

Joining Brahmā at this juncture is the proposed image of Viṣṇu, at the base of the tower, inside the main sanctuary. The pillar of Mount Meru and Mount Mandara, which rises upward as the architectural thrust of the tower, marks a spring equinox center between the solstice gateways. The *Indrābhiṣeka* of the king was probably celebrated at the spring equinox, and so, once more, we are back with King Sūryavarman.

The central entrance not only encapsulates all the information we found on the bridge but adds mandala numbers and a solar component (366-unit circumambulation path) in a lunisolar pairing with the other entrances in the enclosure. That pairing is repeated in the circumference and axes, and in the deity and consorts (perhaps visual metaphors for the king and queen as inheritors of the line of Kauṇḍinya and Somā) as seen on the lintels.

With that first step up to the main western entrance, we are not only entering this multilevel world of meaning in the central tower. We are starting a *dvāpara yuga* distance that coincides with an arena of practical astronomy. We are entering the area where most solar and lunar observation was conducted, using the central towers of the temple. The next stage in the journey takes us past the lofty introduction of the central entrance towers and into a more practical application of measurements and axes.

4

From the Western Causeway through the Third Gallery: The Moon, the Libraries, and History

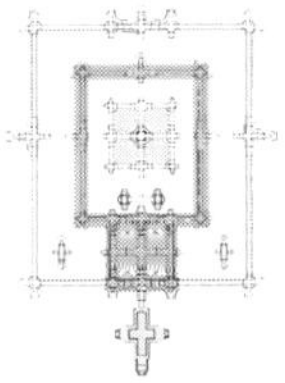

AFTER leaving the spacious chambers of the western entrance behind, the external world fades away as the visitor enters the temple grounds. New vistas are opened by a grand courtyard that ends in the far distance at stands of tall trees and dense jungle growth. Hidden behind the forest of trees, the lunar enclosing wall is 400 m away on each side of us, and straight ahead are the central galleries. At this point, we are on the broad, elevated western causeway, which rises high above the scrub-filled terrain. The sandstone surface is 10 m wide, or about 30 ft, a good proportion for the 350-m length of the causeway. This imposing sandstone walkway is interrupted by six sets of projecting stairways at regular intervals, and it is bordered by an impressive, shoulder-high *nāga* balustrade on each side (Fig. 4.1).

The lunar alignments that join the causeway to the central towers help to explain why it is elevated and divided into six sets of stairways.[1] In the latter instance, the stairways mark off observation points. In the former, the height of the causeway would provide a good view of the temple's towers and the ponds ahead. The ponds flank this axis on the north and south, just in front of the central galleries. By gauging the altitude of a star from its reflection in the water of the ponds, the astronomers could obtain very precise data on the star's location at a given time. The angle formed between the star and its reflection would be divided in half to give an accurate reading of the star's position in relation to the horizon at that time. The horizon line itself, by contrast, is not only obscured by trees and shrubs; it is opaque anyway. Locating it would be like trying to find a length of black thread in the dark.

Focusing on the staircases alone, at intervals starting from the first set of stairways at the west end of the causeway (6 in diagram), to the next-to-last set on the east (4 in diagram), the lunar alignments are (Fig. 4.2):

1. From first staircases (6) to second gallery, southwest tower (D)
2. From second staircases (7) to second gallery, northeast tower (A)
3. From second staircases (7) to second gallery, southwest tower (D)
4. From third staircases (8) to second gallery, southeast tower (B)
5. From fourth staircases (2) to first gallery, northwest tower (C)
6. From fourth staircases (2) to second gallery, southeast tower (B)
7. From fifth staircases (4) to first gallery, northwest tower (C)

Angkor Wat, as shown by these alignments, was a sandstone observatory. The rituals that once filled its chambers with harmonious music, aromatic incense, bright flower garlands, and chanting priests were crucial to the nation's well-being. In turn, these rituals had to be performed at exactly the right day and the right time, or their efficacy was blunted if not completely nullified. What would be more appropriate than to build the temple as its own timepiece for its own rituals?

Except at the center, where two libraries stand like silent guardians, the staircases in the grand western causeway do not lead anywhere. Although this temple is characterized by architectural and arithmetic symbolism, the functional side of architecture was of primary importance. The Khmer builders were practical: they did not build ivory towers. Therefore, the staircases would be an odd trait, at the least, and an inexplicable exception if they really did not lead somewhere.

A few sets of staircases now point to an empty field or an occasional grazing cow. Might these staircases have once been aligned with wooden, palace-like structures that accommodated the preparations for temple functions, temple maintenance, and all the accoutrements for grand processions and rituals involving hundreds of onlookers and participants? Among these structures would have been a building to house the records, texts, and other implements connected to actual observation of the sun, moon, planets, and stars. There could be no better place for such a structure than somewhere near the causeway itself, on the western half of the temple. At the same time, no building would have been placed so close to the causeway that it obstructed a sight line.

The causeway staircases not only served as markers for observation points, and possible means of access to buildings in the western courtyard, but the distance between each successive staircase had a 28-*phyeam* lunar meaning as well (Fig. 4.3).[2] (See Appendix A, Table 4.1.)

A numerically perfect 29.53-unit lunar month, constructed by a nearly perfect 29.51-cubit module begins at the first step up to the main western entrance and stops at the east end of the causeway. There is yet another exact 28-unit length constructed by another, near-perfect 28.05-cubit module, between the last step out of the western entrance to the same point at the end of the causeway (arrows at bottom of Fig. 4.3).

If we wanted to do so, we could focus solely on the lunar calendar all the way up to the main Viṣṇu image in the central tower. The causeway ends at the 354-*phyeam* lunar axes underneath the central three galleries of Angkor Wat (Fig. 3.19), exactly where a 354-cubit path to the base of the upper elevation begins. Once we have climbed up the stairs to the top elevation, a circuit around the gallery represents one lunar year, but now in terms of the gods on Mount Meru, as will be shown. There are no more explicitly lunar paths to Viṣṇu but the moon is implicit in several of the mandala representations that lead us to the supreme deity at Angkor Wat. The ultimate and highest definition of the lunar calendar then, is in terms of the gods and the mandala. Along the way to that definition, the successive galleries will also paint the lunar month and year in progressively increasing detail. The lunar calendar as seen from these several perspectives, divine and human, could be the only focus of our journey to Viṣṇu if we so desired.

Phnom Bakheng (A.D. 900) has 12 towers on 5 terraces, symbols for a 5-year yuga period that is the oldest yuga cycle in Indian literature.[3] Compared to Phnom Bakheng, the 5-year cycle in the causeway at Angkor Wat is more a footnote than full text. The 12 staircases along the causeway do not have the same scale, but their numerical allusion to 12 × 5 for a total of 60 steps refers back to the axes and circumference of the temple and the many sets of 60 and 12-unit combinations at the base of time and space measurements. This 5-year cycle and the number 60 unify the solar and lunar calendars, bringing them into conjunction every 5 years (or every 60 solar months). And this brings up another point.

Despite the lunar nature of the walkway, there were three consecutive days each year when Sūrya, the sun god, held court over both causeway and temple. At dawn on the spring equinox day, an observer standing at the edge of the steps in the first stairway on the north side of the causeway will see the sun rise directly over the central tower of Angkor Wat (Figs. 4.3 and 4.4).[4] The sun's brief

Fig. 4.1. Western causeway and courtyard from northeast.

The central triad of western entrances is at the west end of the causeway, and a segment of the cruciform terrace is in the foreground. To the right is one of the causeway libraries.

but spectacular conjunction with the top of the tower is also seen 3 days later from the center of the causeway, between the first set of staircases, just in front of the central western entrance. The stunning vision of the sun as it comes up over the tower transforms the previously abstract solar symbolism into a living experience. For a rare moment, the observer actually sees the calendrical function of Angkor Wat in action.

Surya's solar disk would appear to rise up "out of" the central sanctuary, issuing forth from the interior image of Viṣṇu twice in a 3-day succession. The 3-day difference between the two equinox alignments agrees with the suggested 3- or 4-day equinox period symbolized by Mount Mandara at the center of the bas-relief of the churning scene at Angkor Wat. Because of the alignments and the bas-relief, we can also postulate that the 3-day equinox celebration period was observed in the early twelfth century at Angkor.[5]

Like the solar disk on the equinox day, Viṣṇu generates the horizontal axes of the temple and the vertical tower that rises above him like the lotus stalk at the time of creation. By inference and association, the solar character of the central sanctuary would propagate outward to the kingdom along the axes of the temple and the city beyond. Viṣṇu in the tower is at the center of Angkor Wat, at the center of the city-nation, at the center of the solar

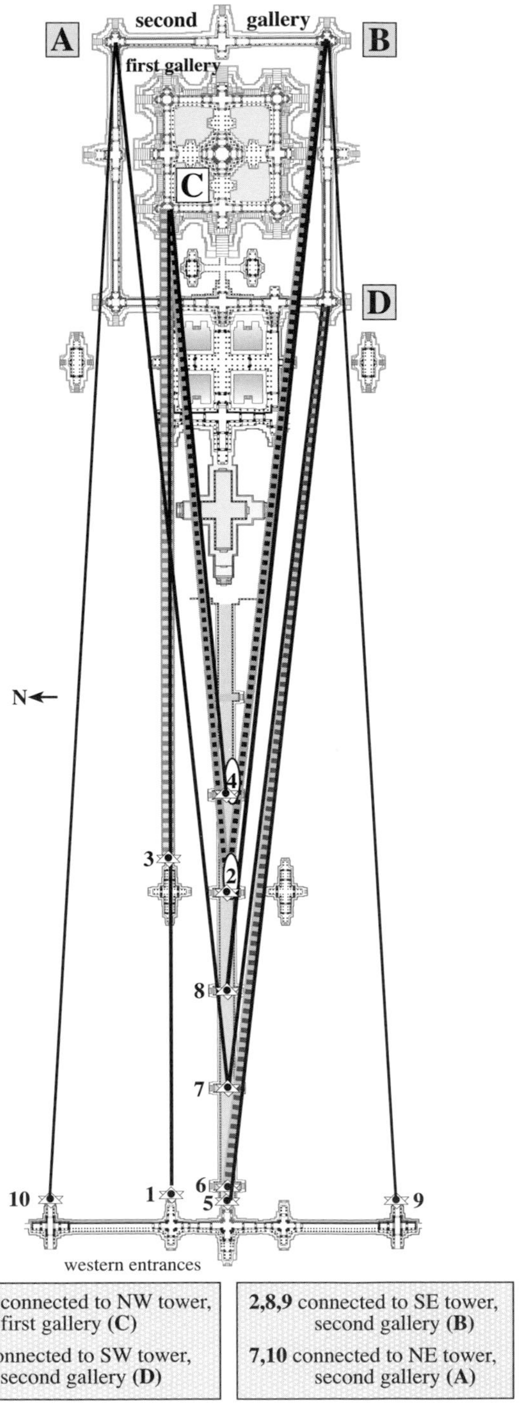

Fig. 4.2. Lunar alignments.

There are 12 different lunar alignments with four of the towers in the first and second galleries from observation points on the causeway, on the porch of the north causeway library, and in the western entrances. Eight alignments are with the second gallery (A, B, and D) and four are with the northwest tower of the first gallery. Most of the alignments are over 500 m in length. They create a spectacular connection between the central area of the temple and its approach from the west.

year (spring equinox), and at the center of the gods on Mount Meru.

The most direct solar connection to the image of Viṣṇu at the hub of Angkor Wat and the hub of King Sūryavarman's larger world starts with the solar axes in the outer enclosure of the temple. Rather than follow the circumference around the enclosure and then continue on the previous lunar journey, we cross directly through the main western entrance in a 366-cubit circumambulation path. The solar year (365.24 × 12) along the axes starts with this alternate version of the solar year into the temple grounds. At that point, we are at the equinox alignment with the central tower, and are joined directly to Viṣṇu and the rising sun on March 21. The six staircases on the north and south sides of the causeway are also symbols for the six months that the sun is north or south of due east on the horizon. This north-south split in the solar year was first introduced on the bridge with its solstice alignments to the end gateways on December 22 and June 21.

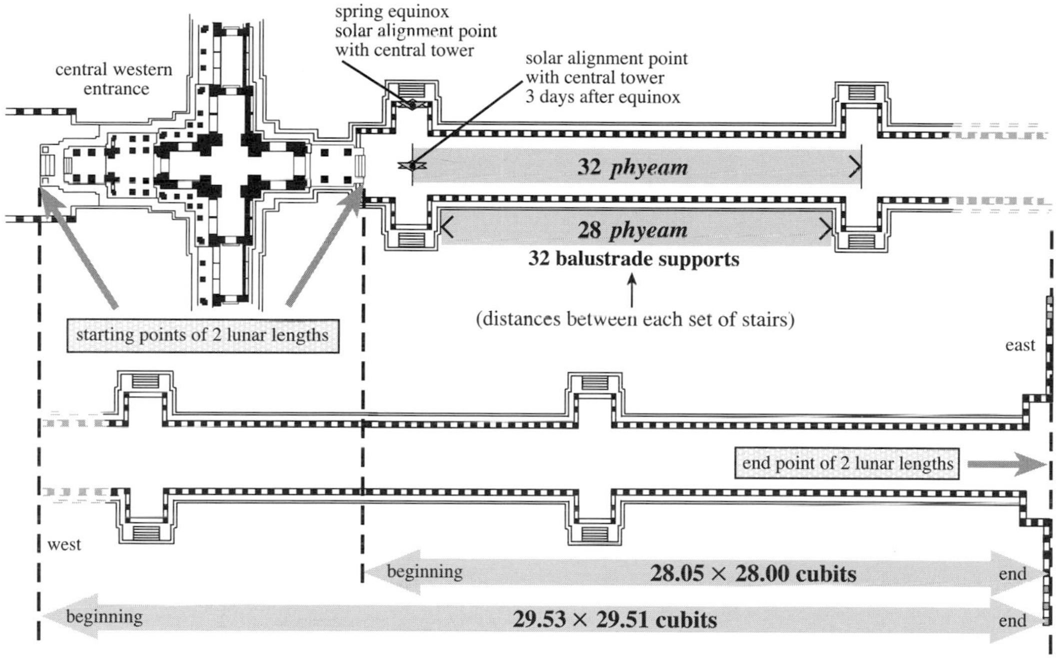

Fig. 4.3. Western causeway, lunar measurements.

The lunar alignments along the causeway arise from a lunar numerical environment. Two alternate lengths involving the causeway and the main western entrance provide exact totals for the lunar month, measured in days or in terms of *nakṣatra* (29.53 and 28). Aside from the lunar measurements and those numbers related to the 32 gods, the most outstanding solar alignment at Angkor Wat is found right at the beginning of the causeway on the west. On March 21 at the vernal equinox and beginning of the solar year, we can see the sun rise over the central tower if we stand at the top of the first northern staircase on the causeway. Three days later, if we stand at the center of the causeway between the first set of staircases, we see the sun rise directly over the top of the central tower once more. The three-day period between the two solar alignments was the traditional period for celebrating the new year at the time Angkor Wat was constructed. (See Appendix A, Table 4.1.)

Fig. 4.4. This photograph of the sun rising over the central tower of Angkor Wat was taken on March 21, 1992. The photographer was positioned at the top of the first northern staircase on the causeway, the spot marked by astronomers in 1976 as the point where this alignment would occur. (Photograph courtesy of Yoshiaki Fujiki.)

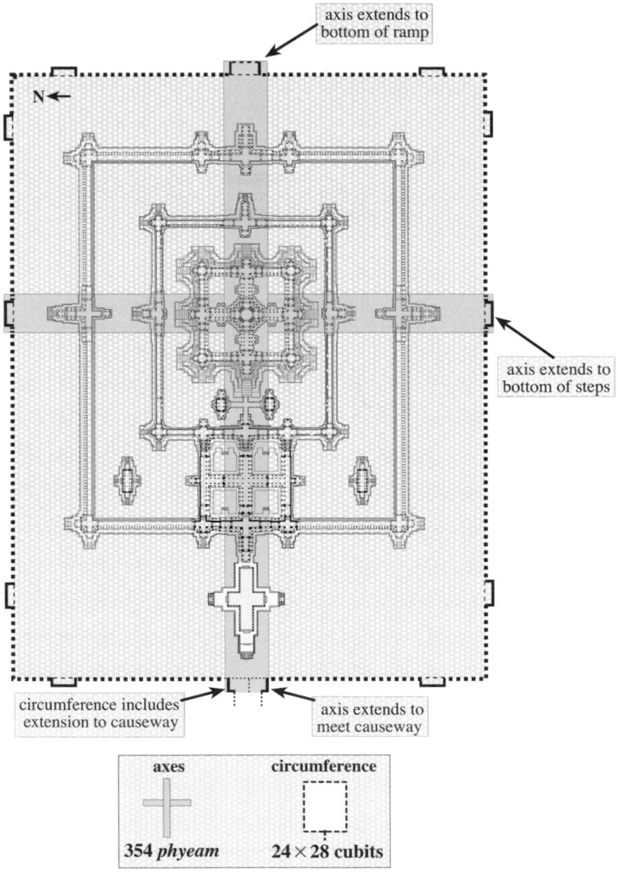

Fig. 4.5. Nāga *terrace, axes and circumference.*

The 354-*phyeam* axes and 24-unit component of the circumference of this terrace define the lunar year by days and lunar half-months. Also, the 28-cubit module in the circumference measurement provides the length of a lunar month calculated by the number of *nakṣatra* crossed by the moon in that period of time. Likewise, the 12 staircases around the lunar terrace would refer to the 12 full months in one lunar year, in approximately three-month segments between the equinox and solstice days. In this aspect, the terrace mirrors the 12 staircases in the upper elevation—solar in meaning at that level, however. In a fitting complement to the lunar measurements of the terrace, the *nāga* balustrade that circles it places its own zoomorphic symbol for the moon around the perimeter.

Outer enclosure, western entrances, south end (solstitial) gateway.

During the winter solstice period, the sun rises directly over the pediment of this gateway when viewed from the west end of the bridge across the moat.

Second and third galleries, northeast corner, eastern corridors.

The recently cleaned sandstone of the third gallery stands in dramatic contrast to the rest of the temple, and to the green jungle beyond.

Second gallery, southeast corner tower, view from the eastern entrance of the third gallery.

When this photo was taken in early 1992, the roof over the eastern entrance had not been put back yet. Now it is no longer possible to see this tower from inside the entrance.

Upper elevation, northwest corner tower, south facade.

The counterpoint between the faceted tower and the smooth surface of the wall enhances the dynamic of these strong vertical and horizontal architectural components.

Upper elevation, grand western staircase.

The steep angle and tall steps of Angkor Wat's most famous staircase are in keeping with the majestic facade of the topmost level of the temple.

Upper elevation, southwest courtyard, southwest corner.

A promenade of vaulted and pillared corridors circuits the upper level of the temple, allowing for a panoramic view out the windows in all directions.

Preau cruciforme, *center, at winter solstice.*

The play of light and shadow across the center of the *preau cruciforme* is not accidental but was carefully planned to precisely highlight the place where a reliquary was once buried underneath a statue of Brahmā.

Preau cruciforme, *northeast corner, view up along corner of roofs.*

The rich and delicate, organic surfaces of the roof and tympana give the hard stone a lightly textured and lively ambience.

Preau cruciforme, *northeast corner, telescoping roofs leading up to the second gallery.*

The ornately carved, decorous roofline populates the *preau cruciforme* with *nāgas*, meditating yogins, and *garuḍas*.

North library between the third and second galleries, southeast facade.

Elegant and isolated, its chambers now empty, the library's current presence belies an active and ritual-filled past.

Upper elevation, southwest courtyard, view to the east.

The central tower begins its vertical ascent at the left, the south entrance to the gallery is in shadow at the right. They are connected by one of four axial corridors that lead right up to the tower.

Central towers and north pool, from the west.

On a still and clear day, Angkor Wat seems to float in space when viewed from the edge of the reflecting pool.

The axes of the third gallery are expressed as a series of historical dates, recorded in the passage of 365.24-day solar years. The axes of the second gallery include the solar months as 12 *ādityas* in their 44-unit total. The axes of the upper elevation define the solar year as 366 days again, and the axes of the central tower define the 91 days between equinox and solstice points each year. We thus travel along axes that are singled out as solar in meaning by their own measurements, by the equinox alignment from the west-east axis to the central tower, and by the solstice observation point along the west-east axis of the bridge. If we so desired, we could in this manner follow a solar path from the entrance bridge right up to the central tower of the temple.

In the preceding chapter, we noted the pyramidal progression of the axes of the temple. The *nāga* terrace at the end of the causeway is the last element in the first half of this progression. It is at the same level as the causeway: one simply walks onto the terrace without noticing it very much. Its axes measure 354.67 *phyeam,* or exceedingly close to the 354.36 days in one lunar year.[6] Its circumference is equal to 24 × 28 cubits (Fig. 4.5). No wonder a series of *nāgas* circle the periphery of the terrace as a balustrade. Their lunar nature is right at home with the measurements beneath them (Figs. 1.7 and 1.8).

Setting aside the solar perspective for a moment, the axes have taken us steadily upward from the 60-unit basis for measuring time, through the yuga periods and the solar year, to the lunar year in the *nāga* terrace. At each new axial length, the time period represented gets smaller and smaller, and so does the space involved. The conceptual basis for the organization of the axes lies in their vertical succession. The axes above or below a gallery, it turns out, are not relevant to the meaning of that gallery. Only its own axes convey its relation to a time period. Nevertheless, from the point of view of a journey into the temple, we climb onto each level of the west–east axis in turn and therefore go up through each smaller and smaller expression of time. As our spatial focus narrows, as the walls literally close in, the time frame narrows also. Ultimately, we will find ourselves in the smallest unit of time yet: the dates within the *śāka* era that are recorded in the axes of the third gallery.

The vertical separation of each axis does not affect the concept of a central Viṣṇu emanating solar and temporal blessings along the axes of the temple and out to the world. The central tower is itself along a vertical axis that extends to just below ground level, where a sacred deposit was once buried before construction began. This vertical axis is the hub of every single horizontal axis at the temple: it goes through all of them like an axle through the hub of a wheel. For the literal-minded, it is this vertical connection that "allows" Viṣṇu to extend his beneficence throughout Angkor Wat and beyond. For the less literal-minded, a supreme deity does not always need a logical explanation. Finally, Viṣṇu also emanates along the vertical axis, sending the same solar and temporal blessings to the world of the *devas* above and the *asuras* below.

The horizontal and vertical axes at Angkor Wat and their striking conjunction in the central tower, especially at the spring equinox, cause most other aspects of the temple to pale in comparison. To rectify that impression and achieve a lunar balance with the preceding solar iconography, let us pause to look at the six independent structures known as libraries.

LIBRARIES ON THE LUNAR SIDE OF MERU

Uniquely paired libraries flank the main west–east axis of the temple. The first set falls on either side of the western causeway at its center point; the second set is in front of the second gallery; and the

third in front of the first gallery. All are on the west half of Angkor Wat, and all are paired north–south across the entrant axis of the temple.

Libraries are found in many Khmer temples. They functioned as repositories for ritual implements and manuscripts.[7] When only one library was constructed, it is generally to the left upon entering the temple—to the south in temples facing east. Otherwise, the libraries are always paired north–south across the entrant axis and in front of the central area of the temple. The structures at Angkor Wat are twins and may have alternated their ritual functions between the light and dark halves of the month. George Coedès has defined these sets of structures in reference to another temple:

> One might suppose that the temple [Wat Baset] had two depositories, one for each half-month, which accords well with the rigorous division in the service [of the temple] for the two halves of the month, which one finds throughout the epigraphy. These depositories, in most cases, would correspond to the two buildings annexed to the temples which we call "libraries" that could have contained, in effect, sacred books. . . . They would have served to keep in order the utensils for the cult and the precious objects offered to the deity, in brief, the treasure of the temple.[8]

Innumerable Khmer inscriptions, most dating from the tenth and eleventh centuries, divide the workers and servants of a temple into two lunar groups: one for the period of the waxing moon and the other for the waning moon.[9] I imagine the temple's chores were divided to give people time to work in the fields or at personal, life-sustaining tasks. The priests were assigned to even narrower periods of time, receiving such titles as "Venerable One of the Afternoons of the Waxing [or Waning] Moon."[10]

Measurement patterns and the reliefs found in the third gallery indicate that the temple's northern half was particularly dedicated to the gods and the southern half to the ancestors, or "fathers." Bas-reliefs on the north side of the third gallery depict the gods and their realm in contrast to the south side's portrayal of the king and his realm. The "fathers" are also shown in the southern bas-reliefs as 19 men seated in celestial palaces. The "mothers" are there, as well, 18 of them, alternating with the "fathers."

The *Śatapatha Brāhmaṇa* states that the waxing moon "represents the gods" and the waning moon represents the "fathers."[11] This fixed rule, which is expanded at great length, agrees with the findings at Angkor Wat. The fathers, the south, and the waning moon are grouped in the third gallery opposite the gods, the north, and the waxing moon. This dichotomy suggests that the southern libraries were used for ritual observances during the period of the waning moon and the northern libraries during the waxing moon. Along with this ritual division, the architectural design and location of the libraries argue for their association with specific areas of the temple.

The libraries at the middle of the western causeway, as noted earlier, are the architectural duplicates of the northern, southern, and eastern entrances in the outer enclosure (Figs. 4.6–4.8). They have the same dimensions and design, the same 24 interior pillars, 24 windows, and 3 interior chambers (Fig. 4.9). Their measurements are different in their organization, but not in their totals, from those of the entrances.[12] (See Appendix A, Table 4.2.)

It is remarkable that the only significant measurements in this set of libraries are either 24 or 27/28, indicative of the lunar month and half-month. Very few sectors of Angkor Wat have such exclusivity—and in this case, the exclusivity goes well with the lunar causeway, the lunar observation points, and the basically lunar measurements of the

Preau cruciforme, *northeast corner, double pillar alongside the entrance up to the second gallery.*

After surviving over 800 years completely intact, this double pillar shows the effects of a random and mindless target practice.

Third gallery, west side, south half, Battle of Kurukṣetra, central figures.

Frozen in the moment just before the decisive end of the battle, these two leading commanders may dramatize King Sūryavarman's own act of regicide.

northern, eastern, and southern entrances of the outer enclosure. It seems reasonable to postulate that an image of Candra or perhaps a Śiva lingam was once installed at the center of these two library structures.

While the causeway libraries are elongated and sprawl from west to east, the middle libraries are strikingly vertical and stand tall in front of the second gallery, resembling miniature high-rises (Fig. 4.10). Their roofs peek over the corridors of the third gallery and can be seen from the courtyard. Their design is traditional in that most libraries seem to have been quite tall, with a clerestory on top, as these demonstrate. They are not joined to the third gallery at any point, however; no doorways lead to that area, no entrances beckon. Instead, one has to walk through the north–south connecting corridors to the second gallery in order to get to the libraries—or else walk down from the second gallery itself. Indeed, it is difficult to see how these libraries related to the third gallery. If they did not, then none did. This may be one of the most telling comments yet on the organization of Angkor Wat, a point to be kept in mind for later retrieval.

Logic and inference place these libraries, moored on the green grass of the inner courtyard, in association with the second gallery right next to them. Their location, their exceptional height, and their exclusion from interaction with the third gallery argue the point. Their measurements, however, are unequivocal. They reveal that the libraries share one of the most outstanding numerical traits of the second gallery: the numbers 20/21 (Fig. 4.11).[13]

On examination, the examples of the number 20 in the libraries implies an all-encompassing twenty-first unit. In the circumambulation path, the central image is a twenty-first unit. In the path up to the image, the image is again a twenty-first unit. In the west–east axial total, the axis itself is a twenty-first unit. In the number of total pillars, either the library or the central image can function as a twenty-first unit. A single, consistent statement

Fig. 4.6. North causeway library, south facade.

Framed by the pillars of its companion library, the north library is much like the southern entrance in Fig. 3.17. The north–south axial pairing of each set of libraries is apparent as one looks through from one doorway to the next.

Fig. 4.7. South causeway library, north facade.

According to architectural tradition, all libraries are rectangular, with a raised central roof and the short side facing the main temple. They tend to occur just inside an enclosing wall and not far from the central axis. In smaller libraries, the entrances are only on the short sides of the structure.

Fig. 4.8. North causeway library, interior, main chamber, view west.

The 24 pillars in each library make a visually faceted environment out of a simple cruciform plan. The inside is well lit by 24 windows as well.

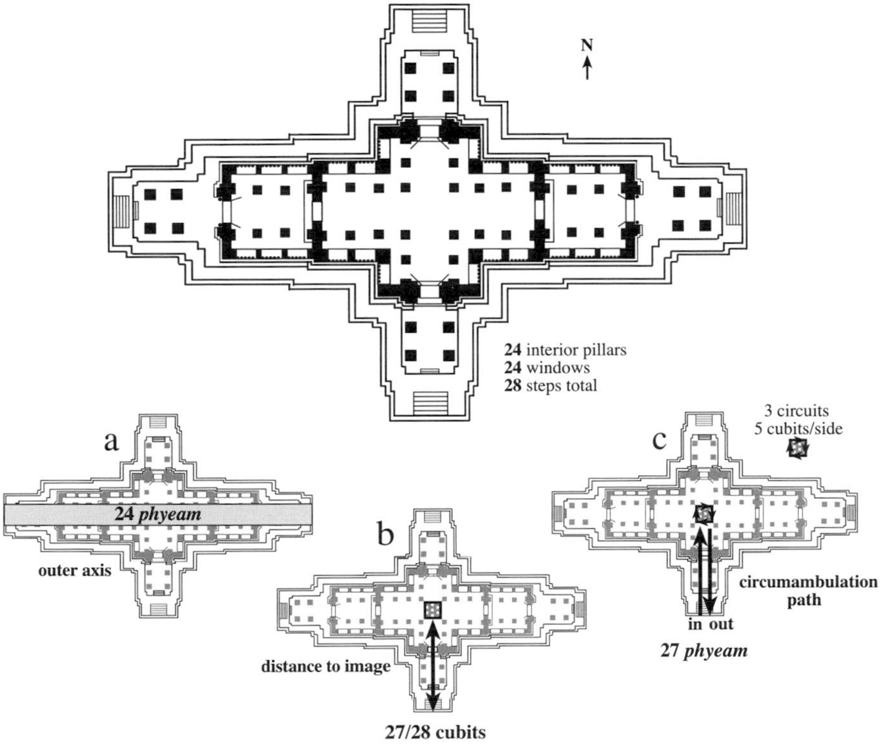

Fig. 4.9. Causeway libraries, measurement patterns.

There are only lunar references in the circumambulation path, pillars, windows, steps, and axes of the causeway libraries. Their architecture reproduces the architecture of the axial entrances of the outer enclosure, also lunar in meaning. The moon may be more dominant in these libraries due to their association with the lunar outer enclosure of the temple. (See Appendix A, Table 4.2.)

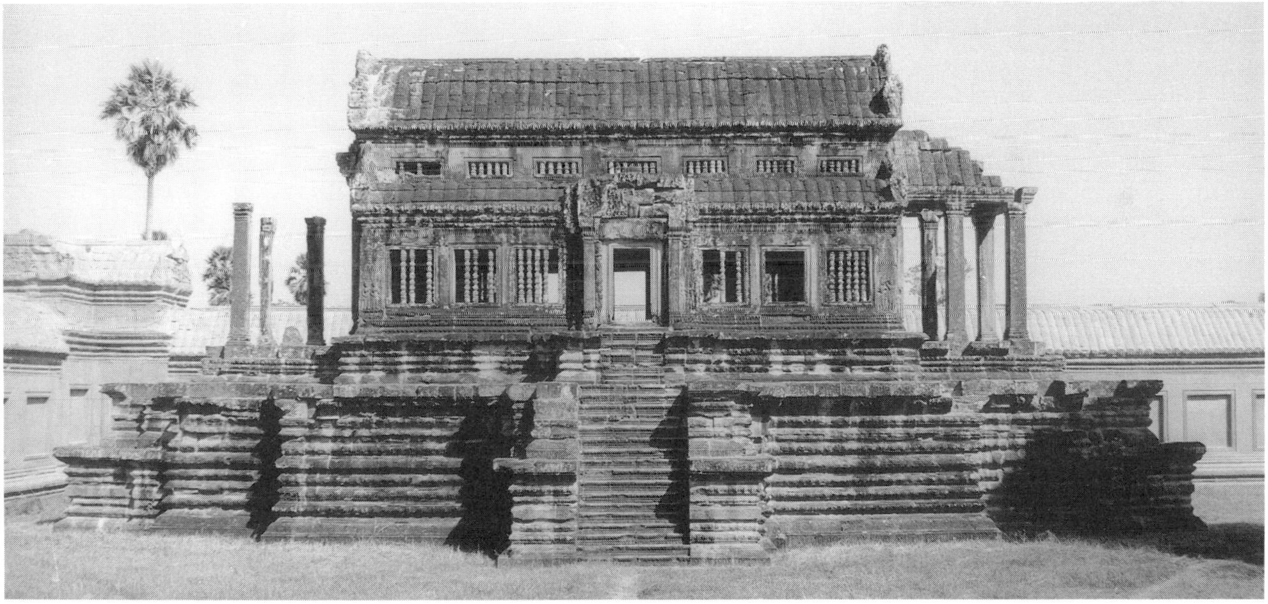

Fig. 4.10. Second level, north library, south facade.

This library is just across from the only exit from the *preau cruciforme* onto this side of the courtyard. The architecture of the library is somewhat more traditional than the other libraries, in that it has a clerestory. Just like the second gallery, it is raised on a high plinth and has a total of 21 steps in its northern or southern set of two staircases.

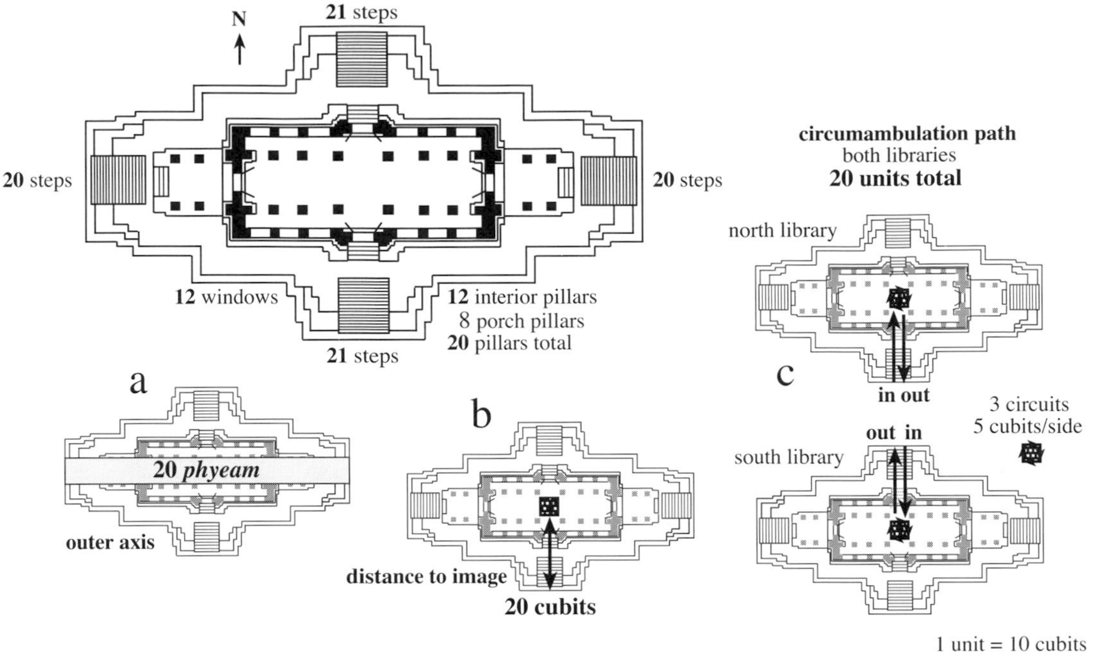

Fig. 4.11. Middle-level libraries, measurement patterns.

These libraries may have one lunar reference in their set of 12 interior pillars and 12 windows each (12/12 paired in both libraries together symbolize the half-months in the lunar year). But that ends their numerical connection to the moon. All of their remaining measurements and total number of steps and pillars, and their circumambulation path refer to 20/21, a definition of the supreme deity and lesser deities. Even though these libraries have no demonstrable connection to the third gallery, the number 20 occurs in both the second and third galleries as a definition of a royal or divine king. Therefore, while these structures are directly accessible from the second gallery and not the third, they may still allude to King Sūryavarman in their measurements. (See Appendix A, Table 4.3.)

comes out of this pattern: a "supreme" twenty-first unit embraces or embodies all the "lesser" deities. Jean Filliozat first emphasized this concept in an article on the Bakheng published in 1954.[14] This is an example of a nonarithmetic instance in which one can mean 21 when examined in a certain light. Therefore, whatever deity may have been represented at the heart of this central set of libraries, it was understood as an all-embracing divinity, probably allied with or identical to Brahmā, the god who dominates the second gallery of Angkor Wat.

From their appearance to their measurements, it is clear that this pair of libraries is not especially related to the preceding set. The libraries may share a common ritual purpose, but they seem to have been designed to be part of only one gallery. This aspect of their placement and meaning is postulated here for the first time.

The libraries on the next level are two diminutive structures dwarfed by the massive, high plinth of the first gallery. They are crowded between the enormous plinth and the blank wall of the second gallery; there is very little room to

Fig. 4.12. Third level, north library, south facade.

The last set of libraries is tightly situated between the first and second galleries. These are the smallest structures at Angkor Wat. There is enough light from their four doorways to allow for blind windows—blind so that there would be wall space inside for placing texts, ritual implements, or images.

maneuver around them (Fig. 4.12). They themselves are connected by a short, raised, cruciform walkway, however, which also connects the first and second galleries to each other (Fig. 4.13). Doors open up from the north and south corridors of the second gallery onto this courtyard, in alignment with the doors of the libraries. Another pair of similar doors opens onto the eastern courtyard. These two sets of doors do not occur in the third gallery, where they would have interrupted the bas-reliefs. Their presence here indicates a close connection between the two top galleries of the temple.

Unlike the two preceding sets of libraries, which show a singular focus, these last libraries have an eclectic numerology (Fig. 4.14).[15] For example, Mount Meru, in the form of the upper elevation, casts its shadow over the libraries in several ways at once. The four rivers that flow from Meru cross through seven concentric oceans. The four continents surrounding Meru are each characterized by special traits and scenery; the four mountains around Meru (including Mandara on the east) are present as the four corner towers of the upper elevation. At the same time, these towers correspond to the four towers around Indra's palace on the summit of Mount Meru. The 27/28 *nakṣatra* circle Meru, and the god Brahmā above the top of this cosmic mountain is defined as a twenty-first deity (Fig. 4.11b, c). Nearly all the measurements of the last set of libraries are related to Mount Meru and its gods in one way or another. They also tend to summarize the measurements in the preceding sets of libraries.

The 11 *karāṇa* that alternate in presiding over the 60 half-days in a lunar month are found in the outer west–east axes. They first appeared in the northern, southern, and eastern entrances of the

Fig. 4.13. Cruciform walkway between second gallery and upper elevation.

The walkway reaches from the exit out of the second gallery (upper left) to the great western staircase (lower right) a distance of 32 cubits. The cross-arm connects the libraries at upper right and lower left (out of camera range).

Fig. 4.14. Topmost libraries, measurement patterns.

Unlike its predecessors, this set of libraries has a variety of measurements that refer to the moon (4, 7, 11, 27/28) and in some cases, to Mount Meru as well. Meru has four mountain peaks around it, and seven oceans that circle it as well. Other than these references found in the axes, pillars, windows, and doorways, there is a 21-unit circumambulation path into and out of each library. In some ways, it seems as though this last set of libraries summarizes the traits found in the other two sets. (See Appendix A, Table 4.4.)

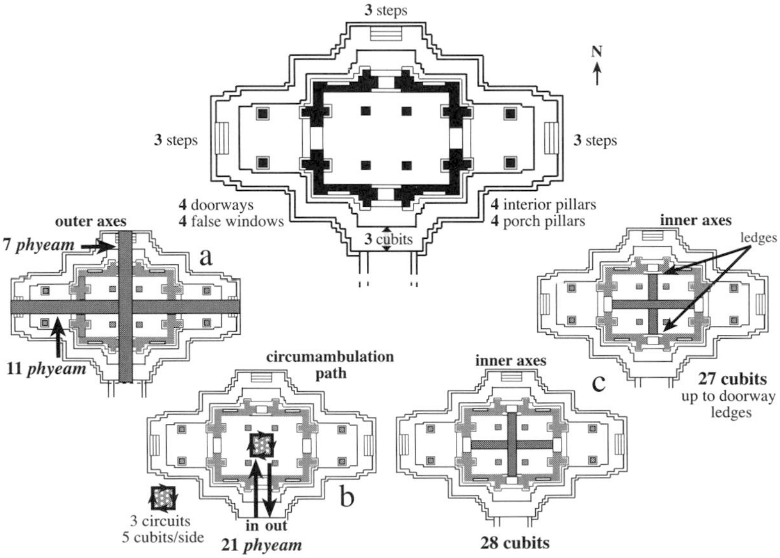

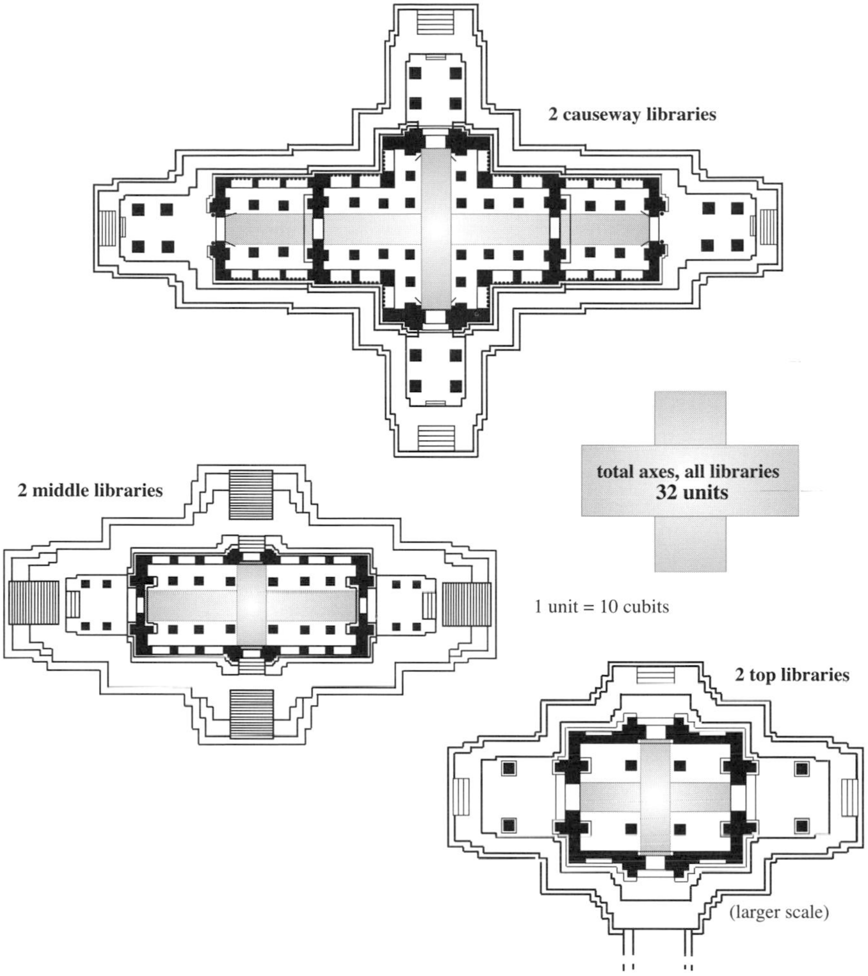

Fig. 4.15. Three sets of libraries, total inner axes.

The interior axes of all six libraries at Angkor Wat come to 32 units. Other than 20 or 21, this is the only instance of a library measurement that is directly joined to the gods. It is one indication of a need to specifically incorporate the 32 gods into every aspect of the architecture at the temple.

outer enclosure. These lunar gods are related to astrology and calculating the best time for activities and events.

The gods on Mount Meru may also be present in a final measurement of both libraries together. When the central circumambulation space is subtracted from the outer axes of both libraries, the result is 32.34 *phyeam*. The action of deleting a circumambulation space from the axis, or from any measurement that runs through a sanctuary, is the key to understanding the upper elevation of Angkor Wat. The number 32 is also the most repeated measurement on the upper level. Both the number 32 and the way it is derived in these two libraries connect the libraries to the upper elevation.

Architecturally speaking, the six libraries form a distinctive set of structures placed in the same relationship to the western axis. When examined as one set, the inner axes of all six buildings total 319.64 cubits, or 32 × 10 (Fig. 4.15).[16] This final measurement is the only measurement shared by the libraries as one set. It joins them one to another, as it joins them all again to the gods on Mount Meru.

The implication is that all libraries, beyond their association with individual galleries, ultimately belong to the deities on Mount Meru. This may explain why there are no libraries connected to the third gallery of King Sūryavarman—the only sector of the temple that is explicitly an expression of worldly time and space. If the libraries belonged to the 32 gods on Meru, there could be no set next to the third gallery. On a much more practical level, where would they fit? The absence of libraries is the first indication that the third gallery of the temple has a special role in the organization of Angkor Wat. Other indications will follow.

As the priests performed rituals alternating between the light and dark halves of the lunar month, the three sets of libraries fulfilled their functions according to the same alternation. This north–south oscillation between the libraries is the lunar version of the north–south solar oscillation between the solstice gateways. In fact, since the moon also has its own north–south oscillation, like the sun, this symbolism may fulfill a dual purpose in this instance.

THE THIRD GALLERY AND ITS CRUCIFORM TERRACE

The seven-headed *nāga*s that rise up at the end of the causeway spread their protective hoods toward the temple, the balustrade that is their body extending behind them (Fig. 4.16). They signal a major change in the architectural ambience.

Like the *nāga* heads, the viewer's back is now turned to the vast, open courtyard. Ahead lies the increasingly steep ascent up to the "master mountain," the central tower and Mount Meru, home of Viṣṇu and the *deva*s. The horizon looms higher and higher as we approach the center, until there is no horizon and we are enveloped in the stone casing of sanctuaries and galleries. The open, unbounded, and horizontally extensive plains of Angkor, and the lesser but still broad vistas of the courtyard of Angkor Wat, are gone. At the end of the journey into the temple is the solitary, dark, and vertical central sanctuary. The priests focusing on ritual practices there would have been enclosed within a concentrated, narrow environment, stripped of all distracting sights and sounds. The change from open vistas to a closed space, from a broad horizontal expanse to a narrow vertical height, from daylight to no light, from mundane sounds to silence, from social interaction to solitude, begins at the end of the causeway and the start of the central galleries.

The Cruciform Terrace

The rising central galleries of Angkor Wat are preceded by a massive terrace, in the shape of a cross, with access stairs on the west, north, and south ends. On its east side, the terrace leads into the steps of the entrance to the third gallery. Like the temple itself, the terrace rises in graded stages (Fig. 4.17). The horizontal stretch of the terrace balances the vertical thrust of the upper elevations of the temple and helps to anchor the ascending galleries to terra firma. The terrace is an architectural cousin of the bridge and causeway: there is a diminutive *nāga* railing on its upper platform, and vertical columns striate its long sides (Fig. 4.18). As on the bridge itself, the axes of the upper cruciform and the north–south axis of the main body of the terrace are both measured between slightly raised ledges. The rest of the axial measurements on the terrace extend between the bases on the north and south or between the outermost bottom step of the sections being measured.

The terrace measurements are as eclectic as those of the last set of libraries, perhaps because the terrace introduces all the galleries at the heart of the temple and thus contains a little of each in its dimensions (Fig. 4.19).[17] Of these measurements, the numbers 12, 32, and 108 (108 total columns) are connected with the Mount Meru symbolism of the upper elevation; 24, 27, 28, and 21 are related to the moon and Brahmā in the second gallery; and the 54/54 split in the columns recalls the Churning of the Sea of Milk and the *Indrābhiṣeka* of King Sūryavarman in the third gallery. With its scattering of numbers characteristic of the galleries ahead, the terrace brings us to the main themes of the central temple. At the same time, it effects a transition from the format of the causeway behind us to the enclosed and restricted corridors of the galleries in front of us.

The Third Gallery and Its Time Periods

King Sūryavarman is praised as bringing the *kṛta yuga* to Angkor when he came to power—according to the composite of information that can be

Fig. 4.16. Western courtyard: causeway, libraries, and main entrances (east facade).

The long, lunar causeway and pair of libraries, along with the main western entrances and their solar alignments, provide an expansive introduction to the heart of Angkor Wat. As the lion guardians survey the landscape, the ascent up the first of many staircases begins.

gleaned from the story of the Churning of the Sea of Milk, the bridge, and inscriptions. Apparently he not only brought the golden age and all its perfections to Angkor, but he installed this auspicious era at Angkor Wat along the west–east axis, the north–south axis, and in the third gallery as well. The circumference of the third gallery is 1728.40 cubits (Fig. 4.20). As always, the circumference measurement is equal to the inner west–east axis of the main entrance chamber, plus the circumference itself.[18] But this time the circumference contains more than a relationship to the western entrance alone. The sets of corner pavilions and lateral entrances on the west and east, and the northern and southern entrances are also connected to the circumference by a *kṛta yuga* total.[18] Based on measurement patterns, the circumference in each of the three central galleries is related to the images in the various chambers of each gallery. Nevertheless, the connection to the image in the western entrance is singled out as a special occurrence. This gallery provides one example of that unique connection. The image in the main western entrance here was preceded by the image of Viṣṇu symbolically inclusive of Brahmā and Sūryavarman in the main western

Fig. 4.17. Cruciform terrace and main entrance, third gallery, west facade.

The cruciform terrace rises in short stages, each level marking different measurement boundaries. The terrace may have been a place for open-air ceremonial events.

entrance of Angkor Wat. The latter image generates a 354.36-unit lunar circumference while being joined to solar axes. Here, the image similarly generates the *kṛta yuga* along the circumference while being connected to the suggested historical dates along the axes, discussed later. Other western entrance images agree with the general circumference/axes pattern. Brahmā in the second gallery generates the grid of a mandala along the circumference and is connected to the 44 mandala deities along the gallery's axis. The western entrance image on the top level generates a lunar circumference while connected to the solar axes of the gallery. Because of these analogies and the combination of historical dates and the *kṛta yuga,* an image of Sūryavarman in the guise of Viṣṇu may have occupied the place of honor in the western entrance chamber of the third gallery, generating the *kṛta yuga* from there.

Nevertheless, if the sets of axes in the entrance chambers were not added to the circumference of 1698 cubits, no *kṛta yuga* total would result. But they are added. Presumably King Sūryavarman's golden age was meant to permeate each chamber, explicitly joining the image to the era actualized by the king. Except for the image in the main

Fig. 4.18. Cruciform terrace, northeast facade, view from third gallery.

The graceful sweep of the terrace transforms the linear approach of the western causeway into a gradual, upward climb to the central galleries. The columns alongside the terrace ameliorate its flat horizontal movement and repeat the design of the pillars along the corridors of the third gallery. This same pattern of columns and pillars was seen in the bridge and the corridors of the main western entrances (Figs. 1.2, 1.4, 1.6).

western entrance, no other image is included in the circumference total. This implies that the other images do not generate the *kṛta yuga* on their own, they simply enjoy its effects in each chamber.

The main eastern entrance at this level is opposite the main western entrance in more ways than simple location. The eastern axial entrance is almost like a pariah: it has no entrance staircase, no auspicious measurements, and no *kṛta yuga* total in connection with the circumference. We assume then, that the image in the central eastern entrance was excluded from the time period that fills every other chamber in the gallery. A few reasons for this curious exclusion and for the missing staircase will be suggested after the historical dates along the axes are considered.

Two final *kṛta yuga* lengths at Angkor Wat (Fig. 4.21) extend between the base of the southern staircase up to the third gallery and the outer border of the moat on the north (1729.48 cubits) and the base of the northern staircase to the southern border of the moat (1720.31 cubits).[19] The discrepancy in the southern distance is due, in part, to the 1.72-m southward displacement of the center of Angkor Wat.

These two *kṛta yuga* lengths lie along the same axis as the total of 1728 cubits between the northern or southern entrances (in the outer enclosure) and the upper elevation of the temple. All seven representations of the golden era at Angkor Wat, counting the circumference of the third gallery as one, are either directly associated with King Sūryavarman's third gallery or cross through it.

If one were to enter each chamber of the third gallery from the outer perimeter, circuit the image inside three times, and leave toward the outer

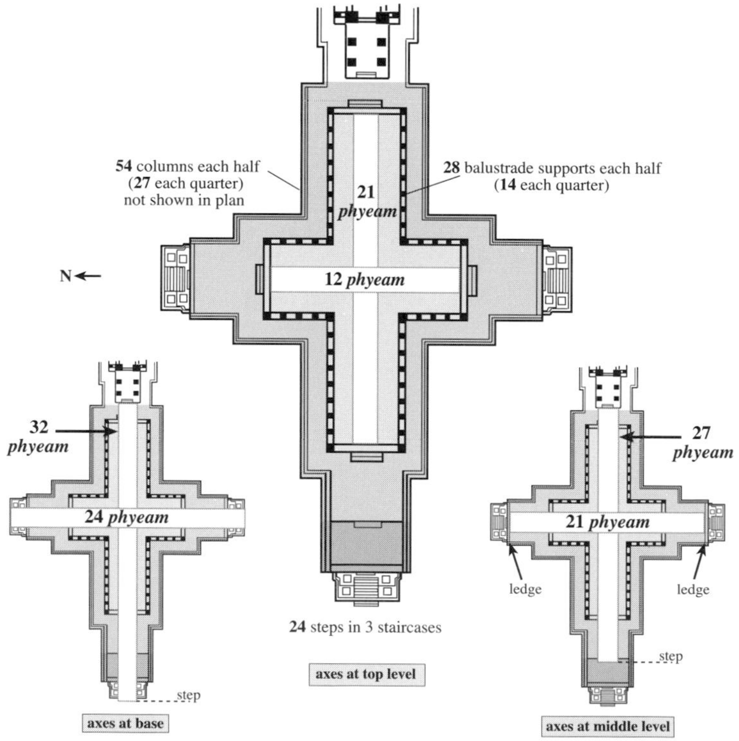

Fig. 4.19. Cruciform terrace, measurements.

The cruciform terrace in front of the third gallery is eclectic in its measurements. The 32-*phyeam* length of its longest west–east axis is exactly the distance between the staircases in the western causeway, and numerically equal to the 32-cubit length of the cruciform walkway in front of the upper elevation. The lunar symbolism inherent in the terrace's 24-, 27-, and 28-unit measurements matches the environment of the *nāga* terrace on which it rests. As an introduction to the central galleries of the temple, the cruciform terrace seems to cover most of the measurements we will encounter in the levels ahead of us. (See Appendix A, Table 4.5.)

perimeter again, the total distance covered would approximate a *tretā yuga* (1293.16 cubits). This same type of path around a perimeter occurred in the outer enclosure and described a lunar year.[20] Now the path around the gallery places the *tretā yuga* as a larger concentric ring around the circumference, a kind of "safety margin" to further insulate the king and his ministers from the negative connotations of time beyond the gallery.

ARE DATES RECORDED IN THE AXES?

The axes in the third gallery come to 1048.55 cubits from base to base and to the farthest step on the west (Fig. 4.20).[21] If the axes are measured to the first step into the gallery on the west (excluding the porch), they total 1034.42 cubits.[22] If the circumambulation space around the image of

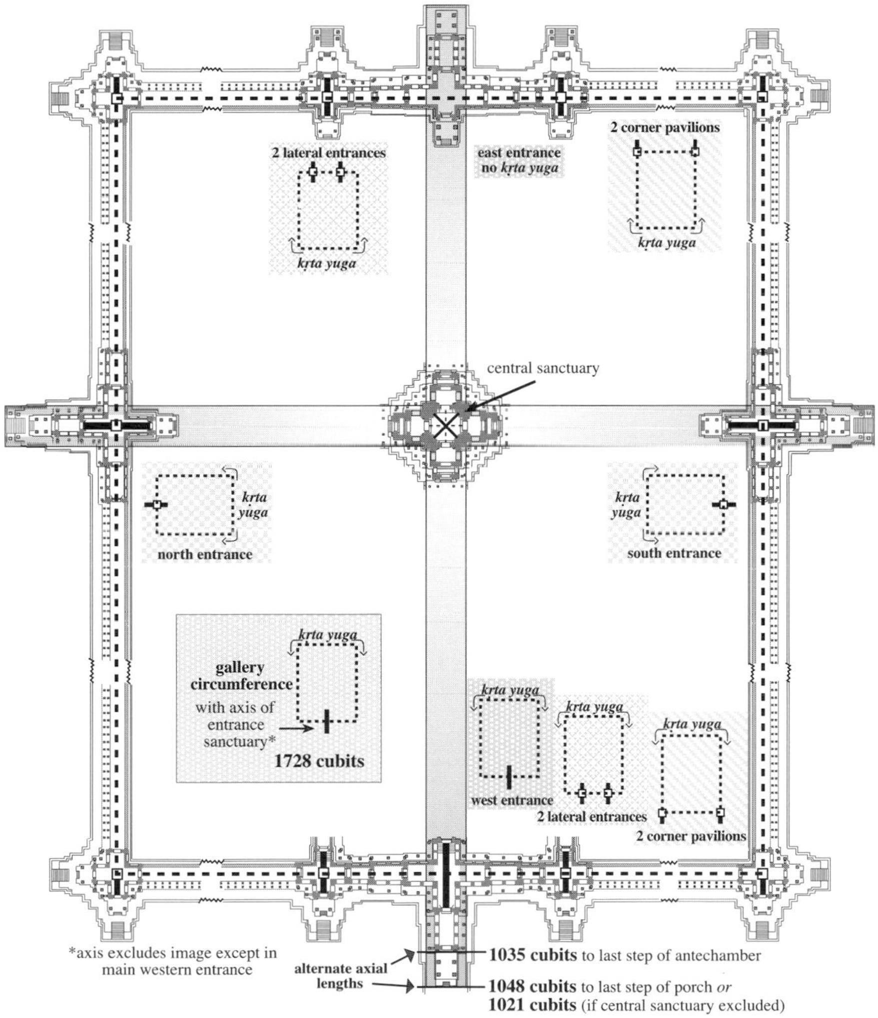

Fig. 4.20. Third gallery, axes and circumference.

The *kṛta yuga* that surrounds the gallery is precisely reproduced by a combination of the axial approach to the circumference in each chamber or set of chambers, and the circumference measurement. Only the image in the main western entrance is included in the *kṛta yuga* total (1728.4 cubits) which indicates a possible association between the image and the creation of the yuga itself. A strong connection between King Sūryavarman and the image in the central western entrance arises when the series of three different dates in the axes are paired with the *kṛta yuga* circumference.

Viṣṇu in the central sanctuary of the temple is excluded, the full axes equal 1038.55 cubits including the western porch; if the central sanctuary itself is excluded, the full axes measure 1021.89 cubits.[23] This series of 1021.89, 1034.42, 1038.55, and 1048.55 clusters around the year of the king's battle for the throne and his installation at Angkor: 1035 *śāka,* or A.D. 1113. The four variations of axial lengths also include all the possibilities inherent in Angkor Wat's measurement patterns.

Since the bas-reliefs on the south wall of the gallery clearly record events from the history of King Sūryavarman, these axial measurements would logically coincide with the *śāka* years (1035–1071/72) when those events occurred. First of all, if the axes represent dates from the life of the king, then they are brilliantly paired with the *kṛta yuga* circumference of the gallery—driving home the point that King Sūryavarman brought the *kṛta yuga* into existence with his reign.

Placing dates related to the king at the heart of the gallery, in the axial lengths, is another way of not only putting the king at the nexus of these axes and along their lengths but putting him at the nexus of the images of ministers, deities, or kings that may have once occupied the chambers of the gallery, as suggested. He created the conditions of the *kṛta yuga* for these images in the chambers, whoever they represented, and honored the ministers by name and physical depiction on the south wall. The ministers are also the most likely identity of the 19 men shown in the heavens of the gods on the south wall. And the gods are the focus of the northern half of this gallery. When seen as a totality, *śāka* dates along the axes define the gallery in terms that coincide with its circumference measurement, its series of historical and mythological bas-reliefs, and the practice of installing deities related to kings, ministers, and officials, seen at the Bayon in A.D. 1200. Finally, axial dates masterfully unify these disparate elements and harmonize with the allusions to the king as well as Viṣṇu at the center of Angkor Wat—and these axes.

From a second, more concrete, perspective, the king came to power in 1035 *śāka* according to inscriptions, which is close enough to the 1034.42-cubit axial measurement to assume that the latter stands for the year of the king's rise to power and the battle he won for the throne. Third, the number 1021 occurs in other contexts which suggest in their totality that this was the date of King Sūryavarman's birth. If the king were born in 1021 *śāka,* he was 27/28 years old in 1048 *śāka,* 32/33 years old in A.D. 1131, a date recorded in the northwest corner pavilion, and 20/21 years old in A.D. 1119, the date of an inscription describing a major event that took place in the king's royal hall. In this latter inscription, the king's ministers, generals, princes, members of the royal family, and all the rest of the court were recorded as being in attendance.[24] The venerable Divākarapaṇḍita then performed a special ablution ceremony. Clearly this was an outstanding occasion in the life of the king. No similar occurrence has been found in inscriptions before or after that date. This unique and highly prominent ritual celebration in 1119, and the other two dates that may refer to the king's life, bring forth numbers (the king's age) that have proved to be sacred at Angkor Wat: 20/21, 27/28, and 32/33.

Assuming that the king was born in 1021 *śāka,* then the ablution ceremony described in the inscription may have been planned for the first numerically significant change in his life: from 20 to 21. Like the successive yuga cycles to the upper elevation, time in this framework is not a neutral measuring device. As the king completed 21 years of life, his relationship to Viṣṇu may have been felt to be especially meaningful. Likewise, when the king turned from 27 to 28, in 1048 *śāka,* the same viewpoint would have held, and so on through 32/33. This series of 20/21, 27/28, and 32/33 is exclusive. There are no other numerically significant pairs of numbers in the king's age span until 44/45, which is not recorded in the gallery. All three changes in the king's age depend on 1021 *śāka* as his year of birth. Additional evidence for 1021 as the year of King Sūryavarman's birth is varied, but compelling in its totality. It can be summed up in the following three categories.

Category 1: The date of 1021 *śāka* may be only one of a series of "birth" dates. The range of four axial measurements in the third gallery can be interpreted as:

1021 = birth of King Sūryavarman
1035 = birth of Sūryavarman as king *(Indrābhiṣeka)*
1038 = birth of Angkor Wat
1048 = birth of the Viṣṇu image in the central sanctuary of Angkor Wat

Evidence for suggesting 1038 as the "birth" of Angkor Wat depends on two factors. First of all, it is generally accepted that the consecration of the temple grounds and initial construction at the site occurred after the king had consolidated his power. A 3-year preparation is not incongruous for a temple of this stature and degree of perfection. Moreover, the date 1038 occurs in another setting that also indicates a connection to the temple. The distance between the center of the central sanctuary and the northern border of the moat is 1038.62 cubits, while the corresponding southern

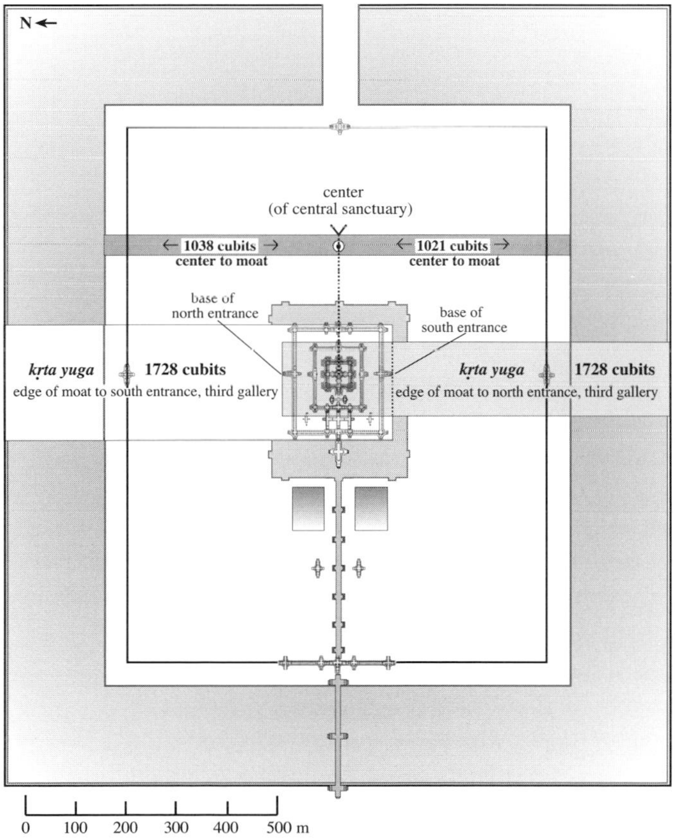

Fig. 4.21. Third gallery, dates and the kṛta yuga *along extended axes.*

Although drawn separately for illustration purposes, the 1038- and 1021-cubit lengths (*śāka* era dates) between the center of the central sanctuary and the inner border of the moat overlap the north-south *kṛta yuga* lengths. These latter two distances reach out between the base of the staircase to the third gallery on the north and south, to the opposite, outer border of the moat. The association of axial dates and the *kṛta yuga* in the third gallery's circumference is repeated here, expressed in a different pattern.

distance is 1021.54 cubits (Fig. 4.21).[25] (The center of Angkor Wat is displaced 1.72 m southward, as noted earlier, and the northern separation of enclosing wall and moat is larger than the southern separation, accounting for the differences in these two paired measurements.) The northern side of the third gallery is dedicated to the gods and their exploits, while the southern side is dedicated to the king. Based on this dichotomy and lacking any other explanation for 1038, I suggest that if 1021 refers to the birth of the king, then 1038 would once again refer to the "birth" of Angkor Wat. Viṣṇu in the central sanctuary would be the ultimate source of both "births." Not only do these axes emanate directly from Viṣṇu, but the four *kṛta yuga* lengths on the north–south axis of Angkor Wat overlap these suggested dates. Once again, King Sūryavarman and Angkor Wat are juxtaposed with a *kṛta yuga* time period; and once again, this suggests that the king changed the era. As a final note, the date of 1021 must have been very auspicious, since it occurs exactly 21 years after the turn of the first millennium in this calendrical system.

The year 1048 has no such corroborating evidence. In keeping with a theme of "births" at Angkor Wat, I propose that this is the date of the consecration of the main Viṣṇu image—the "birth" of Viṣṇu at the temple. Since the full axes of the third gallery radiate outward from this Viṣṇu image, as do the 1021, 1035, and 1038 measurements, the consecration of the main image seems a good possibility for the meaning of 1048 cubits.[26] I realize that the complete picture of a series of "births" is composed of interdependent pieces that, taken alone, are less persuasive than when seen together. Nevertheless, the hypotheses presented here are reinforced by other evidence.

Category 2: Khmer inscriptions state that the king was "quite young" when he came to power: he "was at the end of his studies."[27] From another inscription, we know that young men finished their studies around the age of 16.[28] If the king were born in 1021 *śāka,* then he was 14 or, at the most, 15 years old when he came to power. He would have been near the end of his studies. This timing agrees with the inscription describing the "end of studies" at 16 years of age.

Category 3: There is a four-sided stone stele in the Musée Guimet in Paris, and another in the Conservation d'Angkor in Siem Reap, which have 1020 images of a four-armed standing Viṣṇu (Fig. 4.22).[29] Both steles are in the Angkor Wat style. At the top, they feature a trilobed foliated arch on each side, with a Viṣṇu Caturbuja (literally, Viṣṇu "four arms") under two of the arches, a reclining Viṣṇu under one, and a Viṣṇu on Garuḍa under the other. Beneath these large figures of Viṣṇu, we find 17 rows of Viṣṇu Caturbuja, with 15 figures in each row (1020 total) in the Guimet stele. The stele in the Conservation d'Angkor is damaged, but it originally had the same total of images, arranged slightly differently.[30] As for the date recorded by these steles, a final year is added to represent the stele itself. A stele with 1020 images would thus refer to 1020 past years with the current year equal to 1021, the stele itself. This same process applies to the 20 steps in a staircase that formed a twenty-first unit, or a 20-unit circuit around an image that made the image a twenty-first and all-encompassing deity. The stele expresses the same concept in sculpture.

The Conservation has a second stele with 960 images (16 rows with 15 figures each on each side). If this were also a *śāka* date of 961 (A.D. 1039), it might correspond to the birth date of either Dharanīndravarman or Jayavarman VI, the great-uncles of King Sūryavarman who preceded him in ruling Cambodia. That would make Jayavarman 41 when he came to power in 1080, or Dharanīndravarman 68 in 1107.

Coinciding with the earlier date is an earlier style of sculpture. This last stele is of the Baphuon period by the suggested date, and it is in the

Fig. 4.22. Sandstone stele 6906/N79, Conservation d'Angkor, Siem Reap.

This is one of only four known stone steles that may contain a coded date. This example and another in Paris have 1020 small images of a four-armed standing Viṣṇu that may refer to a *śāka* date and the birth year of King Sūryavarman. A third stele has 960 such images, perhaps a reference to the birth year of one of Sūryavarman's dynastic predecessors. No photographs were available for the fourth stele. The fourth stele dates to the end of the ninth century and has around 800 images.

Baphuon style. A similar stele was found at Luang Prabang in Laos, brought there from Cambodia in the fourteenth century. It is severely damaged but seems to have figures numbering close to 800 also.[31]

These are the only four examples of steles numerated with hundreds of four-armed Viṣṇu figures—no other examples, no representations of a deity other than Viṣṇu. Because of Viṣṇu's ties to kingship and the solar year, and given the rarity of these steles, they may have been a prerogative of kingship joined in union with the cycles of the sun.

In the three later steles there are 60 figures around each of the 17 rows or registers. It is likely that these 60 figures represent the 60-year cycle discussed earlier. The much older Luang Prabang stele has 44 images around each row. The 60-year cycle does not divide evenly into the images on this stele.

The source for all four suggested dates in the axes of the third gallery is Lord Viṣṇu in the central sanctuary. The axes emanate outward from him like rays of light from the sun. Viṣṇu could then be construed as the ultimate cause of the birth of King Sūryavarman (1021), the motivating cause behind the temple of Angkor Wat (1038), the reason why King Sūryavarman came to power (1035), and spiritually present at the "birth" of his own image in the central sanctuary (1048). All these associations with Viṣṇu are brought about through the axial measurements in the third gallery. And related to the realm of King Sūryavarman and the group of images that may have been installed in the main chambers of the third gallery is the curious anomaly of the eastern entrance.

THE ENIGMA OF THE EASTERN ENTRANCE

To call the eastern entrance into the third gallery an "entrance" is somewhat misleading: there is no stairway. There is no way to climb up into the entrance without going through one of its flanking, lateral entrances (Fig. 4.23). Other staircases in this gallery slant at a steep incline that includes 11 steps. On the east, in place of a staircase, there is a straight drop to the ground delineated by a sandstone plinth with roughly cut horizontal moldings (Fig. 4.24).[32] These moldings give the plinth a hurriedly finished appearance—indeed, there is no indication that a staircase was ever started. Because the four numerically significant totals in the axial lengths of the third gallery are measured from this drop-off on the east, we can conclude that no staircase was even planned.

The axial ramp that leads up to the *nāga* terrace is right in front of this eastern entrance with no staircase (Fig. 1.8). The axial ramp is an exception, too, but more readily understandable because it would allow chariots and elephants to enter the compound easily. Based on the popularity of processions as described by Zhou Daguan at the end of the thirteenth century, the vast courtyard of Angkor Wat would make an ideal staging ground for the start of a long parade. In fact, some people believe the eastern drop-off plinth was for mounting elephants with their high litters. Although this is a tempting and practical solution to the case of the missing staircase, it has its problems. First of all, is this the only place royalty mounted elephants? Why do we not find similar areas elsewhere? Second, why use a major entrance to a sacred temple to mount an elephant? Third, if that is what was wanted, there would have been some sort of entablature in place—a loading or unloading dock, if you will—and this is not the case.

The lack of a direct access into the eastern entrance for circumambulation and other rituals coincides with the fact that this chamber has no numerically significant measurements. It does have

Fig. 4.23. Third gallery, east side, main entrances.

The main eastern entrance has no staircase. By coincidence or not it faces an entrance from the *nāga* terrace that, unlike the other staircases to the terrace, is in the form of a ramp (Fig. 1.8). Perhaps there was also a wooden ramp that once led up to the main eastern entrance. To reach the main entrance now, one has to climb up to either lateral entrance and walk through the connecting chambers to the center.

32 pillars on its eastern facade, but that fact more or less begins and ends its claim on auspicious numbers.[33] This may or may not have something to do with the missing staircase. Intuition and logic both argue that something happened. But what?

The design and dimensions of the porch and forechamber of the western entrance to the third gallery already correspond to the forechamber and porch of the eastern entrance with no staircase. There is no staircase on the west, because none was needed. The cruciform terrace leads one right to the porch. Yet this does not obviate a physical need for a staircase on the eastern side of the gallery.

The staircases to both eastern lateral entrances are 4 m long. The porch of the western entrance is 6.05 m long and corresponds in its architectural position to the missing staircase on the east. Based on the temple's design, the missing staircase would have extended outward more than 4 m because the proportions of a central entrance are always greater than its flanking, subsidiary entrances. If the planned staircase was intended to be 6 m long like its counterpart porch on the west side of the gallery, then we may have an explanation for why it was never constructed.

In 1128, the king sent 20,000 men against the Dai Viet in the north of Vietnam and lost the battle. In the autumn following that battle, he sent 700 ships to harass the Thanh-hoa coast and was

Fig. 4.24. Third gallery, east side, central entrance.

In place of a staircase, there is a roughly molded plinth at the end of the porch into the main entrance on this side of the gallery. There is no obvious explanation for the missing staircase, unique in Khmer temple architecture.

chased back.[34] In 1130, he launched another major campaign against the Dai Viet that ended in defeat. During these years he continually coerced the Chams to join him in battle. In 1132, the Chams and Khmers invaded Nghe-an together and lost. In 1133, two men from Champa asked for asylum in the Dai Viet court, indicating that hostilities between the king and the Chams had started already. In 1136, the king carried out another major campaign against the Dai Viet, without the Chams as allies, and was roundly defeated. These defeats were not comparable to battles today. Based on the evidence from extant inscriptions, all enemy soldiers were slaughtered, no captives taken. By 1136, then, the king had lost so many battles that another campaign would not occur until 1144/45, this time against Champa. Buried in the devastating losses of the king—and the cost to the nation in human resources—may lie the reason for the missing eastern staircase to Angkor Wat.

If a 6-m eastern staircase had been added onto the gallery of bas-reliefs, then the dates in the axes would have had the following possible alternatives (the dates in bold type are new in that they are related to the suggested staircase):

1. 1062.44 cubits full axes including suggested east staircase and porch of western entrance
   A.D. **1140** (1062 *śāka*) (possible planned military campaign, actual campaigns began in 1144)
2. 1052.44 cubits full axes minus image of Viṣṇu in central sanctuary
   A.D. **1130** (date of major defeat by Dai Viet)
3. 1035.78 cubits full axes minus central sanctuary
   A.D. **1113** (date of Sūryavarman's rise to power)
4. 1048.55 cubits, axes without 6-m porch on west
   A.D. 1126 proposed date for consecration of main Viṣṇu image
5. 1038.55 cubits axes without 6-m porch or main Viṣṇu image
   A.D. 1116 proposed date for beginning of work on Angkor Wat
6. 1021.89 cubits axes without 6-m porch or central sanctuary
   A.D. 1099 proposed date of King Sūryavarman's birth

The 1034.42 date for the king's accession to power would disappear in this new arrangement, and a date of 1035.78 takes it place. Either is a possibility. The most important aspect of this configuration, however, is that it works with a staircase on the east side of the gallery. This suggests the staircase could have been planned but not executed.

The date of the suggested planetary relief in the northwest pavilion of this gallery is 1131. That relief, discussed in detail later, shows the gods requesting Viṣṇu to incarnate—and help them in battle, it is understood. In 1132, the king launched a great battle in Nghe-an and was defeated. Hostilities with the Chams began as early as 1123 or 1124, a period when both Chams and Khmers were seeking asylum from Khmer attacks at the court of the Dai Viet. These hostilities would be temporarily overcome by Khmer-Cham alliances. A relief on the north side of this gallery shows a battle between the *deva*s and *asura*s that may include a date of A.D. 1122 and represent a battle of the king in that year. The reliefs and their meaning are handled in a later chapter. For now, they are relevant for their possible historical allusions.

Based on the preceding dates and axial measurements, we can postulate that the eastern staircase was planned to perhaps represent a victory or battle in A.D. 1130, but we know that year marked a major defeat for the king. Battles began as early as 1128 against the Dai Viet, (in alliance with the Chams) but they were also not successful. After 1136 and the last devastating defeat, the king had no resources to begin fighting again until 1144/45, and the stairway was never constructed. The time period for marking a victorious battle had come and gone. After 1136, there could no longer be any accommodation to the measurements of the gallery, or to the truth of defeat after defeat.

Even though the preceding scenario is hypothetical, it accounts for the missing staircase without postulating an elephant-mounting dock. It explains, moreover, why the missing staircase is unique in Khmer architecture. King Sūryavarman was the first to record his image on temple walls, as well as the names of his ministers and events from his reign. These axes, then, are likely to be the first in temple architecture to record dates. And since the axes in the third gallery have every possible alternate length in relation to the center of the temple and their own boundaries, and since every possible length is a calendrically meaningful date, it seems the staircase was intended to add to those dates.

The elimination of dates related to military defeats may account for the missing staircase, but not the lack of auspicious measurements in the main eastern entrance. As a tentative suggestion only, it is possible that an image of the slain Dharanīndravarman was once placed in that chamber. King Sūryavarman killed him to gain the throne. Yet he was Sūryavarman's great-uncle, a bloodline that would not disappear with death. Based on tradition and history, Sūryavarman was under a time-honored obligation to pay homage to his great-uncle in the chambers of Angkor Wat. The contradiction between honoring a relative—the preceding king—and honoring an enemy slain in a battle to usurp the throne is obvious. The solution may have been the numerically ill-fated eastern entrance to the gallery.

As for the eastern entrance itself, I would imagine that a wooden staircase or ramp once abutted against the roughly molded plinth, allowing the priests and others direct eastern access to the main chamber for ritual purposes, once the gallery was finished. In reality, the gallery may not have been ready for ritual use on the eastern side for several decades, well into the king's reign. In this hypothetical scenario, since the staircase itself was not there when the rest of the gallery was planned, the priests would have made the circumambulation path through the eastern entrance, as well as any other measurements involving its axes, dependent on the status quo. In other words, it seems that numerically significant paths and lengths had to be established in the gallery without depending on the staircase—and so they were.

As for the ramp in front of this eastern entrance, in the *nāga* terrace, I think it was constructed to allow work to continue on the central galleries. Workers were not going to walk 500 to 700 m to reach this area of the temple when they could reach it more quickly on the short eastern side. The east side of the temple, after all, was its back side. Work in this area was usually left for last, and one imagines the ramp was acceptable as a back door for workers, but not acceptable for the formal western facade of the temple.

MEASUREMENT PATTERNS IN THE GALLERY

When the yuga cycles around the outer enclosure were measured in 108-cubit modules, their time periods disappeared and the 32 gods arose in their place (Fig. 2.23). The third gallery repeats this concept in its own way. An in-and-out circumambulation of the four corner pavilions comes to 107.51 *phyeam,* the four lateral entrances 107.62 *phyeam,* and the 3 axial entrances (east, north, and south) 108.16 *phyeam* (Fig. 4.25).[35] The repetition of 108 *phyeam* in three sets of identical entrances equals exactly 1293.16 cubits, close enough to 1296 to refer to the *tretā yuga.* In effect, the 108 *phyeam* groups around the gallery disappear and the *tretā yuga* arises to take their place when a cubit module is used.

After circling the gallery, one continues the journey into Angkor Wat through the main western chamber. Including a circuit three times around the image in that chamber, the distance

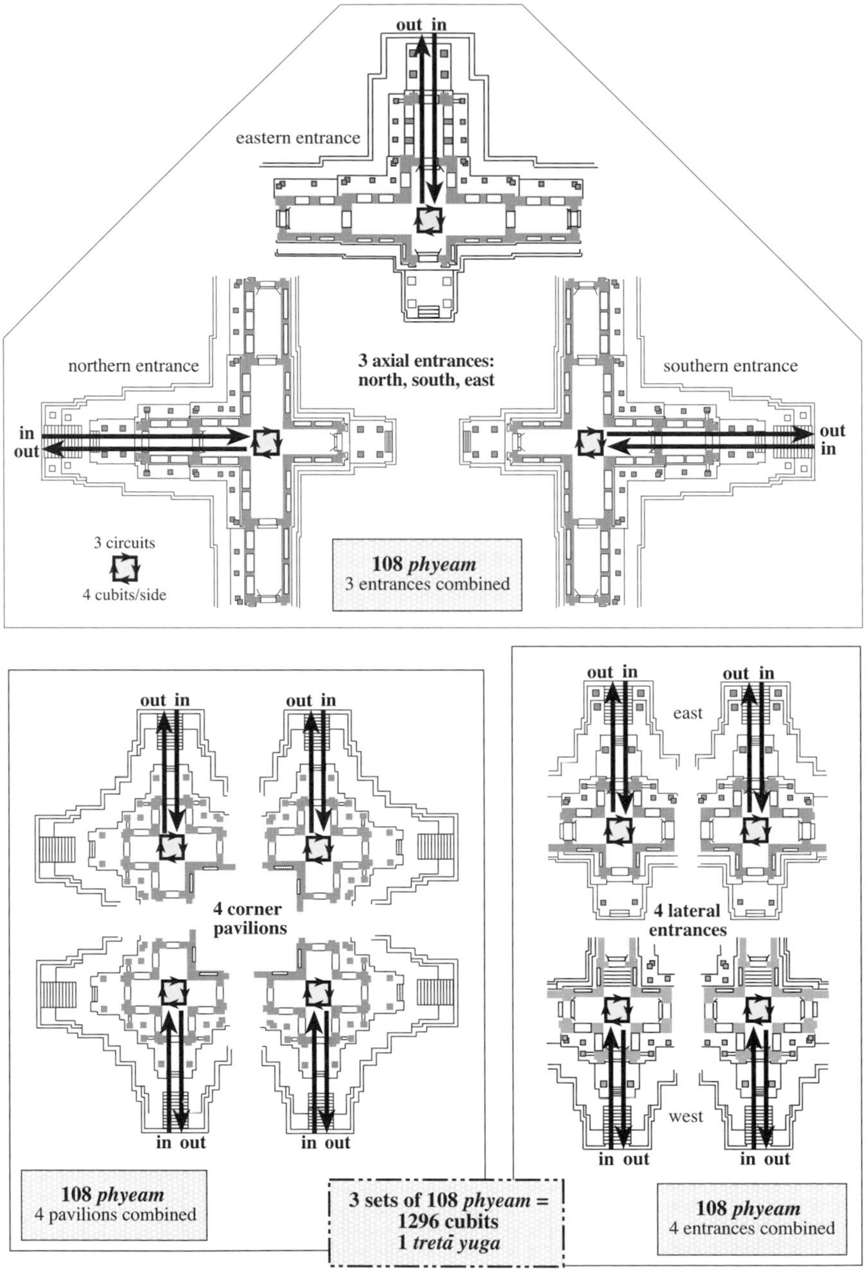

Fig. 4.25. Third gallery, three sets of circumambulation paths around the perimeter.

An in-and-out circuit around the main images in each entrance except the central western entrance produces three identical numerical totals: 108 *phyeam*. In addition to introducing this auspicious number into the chambers of the gallery, the same three sets numerically describe the *tretā yuga* when expressed in cubits.

into the chamber from the west and out of it on the east is 32.19 *phyeam* (Fig. 4.26). The *tretā yuga* sequence, or the three approximately 108, 108, and 108-*phyeam* circuits just outlined, thus ends in a 32-*phyeam* pathway. Perhaps to emphasize the 32-unit path through the western entrance, that entry has 32 pillars in front of it and 33 steps total.[36] This is another example of connecting divinity to time and time to divinity, either through 108 and 32 or the *tretā yuga* and 32. In either instance, it is clear that the 32 gods of the *vāstupuruṣamaṇḍala* have just escorted the visitor out of the third gallery and into the *preau cruciforme* to follow.

If numbers related to King Sūryavarman dominate the axes and circumference and most of the bas-reliefs in the third gallery, measurements connected to the sun and moon and mandala of *devas*

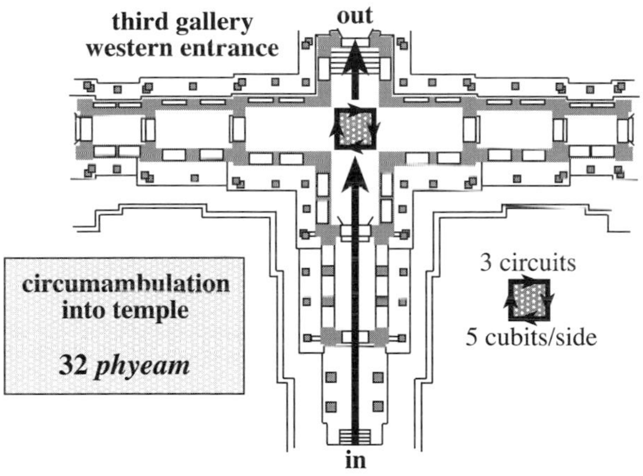

Fig. 4.26. Third gallery, circumambulation through the central western entrance.

After the 108-*phyeam* circuits described in the preceding Fig. 4.25, there is a 32-*phyeam* path that leads directly through the central western entrance into the *preau cruciforme.* The set of 32 and 108 created in this pattern of ritual paths echoes the sets of 32 units formed by 108-cubit modules in the yuga routes to the upper elevation, or along the axes of the temple.

fill in the rest of the numerical traits here. The third gallery has 28 chambers; the outer enclosure has 32. The middle gallery has 49 chambers. There are 12 staircases on the upper level, gods and the central tower itself has 44 pillars around it. In this sequence, the chambers in the outer enclosure and third gallery (32, 28) define the border of a mandala, the 49 chambers in the second gallery define the squares in a mandala, the 12 staircases in the first gallery define the *ādityas* in a mandala, and the central tower places Brahmā at the center of 44 surrounding gods. The history of King Sūryavarman in the third gallery thus becomes part of a vast mandala of gods emanating from Brahmā/Nārāyaṇa, at the center of the temple, and encompassing the reign of the king in a divine enclosure. Nothing within Angkor Wat occurs outside this mandala of *devas*.

The third gallery is distinguished by several measurements around its circumference, symbolic of 1 lunar year (Appendix B, Table 1).[37] The number of pillars on the eastern and western sides of the gallery together come to a total that factors into 28 × 11, lunar mansions and lunar *kāraṇa*. The two western lateral entrances combined have 29 steps while their eastern counterparts have 30 steps. The two sets of steps together, 59, add up to the exact length of two lunar months. Three other lunar-related measurements, 29.53, 27/28, and 14/15 complete the east–west depiction of the moon in the gallery (Figs. 4.27 and 4.28). Because the moon rises in the east and sets in the west and because the full moon and light half of the month are associated with the east (while the new moon and dark half of the month are primarily in the west), the representation of lunar phenomena at Angkor Wat favors an east–west dichotomy. This dichotomy is illustrated in these eastern and western lunar numbers.[38]

The eastern and western corridors define the lunar month in their full lengths, their half-lengths,

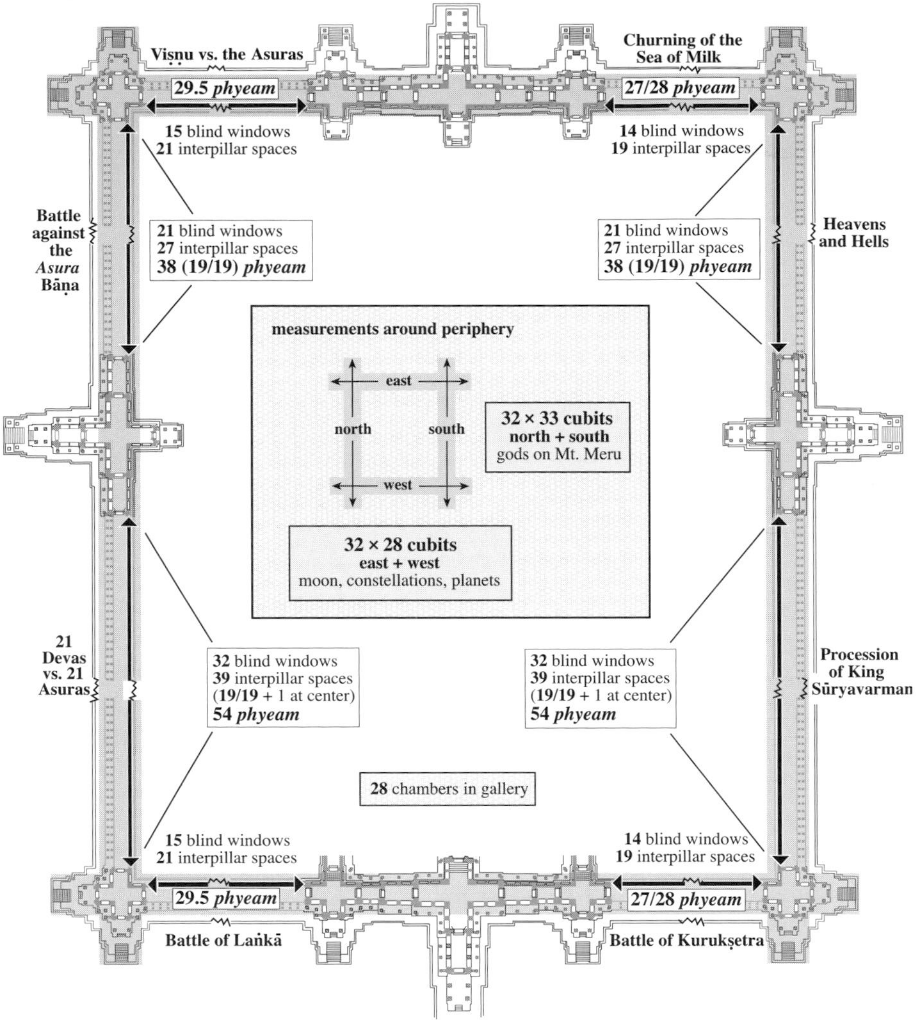

Fig. 4.27. Third gallery, measurements and bas-reliefs around the perimeter.

The bas-reliefs proceed counterclockwise in sequence, beginning with the battle of Kurukṣetra on the west. Otherwise, the blind windows, interpillar spaces, and lengths of the reliefs themselves focus on lunar-related periodicity (14, 15, 27/28, 29.5) on the eastern and western sides of the gallery, and *deva*-related numbers (21, 32) on the north and south. This reciprocity also applies to the content of the bas-reliefs. The measurements of the north and south, east and west sides of the gallery reflect the same lunar/*deva* alternation in meaning. Other than these two themes, the numerical motif of 19 and 21 is a third important component in the definition of the gallery. (See Appendix A, Table 4.6–4.7.)

their blind (false) windows, and their pillars, while the adjunct chambers on the east and west do the same in terms of a measurement (28) and pillars (28 in front, Fig. 4.28). In contrast to the dominant lunar references on the east and west, the north and south sides of the gallery have few, if any lunar measurements at all: they are completely dedicated to the mandala and the *devas*.[39]

In agreement with the second gallery especially, there is a dichotomy between lunar representations on the east and west and *deva* and mandala representations on the north and south.[40] Now that these major characteristics of the gallery are in place, we can stand back and examine it from the perspective of the temple as a whole.

The probable dates recorded in the axes of the third gallery end the series of time cycles represented in the vertical progression from the lowest axes to this level. Once we enter this gallery, we are in the *śāka* calendar and the period of the king's reign; but on leaving, we enter the realm of the gods on Mount Meru. One of the first signs of this transition is the 32-unit passage through the western entrance up to the next segment of our journey. The gods around the perimeter of the mandala are escorting us to the next level.

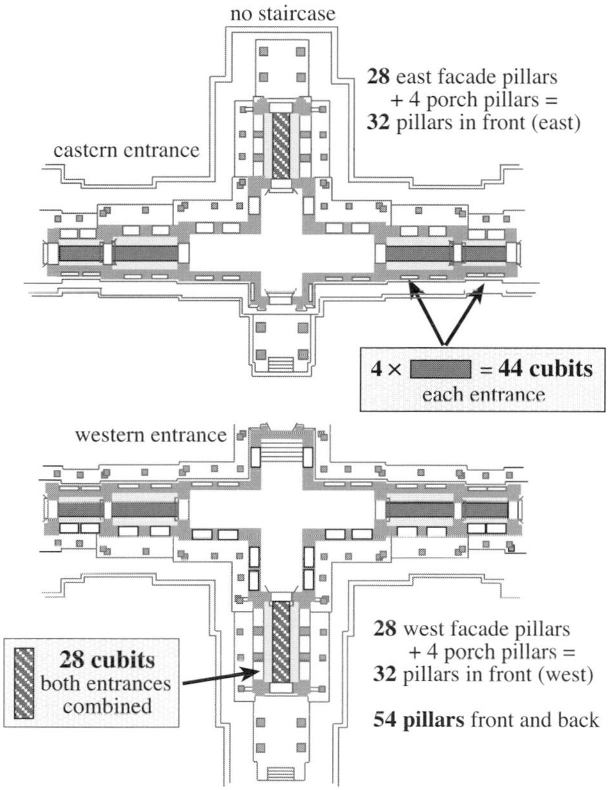

Fig. 4.28. Third gallery, eastern and western entrances, antechamber measurements.

The antechamber sets in these two entrances follow mandala symbolism (44, 32, 28), and west-east lunar emphasis (28). These measurements and the 32 or 54 sets of pillars provide an auspicious environment for the statue in the central chamber. (See Appendix A, Table 4.6.)

Another sign of the changing ambience is the lack of specific libraries that would have provided priests and resources for the rituals in these chambers. Since the six libraries are joined to the gods on Mount Meru by their shared 32-unit inner axes—and due also to their placement and physical association with specific galleries—the historical gallery of the king was left out. It is not a Mount Meru symbol itself, and it has no accessible libraries next to it.

The access doors that open out from the corridors of the second gallery into the courtyard around the first or upper gallery are also significant in this regard because they show a close connection between the two top levels of the temple. No such connection exists between the third and second galleries—quite the opposite. There is a series of transitional corridors and four basins that definitively separate the historical third gallery from the next level of the temple.

All of the time cycles at Angkor Wat can be interpreted as either celestial or terrestrial, since the sun and moon and means of measuring time can be applied both to our mundane world and to the world of the gods. The most notable exception is the *śāka* era in the third-gallery axes. It belongs only to the terrestrial realm.

Having reached Sūryavarman's kingdom, however, we soon find that it is parallel to Indra's kingdom of gods. The ministers are shown as military leaders in procession to Angkor, and possibly also as the 19 men in the celestial palaces of the gods. The bas-relief of Sūryavarman's procession was intentionally placed across the gallery from the panel of Indra and his deities, with several points connecting key aspects of each scene, as we shall see in the following chapter. The measurements themselves show a dichotomy between the nation of the king on the south and the celestial world on the north—interacting in a north–south oscillation as the sun highlights first one area and then the

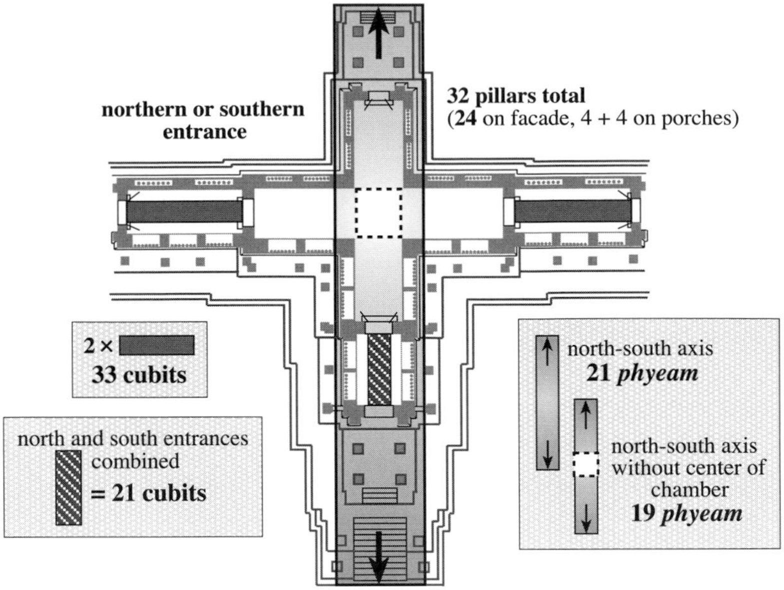

Fig. 4.29. Third gallery, northern and southern entrances, antechamber and axial measurements.

The sets of antechambers follow the same measurement pattern as those in the eastern and western entrances (Fig. 4.28). In this instance, however, the measurements define a supreme deity (21/33). The alternate length of the north–south outer axis of the entrances repeats the 19/21-unit pairing that characterizes this gallery and its focus on kingship and divinity. This is the most precise rendition of a 19/21-unit alternation at Angkor Wat: 19.05 and 21.00 *phyeam* exactly (see chap. 5, n. 20, and Appendix A, Table 4.7).

other. But beyond these concerns, we now are seeing a king and his ministers glorified on temple walls, a space once reserved only for sacred divinitics. This alone brings the king closer to Indra and his ministers closer to the gods.

These ties between Angkor ruled by King Sūryavarman II and the world of the gods are strengthened by the 12 chambers on this level that numerically correspond to the 12 *āditya*s in the inner circle of the mandala. In fact, the normal suffix of male names in Hiraṇyavarman's descendants was *"āditya."* Ministers or male members of Sūryavarman's family including past kings, might have been placed in those 12 chambers, thereby uniting them to the mandala's *āditya*s. If the 12 chambers were indeed meant to symbolize the 12 *āditya*s, then that is another reason why an image of Viṣṇu/Sūryavarman as the twelfth *āditya* is a good possibility for the main western entrance.

The configuration of 12 *āditya*s in the 12 chambers would close one mandala at the level of this gallery before the center is reached in the central tower. A ritual closure at this juncture would further separate the gallery from the next level. Such a closure agrees with the indications that one journey ends here and another begins as we leave King Sūryavarman behind.

From many perspectives, then, we have reached an apex of time and space in the third gallery, an ending to the time and space sequences along the axes. Rather than create an obstacle to reaching the celestial realms, the historical gallery demonstrates that its many connections to the gods are a bridge into their world. Without the link provided by the king and his reign, we would be as far removed from Mount Meru as ever. As we walk out of the gallery into the next segment of the temple, the architecture itself emphasizes a new beginning. In the *preau cruciforme* to follow, four pools provide the ablution water for purification before we step into the god realm. These pools occur only at this juncture, and for good reason. From this point onward, we are ascending Mount Meru.

5

The King and His World: The Southern Bas-Reliefs in the Third Gallery

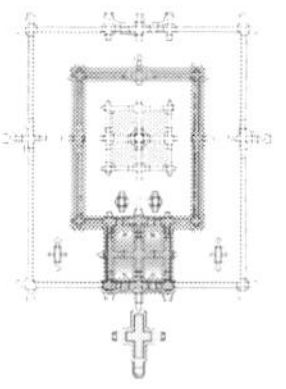

THE third gallery of Angkor Wat was basically constructed to honor King Sūryavarman. The king is shown standing astride an elephant in a military procession moving across the south wall of the gallery (Fig. 5.1). Before the procession starts, the king is also depicted in some official action receiving documents and homage from his chief ministers (Figs. 1.15 and 5.2). This was something unprecedented in Khmer temple architecture—the first time in the history of Angkor that a real king, living or dead, and his men of rank were sculpted onto temple walls traditionally reserved only for the gods and their many manifestations. This ground-breaking change set the stage for the purely historical bas-reliefs at the Bayon, carved about 75 years later. By the end of temple building at Angkor, the Bayon reliefs indicate that history and those who made it had eclipsed Śiva, Viṣṇu, and the Buddha on temple walls. In the third gallery of Angkor Wat, kings and their activities began their transformation to myth and legend.

At Angkor Wat, each side of the third gallery has two large panels of scenes, eight panels in all. Of these eight, the first four are discussed in this chapter and the remaining four in the next. These panels are complemented by reliefs in the southwest and northwest corner pavilions. Starting with the western facade (south half) and proceeding counterclockwise, the reliefs succeed each other in the following manner (Fig. 4.27):

Fig. 5.1. Third gallery, south side, west half, procession of King Sūryavarman.

King Sūryavarman stands on his elephant as he looks back at the commanders behind him. He is tenth from the front of the procession. Transposed across the gallery, he would be facing Indra on an elephant.

Fig. 5.2. Third gallery, south side, west half, procession of King Sūryavarman.

Śrī Vardhana and Dhananjaya sit in allegiance on a raised mat right in front of the king. The audience with the king is high on a mountaintop, Mount Śivapāda, and the procession starts as they descend the mountain on elephantback.

1. West wall, south half: Battle of Kurukṣetra
2. Southwest corner pavilion: Scenes of Śiva
3. South wall, west half: Procession of King Sūryavarman
4. South wall, east half: Heavens and Hells
5. East wall, south half: Churning of the Sea of Milk
6. East wall, north half: Viṣṇu versus the *Asuras*
7. North wall, east half: Kṛṣṇa versus the *Asura* Bāṇa
8. North wall, west half: Battle of *Devas* and *Asuras*
9. Northwest corner pavilion: Scenes of Viṣṇu
10. West wall, north half: Battle of Laṅkā

The two late panels (6 and 7), sculpted in the sixteenth century, just a little more than 100 years after Angkor was abandoned, have no significant numerical grouping of figures, no significant measurements, nothing to indicate that they represent more than the stories they tell. They are exceptions to the rules of organization that governed the original reliefs in the gallery.

Throughout the reliefs at Angkor Wat there are four distinct levels of organization at work. The first is directionality. All three original relief panels on the west and east (the Battle of Kurukṣetra, Battle of Laṅkā, and Churning of the Sea of Milk) have a north–south movement that connects them to the north and south celestial realms of the gods and *asuras*, and to the north–south oscillation of the sun and moon each year. The movement of the large processions on the south wall and the *devas* on the north wall also corresponds to a counterclockwise circumambulation path. In brief, then, directionality organizes individual scenes into a north–south dichotomy or into a counterclockwise movement.

The second level of organization involves scale and placement. Larger figures are not only more important in these reliefs, where "bigger" means "more powerful," but the subsequent grouping of these figures is a significant organizing principle. In the Battle of Laṅkā and the Battle of *Deva*s and *Asura*s, large figures are paired in combat, providing clear reference points across the chaos of battle. In the Churning of the Sea of Milk, larger *asura*s and *deva*s divide a long row of figures into neatly patterned segments. In other reliefs, large figures or pairs of figures are seated or standing at an apex of action: Śiva or Viṣṇu on a mountaintop in the corner pavilions, Sūryavarman receiving the homage of his ministers on Mount Śivapāda, or Kṛṣṇa holding up Mount Govardhana. Both the scale and the placement of a figure or figures, then, are another means of organization in the reliefs.

The third level of organization involves numbers or measurements. Not only do groups of figures arranged in a pattern organize the disparate elements of a scene, but the *numbers* of figures or groups may be played off other scenes, or numbers may have an internal relationship. For example, the 19 ministers of King Sūryavarman are opposite 19 gods under Indra, king of the gods, on the north wall; the 19 leading officers under Rāma in the Battle of Laṅkā on the west wall are fighting the 19 officers under Rāvaṇa: 19 is paired against 19 in both cases. The number 19 organizes these reliefs into recognizable subsets, making it clear that the subsets are meant to be paired. While sets of 19 figures are opposed on the north and south walls of the gallery, the same north and south panels measure 54 *phyeam* each, adding a 54/54-unit pairing and considerable cosmological correlates to the already paired sets of ministers and gods. The measurements and countable properties of relief scenes thus provide distinguishable sets of figures and indicate the type of relationship between those sets: reciprocal, paired, sequential, chronological, or cosmological.

The fourth level of organization, the subtlest level, is implied in the duality and the oscillation mentioned earlier. This type of organization is based on principles of cosmology, geophysics, or religious belief—such as the north–south oscillation of the sun and moon—or the dualism present in many opposite yet complementary phenomena—such as night and day, heat and cold, dry and rainy seasons. This last level of organization is more readily surmised when the other three levels have been defined. For example, the Churning of the Sea of Milk may have been chosen as the topic of the eastern panel in the gallery because it referred to the *Indrābhiṣeka* of King Sūryavarman. But the *Indrābhiṣeka* did nothing to organize the panel. Instead, the north–south oscillation of the sun between solstices gives the panel its composition. It groups the *deva*s and *asura*s into two north–south sets, it determines the exact total of figures (the days between solstices and equinox), and it divides the figures into six segments to represent the months between solstices. The final organizing factor in the reliefs therefore decides what kind of directionality, scale and placement, and measurements or numbers the relief will entertain. In sequence, then, it was the first organizing factor, from which all else derived.

In reviewing the ways in which the relief panels are organized, we find:

1. Directionality
2. Scale and grouping
3. Measurements and countable properties
4. Principles of cosmology, geophysics, or religion

Aside from these four factors it goes without saying that the architecture itself arranges the reliefs in discrete units, provides a space in which they can be viewed, and is the means by which they are opposed or paired across from each other. Moreover, architectural factors such as the number of interpillar spaces in front of a relief panel may complement and enhance the meaning of a relief. Finally, the measurements built into the gallery—which may contain calendrical dates from the reign of King Sūryavarman, as well as references to the *kṛta yuga*—would necessarily coincide with the content of the reliefs themselves.

The observer who enters the gallery from the west is led by the movement of the Kaurava army in the Battle of Kurukṣetra toward the right, or counterclockwise, seeking the final outcome of the fighting. At the opposite end of the corridor, Rāma's monkey heroes in the Battle of Laṅkā are moving toward the right, or counterclockwise, as they engage the demon Rāvaṇa's troops in combat. Following these two battle scenes, the processions on the entire south wall of the gallery continue this counterclockwise flow of action.

On the opposite north wall, battle scenes unfold in the same counterclockwise fashion as the "hero" protagonists move from the back (east) to the front (west) of the temple, attacking their enemies. On the east wall, one follows the movement of the figures observing the Churning of the Sea of Milk toward the center of the panel (although the eastern panels have no set directional movement as a whole). Why was the traditional and auspicious clockwise circumambulation not followed in the third gallery? Surely the architects would not have deliberately built an ill-omened circumambulation path into the temple. Nor is it still seriously suggested that Angkor Wat's function was solely funerary, requiring a funerary counterclockwise circuit of the third gallery. Since these possibilities are unacceptable, we must look elsewhere for an explanation of the unusual circumambulation path. That explanation may lie in the annual movement of the sun, which can be understood as counterclockwise.

Angkor Wat is a solar temple with a striking spring equinox alignment that marks both the beginning of a solar year and the beginning of a journey into the temple. The sun's own journey begins in the east at the time of the spring equinox and continues northward until the summer solstice. From there it moves southward, reaching the autumn equinox after 3 months. Three months more bring the sun to its southernmost point at the winter solstice, and the journey begins again toward the north and the spring equinox.

Although the sun oscillates in its yearly movement from south to north and north to south, the four directions conceptually change the movement to a passage in space: east (spring equinox), north (summer solstice), west (autumn equinox), south (winter solstice), and back to east again. As a reflection of this movement, Khmer astronomers described the sun as traveling counterclockwise around the earth, beginning with the spring equinox (and the new year).

This counterclockwise journey is divided into 12 major sections, corresponding to the 12 solar months, with each section further subdivided. The sequence of these 12 divisions begins at the vernal equinox and continues "toward the left, in the direction opposite to the movement of the hands of a watch."[1] The left, in this instance, is toward the north and the summer solstice.

Thus the Battle of Kurukṣetra on the west and the churning scene on the east are aligned with the sunlight during the autumn and spring equinoxes, respectively. Similarly, the gods on the north wall would face the direction of the summer solstice, which is their midday, and the fathers or ancestors in the heavens on the south wall would face the winter solstice, the midnight of the gods and the midday of the fathers or ancestors. Thus both the counterclockwise and north–south directions of movement in the reliefs appear to be related to the same north–south oscillation of the sun and moon, seen from two different perspectives.

The counterclockwise organization of the panels of bas-reliefs integrates the gallery as a whole into one long sequence of narrative scenes. This sequence starts on the west with the Battle of Kurukṣetra.

THE BATTLE OF KURUKṢETRA

As the visitor enters Angkor Wat from the west and turns to the right (southward), soldiers and charioteers lead the way toward the heart of the battle at Kurukṣetra. This battle was the climax of the epic *Mahābhārata,* the denouement of a long rivalry ending in horrific slaughter on the plains of Kuru (Kurukṣetra) in the region of the modern Delhi. The rivalry started when the blind king Dhṛtarāṣṭra gave his throne to his younger brother Pāṇḍu. On Pāṇḍu's death, the eldest of his five sons, Yudhiṣṭhira, was designated heir-apparent. But the 100 sons of Dhṛtarāṣṭra plotted against the five Pāṇḍu brothers, forcing them out of the kingdom. Before Dhṛtarāṣṭra died, he called the five brothers home and divided the kingdom between them and his sons. Still desiring more power, the eldest son of Dhṛtarāṣṭra, Duryodhana, challenged Yudhiṣṭhira to a game of dice. The winner would gain the entire kingdom. Yudhiṣṭhira lost and in a compromise settlement, the five Pāṇḍu brothers were banished for thirteen years. At the end of that time, they were to regain their kingdom. When they demanded its return in due course, Duryodhana did not reply. Both sides prepared for war, marshalling their own and allied forces to gather at Kurukṣetra for the final battle.

The battle raged on for 18 days, leaving no major commander alive except for the five Pāṇḍava (Pāṇḍu) brothers and Kṛṣṇa. Yudhiṣṭhira was crowned king after this slaughter and ruled for many years until he abdicated. With his four brothers and their common wife Draupadī the Pāṇḍavas left for the Himalayan mountains where they ascended Mount Meru and entered the realm of the gods.

In the battle scene at Angkor Wat, we turn to the right and follow the Kuru army into the center of combat. After only a few steps we come across the dying Bhīṣma, sage of the Kauravas (Kurus), impaled on multiple spears. This is the first sign that Duryodhana and his brothers are doomed to lose the battle (Fig. 5.3).[2] According to the story, Bhīṣma died shortly before the battle ended, and so the moment depicted is approximate to the final defeat. At about six interpillar spaces before the center of the corridor and the panel, the foreground line of foot soldiers loses its formation—chaos reigns—and a neat geometry gives way to total entropy. At the center of the scene, the leading Kaurava horse has his neck pierced by a spear; his dead charioteer is careening toward the ground; death encircles the two central leaders as the victor is about to kill the Kuru commander-in-chief with a powerful downward thrust of a spear (Fig. 5.4). At the axis of battle there is nothing but uninterrupted slaughter. In contrast to the obvious disarray of the Kauravas, the Pāṇḍu army is almost intact. No charioteer is even slightly wounded; the infantrymen form an unperturbed line almost to the very center of the scene. Is this the same battle? There is no doubt as to the superiority of the Pāṇḍu brothers and their army, and no doubt as to whom the victors will soon be. The five Pāṇḍu brothers were cousins and nephews of the Kuru leaders, and the battle at Kurukṣetra was fought so they could not only regain the throne but unite a divided family.

This depiction of the Battle of Kurukṣetra, despite the chaotic segments of fighting and wrestling soldiers (Appendix B, Table 2), is not at all random. On the left or north, there are exactly 43 large figures representing officers in the Kaurava army, all deployed on elephantback or in chariots except for the impaled Bhīṣma.[3] There are 32 opposing Pāṇḍava leaders on the right or south of center, distinguished by their warlike posture, splayed legs, and upraised weapons: 27 of the Pāṇḍavas are on chariots, 2 are on elephantback, and 3 are standing on the backs of horses.

These two sets of 43 and 32 main protagonists are both finalized in the central warrior who is about to kill the forty-forth leading officer and commander-in-chief of the Kuru forces. This central figure will soon become the leader of both groups, as the defeated Kauravas fall under his political as well as military dominion. In numerical terms, the exalted position of the victorious commander is emphasized by making him a thirty-third figure, leader of the 32 Pāṇḍava officers, and a forty-fifth figure, leader of the 44 Kaurava officers, including their commander. These numbers, 33 and 45, are symbols of a supreme deity. The "portion" of Śiva that can manifest through other gods, and resides in the king, is here expressed in terms of sacred numbers. The central figure is numerically on a par with Brahmā at the center of the architectural mandala. Both are a forty-fifth figure at the center of 44 surrounding entities; both are a thirty-third figure at the center of 32 peripheral gods/warriors.

As there were five Pāṇḍu brothers, each one

Fig. 5.3. Third gallery, west side, south half, Battle of Kurukṣetra.

Not long before the Battle of Kurukṣetra ended with the death of almost everyone, Bhīṣma dies impaled (here) on spears and pierced by arrows. Warriors come to pay him homage before he succumbs. Bhīṣma is placed high on the relief wall, near the beginning of the panel on the north.

Fig. 5.4. Third gallery, west side, south half, Battle of Kurukṣetra, center.

The leader of the Pāṇḍu forces is about to slaughter the enemy commander-in-chief by plunging a spear into his chest. The honorary parasols have been knocked down, the charioteer's neck is pierced by an arrow, and there is chaos all around.

was a leader in his own right, sharing the command of their army. Does the Angkor Wat relief focus on a single commander in order to create an axial center, thereby achieving a symmetry with the opposite panel, the Churning of the Sea of Milk? Are there other reasons for this composition as well? The slaughter of thousands, and the near annihilation of all the protagonists, in the battle at Kurukṣetra is rarely depicted in Southeast Asia. The connotations of this scene are horrifying, inauspicious, ill-omened. If there were not an overriding reason for portraying this battle exactly at the point where a visitor should be welcomed, then it would be inconceivable to show it for its own sake.

Since this historical gallery may have measurements related to the reign of King Sūryavarman in the axes, and since King Sūryavarman is depicted in person on the south wall of the gallery, the Battle of Kurukṣetra may likewise have been intended as a historical allegory for the king's own single battle for the throne of Cambodia. This would explain the unique Pāṇḍu commander at the center of the scene, his clear and imminent victory over his enemy, and his parallel placement across from the central Viṣṇu in the Churning of the Sea of Milk on the east wall. When King Sūryavarman fought and won his single battle for the throne, he too united his divided family.[4] He killed his great-uncle, the reigning king, and when the battle was over he ruled an undivided nation. He then held authority over the army of Dharanīndravarman as well as his own. Seen in this context, the Battle of Kurukṣetra becomes a very fitting analogy for King Sūryavarman's rise to power.

The *kali yuga* began with the devastation at Kurukṣetra, and the measurements of Angkor Wat indicate that the *kali yuga* was in effect when Sūryavarman came to power.[5] This time period changed to the *kṛta yuga* with the *Indrābhiṣeka* of the king, a ceremony that may be the focus of the Churning of the Sea of Milk just opposite this relief. The axial measurements of the third gallery also seem to couple dates from the reign of Sūryavarman, including the year he fought his single battle for power, with the *kṛta yuga* of the circumference. The Battle of Kurukṣetra and the Churning of the Sea of Milk may do exactly the same thing. Looking at their unique juxtaposition across from each other on the west and east, respectively, several other paired dichotomies argue for their opposition and reciprocity:

Battle of Kurukṣetra	*Churning of the Sea of Milk*
54/54-cubit axial division[6]	54/54-cubit axial division
warriors face center	warriors face center
destructive	creative
autumn equinox	spring equinox
west, setting sun	east, rising sun
new moon in west, darkness	full moon in east, brightness
entropy increases toward axis	order and symmetry
two warring factions	two cooperating factions
kali yuga	*kṛta yuga*

In brief, principles of cosmology (54/54 division), geophysics (autumn and spring equinoxes, rising and setting sun, new and full moon), and religious belief (the king changing the yuga period, the legends of the gods and antigods, the axial relationship of Viṣṇu and the king, as well as the notion of a center as a generative, hierarchical force) all exemplify the fourth level of organization in these two panels. The reason why the subjects of these two panels were chosen in the first place may be exactly because they symbolize the king's consolidation of power at the beginning of his reign.

When one looks down the western corridor at sunset, or eastern corridor at sunrise, the shadows of the pillars across from the reliefs cast a sharp, striated pattern along the passageway and wall (Fig. 5.5). All segments of the reliefs move in and

Fig. 5.5. Third gallery, west side, south half, view south down corridor at sunset.

As the sun moves across the sky at sunset, the dark striations caused by the shadows of the pillars move too. And they move as the sun changes from north to south and back again at the solstices. The light and shadow created by the sun and the pillars hits the reliefs in ways that seem to be deliberate.

out of the dark shadow of a pillar as the sun travels north and south each year. If we examine the photographs taken during the solstice periods and then look at the panorama of the churning scene on the east wall (Fig. 2.8), we note an interesting correlation. At the winter solstice, the shadow of the double pillars to the left of center reaches from Mandara to a point across from the set of pillars on the right. At the summer solstice, the set of pillars on the right casts a shadow from (and including) Mandara to the pillars on the left. In other words: a solstice shadow will travel across the relief only as far as the next set of pillars, or the distance of one interpillar space. This fact has definite ramifications not only in the churning scene but also in the scenes on the west side of this gallery.

During the winter solstice, the center of the Kurukṣetra scene lies in the shadow of a pillar (Fig. 5.6). Because the gods experience their midnight on the winter solstice day, this shadow might symbolize their night in the god realm. Since the two leaders at the center are in shadow, they are equated with the gods and their winter solstice darkness. At least that seems to be the case. What then happens at the summer solstice? On June 21, the central figures in the Kurukṣetra scene are once again in the shadow of a pillar (no illustration).[7] If they were equated with the gods, they should now be experiencing their midday in bright sunlight. The simple interpretation of "darkness" for the midnight of the gods during the winter solstice and "light" for their noon during the summer solstice does not apply.

In the winter solstice photograph (Fig. 5.6), one can see that a shaft of light brackets the central figures at the left. There is also a shaft of light to the right of the central figures during the summer solstice (no illustration). This bracketing effect at first seems accidental. When the sun is far enough north or south, its rays will shine through the double pillars, creating these shafts of light during the solstice periods. Just for curiosity, I examined the

Fig. 5.6. Third gallery, west side, south half, Battle of Kurukṣetra, center, winter solstice.

At the center of the Kurukṣetra panel, a shaft of sunlight between the two pillars moves up the north side of the central figures during the winter solstice and then moves up the opposite (south) side during the summer solstice. The *nāga* head at the back of the chariot, shown in the shaft of light, marks the end of the 54-cubit distance from the beginning of the panel on the north.

remaining major figures of Viṣṇu on the east and west sides of this gallery on the solstice days: each one was in darkness at both days, and each one shows the same bracketing of light. During the equinox days, these representations of Viṣṇu or his incarnations are in bright sunlight. One could say, then, that the centers of the eastern and western relief panels (all with figures of Viṣṇu or his surrogates) are oriented to the axial equinox days but reflect a relationship with the solstices due to the bracketing effect of the shafts of light. This aspect of the reliefs will be taken up again later in the chapter when we look at the Churning of the Sea of Milk.

THE SOUTHWEST CORNER PAVILION

The southwest pavilion provides an interlude of vignettes—a "story break" in the sequence of panel narratives that stops the visitor for a more intimate and isolated contemplation of each scene. The walls are textured with their illustrations, from top to bottom, in a fine and delicate carving that barely emerges from the gray polished sandstone. The decorative relief on the window frames here and elsewhere in the temple is even more lightly sculpted (Fig. 5.7). Seen in the raking light of the pavilion, the reliefs on walls and windows change tonality and emphasis with the time of day.

To the right as we enter, the Churning of the Sea of Milk features the sun and moon on each side of the central pivot, as a partially effaced Viṣṇu holds onto Mandara (Fig. 5.8). One can still discern the remains of Brahmā's legs on the lotus on top of Mount Mandara. Kūrma supports the base of the pole that represents Mandara, as the *asuras* and *devas* pull on Vāsuki (Fig. 5.9). The Battle of Kurukṣetra has just ended: this scene presages all the good fortune that will come with Sūryavarman's reign.

The southwest pavilion is paired with the northwest pavilion, and the scene to the right as we enter that pavilion depicts Viṣṇu lying on the Sea of Milk.[8] As stated earlier, the Churning of the Sea of Milk and Viṣṇu on the Sea of Milk are compositionally nearly identical, and both are scenes of creation. Their similar composition, as well as their focus on Viṣṇu as an axial, generative

Fig. 5.7. Third gallery, west side, window.

The harsh sunlight and heat are muted by the balusters on the windows, which once prevented animals such as monkeys from climbing into the sanctuaries. The relief on this window frame seems to have been sculpted after the balusters were in place, since it is unfinished.

source of power and creation, link the entrance of both pavilions together.

In the southwest pavilion, there are 10 gods to the right (north) of the churning pivot and 10 antigods to the left (south), all pulling on Vāsuki. That makes Viṣṇu a twenty-first god at the center of the scene—a highly significant number that not only characterizes the second gallery of Angkor Wat but may place Viṣṇu as we shall see, at the axis of the Battle of Laṅkā on the west wall. There are 22 *asuras* seated in registers below this scene (for a total of 32: 22 + 10), but there are 23 gods. When the 10 gods pulling on Vāsuki are added, the total number of *devas* in this scene is 33.

Fig. 5.8. Third gallery, southwest pavilion, north wing, west wall, churning scene.

As we enter the southwest pavilion from the battle of Kurukṣetra, there is a bas-relief of the churning event to the right. Here a heavily damaged Viṣṇu can still be seen holding onto the churning pivot, but unlike the large relief panel in this gallery, he is facing us. There is almost nothing left of Brahmā at the top of the pivot except his legs.

Just as the churning scene augurs future benefit under King Sūryavarman, the scene to the left is of Kṛṣṇa Govardhana: Kṛṣṇa holding up Mount Govardhana to protect villagers and animals from the heavy downpour unleashed by an angered Indra (Fig. 5.10). This benign and all-encompassing protection is another symbol of praise for Sūryavarman. Parallel to this scene in the southwest pavilion, the northwest pavilion shows Kṛṣṇa, carrying Mount Maṇiparvata (the peak of Meru), homeward bound in victory over the quarrelsome Narada (Figs. 3.1 and 5.11). Thus the Sea of Milk and creative energy are placed on the right as we enter the northwest and southwest pavilions; mountains, protection, and victory are placed on the left. Walking between these mountains and the Sea of Milk, the visitor enters each pavilion and encounters Śiva in the southwest pavilion and Viṣṇu (or one of his incarnations) in the northwest pavilion.

Before leaving the southwest pavilion, we find Śiva seated on a mountaintop to the right, receiving homage and perhaps an offering from a royal figure (Fig. 5.12). Before leaving the northwest pavilion, we find Viṣṇu seated on a mountaintop to the right, receiving homage from a royal figure (Fig. 5.13). On the southwest, the homage to Śiva precedes the next panel, whose focus of action is the king and his ministers on Mount Śivapāda. The smaller scene of Śiva on a mountaintop in the southwest pavilion "introduces" the larger panel to come. On the northwest, the homage to Viṣṇu precedes the next panel, whose focus of action is the great Battle of Laṅkā, fought by an incarnation of Viṣṇu. The smaller scene of Viṣṇu on a moun-

Fig. 5.9. Third gallery, southwest pavilion, north wing, west wall, churning scene.

Kūrma is at the base of Mount Mandara with Śrī Devī emerging at the left and the head of the horse Uccaiḥśravas at the right. The gods and *asuras* are pulling against each other. Unlike the large panel of the churning scene, here Kūrma does not wear a crown, and there is no flying *deva* on Mount Mandara, only Brahmā as usual. This scene corresponds in composition, theme, and location to the scene of Viṣṇu lying on the Sea of Milk in the northwest pavilion.

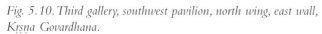

Fig. 5.10. Third gallery, southwest pavilion, north wing, east wall, Kṛṣṇa Govardhana.

Across from the churning scene in the southwest pavilion, Kṛṣṇa stands holding up Mount Govardhana to protect the villagers and animals from the aquatic wrath of Indra. The theme of Kṛṣṇa supporting or carrying a mountain is repeated on the wall that corresponds to this location in the opposite (northeast) pavilion (Fig. 5.11).

Fig. 5.11. Third gallery, northwest pavilion, east wing, south wall, Kṛṣṇa carrying Mount Maṇiparvata.

Garuḍa holds up the peak of Meru, Mount Maṇiparvata, visible in the triangular shape over Kṛṣṇa's head. Garuḍa also carries a multiplicity of figures on the peak itself, as well as the god Kṛṣṇa and his wife.

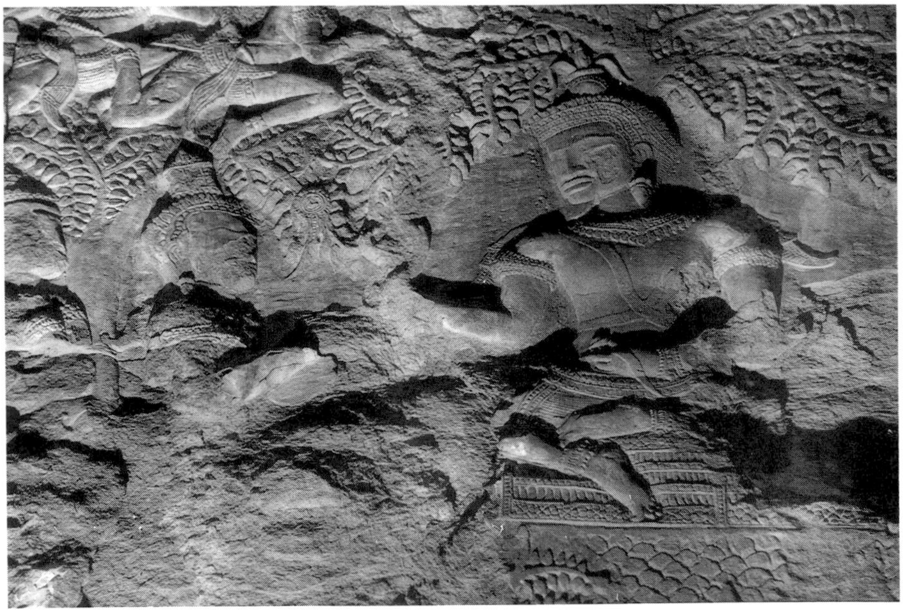

Fig. 5.12. Third gallery, southwest pavilion, east wing, south wall, Śiva on a mountaintop.

Just before we exit to view the panel of Sūryavarman's procession, there is a scene to the right with Śiva, high on a mountaintop, receiving some sort of offering from a *deva* or royal figure. This homage to Śiva precedes the next large panel, that of King Sūryavarman and his army descending Mount Śivapāda. This scene corresponds to a homage to Viṣṇu in the northwest pavilion, parallel in location, function, and theme (Fig. 5.13).

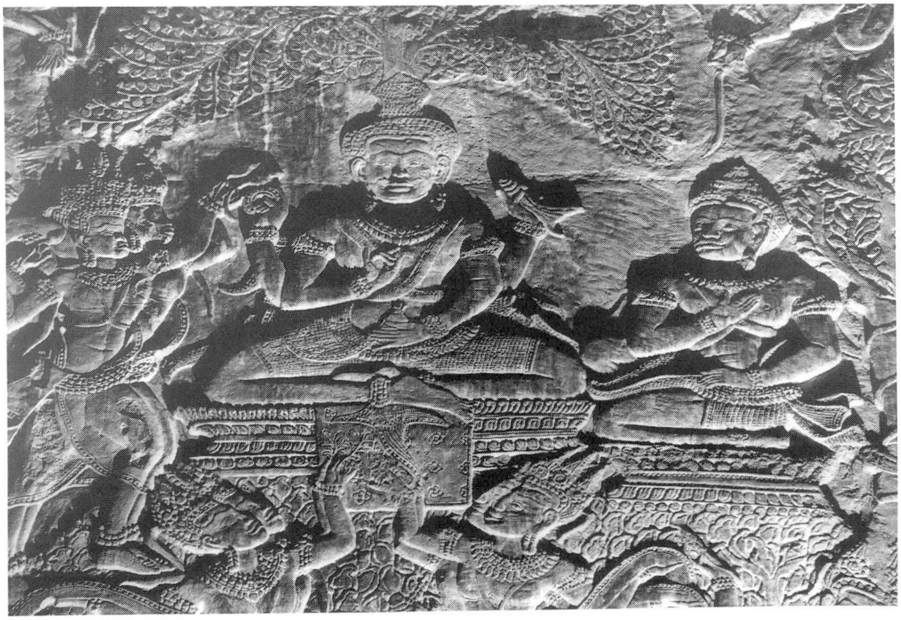

Fig. 5.13. Third gallery, northwest pavilion, south wing, west wall, Viṣṇu on a mountaintop.

Just before exiting to view the Battle of Laṅkā, we find Viṣṇu seated high on a mountaintop with a royal figure or *deva* next to him. He holds a conch tied with a ribbon in his upper left hand (our right), while the upper right hand holds a *cakra*. A small round object like a pearl is held at his chest, and what might be a small jar rests against the hand on his lap.

Fig. 5.14. Third gallery, southwest pavilion, east wing, north wall, water festival.

This scene of a major celebration occurs to the left as we walk out the door to view Sūryavarman's procession. Here a group of foreign (Chinese?) revelers dance and make merry as the oarsmen look on. To the right, a canopied cabin shades two young women, accepting fruit or food from a kneeling servant, and a woman holding a small child. The dragon-headed ceremonial boats must have been deployed along the Great Lake not far to the south of Angkor. This celebratory scene parallels that of the marriage of Sītā and Rāma (combined with the archery test of Rāma) in the northwest pavilion (Fig. 5.15).

taintop in the northwest pavilion equally "introduces" the larger panel to come.

To the left on leaving the southwest pavilion, there are depictions of the great water festival celebrated in mid-November when the Tonle Sap River changes its course and runs southward. The women of the court and children are present in boats, while dancers, acrobats and jugglers, and cockfights entertain the viewer (Fig. 5.14). To the left on leaving the northwest pavilion, there is a scene of the marriage of Sītā and Rāma, as well as Rāma's test of archery to win the hand of Sītā (Fig. 5.15). This scene represents a celebration and involves the queen and the court, too, as does the

Fig. 5.15. Third gallery, northwest pavilion, south wing, west wall, archery test and marriage of Rāma.

Rāma shoots an arrow upward at the target of a bird perched on a spoked wheel—a Khmer version of the test he passed to win the hand of Sītā.

water festival in the southwest pavilion. The parallels between the entry and exit scenes in the two pavilions indicate that despite their opposite emphasis on Śiva (southwest pavilion) and Viṣṇu (northwest pavilion), they function in the same manner. Both corner structures are meant to glorify King Sūryavarman on entering, and both presage his next major activity (the next relief panel) on leaving.

Continuing the counterclockwise circumambulation in the southwest corner pavilion, we encounter three Śivaite scenes in sequence. Around the corner to the Churning of the Sea of Milk, in the west cross-arm, right or north side, there is a relief showing Śiva Bhikṣāṭanamūrti (Lord of Beggars).[9] In this story, Śiva was on his way to Varanasi to purify himself of the crime of cutting off the fifth head of Brahmā. Along the way, he stopped by a forest where many ascetics were practicing yoga. In order to test their level of attainment, Śiva turned himself into an attractive, nude young man and caused the ascetics' wives to rush up to him with great ardor and passion. In response the ascetics cursed the young man—only to realize their lack of achievement when Śiva suddenly disappeared. The scene depicted in the Angkor Wat relief shows Śiva standing in a doorway with a lizard over it, as women rush up to him on both sides (Fig. 5.16). Small figures of ascetics appear in the bottom foreground, yet another indication of the scene's origin. Curiously, the number of women in the registers below this scene, in combination with the women depicted below the relief of the death of Kāma on the south cross-arm, totals 108. These are the only subsidiary females in this pavilion.

The second Śivaite scene (across from the preceding scene) shows Rāvaṇa, the multiheaded and multiarmed *asura* king, shaking Mount Kailāsa as Śiva sits in unperturbed meditation above (Fig. 5.17)—a popular depiction in Khmer temples. Rounding the corner to the south cross-arm, we encounter the third scene: Śiva killing Kāma, the god of desire, who first shoots his arrow upward

Fig. 5.16. Third gallery, southwest pavilion, west wing, south wall, Śiva Bhikṣāṭanamūrti.

The southwest pavilion has several scenes dedicated to Śiva. In this instance, the god is shown raised high on a mountaintop again, standing in a palatial doorway with a curious lizard over the top. Women are rushing up to him on all sides. Ascetics meditate on the mountainside, a feature suggesting the story in which Śiva tempts their wives to test the ascetics' achievement.

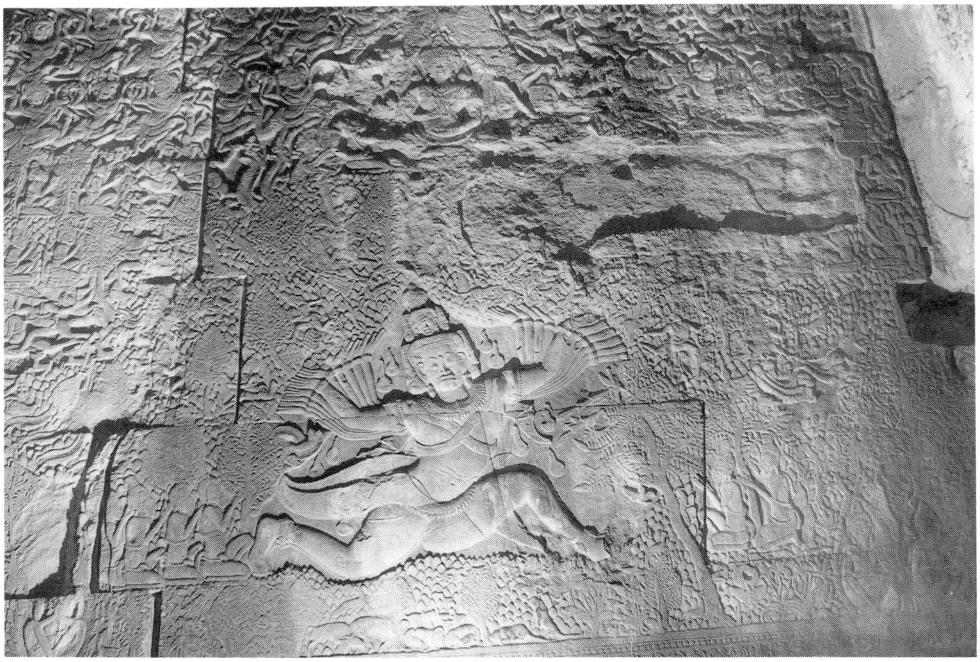

Fig. 5.17. Third gallery, southwest pavilion, west wing, north wall, Rāvaṇa shaking Mount Kailāsa.

The multiheaded, multiarmed Rāvaṇa is shown here shaking Mount Kailāsa while Śiva meditates above. The supremacy of Śiva on a mountaintop, impervious to the attacks of a demon king or the attractions of women, is highlighted in this scene and the scene of Śiva Bhikṣāṭanamūrti opposite (Fig. 5.16).

Fig. 5.18. Third gallery, southwest pavilion, south wing, west wall, death of Kāma.

Kāma, the god of love and desire, lies moribund on the ground while his consort Ratī holds him in grief. Traditionally Kāma is burnt to ashes by Śiva's third eye, which is not quite as poignant an image as the dead Kāma in the arms of his consort. His death, his supine position, and the position of his consort are mirrored in the relief opposite (Fig. 5.19).

at Śiva and then lies dying on the ground, gently held by his consort dressed in regal attire (Fig. 5.18). These three scenes underscore Śiva's role as god of the yogis.

Just opposite the scene showing the death of Kāma is a relief of Rāma shooting an arrow at Vālin, the monkey leader in the epic *Rāmāyaṇa,* and brother of Sugrīva. Vālin appears twice: once fighting Sugrīva, once dead on the ground with his consort holding his head and mourning her loss, the counterpart of Kāma's consort Ratī (Fig. 5.19). Even though this narrative is quite different from Śiva striking down Kāma with his third eye, the compositions of the scene with Kāma and the scene with Vālin and Sugrīva are exceptionally similar.

The legend of Vālin and Sugrīva is taken from the *Rāmāyaṇa,* as mentioned, and rightly belongs in the northwest corner pavilion, which features that epic in its four lintels and half of its wall reliefs. In trying to understand why this particular scene has been excerpted and placed in a Śivaite pavilion, one wonders if the sculptors were simply looking for something that would complement the

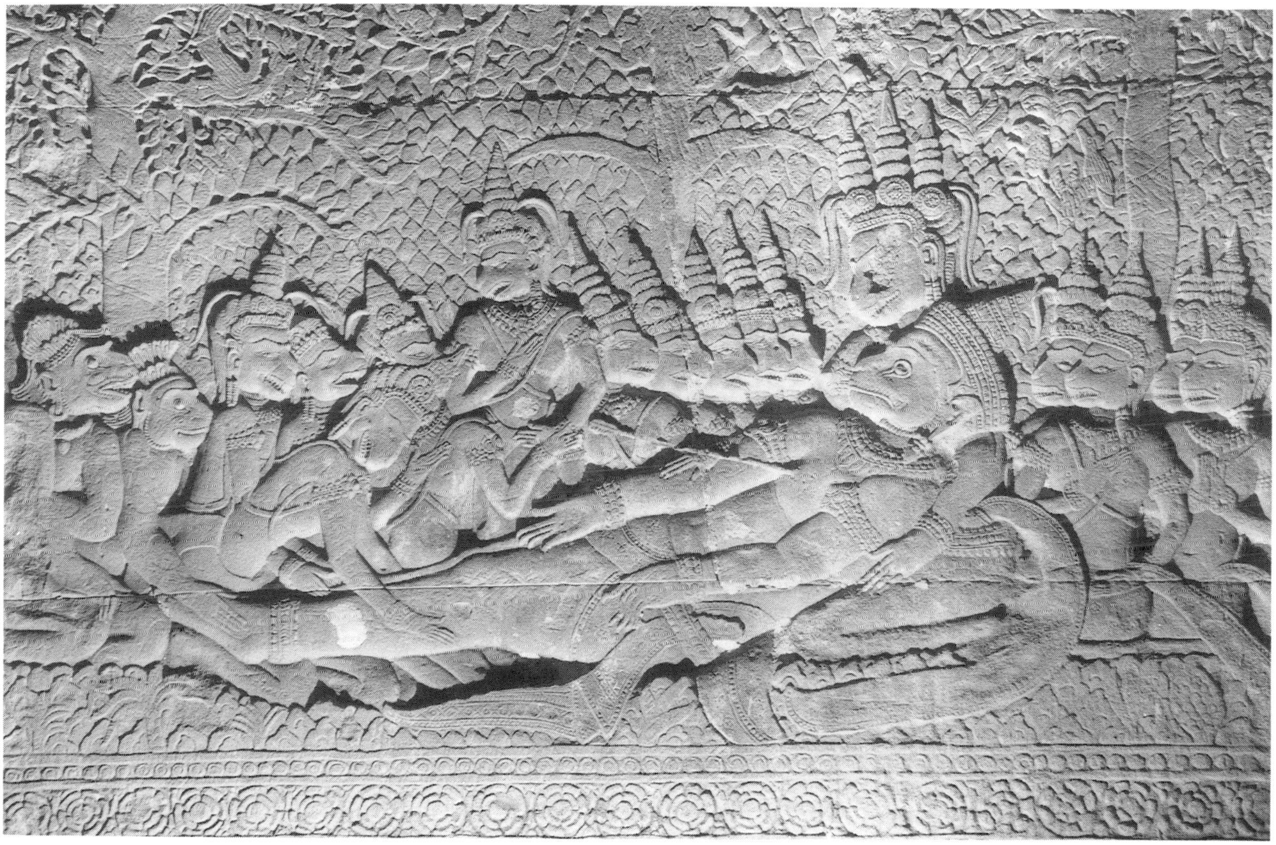

Fig. 5.19. Third gallery, southwest pavilion, south wing, west wall, Battle of Sugrīva and Vālin, death of Vālin.
Pierced by an arrow, Vālin dies while being held by his consort. His mortality is contrasted to the power of Śiva in the relief opposite: Śiva not only was unaffected by Kāma's arrows, but killed Kāma as well.

Fig. 5.20. Third gallery, southwest pavilion, east doorway, lintel, Viṣṇu Caturbhuja.
The Supreme Viṣṇu stands in full hierarchical splendor, worshiped with offerings and exalted by flying *devas*. Although there are Śivaite scenes in the pavilion, all the lintels illustrate Viṣṇu as Rāma, as Kṛṣṇa, or, in this case, as himself.

death of Kāma across from this wall. Or perhaps the scene was intended as an allusion to the death of King Dharanīndravarman at the hands of King Sūryavarman. In the end, there is no obvious explanation for this single Vaiṣṇava episode in a Śivaite context.

Śiva may dominate the walls of this pavilion, but Viṣṇu—as himself, as Rāma, or as Kṛṣṇa—is placed above Śiva in the lintels over the doorways. In both of the western corner pavilions, the lintels over opposite doorways directly complement each other. In the southwest pavilion, Rāma is depicted in the act of killing the demon Mārīca in the lintel over the north doorway; the opposite (south) lintel shows the death of another demon, Pralamba. These demons may have been symbols for the king's enemies conquered in the past, and to be conquered in the future, especially since the lintels follow the military motif of the battle at Kurukṣetra and precede the military procession panel.

Over the inner western doorway the child Kṛṣṇa is depicted horizontally, crawling on his hands and knees, dragging the mortar to which he was tethered, and pulling down two trees in the process (thereby releasing two men from a curse that had kept them imprisoned there). Opposite this scene, a four-armed Viṣṇu, majestic and hierarchical, is illustrated vertically and frontally (Fig. 5.20), with offerings being made to him in a format that is compositionally heraldic. The deity is now seen in full transformation: from Viṣṇu incarnate as a child (Kṛṣṇa) to Viṣṇu as a symbol of power. It is under this inspiring image of the four-armed standing Viṣṇu that the visitor passes to view the panel of King Sūryavarman. There could be no better introduction to the new Vaiṣṇava ruler—and no better balance to the emphasis on Śiva in this pavilion.

THE PROCESSION OF KING SŪRYAVARMAN AND HIS MINISTERS

The panel of Sūryavarman's military procession is really a juxtaposition of three different events (Fig. 5.21).[10] The first 32 cubits of the scene show a procession of 11 courtly women en route to meet the end of the procession of 19 ministers (Appendix B, Table 3).[11] At the end of this group, on the western and left-hand side of the relief, are six women on litters, bracketed by five males standing in a group in front of them, and one larger male who leads a group of servants behind them. The five men who cluster together in this scene seem to be holding rolled documents (scrolls) in their hands. There are six women and six predominant men in this section of the relief: are they somehow paired or connected?

In front of the six women in litters are five more traveling in palanquins. These five women do not have any visible male companions. They are attended by a multitude of servants, including dwarfs, and many seem to be entertained by their retinue or are in the process of fixing their hair or touching up their appearance. At the very front of this procession a kneeling woman holds out an oblong form or forms that may represent scrolls. With a stylus-like implement, a standing male appears about to mark them (Fig. 5.22). The *rājahotar* (royal priest) in the procession also seems to be holding the same oblong scroll and pointed implement (Fig. 5.23). These women are traveling through a densely wooded, jungle-like setting,

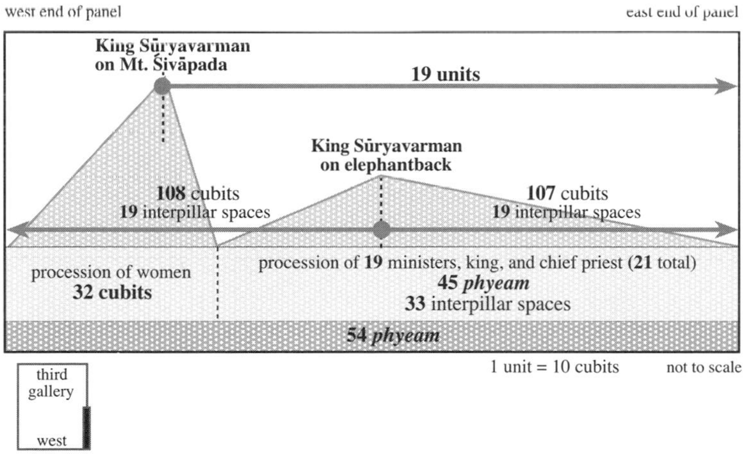

Fig. 5.21. Third gallery, south side, west half, diagram of Sūryavarman's procession scene.

The 19 interpillar spaces (bays) on each side of the king, the 19 ministers, and the 19-unit length between the king on a mountaintop and the eastern end of the panel set the dominant theme of this relief. Other numbers, such as 54, 108, and 19/21 (again) connect this scene to the next in sequence and to the opposite relief across the gallery. That connection lies not only in the measurements, but in the context and manner in which the measurements appear. The 21 figures in the procession are given the highest numerical praise because the space they occupy is defined by 33 bays and 45 *phyeam*, symbolically bringing the supreme deity into the procession as well.

replete with monkeys, deer, and birds interspersed between the trees. The scenery might be a representation of the landscape they passed through in order to join the king's procession.

Along the upper two-thirds of the panel, a mountaintop scene is depicted simultaneously with this caravan of women. King Sūryavarman is seated, facing his left (our right), and is in the act of accepting the homage and allegiance of four of his ministers, most of whom have their hands placed over their hearts in a show of devotion and servitude. This is the second event in the scene. Quite inexplicably, King Sūryavarman is holding a dangling snake in his right hand; his left hand, extended toward the men in front of him, holds a small unidentified object apparently wrapped in cloth (Fig. 1.15). The inscriptions accompanying the scene identify the men in front of Sūryavarman as *tamrvac,* which has been translated as "inspectors." They are, in effect, ministers. Śrī Vīrasiṁhavarman (on his knees before the king, offering him a scroll), Śrī Vardhana, Dhananjaya, and a fourth minister "charged with the inspection of merits and defects" are the inscribed identities of these four high-ranking officials. Śrī Vardhana and Dhananjaya, seated on a raised mat, are larger in scale than the other figures (Fig. 5.2).[12]

These loyal retainers may be taking a well-known oath of allegiance first recorded in the reign of Sūryavarman I and dating to A.D. 1011. This oath says in part:

> If we do not keep this vow [of allegiance], may we be reborn in the 32 hells for as long as there will be a sun and moon... and may we obtain the reward of those who are devoted to their master, after this world, even in the other world.[13]

The *tamrvac* who take this oath swear loyalty to the king, vowing to help him always and never to serve another king. One wonders, then, how many "kings" there were. The statement implies a rather unstable environment. An example of the loyalty oath is found in eight inscriptions carved in the eastern gateway of the Royal Palace of Angkor Thom (Phimeanakas and its environs). These inscriptions, written on the door and window

Fig. 5.22. Third gallery, south side, west half, procession of King Sūryavarman.

At this juncture, the procession of women going to join the king and his commanders arrives; on the upper right, the next procession of men heads down the mountainside. A kneeling woman seems to be offering rolled documents to the standing male figure, so that he may mark or stamp them.

Fig. 5.23. Third gallery, south side, west half, procession of King Sūryavarman.

The *rājahotar,* or chief priest, is carried in a litter in front of the king. He seems to be holding a stylus—or at least a long, pointed object—in his right hand. In his left, he appears to hold a narrow, rolled-up scroll.

frames, repeat the vow to the king and are followed by a list of names of people presiding over a *sruk,* or district. The modern oath of office in Cambodia is similar in wording to this original oath.

As Sūryavarman is receiving homage and a ritual expression of fealty from his ministers, we can assume that the women depicted in the caravan are the women of his own family, and perhaps other royal and courtly families as well, en route to join him and the ministers. The location of this scene of allegiance is given in the reference to Mount Śivapāda, which reads: "The moment when H.M. Paramaviṣṇuloka had his troops descend from Mount Śivapāda."[14] Paramaviṣṇuloka is the posthumous name given to King Sūryavarman, indicating that the inscriptions were carved after his death. The style of the bas-reliefs, however, places them within the bounds of Sūryavarman's reign.

After the king and his ministers have concluded this rite on the mountaintop and the women have joined the court, these two registers of separate scenes converge. At this juncture, we see the back of the full military procession of ministers progressing across the rest of the panel to the far end (Appendix B, Table 3). This is the third and final event shown in the panel.

Sūryavarman appears once again at the center of the procession scene, standing with great dignity on top of an elephant (Fig. 5.1). Presumably his most important ministers flank him. His *rājahotar,* or royal priest, appears in front of him (Fig. 5.23) and then Śrī Rājendravarman, Śrī Vardhana, and the Anak Sanjak Trailokyapura; behind the king are Dhananjaya, Śrī Sūrādhipativarman, and Śrī Narapatīndravarman. Two of these ministers, Dhananjaya and Śrī Vardhana, are named in the scene of allegiance and seated on the special mat.

The ministers in the procession would have ruled over certain regions of the Khmer nation, but it is impossible to know if their distribution in this scene follows a regional order. Whatever the logic behind the sequence of ministers, their order of appearance would not have been accidental.[15] An interesting segment of the relief shows the "sacred fire," or *vraḥ vleṅ,* being carried on a litter (Fig. 5.24). The container for the fire is enclosed and has a conical top that is perforated to allow the smoke (or flames?) to escape. Inside there must have been a flame burning with a wick set in oil (or the sap from "candle trees" that is still used today for candles). The sacred fire was one of the palladia of kingship, but we know nothing about its origins or its specific purpose.

There are 21 major figures in King Sūryavarman's procession. One is the king himself and another is the *rājahotar.* The remaining 19 figures are the ministers whose names and titles are inscribed below them in the relief—with the inexplicable exception of the *"syam kuk"* at the head of the procession (Figs. 5.25 and 5.26). The title is a puzzle, since the nation known as "Siam" or Thailand was not in existence at this early a date. This inscription was chiseled off and erased by vandals in the early 1980s (Fig. 5.27).[16]

The king's central position in the procession coincides with the placement of Viṣṇu in the

Fig. 5.24. Third gallery, south side, west half, procession of King Sūryavarman.

The sacred fire is carried just in front of the *rājahotar,* suggesting that the priest may have been involved with the rituals connected to the fire. The container is fenced around by a *nāga* railing supported on miniature columns and adorned with porchlike extensions on each side. Flames, or perhaps smoke, fringe the upper part of the dome.

Fig. 5.25. Third gallery, south side, west half, procession of King Sūryavarman.

The leader of the striking *syam kuk* holds a bow and arrow as he stands on his elephant. His hair and that of his warriors appears to be long and braided. He wears an apronlike piece of cloth at the back, over his *sampot,* as does his charioteer.

Fig. 5.26. Third gallery, south side, west half, procession of King Sūryavarman.

The foot soldiers in the *syam kuk* group at the head of the procession carry long, curved body shields and spears. Their *sampot* are also belted with beaded strings that end in a metallic point. Their commander, unlike the other 18 commanders, is not named in an inscription. His dress and the lack of a title suggest that—also unlike the other commanders in the procession—he was not Khmer.

Fig. 5.27. Third gallery, south side, west half, procession of King Sūryavarman.

At the head of the procession, the inscription that identified the group of warriors as *syam kuk* for 850 years was recently vandalized and effaced. The subsequent hole, near the tips of the lower two branches in this view, was covered over with cement.

Churning of the Sea of Milk or the Pāṇḍava leader in the Battle of Kurukṣetra, who were on an axis at the center of a panel. In this instance, the king is at the center of power, and from that viewpoint his ministers can be conceptualized as extending outward from him. Again, considering this organization numerically, there are 19 interpillar spaces, symbolizing the 19 ministers, on each side of the king, which place him at a "center" radiating 19 in either direction. The figure of the king is also juxtaposed to the central figure of Indra in the panel across the gallery. The two kings, Indra and Sūryavarman, are placed in such a way that if the reliefs were superimposed, they would be directly facing each other. The great Khmer king and the divine Indra, both on elephantback, would then confront each other as equally majestic figures symbolizing the leadership of men and the leadership of the gods, respectively.

This conjunction of secular and divine kingship is not the only link between these two reliefs (Appendix B, Table 3). The king occupies the tenth position from the front of his procession; Lord Viṣṇu, the supreme deity and the king's divine mentor, occupies the tenth position in the sequence of *deva*s on the opposite north wall. Viṣṇu is the tenth figure from the front and the twelfth figure from the back of the procession: both are significant numbers equal to the 10 incarnations of Viṣṇu and the 12 *āditya*s, respectively. By parallel placement and sequential position, the sculptors have exalted King Sūryavarman to the rank of a human equivalent to Indra and Viṣṇu—or at least represented him as a king imbued with a special divine relationship.

A total of 107.92 cubits lead to King Sūryavarman, measured from the western edge of the procession panel to the first flick of his drapery (Fig. 5.21). The distance from that flick of drapery to the eastern end of the panel is 107.03 cubits. This dichotomy does not place the king between two numerically exact 108-unit halves but, rather, makes him part of a generally auspicious division. Although one half of the panel is 1 cubit shorter than the other, the intent is clear.

As noted earlier, there are 19 interpillar spaces on each side of the central Sūryavarman. The distance between the first representation of the king on Mount Śivapāda and the eastern end of the panel is 191.32 cubits (19 × 10).[17] This distance, which includes the entire procession and all the king's major ministers, is yet another way of associating the number 19 with the leaders in Sūryavarman's government.

On careful analysis, then, the king is numerically and geometrically associated with Indra and Viṣṇu. His terrestrial realm, however, expressed in the depiction of 21 figures (including the king and his priest), is numerically associated with Indra's celestial realm of gods. As noted earlier, the sun's position during the two halves of the solar year would fluctuate between these two reliefs, so that as the north panel was favored by the summer solstice sun, the south panel would be in darkness (and vice versa for the winter solstice). An interesting passage from the *Śatapatha Brāhmaṇa* explains the nature of this alternation:

> The spring, the summer, and the rains, these seasons (represent) the gods; and the autumn, the winter, and the dewy season represent the fathers. The half-moon which increases represents the gods, and that which decreases represents the fathers. And further, the forenoon represents the gods, and the afternoon the fathers.
>
> Now when he (the sun) moves northwards, then he is among the gods, then he guards the gods; and when he moves southwards, then he is among the fathers, then he guards the fathers.[18]

Based on this viewpoint and on the actual movement of the sun, when the "fathers" in the celestial palaces in the scene of heaven and hell—as well as Sūryavarman and his ministers—are in darkness on the south wall, the gods on the north are illumined by the sun and vice versa. At least, the figures receive whatever sunlight filters under and through the vaulted roofs and pillared corridors.

In agreement with this alternation in seasonal and solar periods, the length of the procession panel in the south (and the panel of *devas* and *asuras* in the north) is 53.74 *phyeam* each. This pairing of two 54/54-*phyeam* lengths is normally representative of the *devas* and *asuras*. In this case, however, the *asuras* are replaced by Sūryavarman and his forces, raising the secular realm to a numerically equal footing with the gods. Again the principal intent of the architects seems to have been to equate their king to Indra and Viṣṇu and, similarly, the king's ministers to the remaining *devas*.[19] In a general sense, then, the terrestrial Sūryavarman and his troops are not only contrasted to the gods while these former figures are still alive, but continue to be so contrasted when Sūryavarman and his ministers become "fathers" in the afterworld.

This concept is particularly relevant to the next scene, depicting heavens and hells, which may allude again to the after-death destination of the ministers. The heavenly palaces shelter 19 men; there are 19 interpillar spaces in front of the palaces; and the number 19 occurs in several other instances. Alone it represents the government of King Sūryavarman as personified in his ministers. It is for this reason, aside from simple logic, that the men in the celestial palaces have commonly been identified with the 19 ministers. When the king and his chief priest are included in the count of governing figures, the total is 21, a number that defines the *devas* and their supreme deity. Because the king and the chief priest are able to numerically "transform" the secular kingdom of 19 ministers into a 21-unit realm parallel to the world of the *devas*, they themselves take on a certain divine quality.

The multiple reciprocity between the procession panel and the panel of the 21 *devas* provides diverse links between Sūryavarman and his world, on the one hand, and Indra, Viṣṇu, and their celestial realm on the other. These various connections between the two panels of reliefs seem quite intentional, deliberately pairing 19 and 21. When we reach the Battle of Laṅkā at the end of the journey around the panels of bas-reliefs, we will encounter a detailed expression of 19 and 21 that repeats the allusion to 19 ministers and a twenty-first supreme deity. In fact, there are no original panels of bas-reliefs in the gallery that are not keyed into the 19/21 set in one way or another.

There may be scattered examples of 19/21 on the upper elevation (Fig. 8.12), in the second gallery (Fig. 7.21), and in the outer enclosure (Fig. 3.15e), but the representations of 19/21 at Angkor Wat are overwhelmingly clustered in the third gallery—with more than a dozen occurrences in all. This cluster makes royal and divine government a prerogative of the third gallery, like the 54/54-unit cluster on the bridge and in the western entrances that especially places the churning scene in those areas of the temple.

The basic concept of this unusual set is a definition of either 19 royal ministers under a terrestrial king or 19 deities under a celestial king, both sets of 19 presided over by a twenty-first supreme deity, as noted. A simple head count indicates that the king in each case is a twentieth figure. When a measurement provides a 19/21-unit alternation then, the king and Viṣṇu are joined together. Whenever a 20/21 unit pairing occurs at Angkor Wat, it places the king and ministers or Indra and the gods in one group and the supreme deity alone. This latter type of alternation occurs in instances in which 21 embraces 20 units as a whole, such as a staircase (21) with 20 steps. The former 19/21 alternation can occur in an axis that measures 21 units unless the central chamber (or the circumambulation space) is excluded, at which point it measures 19 units (Figs. 3.15e and 4.29). When the image and its space are removed from the axis, the king and the supreme deity numerically disappear, implying that the king and the supreme deity are inseparable from the image. When the image is present in the axis, the 21-unit total brings back the king and deity. The 19/21 numerical alternation is particularly interesting because images were, in fact, removed from sanctuaries and taken on procession or to "visit" other temples. When the image is not present, neither are Viṣṇu (21) or Sūryavarman (20). In this subtle differentiation, the portion of divinity that resides in the king, and the royal essence that resides in Viṣṇu are joined in the image.

One 19/21-unit alternation occurs in the main western entrance of Angkor Wat. The west-east outer axis is 21.53 *phyeam* but only 18.89 *phyeam* without the central chamber.[20] This is the chamber in which Viṣṇu, the king, Brahmā above, and the spring equinox as well as the *Indrābhiṣeka* were joined together. The second and only other alternating 19/21-unit axis is in the third gallery, northern and southern entrances, and it is much more precise at 19.04 and 21.00 *phyeam* (Fig. 4.30). Although not in the main entrance, the north and south location agrees with a 19/21-figure dichotomy in the northern and southern bas-reliefs. It is the content of the reliefs that first indicated that a king is given the twentieth position between 19 lesser figures and the twenty-first supreme deity.

The basic concept of a 19/21-unit alternation agrees then, with the belief that the "subtle inner self" of the king was in a statue of Viṣṇu or Śiva named and created to be in relationship to the king. When a 21-unit length becomes 19 units with the exclusion of such a statue this same concept is expressed in measurements.

THE SCENES OF HEAVENS AND HELLS

The long and abundantly rich procession of King Sūryavarman on the west comes to an abrupt end at the southern axial entrance to the third gallery. After crossing through the axial entrance, we encounter the scenes of heavens and hells.[21] The 32 hells depicted here are not in Hindu cosmology, which has no hells: they are the only instance of a definite Buddhist representation at Angkor Wat, an indication of the acceptance of Buddhist beliefs. In this case, the hells closely correspond to those in Mahayana Buddhism (Appendix B, Table 4).[22] Despite the change in theme, the eastward procession seen in the preceding panel continues, as two registers of men and women angle upward, making room for a third register of the hells below. There is no relationship between the registers; indeed, the inscriptions and visual depiction of the upper two registers seem to be at odds. The people coming from the second register are shown being thrown into the hells, but an inscription written between the parasols of the people in the middle register reads: "These, the two upper paths, are the paths of the heavens." A second inscription appears along the beginning of the narrow band that runs across the top of the hell scenes, where all the names of the individual hells are written. It reads: "This, the lower path, is the path of the hells."[23]

Yama, the god of death, interrupts the procession in the seventh interpillar space of the corridor, nearly blocking its progress as he sits on his buffalo mount, in the position of royal ease, and brandishes swords in his 18 hands (Fig. 5.28). He points one sword in the direction of his two assistants, Dharma and Citragupta (Fig. 5.29), seated just ahead, while stretching out another hand toward the oncoming line of men and women to our left.[24] His gestures toward the beings in the middle register indicate that these people are being sent into hell; his two assistants reinforce his judgment, as the hells open up in front of them and the condemned are unceremoniously thrown headfirst to their fate (Fig. 5.30).

Oblivious to the horror and uproar, the virtuous men and women of the upper register sit in quiet splendor in the royal palaces of the heavens, attended by a multitude of servants (Fig. 5.31). Their tranquility stands in uncomfortable contrast to the agony just beneath them. These celestial men and women alternate across the top of the relief, almost one pair for each interpillar space. A long series of standing *garuḍa*s, the eagle-like mount of Viṣṇu, supports the heavenly palaces and separates them from the hell scenes below. After each of the 32 hells has been named and duly depicted, and after each of the 19 men and 18 women has been shown enjoying the heavens above the hell scenes, the panel ends without further statement.

On the west side of Angkor Wat, there are two battle scenes; on the south side, there are two procession panels that each have 19 men. These are the only original, consecutive pairs of panels at the temple, and they seem to define the "themes" on the west and south. Unlike Sūryavarman's procession in composition, however, the heavens and hells have no geometrically central figure. The full length of this panel is 37.92 *phyeam,* which divides into two halves of 19 and 19, but neither Yama nor Dharma or Citragupta are the focus of this division (Fig. 5.32).[25] Nevertheless, the 19/19-*phyeam* division here parallels the 19/19 division in the number of interpillar spaces on each side of Sūryavarman in the procession scene. The 19/19 split in the judgment panel, however, might allude to the division between 19 living ministers and the same 19 in the afterworld as the "fathers." That life/death division is one theme of the panel itself.

Fig. 5.28. Third gallery, south side, east half, heavens and hells.

Yama, the god of death and king of the ancestors, directs the flow of traffic toward the heavens or hells, as he stares at us and not those whose fate hangs in the balance. The rigid order and hierarchy that define the relief panels take on a sinister undertone here.

Fig. 5.29. Third gallery, south side, east half, heavens and hells.

Dharma (another form of Yama) and Citragupta (the scribe who records good and bad karma) are two large-scale figures who appear just before the opening to the hells. Dharma sits in a posture close to that of an attendant; Citragupta, the scribe, is seated on a raised lotus mat. As in many other areas of the reliefs, their faces seem to have been deliberately damaged. In addition, this half of the gallery collapsed in 1945 and as a consequence the panel is marred throughout by missing pieces.

The beginning registers of Yama's panel are filled with a crowd of elegant men and women, the latter carried in palanquins and attended by servants. There are 21 major figures in these introductory processions, equivalent in number, if not in identity, to the 21 people in King Sūryavarman's procession.[26] The coincidence of the processions and 19 men specific to each panel, along with the 19/19 division from a central axis, strengthen the evidence that the heavens and hells illustrate the rewards and punishments for those who were loyal—or not—to the new king.

Yama also occupies interpillar space 21 counting from the east end of the panel, and Dharma and Citragupta occupy space 20. Dharma himself is another form of Yama. He embodies the best qualities of our lives, defined by our ability to live according to the "truth" (the approximate meaning of "dharma" that also embraces virtuous conduct). Citragupta records and weighs the karmic actions of the living so that they may be judged at death. The relationship of these two assistants to the god Yama is analogous to Sūryavarman's relationship to Viṣṇu in broad terms, and their placement in the twentieth interpillar space brings to mind Sūryavarman's position in the preceding panel. At the same time, Yama is the king of the ancestors, Sūryavarman is king at Angkor, and Indra is the king of the gods. We can surmise, then, that Sūryavarman's role as king over 19 ministers is amplified by the content of this scene. The 19 ministers have Sūryavarman as their king while living, and Yama as their king after death.

In the procession panel there are 19 interpillar spaces to the right of the king, and in this panel there are 19 such spaces to the right of Dharma and Citragupta (our right, that of the viewer). There are 108 cubits that lead up to Dharma and Citragupta from the east end of the panel and there are 108 cubits that lead up to King Sūryavarman from the west end of the procession panel. So although Dharma and Citragupta are not at the center of the judgment scene, their position is linked to that of the king. In general terms, then,

Fig. 5.30. Third gallery, south side, east half, heavens and hells. As the demons in hell hack at people suspended from trees or crush them with rollers, the newly condemned fall headlong into the torture that awaits them.

the king seems to have a counterpart in Yama as well as in Yama's two attendants. There is a similar dual connection between the king, and Indra and Viṣṇu in the panel across from the procession scene. King Sūryavarman is placed opposite Indra, the king of the gods, and is given the same tenth position in the sequence of ministers as Viṣṇu is given in the sequence of gods.

Over time, there may have been many more than 19 ministers as the decades wore on and battles took their toll, but there were no more than 19 such offices. The 19 men are not identified by inscriptions in the scenes of the heavens. We can assume, then, that the ministerial title and function garnered a heavenly abode as long as the minister kept allegiance to the king. In a certain sense, that undercut the belief that the presence of dharma in each life would be rewarded with a sojourn in the heavens. Loyalty seems to be the determining factor here. Also, the benign Dharma and fierce Citragupta symbolize the king's own character as a fatherly ruler or chastising warrior, benevolent or wrathful as the situation demands.

The 12-*phyeam* length that introduces the heavens at the top of the panel would most likely refer to the 12 *aditya*s, thereby connecting the heavens to the solar Viṣṇu. At the same time, Yama, Dharma, and Citragupta are excluded from the 12-unit length of the panel expressed in 12-cubit modules. This 12-unit length repeated 12 times might refer once again to the sun, or might refer to the 12 light and 12 dark halves of the lunar month. In either instance, the central triad of actors in this drama are excluded. They are also excluded from the 28- and 27-*phyeam* lengths which stretch between them and the eastern end of the panel. We cannot help but conclude that wherever Yama, Dharma, and Citragupta reside, they are not bound by the lunar or solar time that regulates the life of the mortals they judge.

Although the panel covers 27 interpillar spaces

Fig. 5.31. Third gallery, south side, east half, heavens and hells.

Here one of the 19 men that occupy the heavenly palaces sits attended by *apsarases* like those shown on the walls of the temple. A long line of *garuḍas* holds the palaces aloft, a sign that these are celestial quarters.

from beginning to end, as does its sixteenth-century counterpart panel on the north, it is not possible to come to terms with the meaning of that measurement. Without the original scene for the paired panel on the north, the southern panel of heavens and hells lacks a necessary, larger context. If the number 27 were meant to provide the paired panels with a lunar connotation, it is not clear how that would relate to the content and internal measurement patterns discerned in the scenes of heavens and hells.

Before taking a final step past the scene of heavens and hells, the content of their inscriptions is worth noting. These inscriptions paint a colorful picture of life at Angkor.[27] Sleeping with another's wife, for example, was apparently common enough to warrant the capacity and nuances of punishment in 3 hells out of 32. The women in these cases were not expressly condemned to a hell realm, though, just the men. Women are classed as possessions; if a possession is stolen, it is not at fault. In fact, thievery is the most repeated means of descent into one of the hells. A total of 12 different hells are reserved for those who steal land, residences, elephants, horses, vehicles, shoes, sandals, parasols, rice, strong liquor, the goods of priests, the goods of the poor, flowers, and, of course, the wives of others. One senses that thievery might have been a widespread avocation at Angkor.

The hell of Aṅgaricaraya was filled with those who burned villages and towns and the "parks of the sacred bulls"—and those who urinated or defecated in areas consecrated to the gods. Another hell, appropriately called Padma, or Lotus, was reserved for those who took flowers from Śiva's gardens. Śiva and his bull Nandin must have been widely venerated if parks and gardens were dedicated to them. Anyone who cut down trees that were not designated to be cut, or who cut down trees in areas consecrated to the gods, or who dirtied those areas, was condemned to suffer in Tālavṛkṣavana. Parks, trees, flower gardens—the picture of Angkor that emerges from these lists of crimes is attractive indeed.

The hell of Kṛminicaya was set up to receive those who denigrated the gods, the sacred fire, the gurus, the Brahmans, the learned ones, the teachers of dharma, Śiva's followers, their mother, their father, their friends. Another hell was reserved for those who denigrated the objects of sacrifice.

Murder is specifically mentioned just once: the murder of women and children. Killing, however, is certainly implied in the statements about burning down villages and similar acts such as poisoning. But it is the arson and the poisoning that lead to the hell, not the killing per se. It seems as though the Khmers edited this list in that regard. Otherwise, it would be hard to explain why the 19 ministers, who had undoubtedly killed soldiers in battle, were rewarded with celestial palaces but no reprisal. Perhaps their loyalty to the king was enough to overcome negative karma, as suggested.

It was also possible to arrive at a hell realm by eating food that was not consecrated, by vandalizing wells and gardens, by being a charlatan or a liar, by desiring someone's death or misfortune, by being insane, by abusing something said in confidence, by being a glutton, a debtor, or an arsonist, by being avaricious. In all, the list is fairly complete and, for the most part, in accord with what other societies and other times have rightly or wrongly condemned. The list lets us know, too, that shoes were costly, that trees inside temples were left alone, that there were sacred and secular parks and gardens, and that alcohol was consumed, no doubt in the 3-day new year's celebration at least. It does not take great imagination to see that more of these transgressions would apply to the lower classes than to their superiors. This pattern, too, seems to fit with the tendencies in other societies and other times. As we leave this dark but fascinating aspect of the society behind, we find that the next

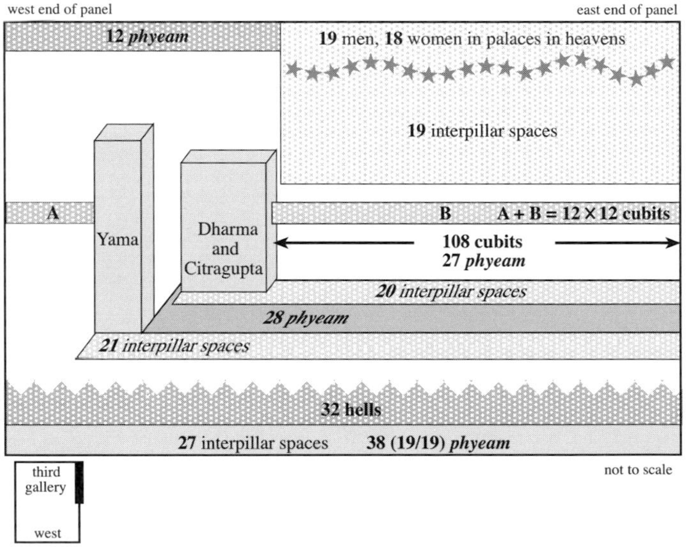

Fig. 5.32. Third gallery, south side, east half, diagram of the heavens and hells.

Even though the hell scenes stretch across the entire base of the panel, the 32 traditional and specific hells are placed directly under the 19 men in the celestial palaces—a caveat to future ministers who might be tempted to stray in their loyalty. Yama, as a judge of the dead as well as king of the ancestors, is placed in the twenty-first bay from the eastern end of the panel. That placement raises his stature above mere kingship, whereas the twentieth position of Dharma and Citragupta make them parallel to King Sūryavarman in the twentieth bay of the procession panel. These types of correspondences suggest a certain ambiguity in the definition of Yama and his assistants and their parallels to Sūryavarman. Nevertheless, the 19/19 halves in the length of the panel, and the 19 bays in front of the 19 ministers in the heavens reveal a close numerical and iconographic connection to the preceding panel of Sūryavarman's procession.

scene around the corner stands in complete opposition to the hells.

THE CHURNING OF THE SEA OF MILK

On the south side of the east wall, after passing through an unsculpted southeast corner pavilion, one soon encounters a crowd of *asura* bystanders looking toward the center of the panel in earnest attention.[28] They evoke an image of the real crowd of onlookers that would have gathered for the king's coronation and enactment of the churning event. Following this group of *asuras*, and dominating the wall for a moment, is the gigantic figure of Bali, their king.[29] He is holding up the multiheaded hood of Vāsuki, the king of *nāgas*, whose body is now being used as the "rope" around the central churning pivot. The fierce *asuras* line up in one long rank, 91 figures, pulling Vāsuki toward the south. Opposite them, 88 gods pull the *nāga* northward. In the middle, a four-armed Viṣṇu holds onto Mount Mandara with two hands and helps churn with the other two (Fig. 5.33, Appendix B, Table 5).

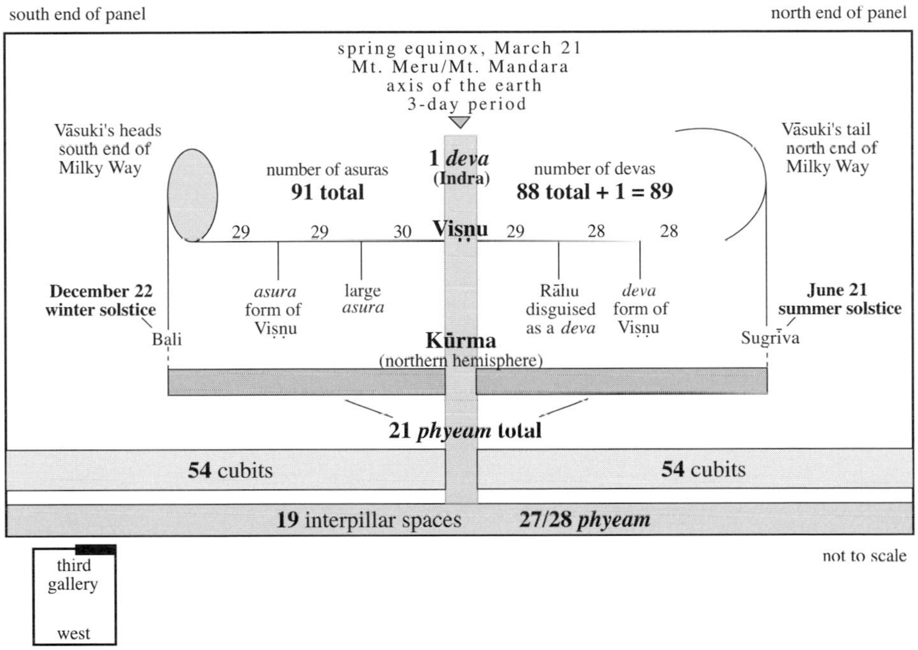

Fig. 5.33. Third gallery, east side, south half, diagram of the Churning of the Sea of Milk.

The churning scene is a calendar of the solar year. At its center is the pivot that marks the three-day equinox period. To our left, the 91 *asuras* stand for the 91 days between the winter solstice and the spring equinox (these dates may change by one day from year to year). To our right, the 88 gods count off the days to the summer solstice. Above the pivot, the god Indra flies down as an alternate eighty-ninth *deva* to make a full 365 days as the yearly calendar moves like a pendulum from one end of the relief to the other. The calendrical content of the relief is emphasized by solar alignments with the major figures on the solstice days (Figs. 5.34–5.36, and 5.38). Other measurements in the relief, such as 54/54, 19, and 27/28 connect this scene to its opposite panel on the west and to the scenes of King Sūryavarman's procession, and the heavens and hells.

There are two interesting aspects of this scene that have not yet been mentioned. One is that the snake Vāsuki lives in the Sea of Milk, which may reflect an origin outside of India. The Babylonian astronomers identified the Milky Way with the "Great Serpent" as early as 1150 B.C., according to cuneiform inscriptions.[30] The serpentine movement of the Milky Way across the night sky, clearly visible outside our light-polluted, smog-bound cities, must have inspired the "Great Serpent" myth in Babylon. The snake Vāsuki and Viṣṇu's support Śeṣa or Ananta, the snake that lies under him in the creation myth, are essentially the same. Their meaning is rooted in astronomy and astrology.

The second novel aspect of the Churning of the Sea of Milk is what happens during the summer and winter solstices. As mentioned briefly in discussing the Battle of Kurukṣetra, at the time of the winter solstice the gods experience their midnight, while the *asuras* on the opposite side of the globe are in full sunlight at high noon. The reverse is true for the summer solstice. During the solstice periods at Angkor Wat, clearly distinguishable shafts of light bracket each side of Mandara and the central Viṣṇu (Figs. 5.34 and 5.35). In effect, the two solstice shafts flank the center of the churning scene just as they flank the center of the Battle of Kurukṣetra.

Because this effect occurs in five separate representations of Viṣṇu on the east and west sides of the gallery, it hardly seems accidental. But before considering why the shafts of light would have been planned, we have more light effects to consider. The tall stand of trees across from the gallery prevents direct sunlight from reaching the Churning of the Sea of Milk until about an hour or so after sunrise. Only a little more than the lower half of the relief, in the best of circumstances, now receives sunlight. Within another hour, the effect is gone and the relief is under the shadow of the roof. And if the trees did not block the light for so long, the flanking shafts of light on the solstice days would be farther away from the figure. The pillar shadows move slowly toward these central figures with the rising sun, about 2 inches (5 cm) every half hour.

The center of the Churning of the Sea of Milk—like all three original relief panels on the east and west—would receive full sunlight only during the spring and autumn equinoxes. Since

Fig. 5.34. Third gallery, east side, south half, Churning of the Sea of Milk, center, winter solstice.

A shaft of light lies to the right of the central Viṣṇu figure during the winter solstice. This same phenomenon occurs in all five representations of Viṣṇu or his avatars on the east and west sides of the gallery. The light shaft runs precisely alongside the central pivot.

the churning event and the Indrābhiṣeka are both associated with the spring equinox, we can assume that the intent was to orient the scene to that time of the year.

During the winter solstice on the northern extreme of the panel, the king of monkeys, Sugrīva, holds onto the tail of Vāsuki—in the shadow of a pillar (Fig. 5.36). Since the monkeys and their king are demigods (their fathers were various gods, their mothers were monkeys), Sugrīva's divine status is signaled by his inclusion in the winter solstice shadow. The father of both Yama and Sugrīva was Sūrya the sun god. Likewise, all the oversize figures of the gods are in

Fig. 5.35. Third gallery, east side, south half, Churning of the Sea of Milk, center, summer solstice.

A shaft of light lies to the left of Viṣṇu during the summer solstice. The same pattern occurs in the other representations of Viṣṇu or his avatars on the east and west sides of the gallery. It does not occur, however, for any other figures. At sunrise the shaft of light would start to move to the left. The light at sunrise is blocked by a stand of trees across from the relief.

Fig. 5.36. Third gallery, east side, south half, Churning of the Sea of Milk, right (north) side, winter solstice.

The monkey king Sugrīva would lie in the shadow of a pillar during the winter solstice period. He marks the summer solstice day in the count of *devas*/calendar days. The gods are in darkness during the winter solstice: it is their midnight.

the shadow of a pillar at this time except for one. One of these figures is in full sunlight—but not accidentally. On closer inspection, this "god" has fangs, slightly larger eyes, a fierce conjoining of his eyebrows, and the headdress of an *asura* (Fig. 5.37). He is most likely the demon Rāhu who insinuated himself into the ranks of the gods to drink the elixir of immortality. The winter solstice sunlight gives him away as surely as if he were labeled and stamped.

While the center of this relief (Viṣṇu, Mount Mandara, Kūrma, and Indra) is in shadow at the winter solstice, and while the oversize gods and Sugrīva are in shadow, the opposite is true for the *asuras*. Bali himself is in light (Fig. 5.38); the oversize *asura* closest to the churning pivot is also in full sunlight (Fig. 5.39); but surprisingly the farthest *asura* on the left lies in the shadow of a pillar (Fig. 5.40). According to this shadow effect, he should be a god.

Fig. 5.37. Third gallery, east side, south half, Churning of the Sea of Milk, right (north) side, large asura *figure in the line of* devas.
This figure must be Rāhu, who stealthily joined the *devas* to drink the elixir of immortality. He is easily identified by his headdress, his fangs, his trimmed beard that frames his lower jaw and comes to a point at his chin, and the added frown line at the joining of his eyebrows. Rāhu failed in his efforts, however, and had his head separated from his body by Viṣṇu's *cakra*. In revenge, he swallows the sun and moon in eclipses.

This latter *asura,* grandiose and elegant, might be none other than Viṣṇu himself. In order to fully assist in the churning effort, Viṣṇu assumed the additional forms of an *asura* and a *deva.* Since the one large *asura* is singled out by the shadow of a pillar and a shaft of light during the winter solstice, he is the most logical choice for the manifestation of Lord Viṣṇu (Fig. 5.41). Similarly, the remaining (and only) oversize *deva* on the north, on the far right, must be the *deva* manifestation of Viṣṇu (Fig. 2.16). He is in darkness during the winter solstice, which is appropriate, but he is also in darkness during the summer solstice (Fig. 5.42). Just why does this happen?

At the winter solstice, all six of the oversize figures in the relief, as well as the central, axial figures, are correctly related to light and shadow. During the summer solstice period, Sugrīva is in bright sunlight (Fig. 5.43) and Bali, at Vāsuki's head in the south, is in darkness. In the winter, the reverse is true. Therefore, the equations of Sugrīva = summer solstice and Bali = winter solstice are

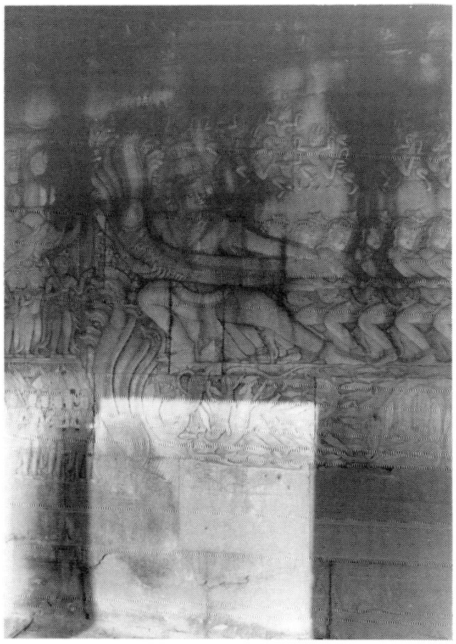

(Fig. 5.38)

(Fig. 5.39)

(Fig. 5.40)

Third gallery, east side, south half, Churning of the Sea of Milk, left (south) side, winter solstice.

At sunrise during the winter solstice, Bali the king of the *asura*s would be in full sunlight (Fig. 5.38). His position and his place in the sequence of 91 *asura*s (including himself) correspond to the winter solstice day. That day marks 12:00 noon for the *asura*s at the south celestial pole.

The first large *asura* to the left (south) just after the churning pivot would also be in full sunlight at sunrise on the winter solstice day (Fig. 5.39).

The remaining large *asura* on the south, closest to Bali, not only lies in the shadow of a pillar on the winter solstice day, but is marked by a shaft of light to the right (Fig. 5.40). Since only figures of Viṣṇu are marked by flanking right or left shafts of light on the solstices, this figure must be the *asura* form assumed by Viṣṇu to help in the churning effort (see Fig. 5.46).

Fig. 5.41. Third gallery, east side, south half, Churning of the Sea of Milk, left (south) side, winter solstice.

During the normal light of day, the large *asura* form of Viṣṇu has no traits that betray his true identity. It is only in interaction with the winter and summer solstice sunlight that he is defined as Viṣṇu.

Fig. 5.42. Third gallery, east side, south half, Churning of the Sea of Milk, right (north) side, winter solstice.

The only large *deva* on the north, closest to Sugrīva and the tail of Vāsuki, must be the *deva* form assumed by Viṣṇu. Not only is there is no other large *deva* in the lineup on the north, but this figure is also flanked to the right and left by shafts of light during the winter and summer solstices, respectively.

indicated by the solstice light and shadow. In the count of 91 *asuras* and 88/89 *devas*, moreover, Bali is the "day" of the winter solstice and Sugrīva is the "day" of the summer solstice. So far, the summer and winter solstice light accords with the positioning of the gods and antigods at the north and south celestial poles.

As we advance to the next oversize figure on each side, however, the light/dark relationships change because these are the suggested figures of Viṣṇu in his guise as *asura* and *deva*. Leaving these two images aside for the moment, we find that the summer solstice light/shadow alternation is not so

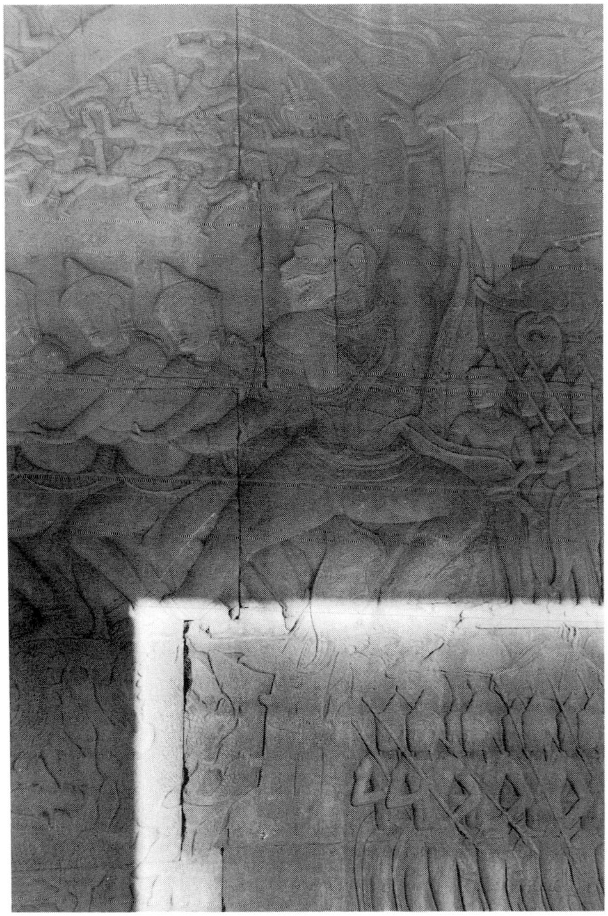

Fig. 5.43. Third gallery, east side, south half, Churning of the Sea of Milk, right (north) side, summer solstice.

Sugrīva at the tail of Vāsuki would be in full sunlight on the summer solstice day, when the sun is farthest north in the sky. Based on his position in the line of 88 *devas*, Sugrīva himself would symbolize the summer solstice day.

well defined in the large *deva* and *asura* that are closest to the churning pivot. On the north, the large *deva* has the face and headdress of an *asura,* and it was suggested earlier that this figure is Rāhu. Rāhu is in sunlight during the winter solstice, which associates him with the *asuras*, but during the summer solstice he would be only partly in shadow (Fig. 5.44), perhaps one-half of his figure at most. The oversize *asura* closest to the central pivot, and parallel in position to Rāhu on the south, is still in sunlight in the summer solstice for the most part (Fig. 5.45). There is no explanation why the iconography of the summer solstice light and shade is less accurate with this figure and partially inaccurate with the Rāhu figure. Nevertheless, the winter solstice effect is accurate for all six oversize figures and the center of the relief, while the summer solstice light is appropriate for four of the six oversize figures and for the center of the scene.

Like the center of this scene, both the *asura* and *deva* forms of Viṣṇu mentioned earlier have the same effect: they have flanking shafts of sunlight at both solstices. The bar of light is to the north side of the figure during the winter solstice and to the south during the summer solstice (Figs. 5.40 and 5.46). At the summer solstice the shaft of light to the left of the *deva* form of Viṣṇu is slim and barely discernible, but it is there. During the equinox days, these figures would be completely illuminated by the sun. With respect to the solar calendar and sunlight, then, these two possible *asura* and *deva* forms of Viṣṇu are no different than the central forms of Viṣṇu on the east and west sides of the gallery. Not only are they identically placed in relation to the sunlight, but there are no other major figures in the reliefs that are similarly placed. These shafts of light also appear on either side of Rāma in the Battle of Laṅkā scene during the solstice days (Fig. 5.47).

The five manifestations of Viṣṇu on the east and west are:

1. Churning of the Sea of Milk: Viṣṇu and

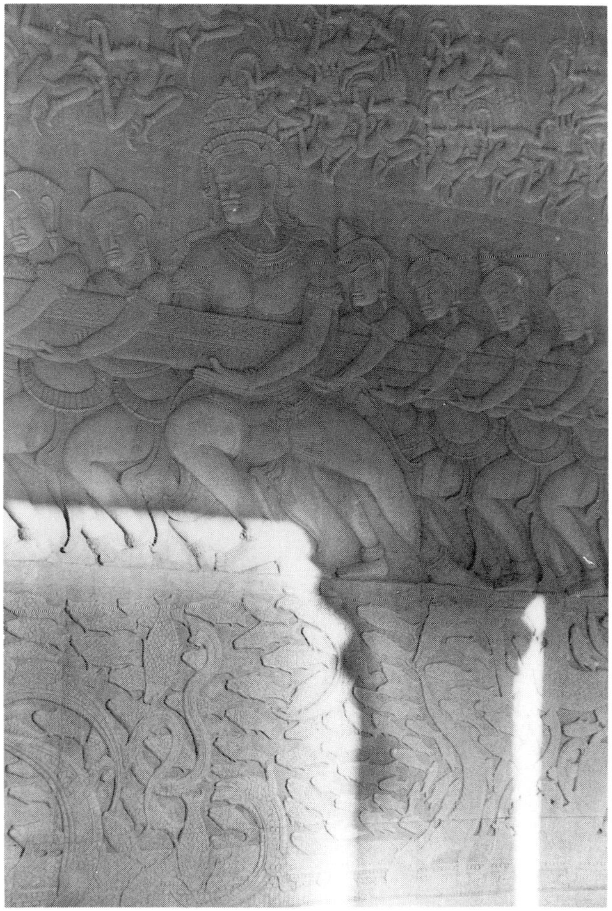

Fig. 5.44. Third gallery, east side, south half, Churning of the Sea of Milk, center, summer solstice.

At sunrise during the summer solstice, the figure of Rāhu would be about one-third in darkness since the shadow of the pillar would cover more of the figure. At this time of year, the shadow moves to the right as the sun rises and the darkness descends down the wall. Perhaps this light and dark dichotomy in Rāhu is appropriate since he swallows the sun in eclipses.

Kūrma, with Indra and Mount Mandara at the center of the scene

2. Churning of the Sea of Milk: oversize *asura* on the far left
3. Churning of the Sea of Milk: oversize *deva* on the far right
4. Battle of Kurukṣetra: Pāṇḍu leader killing an enemy chief
5. Battle of Laṅkā: Rāma on Hanuman

The pattern of the solstice light for each of these figures is the same: the shaft of light is to the south at the summer solstice and to the north at the winter solstice. Because Rāma and the Pāṇḍu leader are on the west side of Angkor Wat, the "right" and "left" directions of the bar of light are reversed, though north and south stay the same.

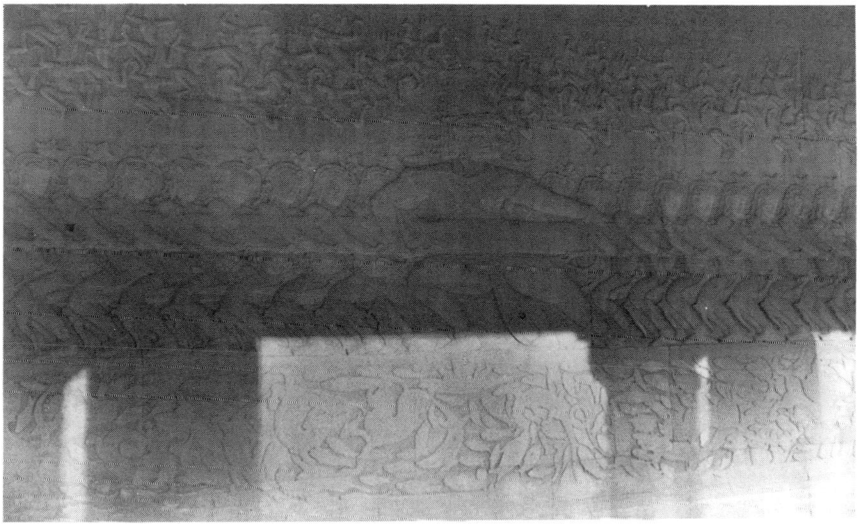

Fig. 5.45. Third gallery, east side, south half, Churning of the Sea of Milk, left (south) side, summer solstice.

The large *asura* closest to the churning pivot would be mostly in sunlight during the summer solstice. This runs counter to the cosmology, however, for he should be in complete shadow. Aside from the anomaly of Rāhu at this same time of year, this figure is the only exception to the pattern of solstice light in the relief.

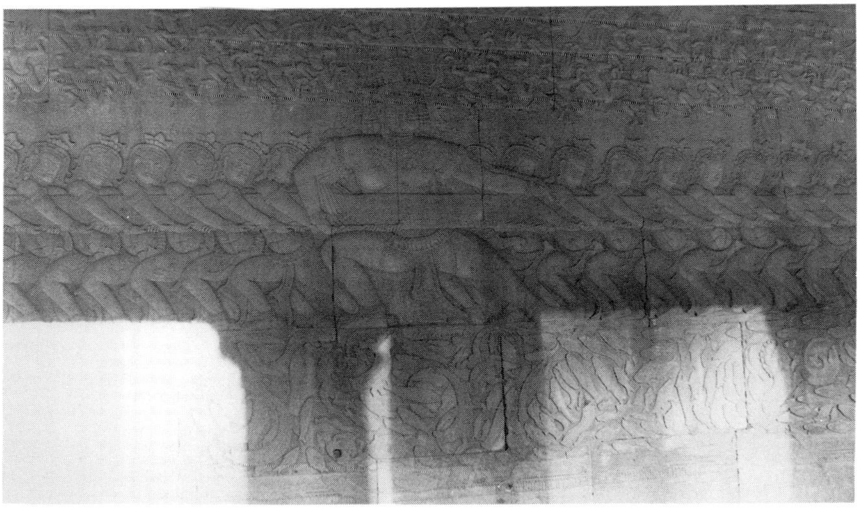

Fig. 5.46. Third gallery, east side, south half, Churning of the Sea of Milk, left (south) side, summer solstice.

The suggested *asura* form of Viṣṇu has a shaft of light to the left during the summer solstice and one to the right during the winter solstice (Fig. 5.40). At sunrise, the shaft of light would be more to the left. It moves to the right (north) as the sun rises and the shadow of the roof descends over the relief.

Fig. 5.47. Third gallery, west side, south half, Battle of Laṅkā.

As the sun sets during the winter solstice, a shaft of light rises to the left (north) of Rāma on Hanuman. Vibhīṣaṇa the brother of Rāvaṇa standing at the lower left next to Lakṣmaṇa, is in the process of emerging into full sunlight. At the summer solstice, the light shaft is to the right (south) of Rāma. Although the right/left correspondence with the light shafts on the east side of the gallery is reversed, the north/south position of the winter/summer solstice light shaft is the same on the east and west.

On the west side of Angkor Wat, the light forms a pattern on Rāma and on the central figures in the Battle of Kurukṣetra that is reversed for the center of the Churning scene, and the large end *asura* and *deva* on the east side of the gallery (Fig. 5.48).

In summary, then, we have five representations of Viṣṇu, or a Viṣṇu-related figure, on the east and west sides of Angkor Wat. All five are bracketed by solstice sunlight; all five receive full sunlight during the spring and autumn equinoxes. The bracketing does not seem to be random. In fact, a similar effect appears in the *preau cruciforme,* as we shall see, in relation to the central image there.

Each of the five representations of Viṣṇu fills the "space" between the shafts of solstice light just as the western entrances and corridors fill the space between the solstice alignments of the end gateways. At the center are Mount Meru, the axis of the earth, Brahmā, Viṣṇu, and the equinoxes: these components occupy the same vertical axis. In the bas-reliefs, each incarnation or image of Viṣṇu appears to be a symbol for all the components at the equinox "center." The very fact that Viṣṇu is superimposed on Mount Mandara (a stand-in for Mount Meru in the ordinary—not astronomical—understanding of the scene), that Kūrma is at the base of Mandara and Brahmā normally at the top, is one type of visual expression of their inseparability. They illustrate the meaning of the measurements and position of the tower in the central western entrance of Angkor Wat.

From another perspective, because the bas-relief images of Viṣṇu are *bracketed* by the solstice sun, the central image of Viṣṇu cannot be placed with the gods at the north celestial pole by experiencing full sunlight as they do during their noon

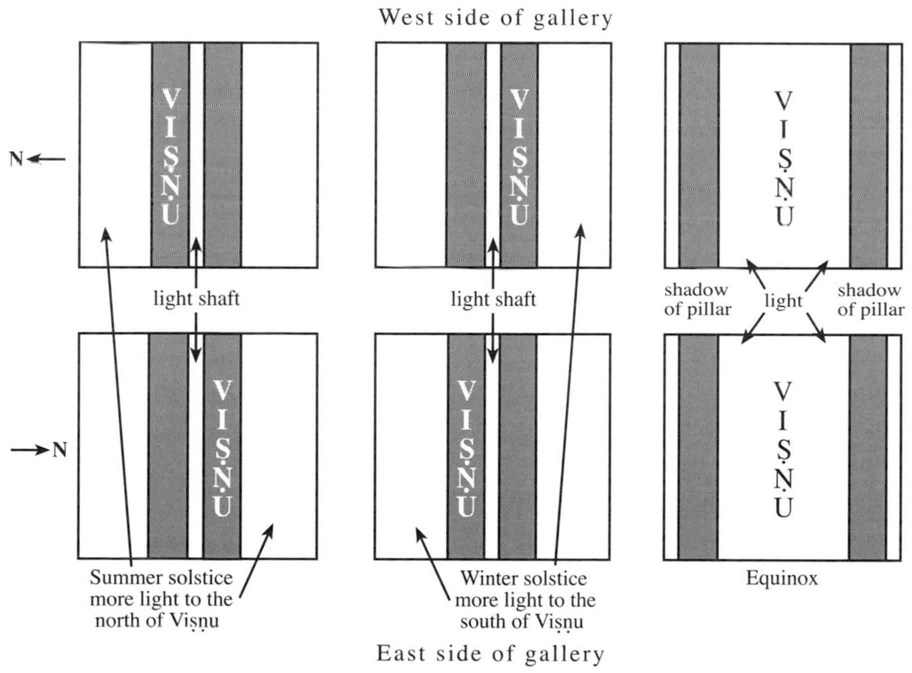

Fig. 5.48. Third gallery, Viṣṇu or his incarnation in bas-reliefs, winter and summer solstice sunlight patterns.

During the winter solstice when the *asuras* are in full sunlight to the south, Viṣṇu or the figures representing Viṣṇu in the bas-reliefs are in the shadow of a pillar. Each Viṣṇu figure has one bay of light to the south and the small shaft of light to the north. The quantity of sunlight flanking Viṣṇu corresponds to the distribution of sunlight on the earth. During the summer solstice, the light distribution is reversed and so is the ratio of light on either side of Viṣṇu.

at the summer solstice. Nor does the main image of Viṣṇu rank with the *asuras* at the south celestial pole, experiencing full sunlight during the winter solstice. He is literally in the center, equated with Mount Meru as an axis, between the gods and antigods, between shafts of light, while the sun is in the northern or southern celestial realms.

This central position of Viṣṇu is in keeping with his placement at the center of all the bas-relief panels and almost every scene and lintel in which he appears, not to mention the center of Angkor Wat. Although he is a god, he cannot be limited to the realm of the gods. He is at the heart of creation: the north celestial pole and the *devas* are above him; the south celestial pole and the *asuras* are beneath him. Thus he is bracketed by the north/south, *deva/asura,* summer/winter solstice light.

The quantity of solstice light on either side of Viṣṇu also places him at the center of the earth and the center of the celestial sphere around us. During the winter solstice the south pole is angled toward the sun and so it receives 24 hours of light. Most of the sunlight hitting the earth at that time is south of the equator and progressively less north of the equator, culminating in 24 hours of darkness at the north pole. During the winter solstice, the Viṣṇu figures have one full bay of sunlight next to them on the south, and the small shaft of light next to them on the north. The contrast in light on either side illustrates the same division in the quantity of sunlight south and north of the equator at this time. The reverse is true for the summer solstice (Fig. 5.48).

The Churning of the Sea of Milk at Angkor Wat is one of the most multifaceted and profound representations of cosmology, history, and the calendar in Khmer art. The number and placement of its figures diagram the 6-month calendar between the winter solstice, spring equinox, and summer solstice. The light and shadow cast by the sun during the solstice periods not only expands and amplifies the meaning of this calendrical division but singles out the major players in the scene in a variety of ways.

Because the churning event was in all likelihood enacted during the coronation of King Sūryavarman, it alludes to that auspicious moment in history. Since it is placed opposite the Battle of Kurukṣetra on the west wall, and since it is divided in half by a 54/54-cubit measurement and two opposing forces just like the Kurukṣetra scene, it suggests distinct parallels between the forces of King Sūryavarman and the gods and between the king and Viṣṇu as well as Indra. The genius, creativity, and inspiration of the unknown Khmer architects of Angkor Wat found full expression in this remarkable panel. When its multiple symbolism is considered in conjunction with the delicacy, precision, and grace of its sculpting, the panel is all the more incredible. Aesthetics, astronomy, mythology, and history are the multicolored threads that weave this scene from Indian epic literature—and continue to form intricate patterns in the bas-reliefs to follow.

6

Warriors Regal and Divine: The Northern Bas-Reliefs in the Third Gallery

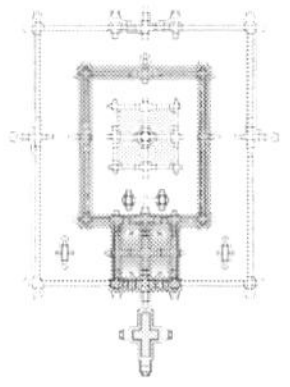

THE remaining bas-reliefs in the third gallery forgo the multiplicity of themes found in the southern half and focus primarily on battles between opposing forces of good yet war-prone *devas*, and bad, equally warlike, *asuras*. Two of these panels were sculpted in the sixteenth century and are discussed in inscriptions carved next to them at their northeast end.[1] The first, dating from September 8, 1546, reads:

> His Majesty Mahāviṣṇuloka had not yet finished two panels; and when H.M. Vraḥ Rājaoṇkāra Paramarājādhirāja Rāmādhipati Paramacakravartirāja ascended the throne, he ordered Vraḥ Mahīdhara, of the royal artisans, to sculpt a story on the panels. . . . in the eighth *śāka* year (of the decade), year of the Horse, Wednesday, full moon of Bhadrapāda.

The second inscription, dating from February 27, 1564, says:

> His Majesty Mahāviṣṇuloka had not yet finished two panels; and when H.M. Vraḥ Rājaoṇkāra Paramarājādhirāja Rāmādhipati Paramacakravartirāja ascended the throne, he had a story sculpted. They were finished in 1485 *śāka,* year of the Pig, full moon of Phālguna, Sunday. The two galleries and the balustrade were solidly finished, as in the past.

The first king (Mahāviṣṇuloka) in the inscriptions is most likely Ang Chan (1529–1546), who would have begun the late bas-reliefs. The second king, with the long name, would have been his son, who was crowned in 1546. The comment that "the two galleries and the balustrade were solidly finished, as in the past," means that the restoration of Angkor Wat began in the sixteenth century.

In a counterclockwise sequence, the first of these later panels opens, continues, and closes with a jumbled mix of *asuras*, riding animal mounts, attacking Viṣṇu who holds his own at the center of the action.[2] Viṣṇu is not in the grandiose scale of his other depictions in the gallery, and the artistry in the reliefs falls short of twelfth-century standards (Fig. 6.1).[3] Nevertheless, the panel is a good attempt at trying to capture the drama of the other scenes in the gallery.

There are 21 interpillar spaces in front of the panel, with 10 of those spaces on each side of the central Viṣṇu, making Viṣṇu a twenty-first component. This numerically significant division was planned in the twelfth century—along with the 29.54-*phyeam* length of the relief. This precise record of the lunar month (29.53 days long) suggests that the intended subject of the original panel must have had lunar connotations. Perhaps Brahmā was meant to be depicted here. Other than these two measurements of 21 and 29.54, the relief has no further significant measurements, directional markers, or figure groupings (Appendix B, Table 6).

The next sixteenth-century panel is the same in this regard. After walking through the northeast corner pavilion, which has no interior reliefs, we encounter the scene on the eastern side of the north wall depicting Kṛṣṇa's victory over the *asura* Bāṇa.[4] The tale revolves around the kidnapping of Aniruddha, who was brought to Śonitapura to marry the daughter of Bāṇa. When the guards tell Bāṇa that Aniruddha was found with his daughter, Aniruddha is captured and bound. Kṛṣṇa, Bala, and Pradyumna hear of Aniruddha's capture and fly to Śonitapura to rescue him. Before fully entering the city, Kṛṣṇa "demolishes the five fires" and then annihilates the *asura*'s army. Kṛṣṇa does personal combat with Bāṇa, cutting off all the *asura*'s arms and then threatening to throw his discus and cut off the *asura*'s head. At this point Śiva intervenes on Bāṇa's part. Kṛṣṇa, acknowledging the similarities between Śiva and himself, says: "That which I am, thou art; and that also is this world, with its gods, demons, and mankind. Men contemplate distinctions but they are stupefied by ignorance."[5] He then spares the *asura*. The three heroes subsequently free Aniruddha and return home.

While the story itself is simple, the panel simplifies it even further. Garuḍa is shown near the beginning of the panel extinguishing a large fire, probably a symbol for the five fires of the legend. Agni is depicted on his uniquely Khmer mount, a rhinoceros. Bāṇa is shown fiercely defending himself. Kṛṣṇa, Pradyumna, and Balarāma, or Rāma, are depicted on the mount Garuḍa six different times. At the end of the scene, Śiva is shown on a mountaintop accepting Kṛṣṇa's homage and, presumably, pleading for Bāṇa's life. There are 27 interpillar spaces across the length of this panel as mentioned earlier in relation to the scenes of heavens and hells. This is its only significant measurement (Appendix B, Table 7).[6]

Following these mid-sixteenth-century scenes there is a return to the twelfth century in the sculpting of a battle between *devas* and *asuras*. A total of 21 oversize *devas*, all in epic battle posture, move across a sea of soldiers and warriors as they each fight an individual *asura* (Appendix B, Table 8).[7] Certain *devas*, such as the sun or Varuṇa, are easily recognizable (Figs. 6.2 and 6.3). As noted earlier, Viṣṇu is the tenth in sequence just as Sūryavarman in the opposite panel is the tenth in his procession (Appendix B, Table 8). King Sūryavarman and Indra are the pivot from which the procession of ministers or fighting gods expands outward in each direction. At the center

Fig. 6.1. Third gallery, east side, north half, battle of Viṣṇu with the asuras.

At the center and top of the scene, Viṣṇu is astride Garuḍa in a less than classic posture. As one indication of the loss of tradition over a 300-year period, Viṣṇu holds the *cakra* in his upper left hand and the conch in his upper right—a mistake in that they are reversed from their traditional position in Khmer representations of Viṣṇu. The god is the same size as the other figures, and Garuḍa is smaller than usual. The figures in these later reliefs are extremely flat, lacking the subtle curvature found throughout the twelfth-century panels. There are also fewer overlapping planes.

of their lineup of figures, Indra and Sūryavarman would be facing each other in royal splendor, each on their respective elephants, if there were no gallery to separate them.

Other than finding Agni in the general vicinity of the sacred fire if the reliefs could be superimposed, there are no other significant correspondences outside of the king, Indra, and Viṣṇu. This means that the commanders in the procession of the king and the fighting *devas* opposite them were placed according to an internal logic, not in relation to each other. In the procession scene, rank may have determined the order of figures, perhaps in conjunction with the ministers' geographic areas. In the procession of *devas*, the reason for their order has been difficult to determine. Nevertheless, based on the characteristics of the planetary deities in the northwest pavilion, explained in detail below, the identity of 6 of these 21 gods might be related to a specific planet. These correlations would be, from right (west) to left (east), that is, from the beginning to the end of the sequence:

Varuṇa	Mercury
Sūrya	Sun
Indra	Jupiter
Skanda	Mars
Agni	Saturn
Kubera	Venus

The planets rose and set in this sequence between September 6–11 and 16–21, 1115; July 27–August 1 and August 6–31, 1117; and from December 23–28, 1121, to February 7, 1122.[8] The sequence does not repeat again very often during King Sūryavarman's reign—not before 1126 at least. In 1123 and 1124, the young king seems to have been fighting the Chams who were causing trouble along the border with Cambodia. Both Chams and Khmers sought protection at the court of the Dai Viet (in the northern part of Vietnam) during the spring of 1123. The coincidence of an early 1122 date, symbolized in this relief, and the fighting

Fig. 6.2. Third gallery, north side, west half, battle of the devas *and* asuras.

Sūrya the sun god is distinguished by the solar disk behind him. As he points his arrow at an enemy, his charioteer, a winged *garuḍa*, brandishes a sword. This is another corroboration that the long-ago association of eagle and sun in the Sumer-Akkadian world found its way to Angkor thousands of years later.

with the Chams might be intentional. In this case the battle scene would refer to the king's first battles after he came to power. Since the procession scene opposite is one of ministers who also commanded soldiers, the military connection between the panels is logical.

There is evidence to suggest that the Battle of Laṅkā in the next panel occurred around 1131 or 1132 and represented one of the king's major battles against the Dai Viet. Thus we might have a connection between the king's victory parade into Angkor (south side, west half) and his first battles against the Chams (north side, west half), followed by a second series of battles against the Dai Viet (west side, north half). This pattern would organize the reliefs on the western half of the temple into one iconographically cohesive unit. In the Kurukṣetra scene we would have the king's battle against the Khmers when he came to power (west side, south half), his victory scene, and his battles against the Chams and the Dai Viet.

Certainly the western half of the temple was the focus of work. The two western corner pavilions are completely sculpted with bas-reliefs, and all the wall panels on the western half are complete. In contrast, the eastern half of the gallery has no sculpting in the corner pavilions, two panels were left blank, and the center of the churning scene is unfinished.

The king was most likely crowned in 1119 when he was 20 years old in one of the major ceremonies of his reign. That event would date the Churning of the Sea of Milk to 1119, with the Battle of the *Deva*s and *Asura*s symbolizing a battle in 1122 or 1123. This would place the events of the two originally intended panels on each side of the northeast corner between 1119 and 1122 if the chronological sequence in the relief program were to continue, following a counterclockwise movement.

Although completely hypothetical, a marriage scene after the churning event, on the east, oppo-

Fig. 6.3. Third gallery, north side, west half, battle of the devas *and* asuras.

Varuṇa rides a multiheaded *nāga* guided by a standing driver holding the reins connected to the uppermost head. Varuṇa is the god of water and thus is intimately connected to the *nāga*s and their world. In this relief, Varuṇa may also be a symbol for the planet Mercury, part of a planetary sequence depicted here.

site the Battle of Laṅkā would have been logical in many respects. First of all, the king obviously did get married since an inscription refers to his first wife. Moreover, the subject would be appropriate for an eastern direction, and the Battle of Laṅkā opposite was fought to return Sītā to her husband. The lunar measurement of this panel would also accord with a female component, and it would be a way of honoring the queen. There is a marriage scene in the northwest pavilion; there is a possible marriage scene in the reliefs of the Bayon; and in the southwest pavilion, royal women are holding children in the nautical scene.

The panel that was to be sculpted across from the scenes of heavens and hells is much more difficult to hypothesize. Perhaps it was meant to depict some sort of ceremonial installation of the 19 ministers, before going to battle. But these two panels were never even started. In the end, it does not really matter what was intended to inform this wall space: the space remained blank.

It does not appear that there was much time to work on these reliefs. Based on the measurements of the axes, the Viṣṇu image in the central sanctuary would have been installed in 1126, and perhaps Divākara died in that year. Two years later, 20,000 soldiers were sent against the Dai Viet and killed. If the date of 1131 or 1132 for a real battle symbolized in the Battle of Laṅkā scene is meant to refer to the history of the king, then the western half of the gallery was planned after those dates. The king continued to suffer defeats against the Dai Viet, and by 1136, the final defeat, he stopped. That left only 8 years of relative peace before major campaigns against the Chams resumed. Other than the death of the king, I cannot imagine what would cause the sculptors to put down their tools and leave the center of the churning scene unfinished. Other decorative reliefs were just as suddenly stopped when only a few more hours of work could have completed them.

Perhaps the relief program was planned after 1136—when the Battle of Laṅkā could no longer symbolize a total victory of the Khmers over the Dai Viet (a victory of Rāma over Rāvaṇa). The relief could not exactly show a defeat, and so the reality of Sūryavarman's loss was presented in the best light: a stand-off between Rāma and Rāvaṇa. Moreover, by 1136 the corridors may have been up in the third gallery. It is difficult to say. The sculptors could not begin work until the gallery was constructed because the walls were not smoothed down until they were in place. Sculpting would have been focused on the center of the temple and western entrances until those areas were fairly finished. It is likely, as a matter of practicality, that the temple was constructed from the top of the pyramid outward and downward. The western entrances, however, would have demanded early attention.

Thus the sculpting of the bas-relief panels was probably begun later in the reign of the king, even as late as the 1140s. In any case, the sculptors did not have time to finish. The story was over before it could be completely told, and the loss to Angkor Wat is our loss as well.

THE NORTHWEST CORNER PAVILION

Just like the southwest corner pavilion, whose scenes create a transition between the large bas-relief panels that precede and follow the pavilion, the northwest corner pavilion provides a transition between the Battle of the 21 *Deva*s before it and the Battle of Laṅkā after it.[9] The Battle of Laṅkā, the epic culmination of the *Rāmāyaṇa,* signals the victory of Rāma over Rāvaṇa (the king of Laṅkā) and his army of *rākṣasa*s.

Upon entering the northwest pavilion after the Battle of 21 *Deva*s and *Asura*s, we see Viṣṇu to the right, above the window, lying on the Sea of Milk

(Fig. 6.4). A procession of *devas* moves in single file beneath him, across the top of the window. These *devas* form the sequence of planets suggested earlier. Eight or perhaps nine of the twelve scenes in the pavilion, including the four lintels, refer to episodes from the *Rāmāyaṇa*. The *devas* under Viṣṇu are most likely on their way to ask him to incarnate as Rāma and his three brothers in order to destroy Rāvaṇa. This request sets the stage for the rest of the reliefs in the pavilion.

Kṛṣṇa, mounted on Garuḍa, is to the left opposite Viṣṇu lying on the Sea of Milk. He is carrying home Mount Maṇiparvata, recently recaptured from the demon Narada (Figs. 3.1 and 5.11). In this story, Indra pleads for help in vanquishing Narada, who has made off with almost all the attractive maidens of the gods and kings. He also took the peak of Mount Meru (Maṇiparvata) and threatened to take Indra's majestic elephant-mount, Airāvata. Kṛṣṇa agrees to help and conquers Narada, bringing home Mount Maṇiparvata in triumph.[10] Taken in conjunction with the request for

Fig. 6.4. Third gallery, northwest pavilion, east wing, north wall, Viṣṇu lying on the Sea of Milk.

Lakṣmī kneels at the feet of Viṣṇu, holding his legs on her lap and rubbing his upper leg to awaken him from sleep. The upper torso and head of Viṣṇu, as well as the heads of the *nāga* Ananta, have been defaced. The series of suggested planets travels in single file to our right, beneath the reclining god.

Viṣṇu to incarnate, these two panels (the request and victory scenes) might have been intended to symbolize the beginning of the chain of events that ended with the Battle of Laṅkā and victory. The two reliefs, as noted earlier, also parallel their counterparts in the southwest pavilion.

Turning the left corner and walking south, we encounter a depiction of Rāma shooting his bow at the target of a bird perched on a wheel (Fig. 5.15). The various figures in the relief, such as Sītā on a throne, establish the scene as both the marriage of Sītā and Rāma and also his "test" to win her hand.[11] In the southwest pavilion, a scene of the annual water festival parallels this test of Rāma and his marriage (Fig. 5.14). Both scenes feature queens, both are celebrations, and both contain members of the court.

Across from this scene, a four-armed Viṣṇu is depicted seated on a mountaintop (Fig. 5.13). A kingly figure is paying him homage on the right; many women, or celestial maidens, are coming hurriedly up the mountain to offer Viṣṇu flowers. In the lower registers, the same women dance and rejoice. Viṣṇu is holding a pearl-like object between the thumb and forefinger of his right hand; his lower left hand holds a small conical container in his lap.

The only section of the *Rāmāyaṇa* in which Viṣṇu appears as himself and not an incarnation is in Book I, when Viṣṇu decides to incarnate as Rāma and his three brothers to kill the demon Rāvaṇa.[12] The rejoicing and offerings in this scene might be in response to that decision. Viṣṇu on his mountaintop is directly parallel to Śiva on a mountaintop in the southwest pavilion (Fig. 5.12). Both these scenes are to our right as we exit their respective pavilions to view the next major relief panel, and both are identical in composition and content.

All but one of the four remaining scenes in the pavilion are from the *Rāmāyaṇa*. On the northern and western arms of the pavilion, Rāma's wife Sītā is praised for her virtue and endurance. In the former instance, she is put through a trial by fire to test her fidelity; in the latter, she hands Hanuman a pearl that would identify her to Rāma. After being captured by Rāvaṇa and taken to Laṅkā, Sītā remained faithful to Rāma throughout her captivity. Hanuman, the commander of the monkey warriors who helps Rāma defeat Rāvaṇa, is dispatched to find Sītā and report back to Rāma. He does so, and Sītā is then rescued and the battle at Laṅkā won by Rāma's forces. Sītā's virtue, however, is called into question. When she survives the fire to test her purity, her loyalty to Rāma is proved (Fig. 6.5).

On the wall opposite Hanuman and Sītā, Rāma and his allies return triumphantly to Ayodhyā, their capital city, after the victory in Laṅkā. Their mode of transport is the flying chariot Puṣpaka, here shown on the wings of several *haṁsa* or mythical geese. Originally there were two figures next to Rāma in the relief, but today they are eroded (Fig. 6.6). According to the story, the figures with Rāma should be Vibhīṣaṇa (the brother of Rāvaṇa and ally of Rāma), Lakṣmaṇa (Rāma's brother), Sugrīva, and Sītā.[13] Two of these four figures would have been placed to the right and left of Rāma and two just below him.

The remaining panel on the east wall of the northern arm of the pavilion is opposite Sītā's trial by fire. It is a scene of Kṛṣṇa receiving homage and allegiance from a few seated men, in particular from one royal figure next to Kṛṣṇa (Fig. 6.7). The scene cannot be specifically identified and is all the more curious for what look like the bodies of two drowned men stretched out under Kṛṣṇa and his visitors. Whatever the legendary or historical allusions may have been, the scene is obviously meant to praise Kṛṣṇa by using a narrative or episode from stories familiar to the Khmers in the twelfth century.

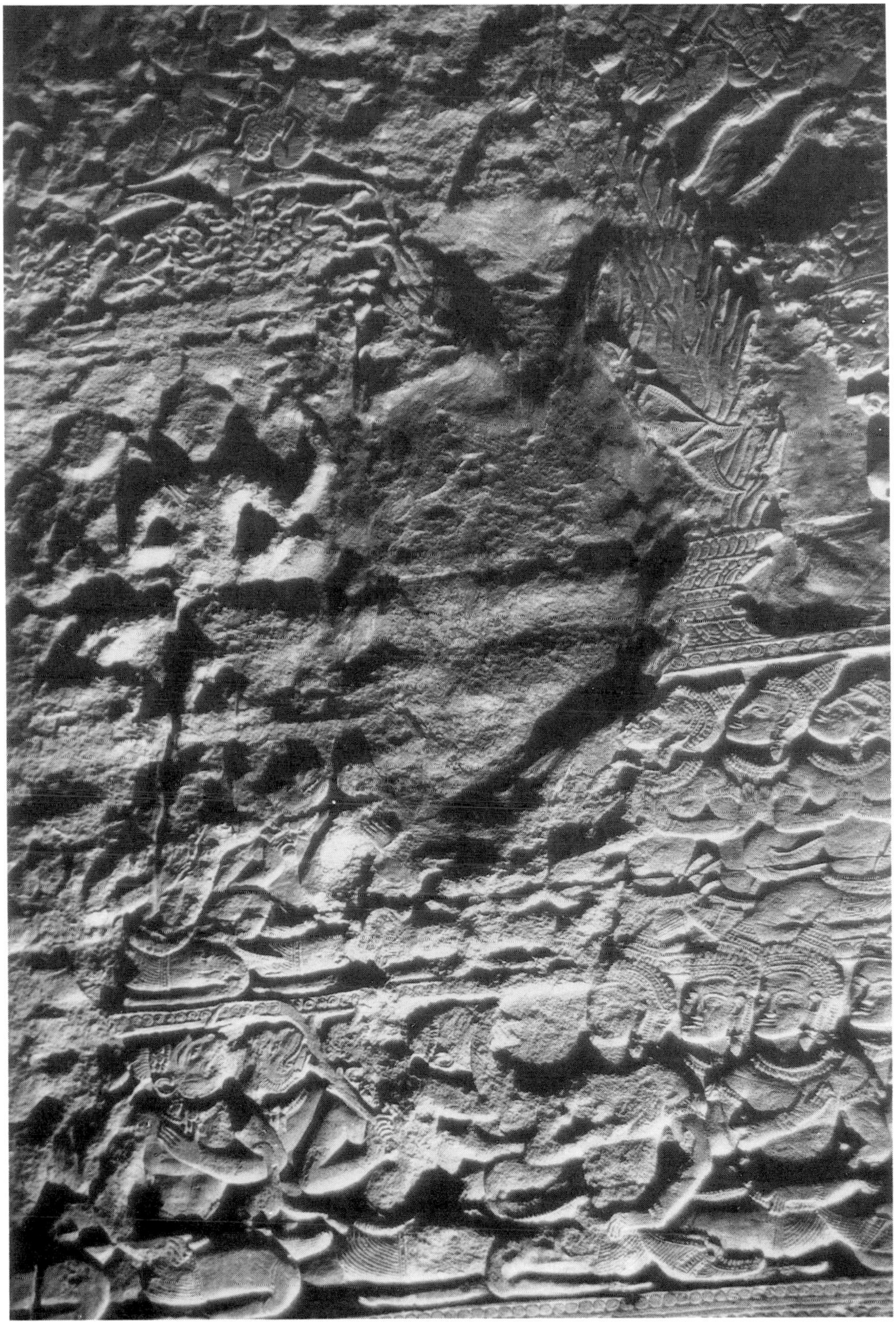

Fig. 6.5. Third gallery, northwest pavilion, north wing, west wall, trial of Sītā by fire.

The entire body of Sītā, except for a small segment of her flying drapery at the upper right, has been intentionally effaced. The flames of the fire rise in a triangular movement from an ornately carved, waisted pedestal. Sītā is present in all four of the panels that explicitly refer to the *Rāmāyaṇa* in this pavilion.

Fig. 6.6. Third gallery, northwest pavilion, west wing, north wall, return of Rāma on Puṣpaka.

Whether eroded or effaced or both, the major figures that sit next to and under Rāma in this victorious return to his capital city are now missing. There would have been Sītā to the right, Lakṣmaṇa to the left, and Vibhīṣaṇa and Sugrīva below. This victory scene happens after the Battle of Laṅkā, the subject of the large relief panel just after this pavilion.

The two pairs of lintels in this pavilion complement each other, as they did in the southwest pavilion. Over the eastern entrance to the pavilion, Rāma and Sugrīva pledge their alliance; over the western doorway, the alliance of Rāma and Vibhīṣaṇa is depicted. In contrast to these alliances, essential for victory in the Battle of Laṅkā, Rāma and Lakṣmaṇa are shown in combat with the demon Virādha over the doorways on the north and south. On the north, Virādha captures Sītā; on the south, Virādha carries Rāma and Lakṣmaṇa into the forest.[14] The themes of captivity and alliance emphasized in the two sets of paired lintels would have their historical counterparts in the many times the king forged—or forced—alliances with the Chams.

The scenes from the *Rāmāyaṇa* in the northwest pavilion follow no particular sequence: stories from that epic are interspersed with events completely unrelated to it. Nor is there any obvious sequence to the reliefs in the southwest corner pavilion. If sequence is not a factor in the arrangement of the reliefs, either their depiction is random or it follows some other logical pattern. In fact, there seems to be a certain geometrical outline in the placement of the reliefs. The scenes in the northwest pavilion may form two swastika patterns based on their content, composition, and position in the chamber (Fig. 6.8). When seen as a totality, the scenes divide into four pairs:

1a. Kṛṣṇa returns victorious on Mount Maṇiparvata
1b. Rāma returns victorious on Puṣpaka
2a. Test of Rāma with bow and arrow
2b. Test of Sītā by fire
3a. Homage to Viṣṇu on a mountaintop
3b. Homage to Kṛṣṇa (at the top of the scene)
4a. Gods request Viṣṇu to incarnate to rescue them from defeat at the hands of the *asuras*
4b. Hanuman tells Sītā that Rāma will rescue her from captivity

These pairs would be connected via the two swastika patterns through the center of the chamber. The counterclockwise swastika, one could say, connects the male-dominated scenes of victory or

Fig. 6.7. Third gallery, northwest pavilion, north wing, east wall, Kṛṣṇa in audience.

To our left, Kṛṣṇa sits receiving homage from a royal figure, while seated men on either side and in two lower registers look on. Inexplicably, two prostrate men, apparently quite dead or drowned, lie face down in the register below Kṛṣṇa.

homage. The clockwise swastika, by contrast, joins the scenes with Sītā together. Thus, although the swastika is usually accepted as a traditionally solar symbol, these two sets tend to fall into solar (male, counterclockwise) and lunar (female, clockwise) patterns.

In this arrangement, the central image in the chamber might have been conceived as "generating" both swastika patterns. Since Viṣṇu's incarnations are manifest on the walls of the pavilion, an image of Viṣṇu would be logical at the center, acting as a pivot around which all these activities revolve. There is no problem in the female/lunar nuances of the clockwise swastika, since Viṣṇu and Brahmā are joined in the iconography of Angkor Wat and in the scene of creation, as the lotus stalk rises from Nārāyaṇa's navel. Among other connections, Brahmā and the moon share the second gallery between them. Therefore, Viṣṇu and the moon are brought together through the persona of Brahmā.

The reliefs in the southwest pavilion appear to form a series of pairs, as well, but across from each other (Fig. 6.9). These pairs are as follows:

1a. Churning scene (Viṣṇu steadying a central mountain)

1b. Kṛṣṇa holding up Mount Govardhana
2a. Śiva on a mountaintop with women rushing up to greet him
2b. Śiva and Pārvatī on a mountaintop with Rāvaṇa below, shaking the mountain
3a. Vālin versus Sugrīva, Vālin dead on the ground
3b. Kāma shooting at Śiva, Kāma dead on the ground (identical composition)
4a. Śiva receiving offerings on a mountaintop
4b. Water festival

If these pairs are seen in relation to an image in the center of the chamber—most probably the god Śiva—they form a lotus or flower pattern of four petals. Śiva is connected to the lotus because of their shared association with water, compassion, females, purity, and the moon. An image of Śiva at the center of the pavilion would agree not only with the themes of the bas-reliefs themselves but also with the north/south dichotomy in the general iconography of Angkor Wat. The south, the ancestors, fertility, the waning moon—all go well with Śiva. That set would be opposed to the north, the gods, Mount Meru cosmology, the waxing moon, solar symbolism, and Viṣṇu in the northwest

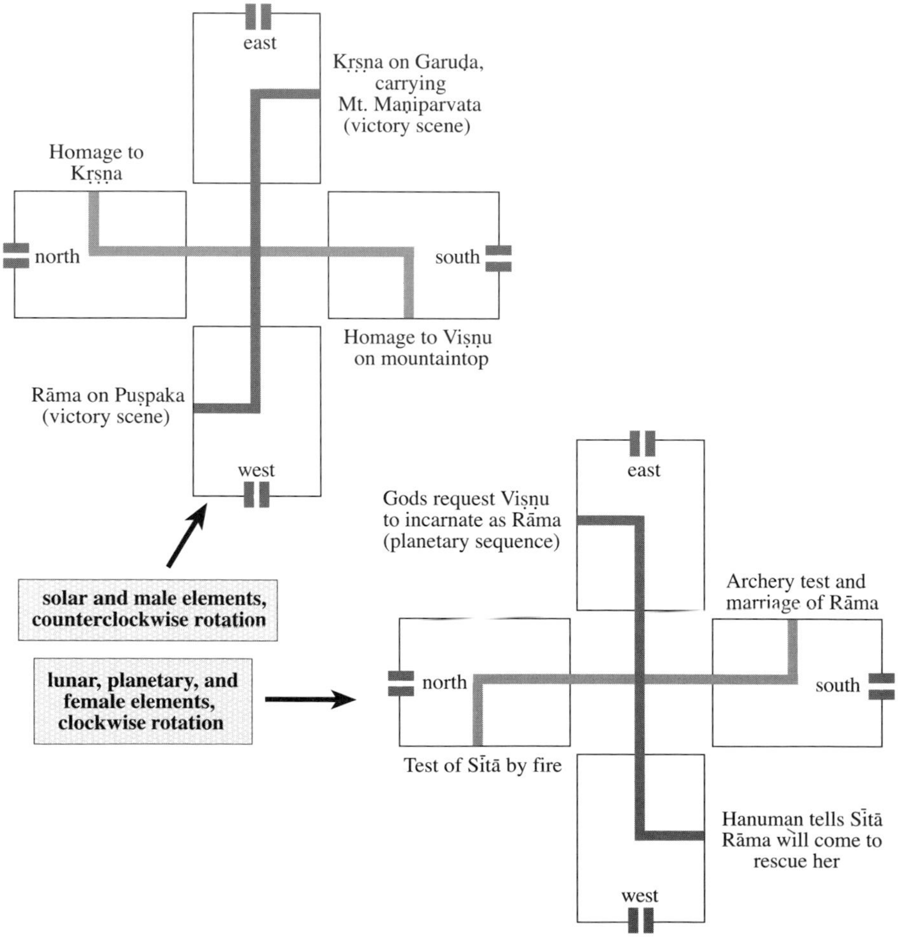

Fig. 6.8. Third gallery, northwest corner pavilion, scenes paired in a swastika pattern.

The scenes in this pavilion can be paired according to their subject matter. When the pairs are connected with each other through the Viṣṇu image that must have been situated at the center of the pavilion, they form two opposite swastika patterns. Since the swastika is an ancient solar symbol, it is a fitting design for a chamber dedicated to Viṣṇu, a solar god.

pavilion. In this general scheme, images of Śiva and Viṣṇu at the center of the southwest and northwest pavilions would have been in keeping with the temple as a whole, with the major bas-relief themes in each pavilion, and with the suggested flower/swastika patterns that connect the center of the pavilions to their reliefs.

Over the north window, on the east wing of

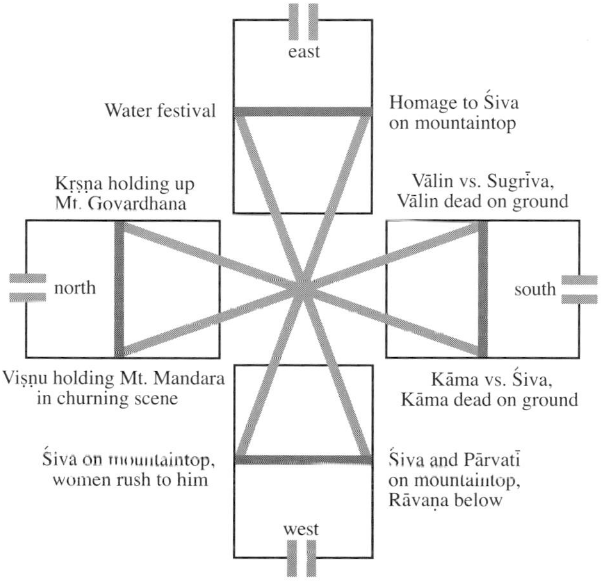

Fig. 6.9. Third gallery, southwest corner pavilion, scenes paired in a lotus pattern.

The reliefs in the southwest pavilion can be paired not only according to their subject matter, but in several instances according to their composition as well. The four bas-reliefs that praise Śiva in the pavilion suggest that a lingam or statue of Śiva was once placed at the center. If the pairs of reliefs are also connected to the central statue, then a lotus or flower pattern of four petals is formed. The association of the lotus with water, women, the moon, and the color white makes it an appropriate symbol for Śiva. Śiva, who wears the crescent moon in his hair, has several consorts and is associated with fertility. He is also the Lord of Yogis.

the pavilion, the stately procession of gods that appears to represent a series of planets is on the way to see Viṣṇu (Fig. 6.10).[15] Viṣṇu's star Altair is 29 degrees north of the ecliptic. That might have been a reason for placing Viṣṇu above this sequence of deities, but in this case there was nowhere else to put him.[16] At the front of the procession is Ketu riding a lion; at the back is Nirṛti on the shoulders of a *yakṣa* (Fig. 6.11). The sun and moon are below the procession, to the left of the window (Fig. 6.12). From the front of the procession on the right to the last figure on the left, the sequence is (Figs. 6.11, 6.13, 6.14):

1. Ketu ("comet") on his lion
2. Agni on a rhinoceros
3. Yama, with a fierce expression, riding on his buffalo
4. Indra holding a *vajra* and riding on his elephant
5. Kubera mounted on a horse
6. Skanda, multiarmed and holding weapons, on a peacock
7. Varuṇa, holding a *pāśa* or noose, riding on his *haṁsa*
8. Nirṛti on the shoulders of a *yakṣa*

This sequence is particularly odd because, in a sense, it is backwards. Planetary sequences in Cambodia begin with the sun and moon and end with Ketu. The sun and moon, as here, are always on the left and Ketu, as here, is always on the right. But here Ketu is leading the sequence rather than trailing like the tail of a comet. Before we explore the reasons for this orientation, some other aspects of the relief need attention.

Sūrya, Candra, Yama, Varuṇa, Indra, Kubera, Agni, Rāhu, and Ketu are the usual planetary deities throughout Khmer art from the seventh century on. A total of 41 of these series, called *navagraha* when discussed as planets, was studied by Louis Malleret.[17] Their order almost never varied. Curious as to why that was so, I discovered that again the reason may be found in Mesopotamian astronomy. Our days of the week, planets all of them, originate from that area of the world—and the sequence of the planetary deities in Cambodia, it appears, follows the days of the week. In case there is any doubt that our 7-day week was current in twelfth-century Cambodia, recall that the days were used to date inscriptions all the way through the Angkor period. Even though the planets in the inscriptions have the same names as in India, the theomorphic forms of the planets in India have different attributes, usually no mounts, and they are never represented in Cambodia.[18] So the Sanskrit terms for the planets (and days of the week) occur in Khmer inscriptions, but these planets are never represented in Khmer art as they are in India. Instead, we have the following sequence (again) and its correlation to the planets:

1. Sūrya	Sunday	Sun
2. Candra	Monday	Moon
3. Yama	Tuesday	Mars
4. Varuṇa	Wednesday	Mercury
5. Indra	Thursday	Jupiter
6. Kubera	Friday	Venus
7. Agni	Saturday	Saturn

Rāhu and Ketu—the demon who swallows the sun or moon in eclipses and the comet deity, respectively—are extra celestial phenomena that are always joined to the planets. They are not, as is often mistakenly stated, the ascending and descending nodes of the moon.

Now let us return to the opening question. The reason why the Angkor Wat sequence begins with Ketu on the right with Saturn behind him is that Ketu simply points out the start of the planetary lineup. The rest of the planets follow in order after Saturn. Saturn is first—and Saturn is at the far right in the traditional Khmer *navagraha.* Mars is at the left in this sequence—and that is where Mars would be placed in the sequence of the days of the week. Finally, Indra is in the center, where he should be. At first glance, the order seems to be connected to the traditional order of the days of the week; on closer inspection, however, we find

Fig. 6.10. Third gallery, northwest pavilion, east wing, north wall, planetary procession and Viṣṇu lying on the Sea of Milk.

Eight deities move to our right across the wall, over the window, and under the reclining Viṣṇu. This procession was formed, it is suggested here, to request Viṣṇu to incarnate as Rāma and kill the demon Rāvaṇa. At the same time, the sun and moon to the left of the window, and Ketu at the head of the procession, call to mind sequences of the planets in Cambodian art.

that it is not. Once I found the correlation to the planets through the days of the week, it was not difficult to find corroborating evidence in many places.

Indra is the king of the *devas*, the god of lightning and thunder and rain. He is very similar to the Western gods of Thursday: Thor, the Germanic god of thunder, and Jupiter or Zeus, the father or the ruler of the Greek and Roman gods. Indra corresponds to Thursday in the preceding sequence.

The *Bṛhat Saṁhitā* specifically associates Mercury, the planet for Wednesday, with water.[19] Of all the planets, Mercury is the one chosen to preside over seven major rivers in India, as well as all other rivers, bridges, waterways, dikes, and reservoirs. The only other "planet" with an aquatic association is, quite logically, the moon. In agree-

Fig. 6.11. Third gallery, northwest pavilion, east wing, north wall, planetary sequence.

The god Nirṛti on the shoulders of a *yakṣa* is at the far end of the procession (far left). In front of him is Varuṇa holding his *pāśa* (noose) and riding a *haṁsa*. In front of Varuṇa (a symbol for the planet Mercury) is Mars, or Skanda, the multiheaded and multiarmed god of war, riding a peacock. Skanda, the son of Śiva, holds a trident. These two figures would put Mars and then Mercury at the end of a planetary sequence.

Fig. 6.12. Third gallery, northwest pavilion, east wing, north wall, planetary sequence.

The sun (bottom) and moon (top) introduce the sequence of planets as they occupy the space between the window and the edge of the wall. By their exalted size and the space allotted them, as well as their frontal position, they are the first major figures in the scene. Above them we come to the rest of the procession. Going still higher, we arrive at Viṣṇu, the objective of the caravan of gods.

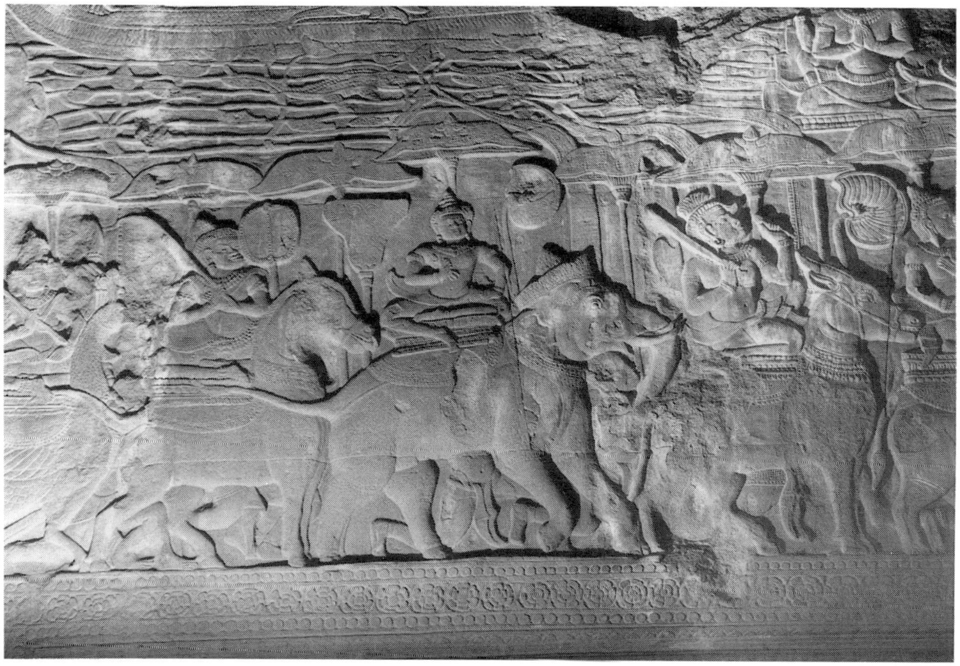

Fig. 6.13. Third gallery, northwest pavilion, east wing, north wall, planetary sequence.

At the center of the sequence is Indra on his elephant, a symbol for the planet Jupiter. Behind Indra, to our left, is Kubera, the god of riches, on a horse. Kubera would represent the planet Venus. Thus Jupiter and Venus would precede Mars and Mercury at the end of the sequence, in that order.

Fig. 6.14. Third gallery, northwest pavilion, east wing, north wall, planetary sequence.

Ketu, the comet, leads the procession seated on his lion. Behind him is Agni on his rhinoceros. Agni, the only planetary deity of these three leading figures, represents Saturn. The figure behind Agni is Yama on a buffalo—a reference to the southern position of Agni (Saturn) in the sky at sunset, the start of the "procession" of planets. Saturn thus leads off the planetary sequence in the east at sunset.

ment with the relationship of Mercury to water, the Chinese (and subsequently Japanese and Korean) cosmological systems assign Mercury the element "water" as its symbol.[20] Wednesday would correspond to Varuṇa in the fourth position of most Khmer *navagraha* sequences. Varuṇa is the god of water.

In Indian descriptions of the planets, Venus (Friday) is always placed on the north, the direction ruled over by Kubera, the god of wealth. This is so even though the directions of the other planets may vary considerably.[21] Once again, the Chinese character meaning "gold" or metal (*jin*) is given to Venus.[22] Gold, of course, is another fitting symbol for Kubera. Venus is also the guardian of treasure and the Lord of Riches, according to the *Mahābhārata*.[23] Finally, there is an inscription from the northern sanctuary of Prasat Prom, in Promtep province, that identifies Venus as "Dhaneśa."[24] Dhaneśa, another name for Kubera, derives from the root "*dhana*," which means wealth. These various sources associate the planet Venus with Kubera by means of riches, wealth, gold, and a northerly direction. Friday is the sixth day in the week and Kubera is in the sixth position in the *navagraha* series.

Finally, Agni, who is often described as black and malevolent in his role as "eater" of corpses in cremation, is an appropriate regent for Saturn, a planet depicted as both black and nefarious. Saturday, the seventh day in the week, would correspond to Agni as the seventh deity in the Khmer planetary sequence. This completes the identification of the gods with the planets.

In the Angkor Wat relief, Skanda and Nirṛti are two extra deities, beyond the count of 9 planets. Why, then, are they in this relief and what do they mean? As Nirṛti is the guardian of the southwest, he would have to be a symbol of the southwest here since there is no other alternative.[25] He has no known planetary associations. Skanda, the god of war, is the regent for the planet Mars and does occur in a few Khmer *navagraha* sequences. But if Skanda is Mars, then Yama could not represent that planet in this sequence. Following the pattern of Nirṛti, Yama might symbolize the south, since he rules over that direction of the compass, especially at Angkor Wat. (Yama is shown as the Dharmarāja on the south wall of the third gallery and Skanda has no directional association.) This would place the south in the third position in the line of deities and give the following sequence:

1.	Ketu	comet
2.	Agni	Saturn
3.	Yama	south
4.	Indra	Jupiter
5.	Kubera	Venus
6.	Skanda	Mars
7.	Varuṇa	Mercury
8.	Nirṛti	southwest

The first planet in the procession is Saturn (Agni), who comes just after Ketu, followed by the other deities in a linear progression. Saturn is followed by Yama (the south) and Mercury by Nirṛti (the southwest), which, it turns out, describes their positions.

At the end of July 1131, the planets followed this sequence based on the order in which they rose over the eastern horizon.[26] When the sun set at Angkor at 6:22 P.M. on July 27 (as a median example), Saturn and Jupiter were already in the night sky. Saturn would have been about 62 degrees from the western horizon and Jupiter about 7 degrees above the eastern horizon. Thus Saturn began the planetary sequence before nightfall with Jupiter a distant second. At 11:42 P.M., Saturn set in the west, followed several hours later by Jupiter at 5:07 A.M. Before Jupiter set, Venus, Mars, and Mercury rose in close succession in the east (at 3:47, 4:18, and 4:25 A.M.). Therefore, the passage of Saturn and Jupiter was followed in the small hours of the morning by the rising of Venus, Mars, and Mercury. This sequence conforms to the order of planets behind Agni in the bas-relief of the northwest corner pavilion. About 1 hour and 22 minutes after Mercury rose in the east, the sun ascended over the horizon to begin a new day.

At sunset, Mercury/Varuṇa would have been 17 degrees below the western horizon—or in other terms, "south" of the western horizon, as well as south of the celestial equator. Similarly, Saturn/Agni is south of the celestial equator and in the western half of the sky. Since both the south and the west were already represented by Nirṛti (southwest) for the position of Mercury, Yama (south) was the only logical choice left to indicate Saturn's position. And since the first and last planets in the procession are so specifically placed in relation to the horizon and the celestial equator, the date implied by the relief is even more exact. This precise configuration occurred only between July 24 and July 29, 1131, and at no other date within centuries of that time. Since this time of year falls within the month of Śrāvaṇa as well as the zodiac sign Leo, Viṣṇu himself presided over this unusual planetary sequence.

For reasons summarized earlier, it appears that the king pushed an alliance with the Chams in this year, because in 1132 they fought an important battle against the Dai Viet at Nghe-an and lost. At the same time, it is possible that the year 1131 marked a change in King Sūryavarman's age (in completed years of life) from 32 to 33, assuming that the king was born in 1099 (1021 *śāka*). If the king were also born under the sign of Śrāvaṇa, as postulated here, he would have been joined to Viṣṇu from birth. The extraordinary conjunction of a rare planetary sequence under the sign of Viṣṇu on the king's thirty-second birthday would have been enough, I believe, to recommend that the king take Viṣṇu as his personal deity and build his royal temple to him. It would also have been sufficient to encourage a major campaign against the Dai Viet during that year in the king's life.

THE BATTLE OF LAṄKĀ

The panoramic Battle of Laṅkā ends a long, counterclockwise circuit around the third gallery. The end of the day, the end of the bas-relief sequence, even the setting moon at the end of a full-moon night—all would lend a tone of finality to this chaotic battle scene. And yet the action in this relief is curiously neutral and no evident conclusion is in sight. Given that the alliance with the Chams fell apart and the battle of 1132 ended in defeat, however, this moment before Rāma's victory was in fact ideal.

For whatever reason, Rāma is not shown vanquishing Rāvaṇa. Rather, he stands on Hanuman and faces to our right, brandishing his bow in a heroic posture (Fig. 6.15). Exactly 21 cubits away, a multiarmed and multiheaded Rāvaṇa rides in his chariot (Fig. 6.16), besieged by his enemies, and faces Rāma in defiance.[27] His ultimate defeat may be intimated by the intense fighting all around him. Closely beset by the enemy, he is not nearly as removed from danger as the majestic Rāma. These two leading figures bracket the center of the panel, which is spanned by the exact 21-cubit measurement. In this 21-cubit space, three pairs of fighting warriors have been locked in battle for 800 years now.

The apparent chaos of this 51.25-m jumble of arms, legs, gnashing teeth, and flying arrows is not nearly so anarchic as it seems. First of all, Sugrīva's monkey warriors enter from our left, or north, and are fighting their way southward. Opposing this advance is the *rākṣasa* army, entering from our right, or south, and moving northward against their enemy. This north/south dichotomy is in keeping with geographic reality. Rāma did in fact attack Laṅkā from the north, placing Rāvaṇa and his forces in the south by comparison. The north/south division at Angkor Wat lends

Fig. 6.15. Third gallery, west side, south half, Battle of Laṅkā.

Hanuman, whose father was Vayu the wind god, appears to fly through the air carrying Rāma into battle. During the summer and winter solstices, Rāma and Hanuman are flanked by a shaft of sunlight to the right (summer) and left (winter, Fig. 5.47).

Fig. 6.17. Third gallery, west side, south half, Battle of Laṅkā, Vibhīṣaṇa and Lakṣmaṇa.

Vibhīṣaṇa stands to the left, Lakṣmaṇa to the right, large in scale. As the winter solstice sun sets on the horizon, Vibhīṣaṇa slowly emerges from the shadows. At sunset, he is completely in light while Lakṣmaṇa remains in shadow (Fig. 5.47). This division between light and shadow corresponds to the division between the south and the *rākṣasa*s (Vibhīṣaṇa) and the north and the *deva*s (Lakṣmaṇa).

Fig. 6.16. Third gallery, west side, south half, Battle of Laṅkā.

Rāvaṇa is placed on his chariot 21 cubits away from Rāma. As he faces us directly with his multiple heads and arms, the curvature of his torso denotes his energy and exertion in battle. Nevertheless, figures like Rāvaṇa take on the aspect of an icon with their frontality, calm faces, and "posed" appearance. The weight of their symbolic meaning seems to have frozen many figures into a stiff, heraldic posture.

verisimilitude to the battle, therefore, authenticating its action.

The same north/south dichotomy is echoed in the composition of the Battle of Kurukṣetra and the Churning of the Sea of Milk. Thus, in the only three original bas-relief panels on the east and west, protagonists and antagonists parallel the north/south division of the *devas* and *asuras*, undoubtedly the archetypal model for this geographic split between "good" forces and "bad."[28] The organizing principle of directionality, then, not only comes to bear on this scene but colors it with divine overtones of epic battles between the gods and antigods. The north/south division is yet another piece of evidence that the reliefs were planned in coordination, one with another, each in relation to the others.

The north/south dichotomy in the reliefs originates in the north–south movement of the sun and moon each year. Just as in the Battle of Kurukṣetra and the Churning of the Sea of Milk, there is a shaft of sunlight to the left (north) of Rāma at the winter solstice and another to the right (south) at the summer solstice (Fig. 5.47).

Vibhīṣaṇa and Lakṣmaṇa, who are in shadow to the left of Rāma on December 22, are involved in the solstice light also. They are both in shadow until the sun is close to the horizon. Just before the sun sets on December 22, Vibhīṣaṇa emerges into full sunlight and Lakṣmaṇa, the brother of Rāma, remains in darkness (Fig. 5.47; left side, Fig. 6.17). Vibhīṣaṇa is a *rākṣasa,* the brother of Rāvaṇa. The light/dark, *deva/rākṣasa,* distinction between Rāma and Vibhīṣaṇa is made obvious by the final rays of the winter solstice sun.

The figure of Rāvaṇa, who faces Rāma at a distance of 21 cubits, would be in partial sunlight during the winter and summer solstices (Figs. 6.18 and 6.19), never in full light or darkness at either. Rāvaṇa was actually one-half *rākṣasa* and one-half god (his father was Vaiśravaṇa, the god of the north, and his mother a *rākṣasī*). Perhaps that is why the figure is divided by light and shadow at the solstices: there was a split in his ancestry—at the summer solstice, it looks as though the shaft of light will cut him in half up the middle. At the

Fig. 6.18. Third gallery, west side, south half, Battle of Laṅkā, winter solstice.

As the sun sets on the winter solstice day (and a week or so before and after), the shadow cast at the left by a pillar to the right of Rāvaṇa moves to cover about half of the demon king's body. On the winter solstice, then, Rāvaṇa would be half in light and half in shadow. This corresponds to the fact that he is half *deva* and half *rākṣasa.*

Fig. 6.19. Third gallery, west side, south half, Battle of Laṅkā, summer solstice.

As the sun sets on the summer solstice day (and, again, a week or so before and after), the shaft of light between the shadow of the two pillars widens and moves closer to the center of the figure of Rāvaṇa. He is therefore bisected by the light shaft, another way of illustrating his half-*deva* and half-*rākṣasa* parentage. A stand of trees on the horizon blocks off the sunlight before actual sunset, so the shadows disappear into a diffuse light before the whole relief is illuminated. Clouds often intervene as well, preventing the pillars from casting shadows on the wall.

winter solstice, he would be half in light and half in shadow.

The remaining figures, to the south behind Rāvaṇa and to the north behind Rāma, also follow a summer/winter solstice light pattern. Since the good and bad forces are paired in combat, they cannot be separated by geographic position. Instead, the oversize commanders to the south are in the shadow of a pillar during the summer solstice. The opposite is true for the commanders paired off on the north.

In summary, then, with their sensitivity to sunlight and shadow, the sculptors of the Battle of Laṅkā were able to highlight Rāma and Hanuman with shafts of flanking sunlight during the solstice periods, excise Vibhīṣaṇa from the ranks of the gods during the winter solstice, allow Rāvaṇa a slight *deva* quality, and create a north/south split in the relief. This splendid achievement forged a bond between the sun and the Laṅkā scene—joining Angkor Wat once again to the solar calendar and the movements of the god Sūrya throughout cyclical time.

The Role of 19/20

The pairs of commanders joined in individual combat stand out against the backdrop of fighting warriors because of their large size (Fig. 6.20). Each pair of combatants is placed exactly in a space marked by the distance between two pillars (Fig. 6.21). There are 19 pairs of oversize combatants placed by themselves in 19 interpillar spaces (Appendix B, Table 9). Rāma on Hanuman occupies another space, and Rāvaṇa in his chariot has his own interpillar space. That makes a total of 21 spaces. Thus Rāma and Rāvaṇa, the twentieth pair of combatants, are larger and more important than the others.

Rāma, Rāvaṇa, Indra, and Sūryavarman are all kings. There are 19 ministers in King

Fig. 6.20. Third gallery, west side, south half, Battle of Laṅkā.

The large-scale pair of combatants on a chariot—monkey and *rakṣasa* commanders—are one of 19 such pairs placed across the relief, one pair to each interpillar space or bay. These large figures on the south side of the relief are in shadow during the summer solstice, while their counterparts on the north are in light.

Sūryavarman's procession, with the king as the twentieth figure. In the next scene of heavens and hells, there are 19 men in the celestial palaces, with Yama, king of the ancestor as the twentieth unit—analogous to King Sūryavarman. On the north wall opposite Sūryavarman's procession, there are 19 gods under Indra, their king, making Indra the twentieth figure. Rāma and Rāvaṇa are each twentieth figures and kings. Where is the twenty-first supreme deity, then? Viṣṇu cannot be represented as himself at the Battle of Laṅkā: he is incarnate as Rāma. Viṣṇu is, however, at the axis of the churning scene, and, by proxy, he is at the axis of the Battle of Kurukṣetra in the form of the conquering Pāṇḍava leader. Only these three panels of reliefs—Kurukṣetra, the churning, and Laṅkā—are organized along a north–south symmetry. With Viṣṇu at the center of the first two scenes, one is justified in asking if he might not also be present at the center of the Laṅkā scene. But Viṣṇu was not at the battle. He could not be shown between Rāvaṇa and Rāma at the center of the panel.

Nevertheless, we know the number 21 is a symbol of the supreme deity. Could Viṣṇu then be represented in the "form" of the 21-cubit measurement between Rāma and Rāvaṇa? This would accommodate Viṣṇu along the axis of the scene, matching it with its counterparts (Kurukṣetra and the churning); but more important, Viṣṇu would be both invisible and, though unseen, at the very heart of the action. How better to indicate the pivotal role of the supreme god, his unseen presence at the nexus of power, generating energy and inspiration to the forces of Rāma?

The 19/21-unit dichotomy, with its inherent definition of a twentieth figure who is a king, is the primary unifying factor between the reliefs related to King Sūryavarman on the south and the relief of the gods fighting the *asuras* on the north. Because 19 and 20 are highlighted in an identical manner in the Battle of Laṅkā, and because the 21-cubit measurement at the center may imply the presence of Viṣṇu as a supreme deity, the Battle of Laṅkā is immediately tied to the northern and southern reliefs in the gallery. But that is not all. This battle scene, as we shall see, is also clearly connected to the Battle of Kurukṣetra by yet another theme: lunar dualities.

Lunar Dualities

For reasons that may relate to the emphasis on the moon on the western and eastern sides of a gallery, the length of the Laṅkā panel is 29.42 *phyeam,* almost equivalent to a lunar month of 29.53 days. The opposite panel across the gallery, sculpted in the sixteenth century, is 29.54 *phyeam* long. The panel next to the Laṅkā scene, the Battle of Kurukṣetra, is 27.76 *phyeam* long,[29] another reference to the lunar month.

The reciprocal lunar lengths of the Battles of Laṅkā and Kurukṣetra are joined by another lunar signifier. There are 15 false windows that run along the back of the Laṅkā panel and 14 false windows behind the Battle of Kurukṣetra. Each lunar month is divided into 14/15 days of the waxing/waning moon.

These lunar ties provide a key to understanding one of the remaining characteristics of the Battle of Laṅkā: the number 12 (Fig. 6.21).

These are 12 commanders, 12 interpillar spaces, and a 12-*phyeam* north/south division in the panel, suggesting the division between the 12 light and dark lunar half-months. At Angkor Wat and in the Hindu *purāṇas,* the north, the gods, and the waxing moon correspond to the light half of the month, while the south, the ancestors, and the waning moon define the dark half. For these reasons, and because of the other lunar references in the panel, the Battle of Laṅkā has a considerable amount of lunar symbolism. This is yet another instance of lunar elements in Viṣṇu's iconography. The shared identity with Brahmā as Nārāyaṇa, the association with Aquila and the night sky, the inclusion of a possible swastika pattern with lunar nuances in the northwest pavilion dedicated to the *Rāmāyaṇa,* and now the suggested lunar divisions in the Laṅkā scene—all agree in attributing a lunar component to the supreme solar deity.

BEYOND LANGUAGE AND FORM

The north–south oscillation of the sun is emphasized in the Churning of the Sea of Milk, along with the solar calendar between solstices each year. Similarly, the churning scene and the Battle of Kurukṣetra are opposite each other on the east and west sides of the temple and share a dichotomy created in large part by the sun (rising and setting sun, spring and autumn equinox). The Battles of

Laṅkā and Kurukṣetra, however, are connected through a shared lunar symbolism (lunar month, lunar half-month). And based on the 29.54-unit measurement of the panel opposite Laṅkā, one assumes that the reciprocity originally intended between these two east/west panels was lunar. That would complement the solar reciprocity between the east/west churning and Kurukṣetra panels. Thus we find that the relationships between the panels in the gallery are based on specific themes that characterize their content.

The parallels between the historical realm of King Sūryavarman and his 19 ministers and the realm of Indra and his 19 *devas*, plus Viṣṇu, define the dynamic between the southern and northern panels of bas-reliefs. At the same time, the number 19 ties King Sūryavarman's panel to the 19 men in the celestial mansions in the panel of heavens and hells and to the 19 commanders under Rāma (and under Rāvaṇa) in the Battle of Laṅkā. While the sun and moon and calendar come into play in almost all the panels, in one way or another, one cannot deny the historical allusions that constantly surface—either through measurements, such as 19/21, or through surrogate symbols, such as the Pāṇḍu leader/Viṣṇu, Yama/Sūryavarman, and the churning scene/*Indrābhiṣeka*. The multiple relationships between these panels strengthens the possibility that the three battle scenes on the western half of the temple were connected to actual campaigns during Sūryavarman's reign.

If it were not for the explicit merging of numerical, solstitial, and directional symbolism with the content of the reliefs in this gallery, the

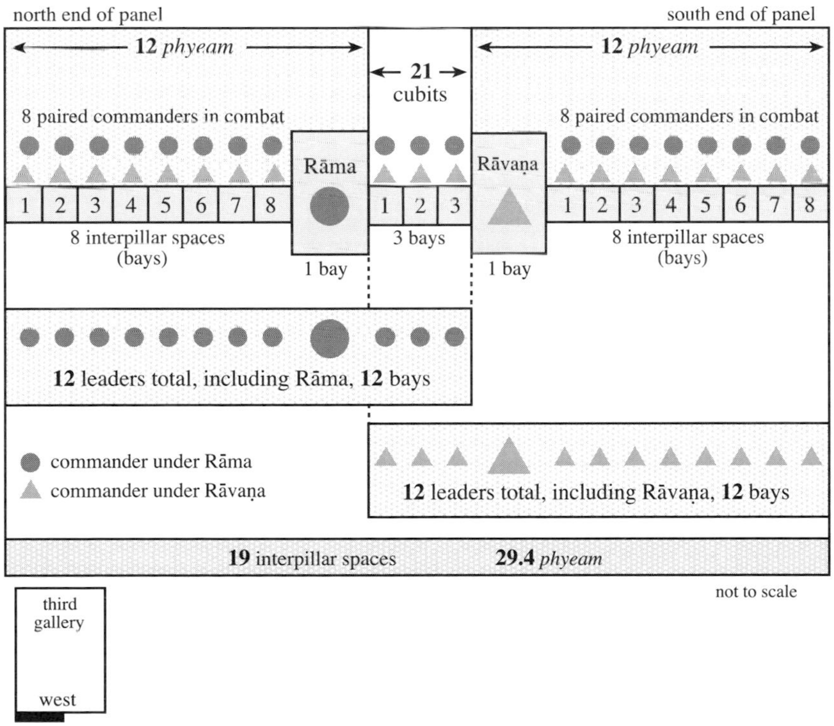

Fig. 6.21. Third gallery, diagram of Battle of Laṅkā scene.

Each pair of oversize combatants in this panel is more or less in each interpillar space (each bay). Rāma and his forces cover 12 bays in front of Rāvaṇa, and Rāvaṇa and his forces cover 12 bays in front of Rāma. Rāma is at the front of a 12-*phyeam* distance and so is Rāvaṇa. The 12/12 split in the relief is its most dominant numerical theme, followed closely by 19 and 21. The 21 cubits between Rāma and Rāvaṇa would readily symbolize an invisible Viṣṇu at the center of the action. And the 19 commanders under each leader, as well as the 19 bays across from the scene numerically join the panel to King Sūryavarman and his 19 ministers.

full implications of the measurements and alignments at Angkor Wat would have remained unknown. From King Sūryavarman's *Indrābhiṣeka* to the meaning of 19/20 and 21, the reliefs give us a literal picture of Khmer culture and beliefs that is not available from written texts. The stories they tell reach beyond the barriers of language and form: they breach the confines of time and place to illuminate our understanding of a past long irretrievable.

7

The Preau Cruciforme *and Second Gallery*

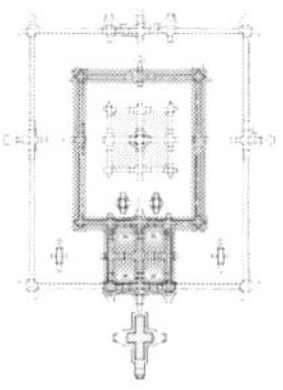

ON January 1, 1993, classical dancers performed on the cruciform terrace at Angkor Wat (Fig. 7.1). During rehearsals the day before, the main western sanctuary of the third gallery was filled with at least 75 people. When the temple was in use in the early twelfth century, a small gamelan orchestra, officiating priests, and perhaps as many as 30 or 40 devotees could have easily been accommodated in the entrance. Together the triad of entrances could handle more than 100 people without crowding. In brief, activities like the dances at Angkor Wat give some indication of the numbers of people that might have been involved in only one segment of the temple on any given day.

THE *PREAU CRUCIFORME*

On looking out a northern, southern, or eastern doorway from the third gallery to the center of Angkor Wat, there is a green, grassy courtyard in the rainy season that contrasts sharply with the black-stained sandstone of the plinth, staircases, and towers of the second gallery (Figs. 7.2 and 7.3). An approach to the second gallery from any side except the west means crossing the courtyard and climbing the steps to a structure that seems independent (Fig. 7.4). On looking through the western entrance of the third gallery, however, we find there is no view at all of the second gallery. Instead, after just a few brief steps, we enter a

Fig. 7.1. Dancers on the cruciform terrace.

Dancers, dressed partly according to the costumes worn by the *apsarases* at Angkor Wat and partly according to current Khmer custom, perform on the cruciform terrace for Japanese national television on January 1, 1993. Whether the terrace was originally used for dance dramas or simply for elaborate rituals, it has provided a stage for modern performances in this century.

Fig. 7.2. Second gallery, east side, central and southeast entrances from the northeast.

With a plinth several meters high and 21 tall steps in the entrance staircases, the second gallery is not easily accessible. Except for the two corner towers and main entrance, the windows on the outside are blind, shutting off the facade even more. By its height, its three solitary entrances, and its closed facade, the second gallery seems built to exalt the rituals once held in its chambers.

Fig. 7.3. Second gallery, east side, northeast corner tower from the southeast.

The sandstone used in these towers is different and softer than that of the corridors, according to conservators. Here the severe erosion is clearly evident along the sides of the tower and at its entrance.

Fig. 7.4. Second gallery, northeast corner, view across the courtyard from the northeast.
The newly cleaned gallery rises like an independent unit from the grassy courtyard around it. From this angle, the top of the central tower can be seen over the partially ruined northeast corner tower in the foreground. The corner towers of the upper level form an exact symmetry with the facade of the second gallery.

pillared, cruciform area filled with filtered sunlight (Fig. 7.5). Activities and rituals would have also filled this space with movement and sound.

For the first time on our journey into the temple, a large entrance leads directly into a much larger space that is still enclosed—half-exterior and half-interior in construction (Figs. 7.6–7.8). The effect is like walking into a private sandstone garden with pillars for trees, corridors for shade, and, originally, four pools for ritual ablution (Fig. 7.9). On the north and south, the space is closed in by the outside wall of the corridors. On the east, the dark tunnels formed by the three flights of steps, leading up and out of the three parallel west–east corridors, do not invite a climb to the top. On the west, the walls of the third gallery block a view out to the courtyard. It is solely from the perspective of the edges of the four pools that one can actually see the outside of the entrances to the second and third galleries (Fig. 7.10). Otherwise, the architecture of this small space—small relative to the grandiose scale of the rest of the temple, that is—creates its own singular environment isolated from what comes before it or after.

The three corridors that connect the second and third galleries are crossed in the middle by a fourth. Hence the French name for this area: the *preau cruciforme*, or covered courtyard in the form of a cross. As *preau cruciforme* says it best, the French term is kept here. The *preau cruciforme* offers one exit through the walls on the north and south (Fig. 7.11). If a visitor wished to circumambulate the second gallery—which is effectively an unknown from here—it would be necessary to step through

Fig. 7.5. Third gallery, west side, main entrance, view through the eastern doorway into the preau cruciforme.

The vistas at Angkor Wat give new meaning to the term "tunnel vision." Looking westward through the doorway we see the vaulting in the *preau cruciforme,* the main western lintel at the central cross-arm, the stairs up to the main entrance to the second gallery, and just a bit of light showing through from the opposite (exit) doorway out of the main entrance to the second gallery. Unlike the view in Fig. 7.4, this is clearly an integrated, well-defined passageway up to the next level of the temple. Nowhere, however, is the actual second gallery in evidence.

Fig. 7.6. Preau cruciforme, *central west–east aisle, view west to entrance.*
A total of 32 pillars radiate outward from the center of the cruciform in all four directions. In this view, a statue of Brahmā on a pedestal may have occupied the central square. That spot is indicated by the dark area on the floor about halfway down the corridor.

these exits. There could not be a more eloquent statement on the isolation of this sector. From the inside, the two lateral exits are barely noticed. Beyond doubt, the *preau cruciforme* is meant to function as an independent construct, excerpting the western entrances from the second and third galleries and placing them in a shared, defined, complete architectural unit. One would expect the measurements to follow this format, and they do.

The character of this transition out of the historical setting of the third gallery and into the mandala of Brahmā in the second gallery underscores the difference between these two levels. The axes that record the king's major dates and the reliefs that tell his story are now cut off, out of view, behind us. Terrestrial time has ended, the architecture has changed, the ambience has changed, and we have walked out of the world of the king that brought us to this level. Throughout the cruciform corridors, the measurements describe the world of the gods.

As though to escort the visitor well into

Fig. 7.7. Preau cruciforme, *view to the southwest from the center of the cruciform.*
From the bright sunlight over the southwest basin to the dark shadow in the main corridor, the cruciform is enhanced by a variegated, multifaceted play of light and shade. Overhead one can still see the red and white painting that details the lotuses on the "beams" between the pillars.

Mount Meru, however, the *kṛta yuga* that began with our first step up to the western entrance bridge is still in effect. This last earthly time period will terminate as we step out of the western entrance of the second gallery at the east end of the *preau cruciforme*. It is our only connection to the reign of King Sūryavarman at this point.

The exits out of the cruciform on the north and south lead to a tiny chamber barely 4 cubits across, too small to have held an image at its center. On the north, the small chamber is popularly called the "echo chamber" (Fig. 7.11). The favorite echo effect is to stand against a side wall and thump your chest. The resultant sound is like standing inside a stethoscope. The "thump," normally barely audible, resounds here in deep, vibrant tones from all around. It is like hitting a bass drum, hard, with a padded stick.

The echo chamber, in turn, opens onto a porch from which a staircase leads down to the courtyard of the second level. More than 20 m away, a tall library is moored across from the doorway to the

Fig. 7.8. Preau cruciforme, *central north–south cross-arm, view south down the demivault from the center of the cruciform.*

This small passageway echoes the telescoping effect found in the central corridor and indeed along all the corridors of Angkor Wat. The base of some of the pillars has eroded away because of the effects of stagnant water in the rainy season—often mixed with the sulfuric acid in bat guano.

Fig. 7.9. Preau cruciforme, *northwest basin, view from southeast corner.*
Water would have once filled the basin, at least to the level of the bottom molded step in the staircase. There is a drainage hole visible in the far corner of the basin. When in actual use, some sort of caulking must have been put on the floor to prevent seepage.

preau cruciforme (Fig. 4.11). To the right (east) side, the equally tall foundation of the second gallery seems to raise that sector out of easy reach. The corner tower of the gallery is also an unlikely destination from here, and the nonfunctional windows of the gallery discourage the curious. Their frames and ornate balusters rest against a solid, blank wall. To the left (west) side, the similarly blind windows and doorless walls of the third gallery turn their back on the temple: there is no venturing forth in that direction. With no obvious destination in view other than the library, a visitor is likely to retreat back into the enclosure of the *preau cruciforme* and continue the journey from there.

At the center of the cruciform, there are cement-covered holes identical to the holes at sanctuaries in the Bayon (Fig. 7.12), which mark the place where the center of a pedestal would have been and the corner posts for a canopy. The corner holes are late additions, but the holes at the center, late or not, would have marked the place of an image according to the measurements here and the architecture.

The same pattern of holes occurs just to the

north and south of center, indicating that the main image was flanked by a statue on each side. These flanking statues were one interpillar space away from the main image. Measurements of possible circumambulation paths agree with this configuration also. Moreover, measurements place an image at the center of each parallel north–south corridor, even though there are no similar holes in the paving stones. Not all sanctuaries at Angkor Wat have holes in their center, but all had images (see Appendix A, Table 7.1).

A new "latitude" unit of measurement mentioned earlier and connected to astronomy, comes into play in this area. To review briefly, the north celestial pole is about 13.41 degrees above the north horizon when viewed from the west–east axis of Angkor Wat.[1] This means that the latitude of Angkor Wat is 13.41 degrees north, since lati-

Fig. 7.10. Preau cruciforme, *northeast corner, ascent to the second gallery.*

Telescoping roofs rise over the north lateral stairway to the second gallery, connecting the elevated corridor of the gallery with the lower corridor that meets it from the cruciform. In the process, the entrance to the gallery loses its identity as an independent structure, becoming instead a massive architectural link between segments of disparate height.

tude is equivalent to the height of the celestial pole over the horizon (Fig. 1.14). Because Brahmā is at the center of the universe above the north celestial pole, he can also be placed in space at the same location: 13.41 degrees above the northern horizon.

The "latitude unit" was first derived from the central sanctuary of Angkor Wat. The sanctuary has many coordinates that place it in relation to the earth, conceived as a globe floating in space. One of these coordinates is the north–south axis between doorways: 13.43 cubits. Since latitude is one's position on a north–south meridian, the north–south measurement is appropriate in orientation as well. If this unit were confined to the central sanctuary it would be interesting in its own right. But it turns out that 13.43 cubits was a construction module in the *preau cruciforme* and second gallery as well. It is close enough to 13.41 to be acceptable as the temple's latitude, and so I have

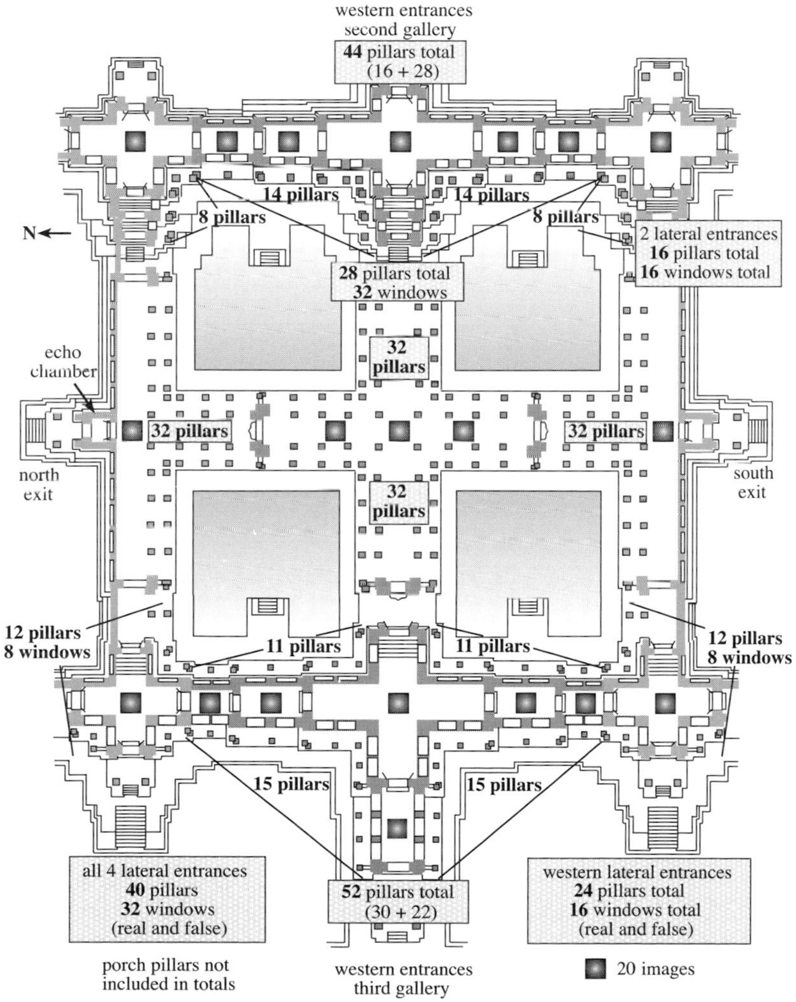

Fig. 7.11. Preau cruciforme, *pillars, windows and exits.*

The pattern of pillars and windows in the cruciform portrays various arrangements of the deities in the architectural mandala. When double pillars occur at both ends of an entrance facade, each supports a different roof, not visible on a ground plan. Therefore, the architecture splits the double pillars as different segments of the facade. This determines how the pillars are counted. On the east side of the *preau cruciforme,* the triad of entrances to the second gallery is raised high above the level of the corridors inside the cruciform. They are out of sight except for their dark staircases. On the west side, the floor of the entrances to the third gallery is below the floor level of the cruciform. The architectural result isolates the corridors here, providing solitude, shade, and quiet. The only direct exits to the outside are in the middle of the north and south walls, and both lead to a library. The "echo chamber" is noted here for its curious sound effects.

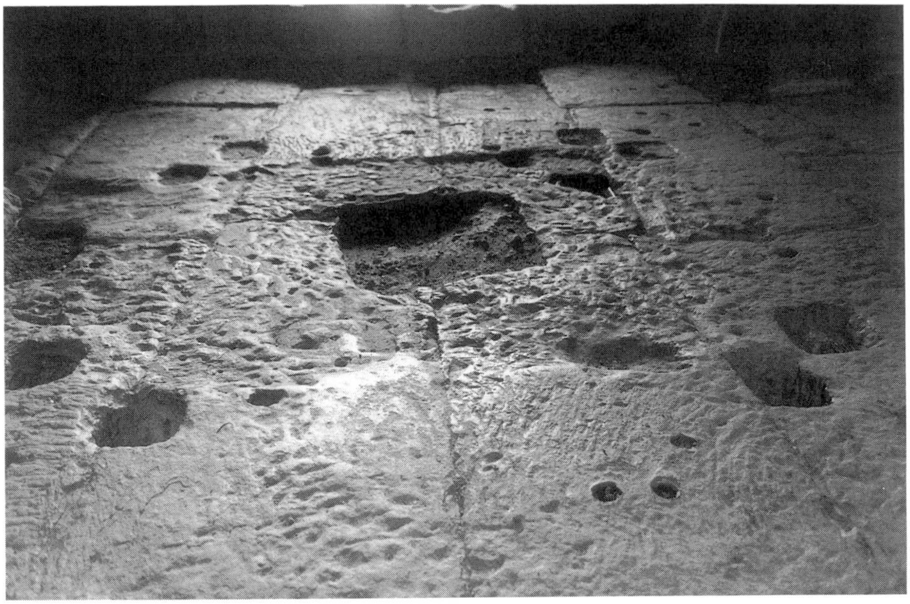

Fig. 7.12. Bayon, inner gallery, east side, north lateral entrance.

A central hole, here with a slightly indented square around it, would have contained a typical reliquary cube that fit inside a pedestal. The pair of holes at each corner were the post holes for a canopy. The central square of the *preau cruciforme* has a similar set of holes now filled with cement, as does the square one bay away, to the north and south of center.

called it the latitude unit. Wherever this unit occurs, it brings Brahmā into the space it measures because it defines his location in the night sky over Angkor.

The introduction of the latitude module is one indication that an image of Brahmā once occupied the center of the *preau cruciforme*. In all, there are four types of evidence that place him in this sector: architectural, astronomical, numerical, and solar.

Architectural evidence. The architectural format in the cruciform is ideal for a four-headed image. Brahmā could "look" down all four corridors at once and could be approached from any side. The four basins form spatial quadrants flanking his gaze in each direction—not only reflecting his domain in the night sky but also recalling the oceans around Mount Meru directly beneath Brahmā. The architecture itself, then, is perfectly designed for a four-headed creator of time and space resident in the sky at the north celestial pole.

Astronomical evidence: the latitude unit of measure. As we have seen, the latitude module derives from the position of Brahmā over the north celestial pole as seen from Angkor. It occurs here for the first time in our journey.

Numerical evidence: mandalas, nakṣatra, and lunar cycles. Based on the measurements of this area, the pillars, statues, and windows in the cruciform are related to the architectural mandala which definitely places Brahmā at the center of this space (Figs. 7.11 and 2.27). From his vantage point, 32 pillars emanate outward in all directions (Fig. 7.11). The four lateral entrances that mark the corners of his domain have 32 windows (real and false) and 40 pillars total (28 *nakṣatra* and 12 *ādityas*). The entrances to the second gallery, which he dominates, have 44 pillars total (28 in front) and 32 windows. Even the 52 pillars in the entrances to the west (third gallery) may symbolize the 52 weeks in a solar year, a time period engendered by Brahmā.

As though to emphasize the mandala that is

Brahmā's terrestrial and celestial home, the axes that emanate outward from him, like the pillars themselves, are 32 and 27/28 *phyeam* (27.60) in length (Fig. 7.13).[2] The inner axes are 120 cubits (12 × 10)—a figure that recalls the system of measurement established in the Mediterranean area millennia before Angkor Wat would be constructed: 12 zodiac signs, 10 degrees each sign, or 120 degrees in all.[3] Brahmā as the creator of time is appropriate to these 120-cubit axes, or vice versa. The mandala that configured the 32 windows and 40 pillars in the four corners—the cruciform's lateral entrances—is repeated in two circumambulation paths that go straight down each corridor connecting the lateral entrances together (32 units of 10 cubits each, Fig. 7.12). This time, however,

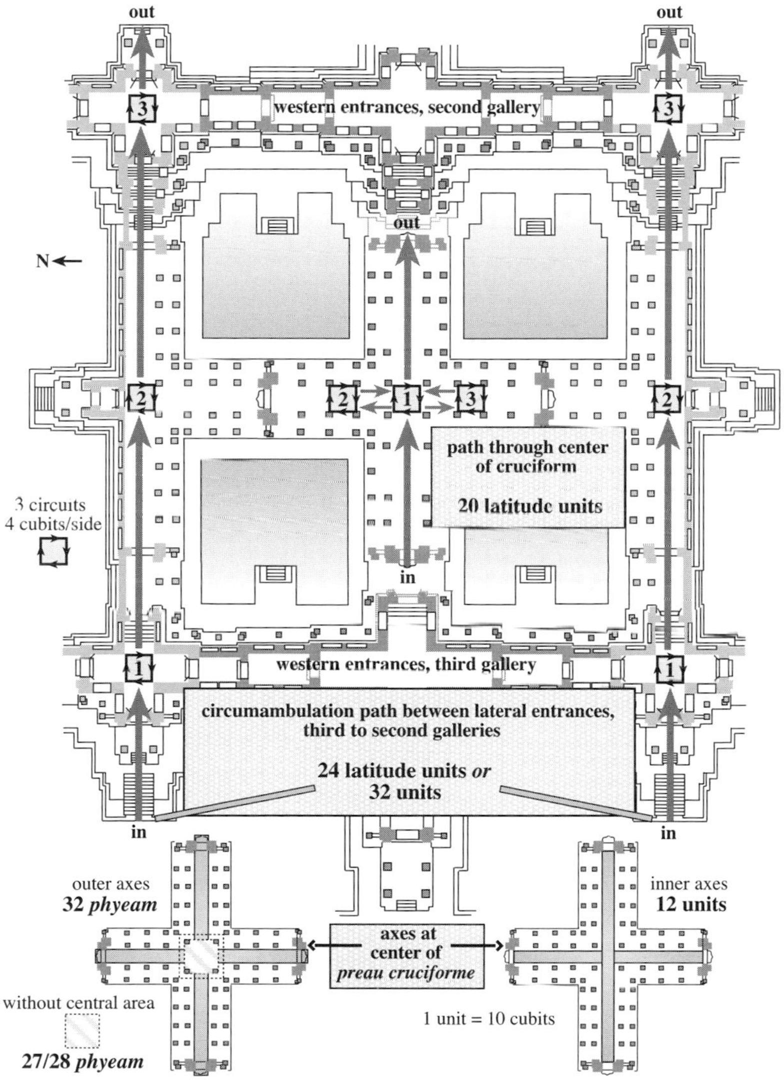

Fig. 7.13. Preau cruciforme, *central axes and three parallel circumambulation paths.*

Except for the central sanctuary and axes on the upper elevation, the latitude module appears only in conjunction with the *preau cruciforme* and second gallery, building the position of Brahmā at the north celestial pole into both sectors. Brahmā as a twenty first deity is the focus of the 20-unit central path. He is flanked on both sides by two 24-unit, lunar-oriented paths. One other central pathway also defines Brahmā as a twenty-first deity (Fig. 7.15). When measurements are taken in cubits, the result describes the deities in an architectural mandala: 12, 28, and 32. The cruciform therefore centers on Brahmā as a twenty-first figure and surrounds him with the gods in the mandala. (See Appendix A, Table 7.1.)

the lunar year is brought into the picture as well when these two paths are measured in latitude units.[4]

There is also a 360-*phyeam* circumambulation path which frames this sector as one enclosed space, like the 360-degree circuit around the celestial ecliptic that circles Brahmā and the earth at the same time (Fig. 7.14).[5] It numerically encapsulates the 360 days in a celestial year and brings the time on Mount Meru into the *preau cruciforme.* By its format and measurement, the 360-*phyeam* circumambulation around the cruciform also puts Brahmā at its center. Because the circuit around the *preau cruciforme* takes us back into the third gallery and effectively eliminates progress to the next level, it must have been an alternative to fully entering Mount Meru, symbolized by both top galleries together.

The latitude unit of measure also puts Brahmā at the center of the three 20-unit circumambulation paths through this area (Figs. 7.13 and 7.15).[6] As a twenty-first unit, he assumes the role of the solar Viṣṇu in the third gallery, incorporating the institution of kingship and 19 subsidiary officials or deities within his status as supreme deity. A 32-unit circumambulation path led us into this area from

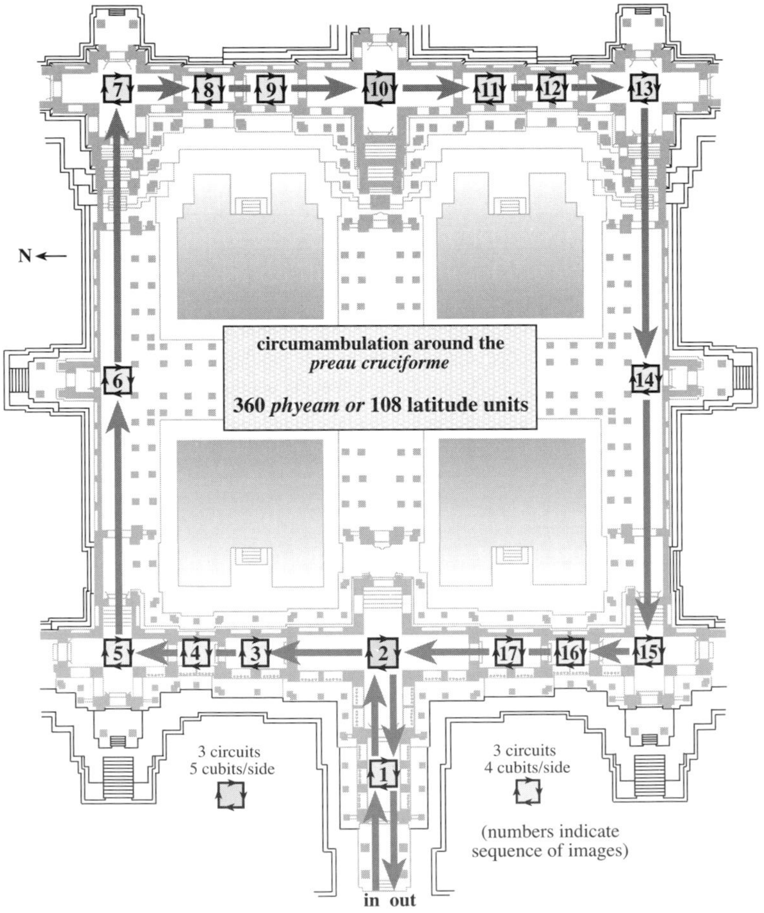

Fig. 7.14. Preau cruciforme, *ritual circuit around perimeter.*

Like the outer enclosure and every gallery in the temple, the *preau cruciforme* also has a ritual circumambulation around each of its images along the perimeter. Unlike the circuits around the galleries, however, there is no need to go in and out of each entrance chamber to pay homage to an image. Instead, the devotee once walked directly from image to image here. After the circuit is completed, it ends at its beginning point. (See Appendix A, Table 7.1.)

the western entrance of the third gallery, and a similar 21-unit path will lead us out of the cruciform through the central western entrance to the next courtyard. Preceded by 32 on the west and followed by 21 on the east, Brahmā is, once again, a fitting deity for the center of this mandala of gods.

Solar evidence. During the winter solstice period, shafts of sunlight start to cross the center of the *preau cruciforme* around 3:00 in the afternoon.[7] As the shafts enter the cruciform from the southwest, their slanting light on the floor shifts in its angle, like the ribs of a folding fan when the fan is opened. With this shift, the movement of light across the center of the cruciform slowly proceeds in a north-northeast direction. By 4:00 or so, one of these light shafts is already shining on the cemented square at the geometric center of the cruciform. This square originally would have held a reliquary. At first notice, the light does not seem particularly significant. But during the next 15 minutes, it becomes apparent that the light shaft might actually frame this square marker before the sun sinks below the roofline. For the viewer, without knowing the outcome, the experience of observing the moving light shaft and rising shadow of the roof is something like watching a race in

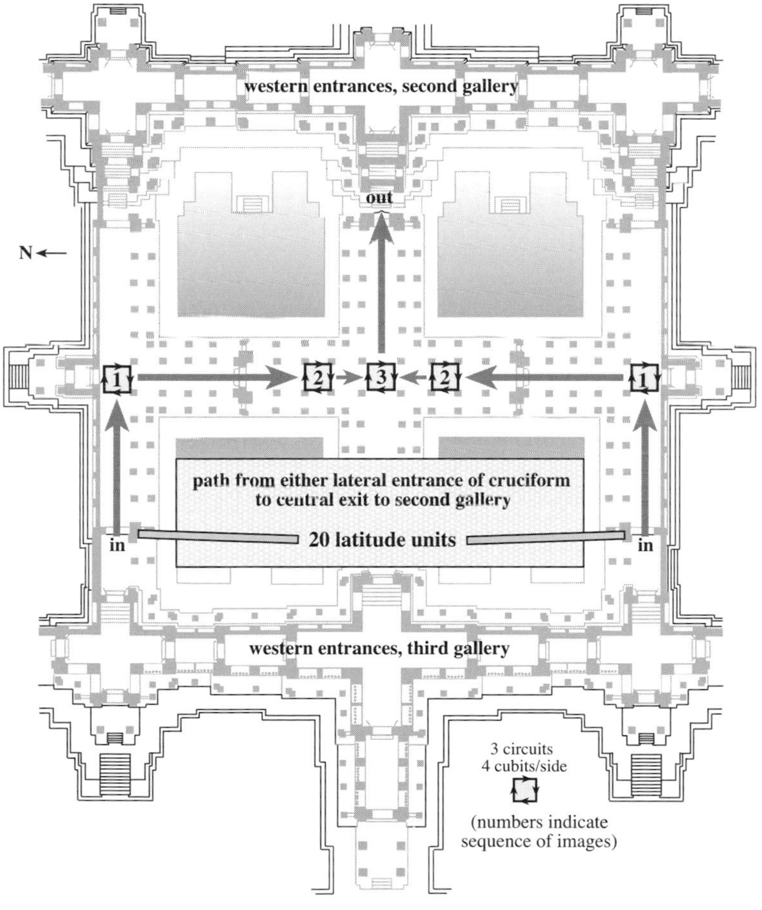

Fig. 7.15. Preau cruciforme, *paired ritual paths from the western lateral entrances to the central eastern exit.*

An approach to the central triad of images from the western lateral entrances to the cruciform, or from the central western entrance (Fig. 7.13), results in a 20-unit path, situating the central image as a twenty-first deity. (See Appendix A, Table 7.1.)

slow motion. When I first observed this phenomenon, I did not know if the roof would "win" and cut off the shaft before the square was framed. At 4:27, the race ended in a photo finish, both symbolically and literally, as I captured the solstice light with my camera. For the next two or three minutes, the square at the center was perfectly framed on two opposite corners by the light shaft and at the "bottom" corner by the shadow of the roof (Fig. 7.16). There was not one centimeter of deviation—the width of the square from corner to corner was exactly the width of the light shaft.

From 4:30 onward, the light shafts continue to move higher and farther into the cruciform before the sun sets below the roofline. The central shaft achieves a maximum height of about 5 feet or 1.5 meters over the covered square at 4:30 P.M., suggesting that a good segment of the statue was in sunlight at this time. The reliquary and the statue, then, were once joined by the sun (and Viṣṇu?) at the winter solstice.

But the reliquary—which usually takes the form of a cube with 16 holes around its upper periphery—was much more tightly aligned with the winter solstice light than the statue. Perhaps these reliquaries can be understood as containing the "essence" of the statue, the heart that gave the statue spiritual significance and life. That might explain why the focus was placed on the reliquary itself. Another explanation also comes to mind, however.

Remember that a portion of the king was in the supreme deity, and a portion of the deity in the king. There is a certain parallel to that concept in the solstice light connection between the reliquary and the statue. It is known that the king's ashes after death were kept in his pyramid temple, but there is no reason to believe that all the ashes were kept only in one temple, or only in the central sanctuary of the main temple. The ashes of the Buddha himself were divided, as are the ashes of

Fig. 7.16. Preau cruciforme, *central square, center hole covered with cement, near the winter solstice day.*

The shadows of two pillars frame the corners of the central hole on each side. Barely visible in this photograph, the shadow of the roof touches the west end of the square (to our right here). Because this image was taken 10 or 12 days after the winter solstice, the shadows of the two pillars have moved slightly into and away from the cemented hole—at the time the shadow of the roof closes in on the west side. On the solstice day, the square area marked by this hole is perfectly framed by shadows on three sides at 4:30 in the afternoon.

many Buddhist priests today. If the ashes of the king were similarly divided, then it is reasonable to assume that a portion of his ashes may have been placed in the central reliquary of the *preau cruciforme.* The *preau cruciforme* is a major juncture along the western entrant axis of the temple, one of just five such sites that precede the central sanctuary. If the king's ashes were also here in this sector of the temple, then the solstice shaft of light once joined the king and the statue together. That would explain why such exceptional care was taken to perfectly align the reliquary with the light shaft.

Whether or not the ashes were those of the king or a relative, an ancestor or a minister, the south is the direction of the fathers. The heavens are depicted on the south side of the monument. They receive a brighter light at the winter solstice while the gods opposite them in the north are in darkness. The winter solstice light comes from the south, shines on the south celestial pole for 24 hours, and brings long hours of daylight south of the equator. The ancestors in their celestial realm are therefore understood to be equally favored by light at this time of year. The solar interaction with the reliquary at the winter solstice would have paid homage to either the deceased king or perhaps a high-ranking father, with light reaching toward the reliquary from the southernmost position of the sun.

As the sun moves toward the spring equinox after December 22, the center of the *preau cruciforme* is gradually left in darkness. Except for a solitary shaft of light it nearly remains in darkness at the summer solstice. This narrow sliver of sunlight moves slowly across the floor—even more slowly it seems if you are watching it—until it passes by the central square at about 12 cm of distance between 5:15 and 5:30 P.M. on the solstice day (Fig. 7.17). The proper right side of the statue would have been illumined by this light since the pedestal extended well past the central square reliquary. Considering that the north and the summer sol-

Fig. 7.17. Preau cruciforme, *central square, center hole covered with cement, summer solstice day, and view north down central corridor.*

During the summer solstice, a narrow shaft of light crosses close to the central, cemented reliquary hole at around 5:15 in the afternoon. Aside from this light shaft and that of the winter solstice period, the center of the *preau cruciforme* remains in darkness all year.

stice lie in the direction of the gods, it seems the architects have taken great care to illuminate the statue. At the same time, they have eliminated the reliquary from any alignment with the northern solstice light, presumably because the fathers would be in darkness at this time of year. As a consequence, only the winter solstice shaft of light comes into alignment with the reliquary at the center of the cruciform.

This solar behavior not only singles out the reliquary and the "essence" of the statue for a special homage on December 22, it also defines an important attribute of the central statue. If Brahmā were at this juncture, he would have been placed between the two solstice shafts of light, symbolically at the center of the earth's axis, rather than at the north celestial pole. Otherwise, the statue would have remained in darkness during the winter solstice and in light during the summer solstice, and that is not the case. Also, during the winter

Fig. 7.18. Preau cruciforme, *central north–south cross-arm, south half, winter solstice.*

During the winter solstice, the corridor to the south of the proposed statue of Brahmā is bathed in sunlight, while the corridor on the north is in darkness. The light/dark effects are reversed for the summer solstice. (Fig. 7.17 shows a view north during the summer solstice.) This solar alternation is in agreement with the location of the *deva*s and *asura*s at the north and south celestial poles, respectively.

solstice in the *preau cruciforme,* the entire south side (*asura* side) of the cross-arm is striated by diagonal shafts of light (Fig. 7.18) while the opposite north side is in darkness. During the summer solstice, the north cross-arm (*deva* side) is brightened by diagonal light shafts (Fig. 7.17) while the south cross-arm is in darkness. This would again place the suggested statue of Brahmā at the center between the *asuras* (and winter solstice light) on the south and the *devas* (and summer solstice light) on the north.

It is said that the *ṛṣis* (rishi; sages or ascetics) are particularly related to Brahmā, who is alternatively their chief or ultimate progenitor. A class of seven Great Sages is found in the seven stars of the Great Bear constellation near Brahmā at the north celestial pole. The ascetics that are shown at the bases of the pillars in the north cross-arm of the gallery are illuminated by the summer solstice sun (Fig. 7.19), but they are in darkness at the winter solstice as the light touches the center of the cru-

Fig. 7.19. Preau cruciforme, *central north–south cross-arm, north half, summer solstice.*

The ascetics at the base of each pillar sit in a shaft of light during the summer solstice. On the other side of the corridor, the ascetics are in darkness. During the winter solstice, all the ascetics are in darkness when the sun reaches through to the center of the cruciform. The two solstice phenomena imply that the ascetics were related to the *devas* and not to the *asuras*.

ciform. During the winter solstice, the ascetics on the north are in darkness like the rest of that cross-arm, but so too are the ascetics on the pillars of the south cross-arm—when the light shaft crosses through the central area. Before then, the shafts of light move slowly away from the pillars, leaving the ascetics in darkness before the sun drops below the roofline. This phenomenon associates the ascetics with the gods in darkness at this time in the north, around Brahmā at the north celestial pole, and eliminates them from a solar connection to the *asuras* or to the fathers in the south. This solar activity in the north-south cross-arm also places Brahmā, like Viṣṇu, at the axis of the earth but aligns the sages with him at the north celestial pole.

Whereas the light shafts pierce the central area of the cruciform and illumine a portion of the statue there, the exact opposite is true for the image of Viṣṇu in the bas-reliefs. The image of Viṣṇu is not pierced by rays of light at the solstices; instead, light shafts flank the deity. He is also in full sunlight on the equinoxes while the statue in the cruciform is in darkness at that time and for most of the year. This light and dark counterpoint seems to paint Brahmā as a nighttime deity and Viṣṇu as a daytime god. In fact, the first indication that Brahmā may assume a noctural identity equal to that of Viṣṇu arises when we look at the constellation of Aquila the Eagle. Aquila is just a few degrees east of the Milky Way, 29 degrees north of the celestial equator. In other words, the constellation figuratively lies on the Sea of Milk, which runs like a serpent from northeast to southwest across the night sky. This tight spatial relationship between Aquila and the Milky Way provides an ancient stellar basis for the cosmology of Nārāyaṇa lying on the Sea of Milk.

In the creation myth, recall that Brahmā as Nārāyaṇa engenders time and space, while Viṣṇu as Nārāyaṇa lies on the cosmic serpent Ananta and engenders Brahmā. Ultimately, there is no distinction between Nārāyaṇa lying on the Milky Way and Nārāyaṇa at the north celestial pole as time and space revolve around him. Both forms of Nārāyaṇa have been bifurcated into Viṣṇu and Brahmā, as though they were actually two separate divinities, but they are not. It is this generally unrecognized reciprocity of Brahmā and Viṣṇu that may add another meaning to the shafts of solstice light through the center of the cruciform.

At the end of the night, the summer solstice rays of morning light dawn about 23 degrees north of due east. During the winter solstice, the sun rises the same distance to the south. The shafts of light that cross through the central area of the cruciform from the south (winter solstice) and from the north (summer solstice) are like the sun rising to dispel the darkness, the "night" at the center of the cruciform. In other terms, the morning light reaches us from 23 degrees north of the celestial equator at the summer solstice, just as the light shaft reaches the suggested statue of Brahmā from 23 degrees north. In the winter, the same phenomenon occurs to the south, except that now the shaft of light in the *preau cruciforme* moves up the center of the statue. These solar metaphors describe Brahmā as a nocturnal deity.

In contrast to Brahmā, a "daytime" Viṣṇu experiences another solstice effect. If we look again at the image of Viṣṇu at the center of the churning scene (Fig. 5.34), the small shaft of winter solstice light that borders him to the north is offset by the light that spans the space between the pillars on the other side of Viṣṇu. This aptly describes a geophysical reality: most of the light is in the southern hemisphere at this time and less light is in the north. At the winter solstice the north pole and latitudes near it remain in darkness for 24 hours. As we move southward on the earth, daylight hours slowly increase until we reach the south pole and 24 hours of light. The reverse is true for the summer solstice. By analogy, the sunlight that borders Viṣṇu not only describes him as a daytime, solar-related deity, but also describes him as centrally located on the earth. This is in accord with the churning scene and the central tower of Angkor Wat where Viṣṇu is placed at the center of the earth's axis.

Similarly, the statue in the *preau cruciforme* is neither at the north celestial pole nor at the south in regard to the solstice light, but between both poles—equivalent to Viṣṇu in the churning scene or in the central tower. Given the reciprocity between Viṣṇu and Brahmā in the myth of creation, this additional equivalency strengthens the hypothesis that Brahmā was once at the center of the cruciform. Once this solar evidence is in place and Brahmā begins to assume the character of a nocturnal alter-ego of the god Viṣṇu, new architectural evidence arises that not only agrees with but augments this diurnal/nocturnal, Viṣṇu/Brahmā alternation.

The reciprocity of Brahmā and Viṣṇu also finds corroboration in the format of the *preau cruciforme* and the upper elevation together. The design of the cruciform connecting corridors is unusual in that it is the same as the upper elevation. The same plan, the same surrounding and crossing corridors, and the same size join these otherwise disparate sectors together, in spite of obvious differences. The cruciform has no massive tower at its center. The floor of the entrances on the west is below the floor level in the cruciform, while the entrances on the east are raised above the cruciform corridors. Unlike the upper elevation, there are no windows here that open onto the surrounding world. But these differences with the upper level of Angkor Wat are due more to the practical and ideological function of the *preau cruciforme* as a transition between two elevations that are quite dissimilar in meaning. They do not negate the unusual connections that remain with the upper elevation, as follows.

The center of the cruciform is not only architecturally parallel to the central sanctuary of Angkor Wat in its location and relationship to axial corridors, but its dimensions are also parallel to those of the central sanctuary. For example, the square space around the statue once at the center of the *preau cruciforme* has a pillar at each corner. There are 4 m between (and including) this inner set of four central pillars. There are also 4 m between the sides of the floor of the central sanctuary (Figs. 7.13 and 8.19). The center of the cruciform has another, outer set of four pillars that enclose the inner set in a square frame 6 m across (Fig. 7.13, large dotted square at center). This 6-m distance between (and excluding) the outer set of pillars is equivalent to the 6-m distance between the doorways of the central sanctuary. In the latter instance, however, there is a discrepancy of about 10 cm or 4 in. because the cruciform distance is larger. These parallels both in ground plan and measurements support a reciprocity between Brahmā in the *preau cruciforme* and Viṣṇu in the central sanctuary on the upper elevation.

If we delete the central sanctuary from the axes that run through the central tower, there are 32 cubits that approach the Viṣṇu image on each side (Fig. 8.9c). If we delete the equivalent sanctuary space around Brahmā there are a total of 32 pillars that approach him from the east and west sides (Fig. 7.11). There are also 32 pillars that cross north-south from door to door in the central cruciform. There are 32 pillars in the east half of the cruciform and 32 in the south half. The various sets of 32 pillars between the doors of the central cruciform are the counterpart to the 32-cubit distances between the doors of the central tower. Although the doorways in the *preau cruciforme* are farther apart than the doorways in the central tower of Angkor Wat, they seem to have the same purpose—they indicate the boundaries of a single, large architectural unit. Unlike the doorways into the central tower, however, the cruciform doorways are only decorative. There are no post holes to indicate that wooden door panels were ever in place. We can also ignore the doorway and walk around it on either side, if so desired.

There are 32 *phyeam* between the steps of these doorways that define and separate a central cross within the *preau cruciforme.* That length changes to 27/28 *phyeam* (27.6 exactly) when the area marked by the four inner pillars around the central image is excluded, counting the pillars as part of that area (Fig. 7.13). The axes of the central sanctuary at Angkor Wat total just under 27 cubits, and the height of the sanctuary is just over 28 cubits, for an average of 27.5 cubits between the two (Figs. 8.19 and 8.21). This 27/28 vertical and horizontal definition of the sanctuary is basically identical to the 27/28 length of the central cross in the *preau cruciform,* although it occurs as a different type of axial total. Furthermore, the 12-cubit length of the central sanctuary between the first step inside each doorway has a resonance in the 12-unit interior distance between the decorative doorways of the cruciform (Figs. 7.13 and 8.19). Aside from these measurements, there are 16 pillars that extend outward from each door of the central tower along a covered axial corridor to the surrounding gallery, and also 16 pillars that extend outward from the doorway in each axial corridor of the cruciform into the surrounding corridors (Figs. 7.13 and 8.7). There may be slight variations such as the exact placement of the pillars, but the connections between these architectural counterparts are clear.

Once the parallels to the upper elevation are put alongside the effects of the solstice shafts of light, the picture of a nocturnal Brahmā alternating with a diurnal Viṣṇu eventually comes into focus. The juxtaposition of measurements, architectural design, the location of a constellation in relation to the Milky Way, cosmogony, and solstice light support the theory offerred here, that an image of Brahmā once looked down all four axial corridors in the *preau cruciforme.*

Brahmā as a nighttime manifestation of Viṣṇu also transforms our perspective on the two upper galleries of the temple. Whereas the second gallery focuses on the night sky and the moon, the first and topmost gallery focuses on the deities on Mount Meru and the sun. These two galleries together celebrate and pay homage to the supreme Nārāyaṇa. It is the two galleries together that fully exalt Viṣṇu as the highest form of divinity. An approach to Nārāyaṇa from the vantage point of Brahmā begins in the *preau cruciforme.* In its own way, the definition of Brahmā found here prepares the visitor for the nighttime association of this deity and the moon, which is looming on the eastern horizon as we climb the tunnel-like staircases into the second gallery.

THE SECOND GALLERY

The hallway in the southern half of the western corridor of the second gallery, with only one window, is nearly pitch-black inside (Fig. 7.20). The northern half opposite has no windows at all. None of the corridors have windows on their outer wall except for the one window just mentioned, and there are only nine interior-facing windows in the full 75-m length of the southern side of the gallery. All the lighting in the corridors is oblique, and it is dimmed even further by the vertical balusters across the windows. Except for the central tower, no other sector of Angkor Wat is as dark as the second gallery—the west side of the gallery in particular.

The dark western corridors are opposite brighter eastern corridors with 12 windows on the south half and 14 on the north half. The southern corridor in the gallery, with its sparse nine win-

Fig. 7.20. Second gallery, west side, south corridor, view to the south doorway.

The remains of sculpture seem to crouch in a corner in this short, dark corridor with only one window on the right. Its opposite companion on the north has no windows and very few visitors feel inclined to walk through its black hallway. These two corridors on the west may symbolize the new moon and the first night of a sliver of moonlight at the start of the lunar month.

dows, is opposite the northern corridor, which has 32 (Fig. 7.21). This unequal distribution is unlike anything else at Angkor Wat, but this does not mean it is accidental.

When the new moon begins the month, the sky is black for one or two nights; then the slowly waxing crescent moon is seen just over the western horizon after sunset. This lunar phase would correspond to the "no window" and "one window" configuration on the west side of the gallery. About 12 days later, the full moon rises in the east. This would explain the 12 windows on the east side (south half) of the gallery. After the full moon, there are 14 more days until we are back to zero again: the new moon. This explains the 14 windows on the east. From the new moon to the full moon and back again, the east and west sides of the gallery record the moon's behavior each month. Moreover, the sheer number of windows on the east, opening onto the full moon as it crosses to the west side of the temple after midnight, makes these corridors as bright as their western counterparts are dark. The lunar characteristics of the east and west sides of the gallery harmonize with the lunar month recorded in three different ways on the east and west sides of the third gallery. Because Angkor Wat faces west, in a sense it faces the start of the new moon period: the beginning of the lunar month. This orientation also allows one to observe the full moon in relation to the towers in the east from the causeway on the west.

The nine windows that are evenly dispersed from west to east across the southern corridor cannot be related to lunar periodicity. But the planetary deities that begin with the sun and moon and end with Rāhu and Ketu total nine altogether. Given no other alternative, the light coming in the nine windows may be connected to the light of these nine planets. Since there are 32 windows on the north that can be numerically factored into the 28 constellations and 4 planetary or directional deities, the sets of northern and southern windows might allude to the band of constellations and planets around the celestial ecliptic. In this case, the alternating periods of the new and full moon depicted on the west and east are placed along the lunar path, defined by the north and south sets of windows. When seen as pairs across the gallery (new and full moon) and as one unified system (band of constellations and planets), the windows on this level may well provide not only the periodicity of the lunar half-month, but the trajectory followed by the moon each month as well.

The alternation of 12/14 windows on the east versus 0/1 window on the west is complemented by eight different lunar alignments between the northeast, southeast, and southwest corner towers in this gallery and the causeway and other sectors of Angkor Wat (Fig. 4.2).[8] These alignments are the

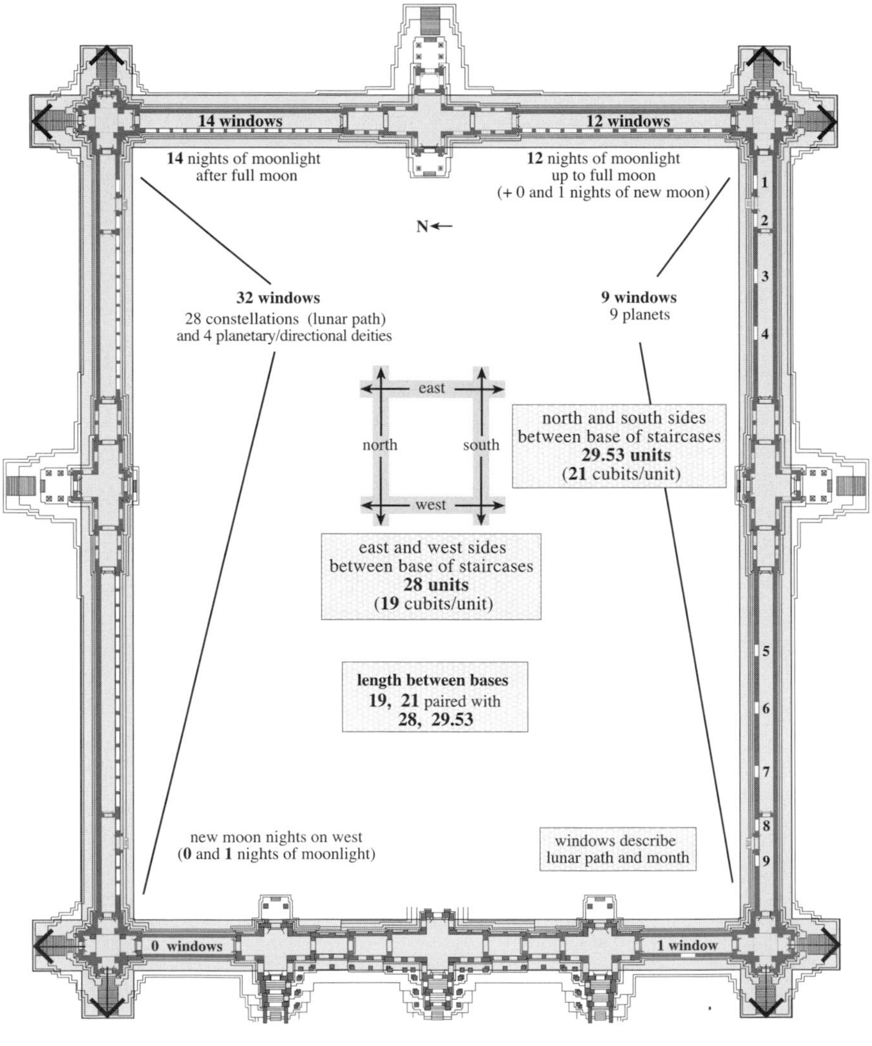

Fig. 7.21. Second gallery, length on each side and distribution of windows.

The sides of the second gallery record two different lengths for the lunar month, the actual length and the days of lunar visibility: 29.53 and 28. The theme is carried into the distribution of windows, itself a description of the lunar path each month and of lunar periodicity. (See Appendix A, Table 7.2.)

largest cluster in any single area of the temple, and presage the overwhelming dominance of the moon at this level. Together the northern and southern sides of the gallery total 29.53 units in length while the eastern and western sides come to 28 units (Fig. 7.21), following the lunar north/south and east/west dichotomy found in the distribution of windows.[9] As it happens, these lunar indicators are just the first sliver of a waxing crescent that will soon become full and bright in a stunning series of measurements. There are four different sets of measurements involving the entrances of the gallery which focus only on the lunar month. These are: 27/28 units (27.6) in ritual paths through the corner towers (Fig. 7.22); 27 or 28 total steps in the northern, southern, and eastern entrances with another total of 27 units in a ritual circumambulation path (Fig. 7.23); and 27 units in the outer axes of all the entrances together (Fig. 7.24).[10] As the drawings illustrate, the measurements in the entrances are recorded in terms of modules of 33 or 13.43 cubits. These entrances express a lunar periodicity that is created by Brahmā as a supreme deity (33) at the north celestial pole (13.43). Because the axial entrances and the corner towers have the same type of lunar circumambulation and their steps total the same 27/28-unit figure, deities connected to the moon must have been featured in the chambers in the second gallery. Along with the emphasis on 54/54 (bridge and western entrances) and 19/20/21 (third gallery), the lunar/*nakṣatra* theme is a special focus here. The moon takes us around the gallery by means of steps, windows, circumambulation paths, alignments, and axial measurements. In fact, within the darkened corridors, there is not a single solar reference.

As the gallery stretches from west to east and north to south forming one architectural construct, its character changes. The moon is primarily constrained to a very active path around the perimeter. But it does not define the gallery as a whole, at least not by itself.

Before we even start to enter the chambers here, the gallery is introduced by the number 21 on all four sides. There are 21 steps in the main staircases on the north, south, and east sides of the gallery. And in a direct path from the *nāga* balustrade we cover a distance of 21 latitude units to the gallery's first step on the west (Fig. 7.25).[11] Between that first step and the last step out of the western entrance is another 21-unit distance that follows a ritual circuit out of the western chamber (Fig. 7.26).[12] We have just passed through the curving vines, flowers, and figures sculpted onto the

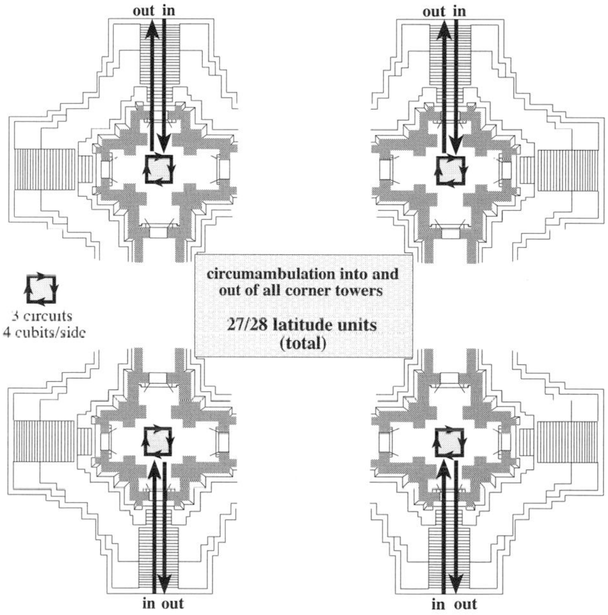

Fig. 7.22. Second gallery, 4 corner towers, ritual path.
The circumambulation path through the 4 corner towers totals 27.6 latitude units, a way of expressing a 27/28-unit possibility indicative of the 27 or 28 lunar mansions. Three of these towers also have several lunar alignments with the causeway and western entrances of the temple. (See Appendix A, Table 7.2.)

stone surfaces of the cruciform. For a moment, we were surrounded by pillared corridors in a seemingly open, yet artfully enclosed and contoured space. The pools once held ablution water that reflected the architectural halls and blue canopy of the sky above. This is the ambience that further sanctified the last stage of the 21-unit journey up to the main entrance of the second gallery.

A statue of Brahmā may have waited for our arrival in the main western entrance. At least, his iconography agrees with the lunar symbolism here, and no other twenty-first deity could preside over the nocturnal environment of the corridors with as much authority. It is possible, then, that we approach the final image of Viṣṇu by means of Brahmā, returning down the lotus stalk to the matrix of creation.

Represented by the 13.43-cubit latitude module, Brahmā at the latitude of the north celestial pole introduces the gallery on the west (21), is present in the lunar circumambulation around the gallery (27/28), and takes us through the main western entrances (21). Until this point, we have considered Brahmā in conjunction with the chambers and approach to the gallery. But he is the nocturnal equivalent of Viṣṇu in the central sanctuary, and from the central sanctuary Brahmā also radiates the axes of the gallery (Fig. 7.27).

Recall that Viṣṇu is located at 13.43 degrees by the north-south axis of the sanctuary, placing him

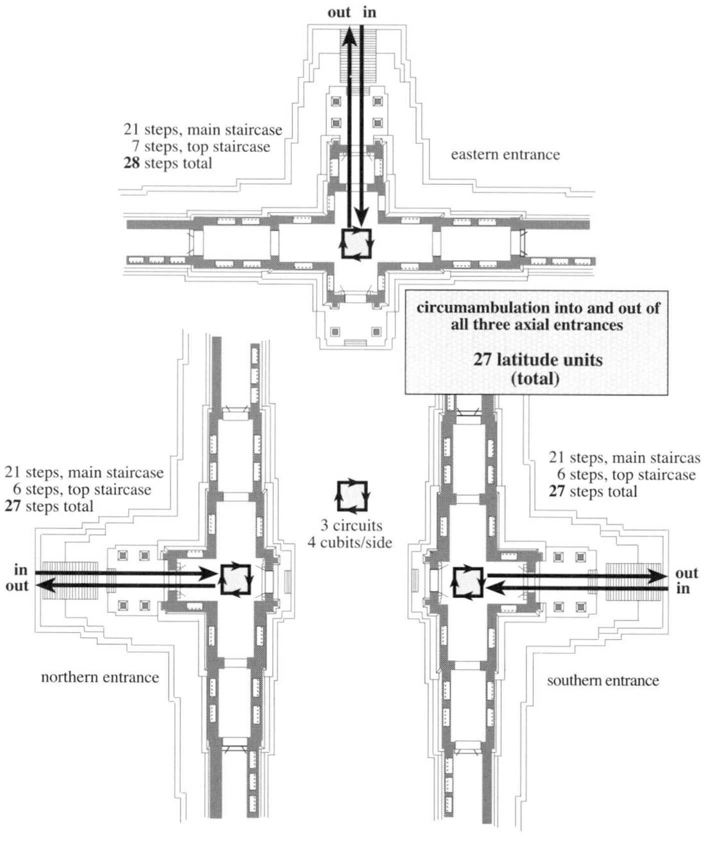

Fig. 7.23. Second gallery, northern, southern, and eastern axial entrances, ritual path.

The ritual circumambulation path through the set of these 3 entrances is identical in format to the path through the corner towers (Fig. 7.22), and identical in meaning. The path here gives a total of 27 lunar mansions in a band around the ecliptic. (See Appendix A, Table 7.2.)

at the north celestial pole as seen from the latitude of Angkor Wat. In that position, he assumes the four heads and persona of Brahmā. From the central tower of Angkor Wat, thus identified as the north celestial pole itself, the axes of the second gallery expand outward for a total of 44 latitude units.[13] The forty-fifth supreme deity is at the point of genesis in the central sanctuary of the temple. In one conceptual stroke, the north celestial pole, Brahmā/Viṣṇu, and the second gallery are joined by all 44 deities in the architectural mandala. To reinforce the union of the mandala and a central Brahmā/Viṣṇu, there are 49 units of 20 cubits each around the circumference of the gallery (Fig. 7.27).[14] The circumference also includes 49 chambers, and 49 steps in its introduction from the western entrances.[15] By numerical allusion, the 49-square grid of a mandala is thereby created, providing the deities with a metaphorical resting place parallel to their places in the 49 sanctuaries of the gallery.

In this instance, the circumference is essentially

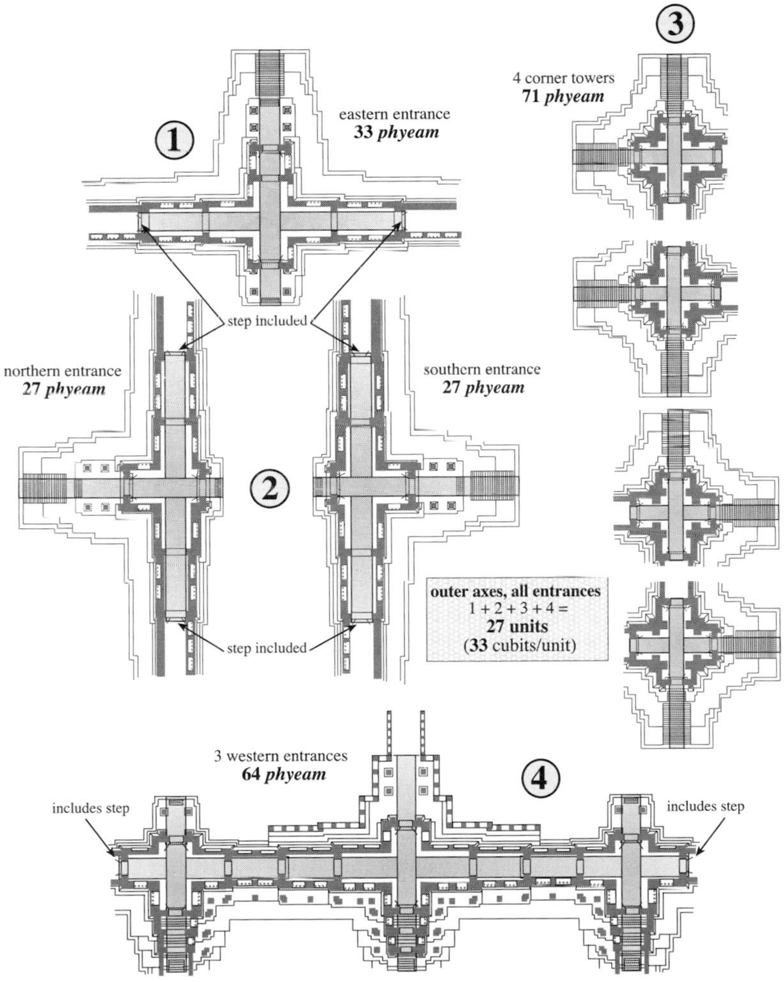

Fig. 7.24. Second gallery, all entrances, outer axes.

When the outer axes of the entrances are taken as one set, they are equivalent to 27 units measured in 33-cubit modules. The number 33 defines Brahmā in relation to the periphery of the architectural mandala, a periphery that is also a description of the 27/28 *nakṣatra*. (See Appendix A, Table 7.2.)

a perfect 49 × 20 cubits in conjunction with the eastern and western entrances, and slightly less in conjunction with the northern and southern entrances (48.90 × 20 cubits), and the corner towers (48.86 × 20 cubits).[16] The pattern of calculating the circumference with the intersecting, internal axis of each entrance is characteristic of the central three galleries of Angkor Wat. We first encountered the pattern in the third gallery, and it will recur on the upper elevation as well. Each time, there is a nuance in the pattern that belongs uniquely to the gallery in question. For example, here the internal axes include the image in every entrance, whereas the opposite is true in the third gallery. Except for the main western entrance there, images were excluded. Their inclusion in the second gallery's

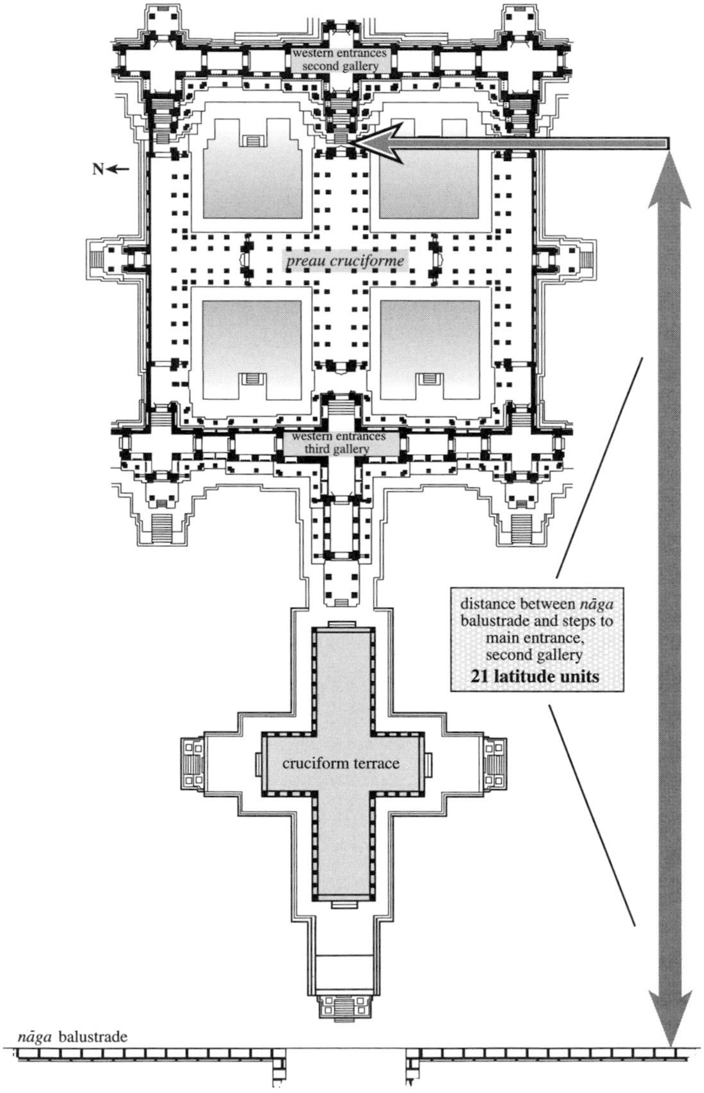

Fig. 7.25. Second gallery, 21-unit introduction from nāga balustrade on the west.

There are 21 latitude units between the *nāga* balustrade at the end of the causeway and the first step up to the main entrance of the second gallery. This is one of a set of distances between the *nāga* balustrade and subsequent sectors of Angkor Wat. (See Appendix A, Table 7.3.)

circumferences places every image actively within the mandala.

Through the 20-cubit module repeated 49 times around the gallery, the lesser deities, in the guise of 19 gods plus Indra, also circle Brahmā/ Viṣṇu in the central tower. One reference to a 19/21-unit alternation has already appeared in the northern and southern sides of the gallery (Fig. 7.21). In that measurement, the multiples of 21 × 29.53 and 19 × 28 join Brahmā to the full length of a lunar month (29.53) and the 19 gods without Indra to the lunar constellations (28).

In the preceding discussion four numerical and conceptual categories emerge: the number 21, the mandala, lunar symbolism, and Brahmā as a nocturnal deity. Within these three categories the entire gallery finds its identity and definition.

Brahmā as the deity at the north celestial pole

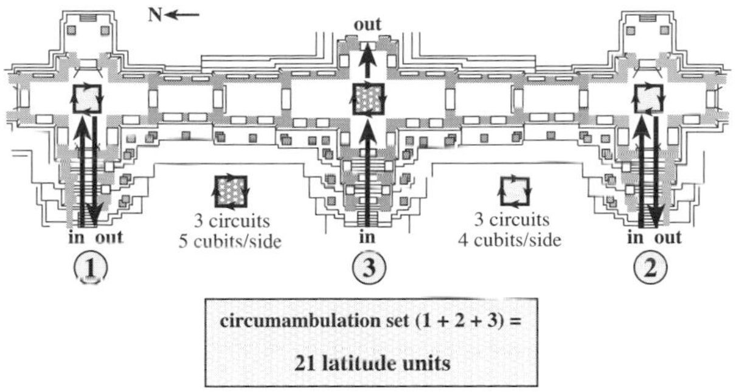

Fig. 7.26. Second gallery, set of 3 western entrances, ritual path.

After completing 27- and 28-unit circuits around the images in the second gallery, the final passage through the gallery and onto the upper elevation is 21 units long. The ritual path through the main entrance involves 3 circuits of the image in each lateral entrance, and 3 circuits of the image in the main entrance before exiting on the west. The total for this set repeats the 21 units that lead from the *nāga* balustrade to the first step in the main entrance. (See Appendix A, Table 7.3.)

disappears during the day when the sun rises and Viṣṇu in his solar aspect rules the world. At night, the sun cedes to the moon and Brahmā reappears. The same night-and-day alternation from the perspective of the gods on Mount Meru has the same source. In Indra's realm, night begins as the sun sets on September 23 and ends when it rises on March 21. Daylight continues until the sun goes down again in September. Once that night ends, Brahmā cedes to Viṣṇu who rises with the sun on March 21—right over the central tower of Angkor Wat, in fact—and begins the 6-month day of the gods. This pattern can be fully appreciated for the first time from the vantage point of the mandala of the second gallery. Up until now, we have seen the north–south oscillation in a limited way: without the perspective of the gods on Mount Meru.

By moving into the mandala of the gods as we enter into the second gallery or walk through its 49 chambers, we attain the temporal viewpoint of divinity. The lunar cycles that alternate from west to east and back again divide the celestial day into 24 periods, 12 light and 12 dark (lunar half-months to us), which ironically or not correspond to the 24 hours in our day, 12 light and 12 dark on the average. The lunar numbers in the second gallery may stay the same, but they function on a different scale.

The moon's cycles connect it both with the western and eastern side of the compass. Again from Indra's point of view, the new moon would start the "light of day" from the western horizon. The new moon is first seen in the west and waxes as it rises farther and farther eastward. Note that all the windows in the second gallery face inward toward the center of the temple except that one window on the west. Was it meant to catch the first rays of moonlight and begin a new day for Indra and the *deva*s in their mandala home in the second gallery?

In a certain sense, then, as we ascend the axes

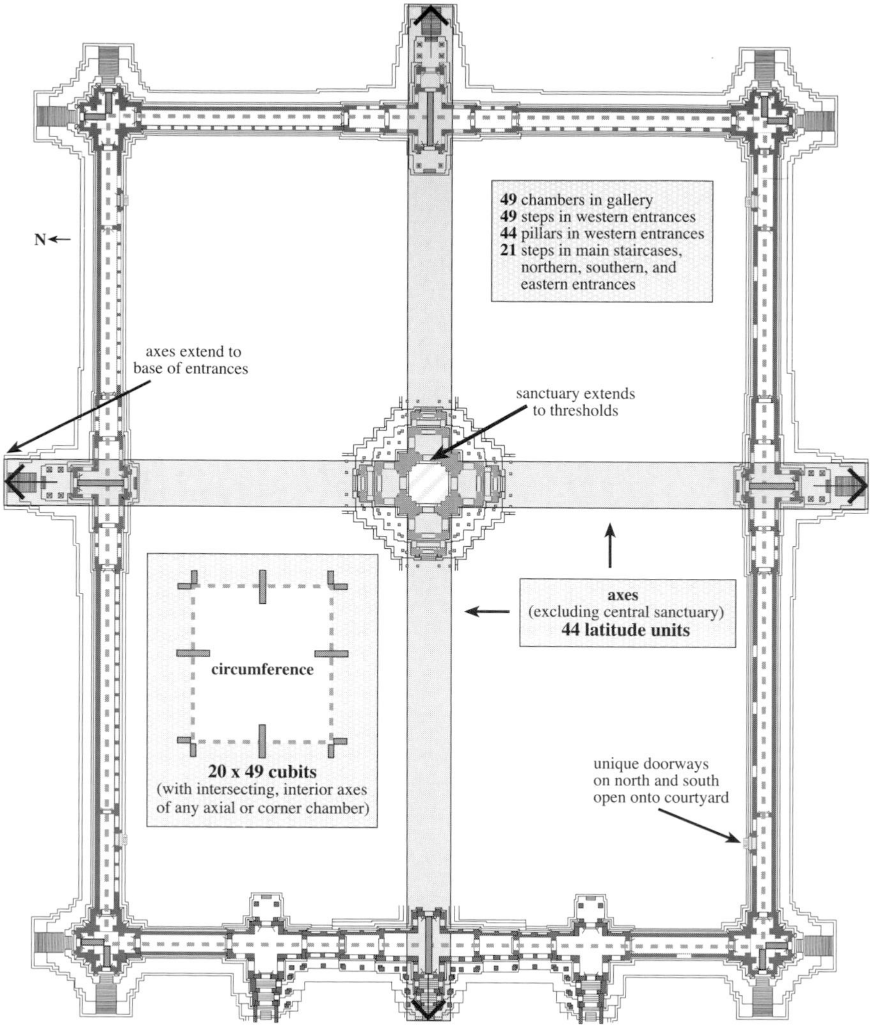

Fig. 7.27. Second gallery, axes and circumference.

The axes of the gallery record the 44 deities in the architectural mandala while the circumference refers to 20 and the 49 squares in the mandala. The circumference measurement is joined to an axis in each entrance, a pattern that is common to the central galleries of the temple. In this instance, the space occupied by each image in the axial or corner entrances is included in the 49-unit circumference total. (See Appendix A, Table 7.3.)

of Angkor Wat and enter this realm of Brahmā and the mandala of *deva*s, we have not only left terrestrial time and space behind us, but we are acquiring the perspective of divinity. As this change happens in us, we are not only approaching closer and closer to Viṣṇu: we are closing the gap between us and the images of ancestor/deities we see all around us. Some portion of divinity is becoming inherent in us, and we are better prepared to step out of the last bit of the *kṛta yuga*, walk across the 32-cubit path to the staircase of the upper elevation, and begin the final ascent to Viṣṇu.

8

Mount Meru at Journey's End: The Upper Elevation

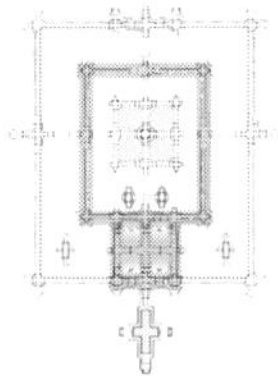

THE topmost gallery of Angkor Wat, a home of Viṣṇu that rests on solar axes, turns the symbolism found in the second gallery from night into day. Whereas the second gallery is hidden from view on the west, its facade obscured in the *preau cruciforme,* the first gallery with its towers and corridors rises upward in the white Cambodian sunlight (Fig. 8.1). Far from being hidden, its form overwhelms the visitor standing at the base of the Brobdingnagian central staircase (Fig. 8.2). The impact of the upper level is all the greater because we have just emerged from the intimate, shaded surroundings of the *preau cruciforme.* It takes only a minute to cross from the cruciform corridors to the courtyard around the upper elevation, but it takes much longer to adjust to the difference.

This change happens just as we step out of the *kṛta yuga* distance and see the upper elevation for the first time, the view shown in Fig. 8.2. We are on the elevated cruciform walkway that spans 32 cubits to the base of the great western staircase and leads to the pair of small libraries on the right and left. We have no choice but to climb the staircase or visit the libraries: there are no steps down to the courtyard from here. Other than going through a library and out its doors onto the courtyard, we either have to jump down or maneuver around the walkway at the grand western staircase—and climb down from there. None of these choices is a likely ritual path. Nevertheless, there are ritual circumambulation

Fig. 8.1. Upper elevation, west facade, southwest corner tower.

There is a magnificent orchestration in the component parts of the upper elevation. The sheer tonnage of the plinth is scaled by the regular repetition of each horizontal step in the staircase. In turn, the vertical ascent of the stairs carries our gaze straight up the axis of the tower. At that juncture, a curving silhouette slowly brings the axis up to its highest point. With this inspired design, the architects have created a dynamic push and pull between the weight of the foundation and the great height of the towers.

Fig. 8.2. Upper elevation, main western entrance and staircase.

This regal and massive staircase—the final ascent up Mount Meru to the home of the gods—is one reason why only the gods reside there. Nor do they have to walk more than a half-mile from the western entrance bridge, in the hot sun, to arrive at this stage. Visitors must walk back, as well, usually subdued by the descent of the staircase. This view does not do justice to the incline, so steep that it is impossible to see the staircase from its landing unless standing very close to the edge.

paths that go around the base of the upper elevation. How could they be reached?

The answer is, by means of the lateral western entrances of the second gallery, which lead right to the courtyard. Once a circuit of the upper elevation is completed, we would go back into a lateral western entrance and exit onto the walkway from the central (not a lateral) doorway (Fig. 8.3). From there, the journey continues up the staircase.

To make a circuit around either the first or second gallery, then, one has to leave from an entrance of the *preau cruciforme*, circle the gallery, and return to the cruciform before continuing along the western axis. The ambience of the *preau cruciforme* adds considerable stature to the approach on the west and isolates the approach from the rest of the gallery.

As discussed earlier, once on the topmost level, we find that the similarities to the design of the *preau cruciforme* are striking. Four roofed corridors lead to the central tower in each cardinal direction, connecting the tower to the axial entrances in the surrounding gallery. These corridors have a double row of pillars along their length—except for the western passageway (Fig. 1.12), which was walled at some point after the temple was completed. At the center of each corridor is a small porch that leads down to the courtyard.

The quadrants formed by the sunken courtyard recall the four empty pools in the *preau cruciforme.* But these quadrants are simple courtyard spaces that today are seldom crossed (Fig. 8.4). Rather than go up and down through the quadrant space from one axial corridor to the next, it is much

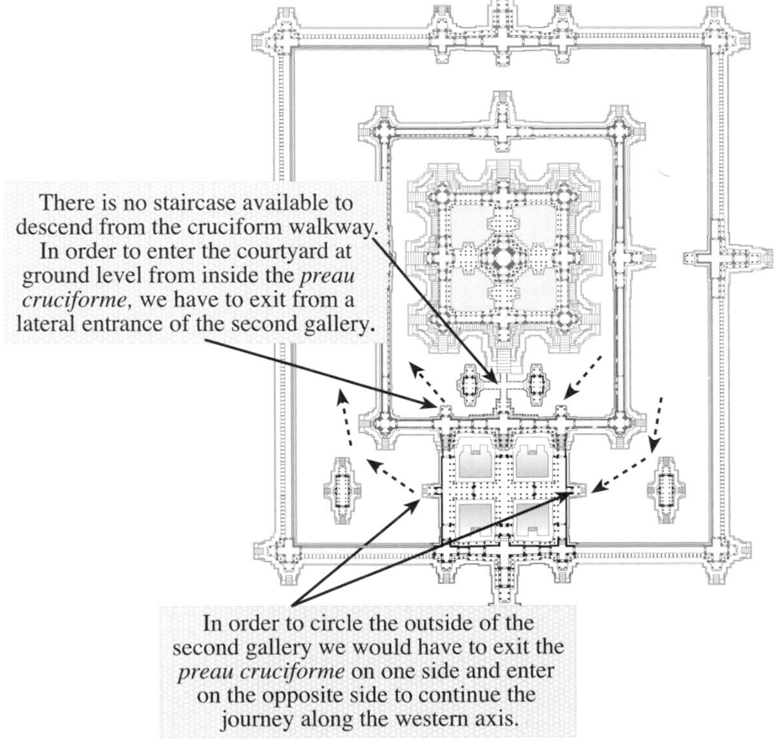

There is no staircase available to descend from the cruciform walkway. In order to enter the courtyard at ground level from inside the *preau cruciforme,* we have to exit from a lateral entrance of the second gallery.
In order to circle the outside of the second gallery we would have to exit the *preau cruciforme* on one side and enter on the opposite side to continue the journey along the western axis.

Fig. 8.3. Central galleries, lateral exits to the courtyards around the second gallery and upper elevation.

There is no direct axial exit on the west to the courtyards that surround the top two galleries of the temple. In order to circle either gallery, we have to leave from a lateral exit in the *preau cruciforme* or from the flanking western chambers of the second gallery.

easier just to walk around the ledges of the central tower and more scenic to walk through the gallery's encircling corridors.

The gallery that surrounds the courtyard has a wall with large windows on its outer perimeter and, on its inner perimeter, a double row of pillars supporting vaulted and demivaulted roofs. Light streams through the broad windows and stately pillars, making these the brightest and most solar corridors at Angkor Wat. They are also the shortest corridors—so short that they seem more like appendages to the corner and axial entrances.

The top of the central tower rises high above this elevation and can be seen only from the inner edge of the gallery or from the courtyard (Fig. 8.5). At the same time, the vast height of the tower is balanced by a graded series of courses that slowly rise from the tower's broad base upward (Fig. 8.6). The horizontally aligned axial corridors reach this base and, with their telescoping roofs, lead

Fig. 8.4. Upper elevation, northwest courtyard, intersection of axial corridor and gallery.

At the left, the balustered windows allow a view out to the lower galleries; at the right, in shadow, an axial corridor connects the north entrance to the central tower. The intimate quarters and high elevation give a feeling of both seclusion and isolation at this level.

Fig. 8.5. Upper elevation, central tower, southwest facade.

The elegant curvature built into the central tower from any angle is enhanced by the multiple *nāgas*, *apsarases*, architectural antefixes, and other figures that inhabit the upper reaches of "Mount Meru." The apex of the tower points to the formless realm of the gods, far above us in space. Measurements define the tower as Mount Meru and place it at the north celestial pole, the northern projection of the axis of the earth.

gracefully into the vertical definition of the tower itself.

Everywhere one finds smiling *apsarases* in bas-relief who now seem to be adorning the interior, rather than the exterior, of the temple. Part of this illusion may be due to the fact that many of these female figures have been placed in the shade by their sculptors. Although the upper elevation is open to the sky, the word that best describes this space is "enclosed."

Because the expanse of the courtyard is undercut by the four axial corridors and the massive central tower, each courtyard quadrant is small, increasing the sense of intimacy at this level. The stilled ambience, the separate quadrants, the tall corridors and towers—all function like protective shields that keep away the clamoring world, by now as psychologically distant in time and place as it is physically remote. All of these aspects recall the *preau cruciforme* that we left behind a short time ago

Fig. 8.6. Upper elevation, central tower, base from the west-northwest.

The tower rises in gradual stages from the courtyard. Its inner configuration of axial antechambers around a central chamber is disguised by pillars, telescoping roofs, and connecting corridors. The final abode of Viṣṇu at Angkor Wat imparts a sense of luxury and mystery with its architectural and decorative complexity.

and not without reason, as we know. The *preau cruciforme* and the upper level of Angkor Wat are both between 47 and 48 m across, north to south, measured from the center of the surrounding corridor. Their west–east axes vary slightly, but the two architectural spaces are essentially the same size and the same design. To put their scale in context, the bas-relief of the Churning of the Sea of Milk is 49 m long.

From ground level far below, the top of the central tower rises as high as a modern 20-story apartment building. In more ways than one, it reigns over the most elevated count of numerical symbolism at Angkor Wat. A total of 80 different significant measurements pay homage to Viṣṇu at this level.

A SOLAR DEITY

The night, the moon, and Brahmā dominate the *preau cruciforme* and second gallery. The sun, the day, and Viṣṇu hold sway over this gallery. Nevertheless, the architects had somehow to create an image in the central sanctuary that was solar in conjunction with this gallery, but not limited to a solar aspect. This was no easy task, but if the measurements are considered, it was successfully executed.

No measurement is of greater importance to a gallery than its axes. The axes emanate from the image in the central sanctuary—directly. There is no intermediary, no intervening bridge, no space between the axes and the image. The axes of the upper elevation define the image in the central sanctuary as both lunar and solar, as both Viṣṇu and Brahmā, as both the 12 zodiac signs and the 28 *nakṣatra* (Figs. 8.7 and 8.8). (The exact measurements are to be found in Appendix A, Table 8.1.)

The 12-unit axes made up of 28-cubit modules are numerically echoed by the 12 stairways made up of 28 steps.[1] Both of these instances depict the 12 zodiac signs and 28 lunar mansions sharing the same space just as they share the space around the ecliptic. Similarly, the 366-unit solar axes are balanced by the lunar axes that define Brahmā (27/28 × 13.43, the latitude unit). Nārāyaṇa is credited with creating all of time, lunar or solar, completely equally. This corroborates the picture in the *preau cruciforme,* which illustrates a solar Viṣṇu and lunar Brahmā determining the daily time period of the gods, our own terrestrial year. The lunar and solar balance of the axes under the topmost elevation of the temple is an eloquent statement on the nature of the supreme deity in the central tower.

The axes of the tower, however, have a solar but no lunar aspect. The closer we get to the central image of Viṣṇu in the main sanctuary, the more solar he becomes. The axes of the central tower, at 91.29 cubits,[2] are one-fourth of the 366-unit axes under the elevation and define one-fourth of the solar year, or the average time between equinox and solstice days (Fig. 8.9a). The staircases to the upper elevation are placed three in each direction and also define one-fourth of the solar year as 3 months in duration. At the same time, the solar connotations of 91.29 are transformed by the expression of the same length as 45 cubits north–south and 45 west–east. This pattern reinserts the Supreme Viṣṇu into the solar year.

More solar measurements show that if we were to circumambulate in and out of the north, south, and east axial entrances before entering this level on the west, the resultant circuit would cover 365.00 cubits (Fig. 8.10a).[3] Each of the four axial entrances on this level has 12 windows, 12 pillars, and two flanking chambers for a total of 12 axial chambers in all. The 365-cubit, in-and-out circumambulation of the entrances, along with their emphasis on 12, indicates that their central image—of Viṣṇu most likely—was solar in orientation. As these entrances are the architectural focus

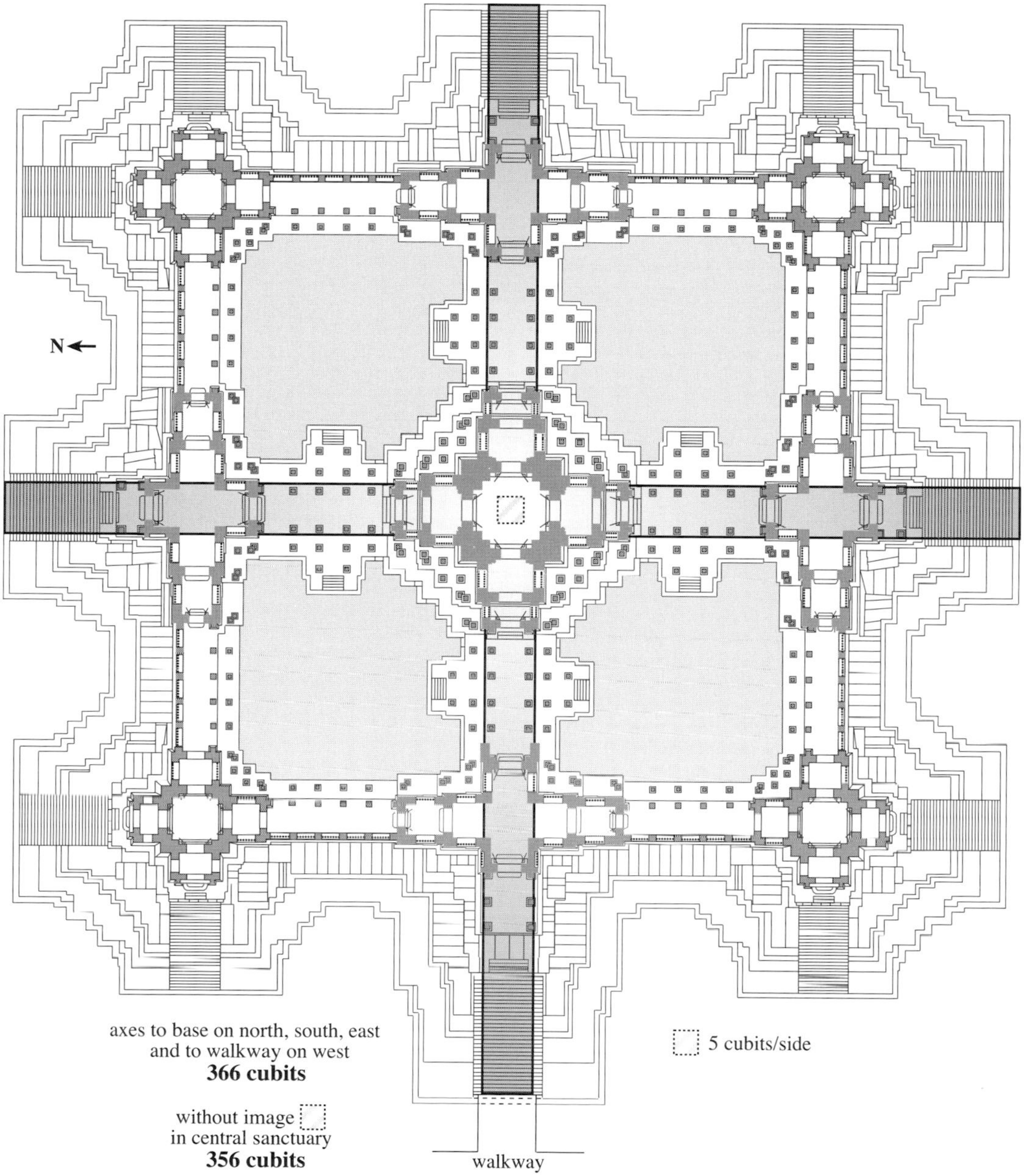

Fig. 8.7. First gallery, axes up to the walkway on the west.

When the axes of the upper elevation are measured between bases and to the walkway on the west, they equal 366.33 cubits or one of the alternate lengths of the solar year (our leap year). If the central image of Viṣṇu (5 cubits on a side) is excluded from the solar axes, the result is 356 cubits, or close to a lunar year of 354 days. (See Appendix A, Table 8.1.)

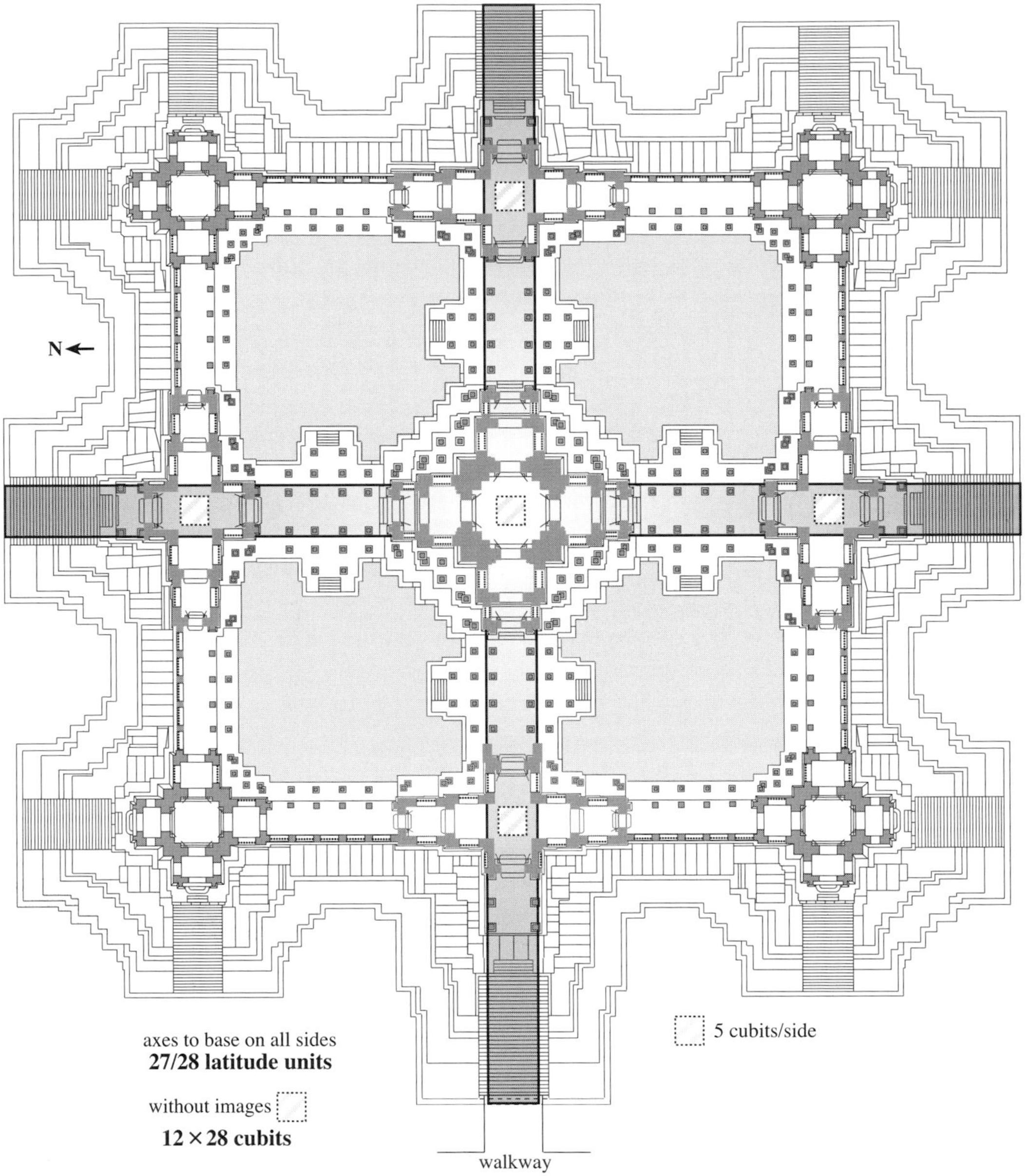

Fig. 8.8. First gallery, axes to the bases on all sides.

The full axes of the upper elevation total 27.43 when measured in 13.43-cubit modules (the latitude unit). In other words, they define the 27/28 lunar mansions in terms of the position of Brahmā at the north celestial pole, as seen from Angkor. If we take away the main images that lie along the axes, the axial total becomes exactly 12 × 28.19 cubits. These latter two multiples describe the 12 zodiac signs and 28 *nakṣatra,* the two sets of constellations that fall within the path of the sun and moon. (See Appendix A, Table 8.1.)

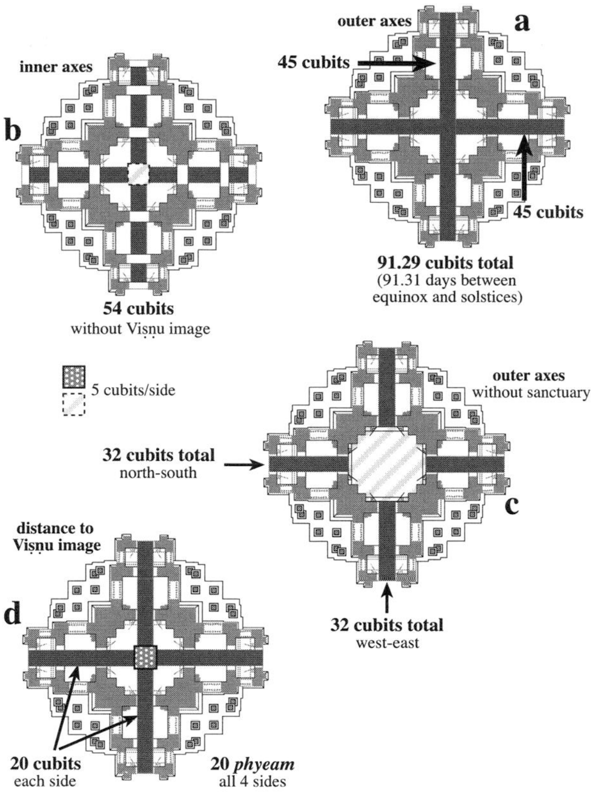

Fig. 8.9. Central tower, outer axes.

When the Viṣṇu image is included in the outer axes of the tower their length is either 45 cubits each way or 91.29 cubits total (a). The former number places Viṣṇu at the center of the architectural mandala as a forty-fifth supreme deity. The latter number places the central tower at the equinoxes, the solar center between the average of 91 days to the winter solstice in the south and 91 days to the summer solstice in the north. By joining 45 and the equinoxes together, the tower assumes the iconography of the central mountain or pivot in the churning scene. In that scene the central axis is joined to the spring equinox, and at the same time it depicts the north celestial pole, equivalent to the central position of a forty-fifth Brahmā in the architectural mandala. The remaining axial measurements of 54, 32, and 20 cubits (b, c, and d) without the central Viṣṇu image describe the three different groupings of gods that surround a supreme deity. (See Appendix A, Tables 8.5, 8.6, 8.7.)

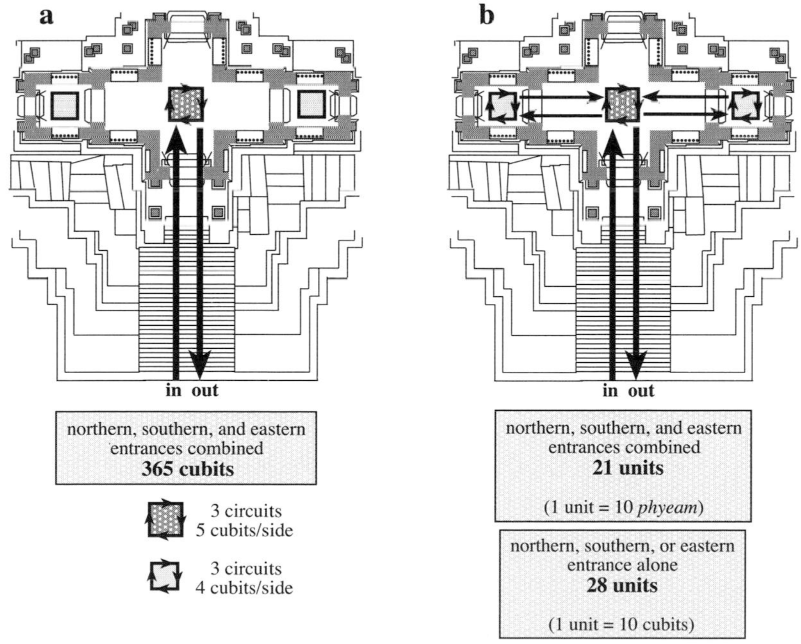

Fig. 8.10. First gallery, northern, southern, and eastern axial entrances, circumambulation paths.

Entering and exiting each of these three axial entrances in turn in order to circumambulate the main image three times produces a total pathway of 365 cubits, or one solar year (a). In contrast, the same in-and-out circuit with the two flanking images included produces a lunar pathway of 28 units for each entrance, and a total pathway of 21 units (of 10 cubits each) for all three entrances together (b). (See Appendix A, Table 8.2.)

of each axis, their connection to the sun is significant.

Just in these 12-unit and 365/366-unit axial measurements alone, the upper elevation has more solar-related numbers than any other area of Angkor Wat. Add to that the spring equinox alignment with the beginning of the western causeway and the 365-unit axes of the outer enclosure, both of which have the central tower as a source, and it is easy to see that the major sun-related measurements at Angkor Wat are inseparable from this level.

VIṢṆU: THE SUPREME NĀRĀYAṆA

When the 365-cubit, in-and-out circumambulation—through the three axial entrances together—includes three circuits of the image in each flanking chamber, then the result is 21 units of 10 *phyeam* each (Fig. 8.10b) for the total of nine images (three triads).[4] This implies that the triads along the axes, grouped together, comprise a supreme deity—not just solar, not just lunar.

For there is a lunar component here. When the in-and-out circumambulation is completed for each individual axial entrance and its lateral chambers, the result is 28 units of 10 cubits each, which is lunar in connotation (Fig. 8.10b).[5] The number 28 matches the 28 steps in the main staircase leading up to the entrance. So when each axial triad is considered as a single set, it has a lunar circumambulation (see Appendix A, Table 8.2).

Summing up these circumambulation paths in the simplest terms, we find that the total of the three single axial images is 365, each axial triad is 28, and all three triads together are 21. This result indicates that the axial images taken as a group were particularly solar, that each axial group has a lunar meaning as well, and that the entire set of triads adds up to a supreme deity.

One circumambulation path through the corner towers leads into the corridors of the gallery and comes to the same total as the path in and out of the axial entrances: 21 units of 10 cubits each (Fig. 8.11a). From northwest around the gallery counterclockwise to southwest, the totals in cubits for each corner tower are 208.79, 209.32, 210.63, and 208.15, for an approximate 21 × 10 cubits, each tower.[6] If these units are expressed in *phyeam,* then all four towers come to 209.22 *phyeam* or approximately 21 × 10 once more. The four corner towers together also have 20 windows and 20 pillars, making the entire group an all-encompassing twenty-first unit. The pathway indicates that the main image in each corner tower also had two flanking images, and that when all of these 12 images are worshiped together they also equal 21, like the set of nine images in the east, north, and south axial entrances. In other words, these 21 images (12 + 9) are venerated as an axial solar group, with a 21-unit circumambulation, and as an intercardinal lunar group with a 21-unit circumambulation.

The status of the images in the corner towers on this level is different than in all the preceding galleries. This is the only time at Angkor Wat in which a circumambulation path can lead into a gallery from a corner chamber. There must have been times of the year or month in which the images on each corner were worshiped separately.

The 21-unit path leads into a circumference that has a lunar meaning like the outer enclosure or the *nāga* terrace. It measures either 19 × 24 cubits or 21 × 24 cubits, depending on its configuration (Fig. 8.12).[7] (See Appendix A, Table 8.3.)

The number 24 in the circumference refers to the 24 lunar half-months. But when seen from the perspective of Mount Meru, these half-months become the 12 light and 12 dark hours of the day and night of the gods. Viṣṇu and the sun regulate diurnal time; Brahmā and the moon, nocturnal. The relationship of divinity and time is clear. The axial images, already defined in a set of 21 (and 365), change the circumference total when they are included to 21 × 24. If the circumference is defined as usual, without these images, it is 19 × 24, or equal to the group of lesser gods in connection with the lunar year. "Defined as usual" means the circumference includes only the main axis of the entrance chamber. Yet as demonstrated in the two preceding galleries, alternate circumference measurements involving all the main entrances are a standard pattern. So, in effect, the circumference measurement on the upper elevation connects the supreme deity and lunar time together when the four axial images are included.

The 19/21-unit dichotomy in the alternate circumference lengths circles this gallery and its central tower. It is joined to all the instances of 32 and 28 around the periphery. The importance of this model of 19 *devas*, the king Indra, and the god Viṣṇu to the government of King Sūryavarman was made clear in the third gallery. The circumference of the upper elevation puts this model of organization at its source: on Mount Meru, in the kingdom of Indra and the gods.

A few lunar measurements remain to be noted, such as the 30 steps in the main western staircase and 29 in the eastern. Together they give a precise total for the length of two lunar months. This complements the 28 steps in all the other staircases (see Appendix A, Table 8.4).

There are 12 cubits between the *nāga* balustrade on the west and the cruciform terrace—perhaps a way of paying homage to the sun after the 12 staircases of the lunar causeway. The 21 latitude units up to the second gallery are clear enough, but there is a 354-cubit introduction to the upper

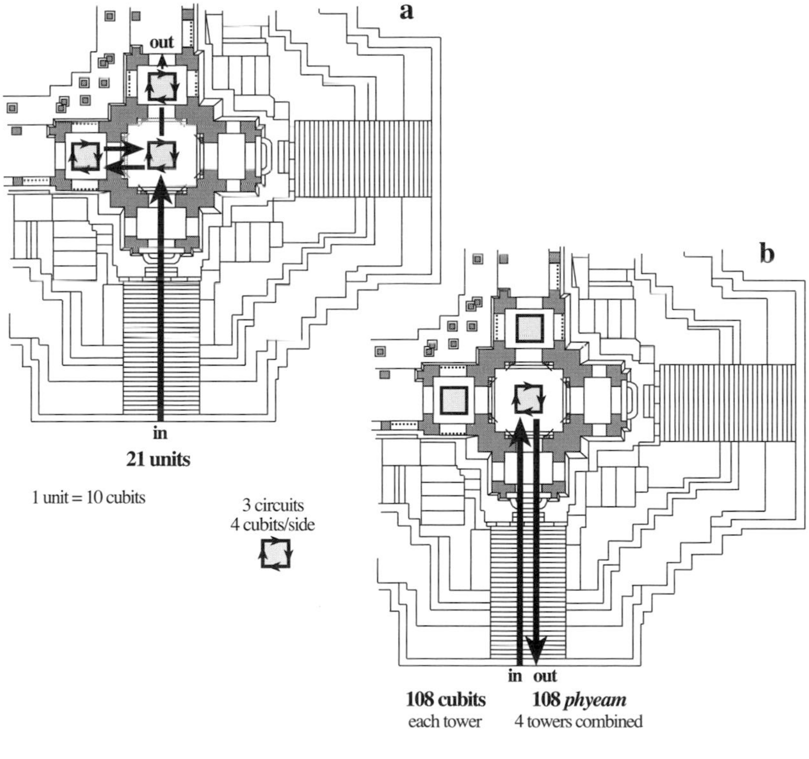

Fig. 8.11. First gallery, corner towers, circumambulation paths.

In spite of a few differences, the 21-unit path that circuits all three images (a) is similar to the 21-unit path in the axial entrances (Fig. 8.10b). The total is the same, is expressed in the same units of measure, and all three interior images are included. In contrast, the circumambulation of the main image alone does not provide a time measurement such as 28, but rather the 108 units that describe the 54/54 *devas* and *asuras*. The number therefore shares in the symbolism of the churning scene and its many connotations. (See Appendix A, Table 8.8.)

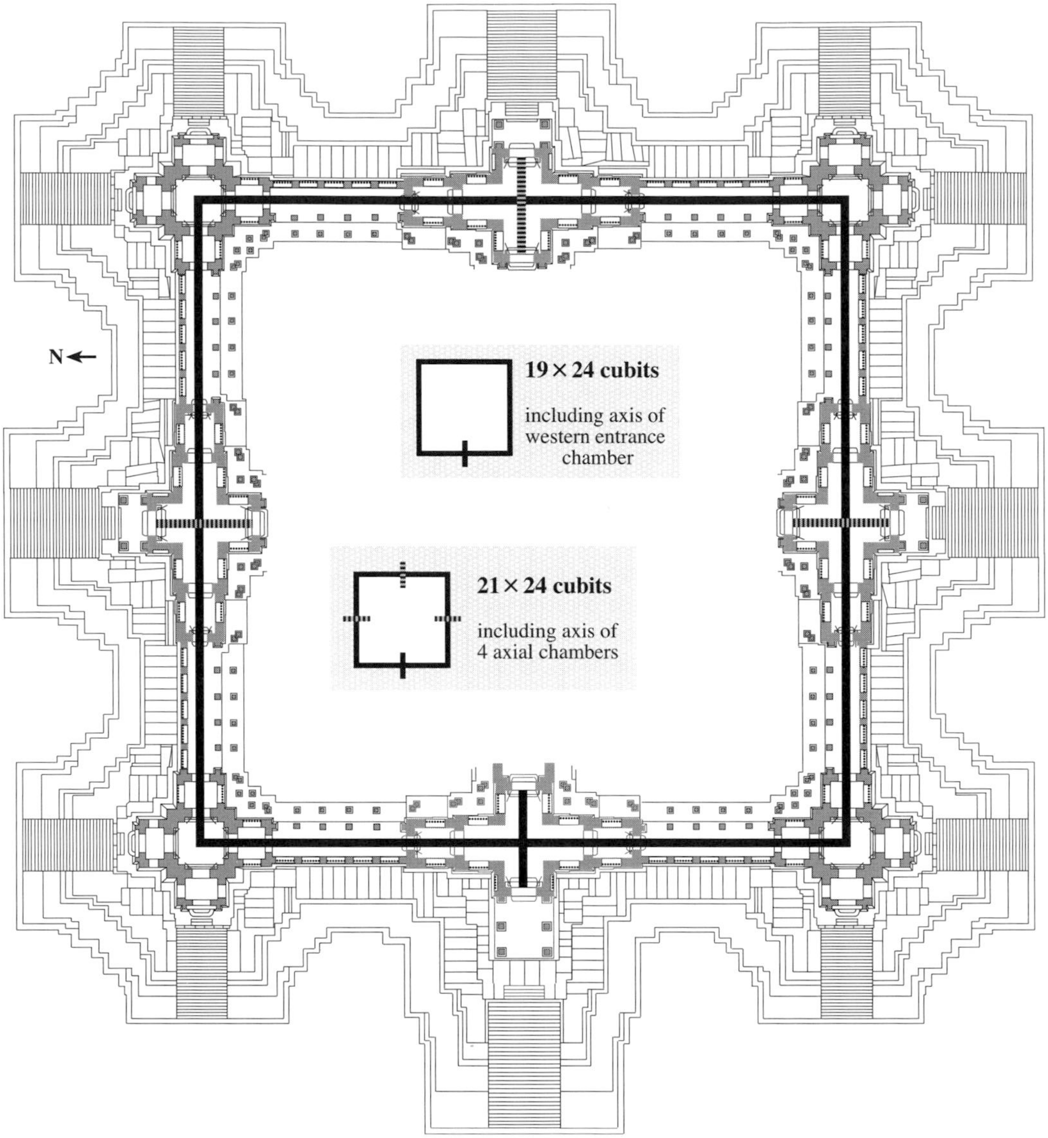

Fig. 8.12. First gallery, circumference.

The measurements of the circumference define it as a lunar year of 24 light and dark half-months. That year is equal to 24 hours of the gods inside the sanctuaries here on the Mount Meru of Angkor Wat. When the four axial images are included in the computation of the circumference, one of the numerical factors is 21. If the circumference is measured in a standard fashion, with only the inner axis of the main entrance (and hence, its image) included in the total, the result is a factor of 19 joined to 24. It can be assumed, then, that all four axial images and the circumference together comprise a supreme, twenty-first deity but only one such image in conjunction with the circumference refers to the 19 lesser gods. (See Appendix A, Table 8.3.)

gallery from the *nāga* balustrade that is hard to understand.[8] The measurement travels the distance through the definitions of the lunar month, on the east and west sides of the third and second galleries, and through the nighttime symbolism of the *preau cruciforme.* It stops at the base of the upper level of the temple, where the days in the solar year begin to be counted. Perhaps because of the numerical terrain it traverses, its lunar beginnings at the *nāga* balustrade, and the start of the solar year where it ends on the east, this 354-cubit distance reinforces the lunar homage to Viṣṇu up to this point in the journey. One thing is certain: the measurement is not accidental.

In the 360-day year on Mount Meru, each day is equivalent to one 365-day year on earth. On the upper level of Angkor Wat, the exact 365-day year was noted in the axial entrances on the north, south, and east, as their combined in-and-out circumambulation path. The 360-day year on the

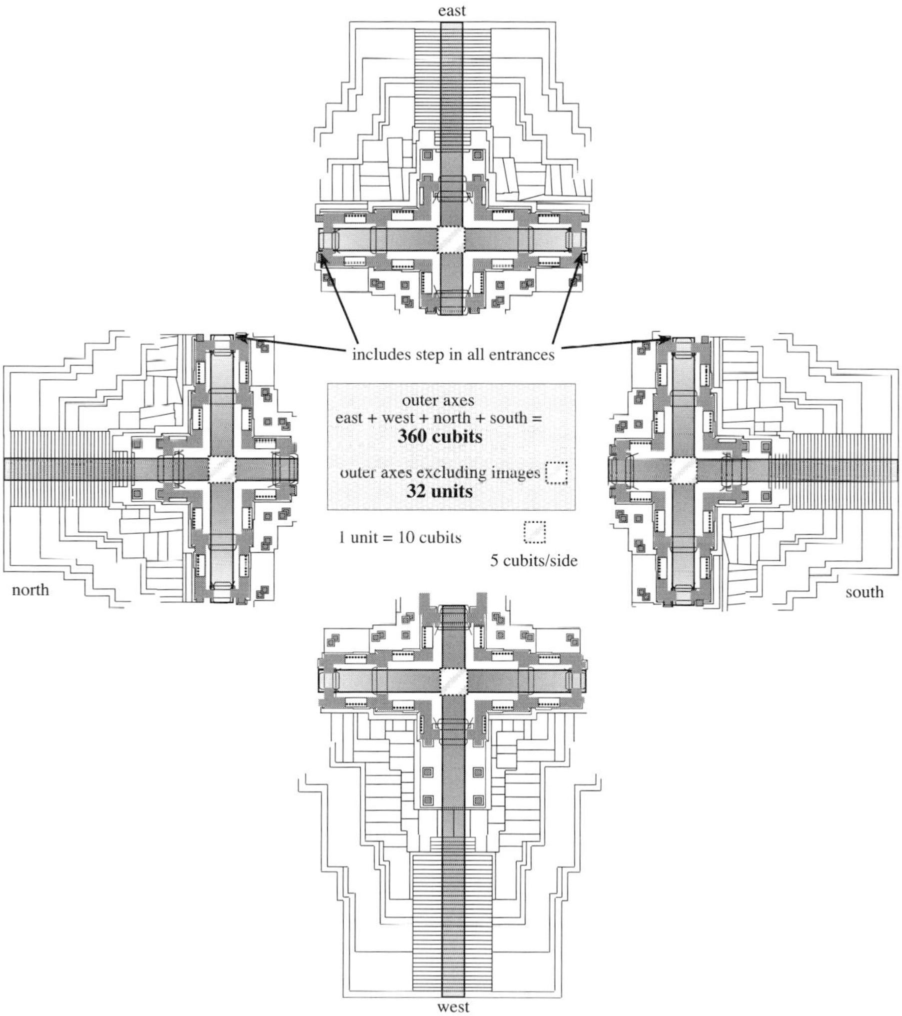

Fig. 8.13. First gallery, axial entrances, outer axes.

If the main images at 5 cubits on a side are excluded from a total for the outer axes of the four axial chambers, the result once again describes the lesser deities (32) and not the supreme Viṣṇu or Brahmā (33). When the images are included, however, the 360-day year of the gods is expressed. The 365-cubit circuit of the images in the northern, southern, and eastern entrances (Fig. 8.10) therefore defines the length of one day of the gods within the axial context of their 360-day year. (See Appendix A, Table 8.5.)

upper level occurs in these same entrances, plus the entrance on the west, as the combined length of their outer axes (Fig. 8.13).[9] In this way, the 365-day solar year, in three of the entrances (Fig. 8.10a) shares much of the same space and the same images as the 360-day celestial year in all four entrances. Since each solar year equals one of the 360 days, this juxtaposition in the axial entrances of the upper level is particularly ingenious. The same four axial entrances are joined to the lunar circumference to create a numerical symbol for a twenty-first supreme deity (Fig. 8.12). With the added reference to 360 and 365, the twenty-first supreme deity of the circumference and four entrances begins to take shape as the solar Viṣṇu and lunar Brahmā combined. The solar numbers associated with the axes join the lunar circumference to create an image of a deity that embraces the sun and moon alike.

Nothing occurs on the upper level of Angkor Wat outside the all-encompassing mandala: not a solar year goes by, not one reference to a time cycle or a deity, outside the borders of the mandala. In order to put these lunar and solar periods in proper perspective, we must pause and examine their environment.

THE NUMBERS 32/33

The sets of numbers that define the architectectural mandala are dispersed around the upper elevation in revealing patterns (see Appendix A, Table 8.5). As the drawings indicate, the large axes and circumference of the gallery, as well as the circumambulation routes around the gallery never include the numbers 32/33. Instead, the circumambulation routes define time periods or the supreme deity with measurements like 21, 28, 108, and 365. If we look back on the nature of the largest axes, circumferences, and circumambulation routes at the temple, a specific character starts to take shape.

All of the axial measurements up to the second gallery recorded time periods or the base units for measuring time: 60, 108, the yuga cycles, the solar year, the lunar year, and historical dates. At the level of the second gallery, that temporal progression stops as 44 latitude units describe the deities in the mandala. Even then, both the number 44 and the 13.43-cubit latitude unit draw a picture of the night sky in the northern hemisphere: the celestial north pole at 13.43 degrees, the 28 *nakṣatra,* 4 directional deities, and 12 zodiac signs. These elements provide a grid-like background for measuring the movements of the sun and moon and planets across the sky. In that sense, the 44-unit axes give us a different kind of information on the measurements of time. But once time has been taken out of the terrestrial sphere and put into the heavens with the constellations, it resides in the realm of the gods. We have literally left the earth at this point. Therefore, when we encounter the 366-cubit axes of the upper elevation we are looking at a description of time on Mount Meru. At that level, one of our years equals one day. When the sun rises over the central tower on March 21, that day on Mount Meru begins. With the 91.29-cubit axes of the central tower (Fig. 8.9a), the day of the gods is divided into four parts, each part a little over 91 units long—the time between the rising sun in the morning and high noon (March 21–June 21), or between 12 noon and the setting sun at 6, or between sunset and midnight, midnight and morning again. So in a general overview, the axes at the temple are devoted to the nature and measurement of time. For that reason, the 32 gods are not represented alone in the axes of the topmost gallery, or in the axes of any gallery.

The circumference measurements of Angkor Wat follow the same time patterns as the axes: 120,

108, the lunar year, and the *kṛta yuga*. At the level of the second gallery, the grid of the mandala in the circumference matches the 44-unit axes: 20 units expressed 49 times over, covering 49 chambers. In this instance, the 49 would refer back to the terrestrial world. Although it literally grids the space for the 44 gods, it is our grid this time, not that of the night sky. We use it in architecture to bind the gods to the site of the temple. It has a terrestrial component in that sense. On the upper elevation, the 24 units of the circumference again record the lunar year but like the solar axes, our lunar year with its 12 light half-months and 12 dark half-months is equal to one day of the gods. Their 12 hours of daylight are comparable to the 12 light halves of the lunar month, and their 12 hours of night to the 12 dark halves of the month, as noted earlier. Although not as rigorous as a one-to-one correspondence between our alternating days and nights, the concept and divisions are similar. Since the circumference measurements at the temple are also dedicated to time cycles (with the sole exception of the second gallery), the 32 gods by themselves would not define a circumference measurement.

The circumambulation routes in a gallery also tend to work together as a set. In the outer enclosure, multiple 54/54-unit paths define the deity in the central entrance as Viṣṇu at the center of the earth's axis, between the *deva*s and *asura*s. Since there is a 366-cubit path through that chamber, Viṣṇu assumes a solar character as well. The circumambulations around the enclosure numerically record the 27/28 *nakṣatra* crossed by the moon each month and each year. In general, then, the lunar constellations complement the solar Viṣṇu in the central western sanctuary. About 100 m away from Viṣṇu on the north and south, the solstice gateways have 32/33-unit paths through their chambers. These paths could be understood as completing the 27/28 constellations with four directional deities, following the same symbolism of a band of stars and planets around the ecliptic. We cross through the central 54/54 location of an axial and solar Viṣṇu in the western entrance in order to enter the temple. The solar and *deva/asura* iconography here contrasts with the lunar circuits around the circumference.

In the third gallery, the circumambulation through the main entrance is 32 *phyeam* long and the circumambulations around the enclosure divide into three sets of 108 *phyeam* each. When the three different sets of 108 *phyeam* are expressed in cubits, they equal the *tretā yuga*. At Angkor Wat when various yuga measurements are expressed in 108-cubit units, the result is 32 (Figs. 2.23 and 2.25). In these cases, the number 32 is changed into a yuga cycle at the temple when multiplied by 108. So the circumambulations in the third gallery give us the relationship between the 32 gods and the measurement of time using a 108-unit key. This is the only instance in which 32 enters into a circumambulation path.

The second gallery repeats the symbolism in the outer enclosure: circuits of 27/28 latitude units go around the gallery. But now the circumambulation through the western entrance is 21 latitude units, connecting the lunar path each month to a twenty-first supreme deity at the north celestial pole (13.43 degrees or one latitude unit at Angkor). The division between the solar Viṣṇu in the main entrance of the outer enclosure and the lunar Brahmā in the second gallery has begun.

The upper elevation of the temple takes every numerical circuit recorded above and puts it in the circumambulation paths around the circumference: 365, 21, 28, and 108. The number 108 in this series is tied to the axial entrances (Fig. 8.14). It defines a circuit of the main Viṣṇu image from the base of the entrance, the same as a 45-*phyeam* circuit found on the west (Fig. 8.15).[10] Once defined in these numerical terms, the 108-*phyeam* paths around the circumference parallel the last 45-*phyeam* path up to the main Viṣṇu image in the central tower. In this axial pattern, the number 108 joins the previous axial circuits of 21, 28, and 365 to Viṣṇu in the central sanctuary (Fig. 8.10), emphasizing the temporal function of 108 as a building block of time periods, and its ability to connect the 32 gods to the yuga cycles that lead up to this level.

If these patterns were ever used in sequence, then it would be logical to enter the courtyard around the upper elevation from a lateral entrance of the second gallery (Fig. 8.3) and circumambulate the main image in each axial entrance on the north, east, and south (365 cubits). At that point, we would turn around and go back, this time circuiting all three images in the axial set of chambers on the south, east, and north (28 each entrance, 21 in 3 entrances together). Having thus paid homage to the sun (365), the moon (28), and a supreme deity (21), we would turn around one more time and go back again. But this time we would enter only one axial entrance and after circuits of the central and

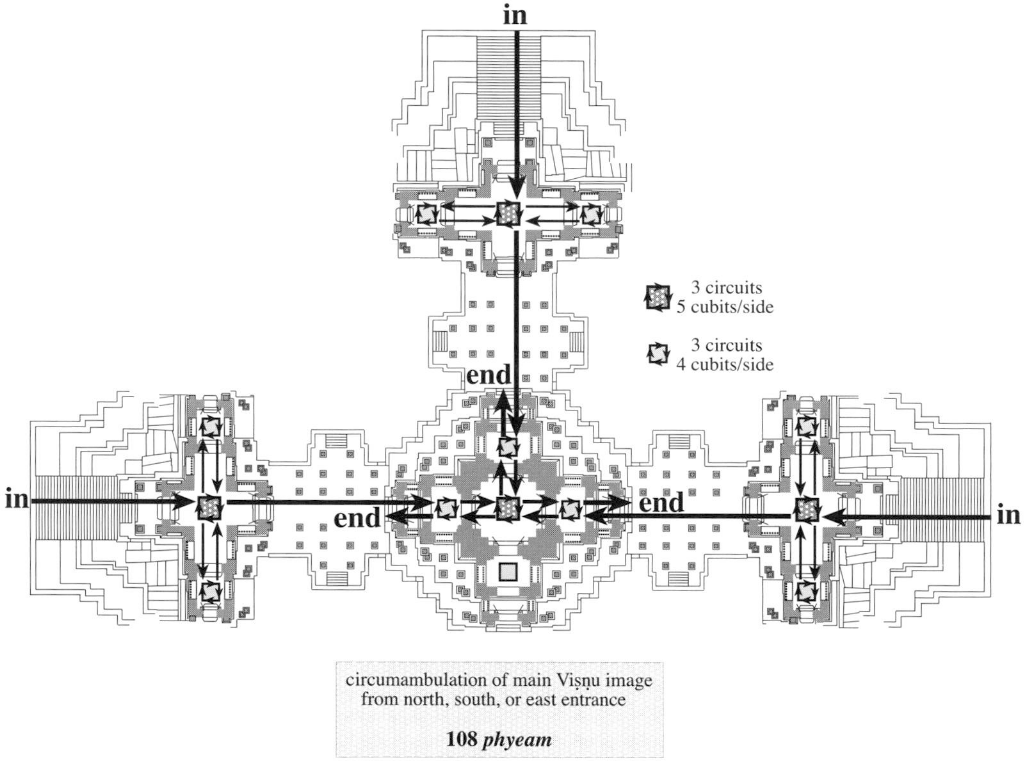

Fig. 8.14. First gallery, circumambulation of central Viṣṇu image from three axial entrances.

From the base on the north, south, or east sides of the axes there is a numerically significant 108-*phyeam* circuit up to the main Viṣṇu image in the central tower. The same circuit is repeated on the west, but with a different total (Fig. 8.15). According to these patterns, the four images around Viṣṇu in the central tower are not addressed as one set—there is no circumambulation path that involves all four images—but are placed axially with the images in the northern, southern, eastern, or western entrances. (See Appendix A, Table 8.8.)

flanking images, continue on to the central tower to pay homage to the main image of Viṣṇu (108 *phyeam*) (Fig. 8.15). Because this last path ends just outside the central tower, it is in fact, a terminus to the preceding series of 365, 21, and 28.

Backtracking yet again, there is a 24-unit path through the lateral entrances of the second gallery that begins in front of the third gallery and ends in the courtyard in front of the upper elevation (Fig. 7.13). Given the 108-*phyeam* ending to our circuits

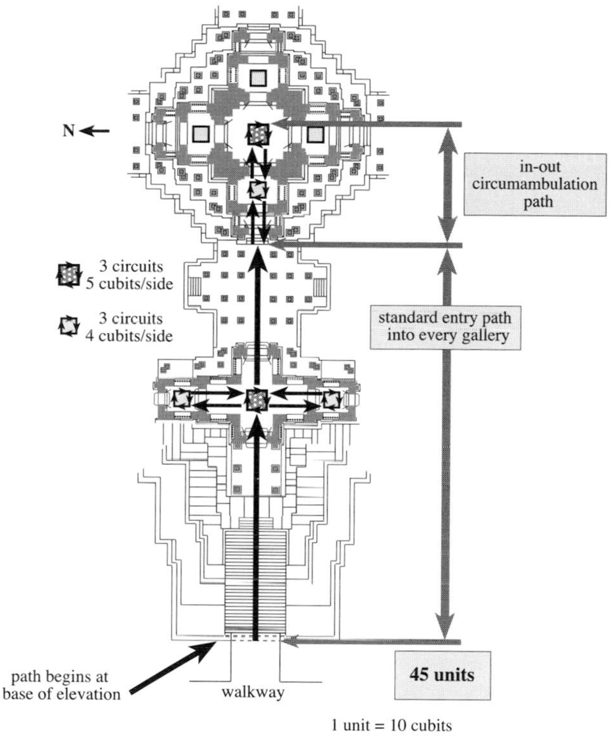

Fig. 8.15. First gallery, circumambulation of central Viṣṇu image from the west.

In this pathway that is repeated on each side of Viṣṇu (Fig. 8.14), the two most common circumambulation paths at Angkor Wat are combined. The total of 45 units puts Viṣṇu at the apex of the mandala of gods—gods that surround him on all sides and bring us to him along the western approach to the upper elevation. (See Appendix A, Table 8.6.)

around the top elevation (365, 21, 28), it would appear that there are a pair of alternate routes to the central sanctuary that lead from the lateral entrances in the third gallery, through the lateral entrances in the second gallery, and then around the upper level, to finally enter the central tower. These circuits are based on time-related elements (365, 24) as well as on allusions to Brahmā (the latitude unit of measure in the 24-unit path through the cruciform, the number 21, the lunar 28). In contrast, a trip straight along the western axis takes us through a 32-*phyeam* circuit in the western entrance to the third gallery (Fig. 4.26), two 21-unit circuits around the statue in the cruciform and the image in the main western entrance to the second gallery (Figs. 7.13 and 7.26), a 32-cubit walk to the base of the upper elevation from there (Fig. 2.26), and the final, 45-unit ascent up to the image of Viṣṇu in the sanctuary (Fig. 8.15). Even before reaching the 32-unit circuit through the western entrance of the third gallery, we cross the full 32-*phyeam* west–east length of the cruciform terrace (Fig. 4.19), and each 32-*phyeam* length between the center of the staircases on the causeway (Fig. 4.3). That is not to say that time elements do not factor into this western, axial approach to Viṣṇu. They do. It is clear, however, that the 32 gods and a twenty-first supreme deity in the cruciform are meant to culminate in the forty-fifth deity that resides in the central sanctuary. They form one conceptual set. This route, defined by Brahmā and the gods on Mount Meru, is flanked on each side by the paths that reflect the lunar (24) and solar (365) years, and other time measurements, as well as the 21-unit reference to a supreme deity. Even though the central, axial approach to Viṣṇu based on the Hindu deities, and lateral approaches based on time cycles are not exclusive (they share in themes of time and divinity), it does seem as though the differentiation between deities (32, 21, 45) and time (24, 28, 365) was planned in these parallel paths.

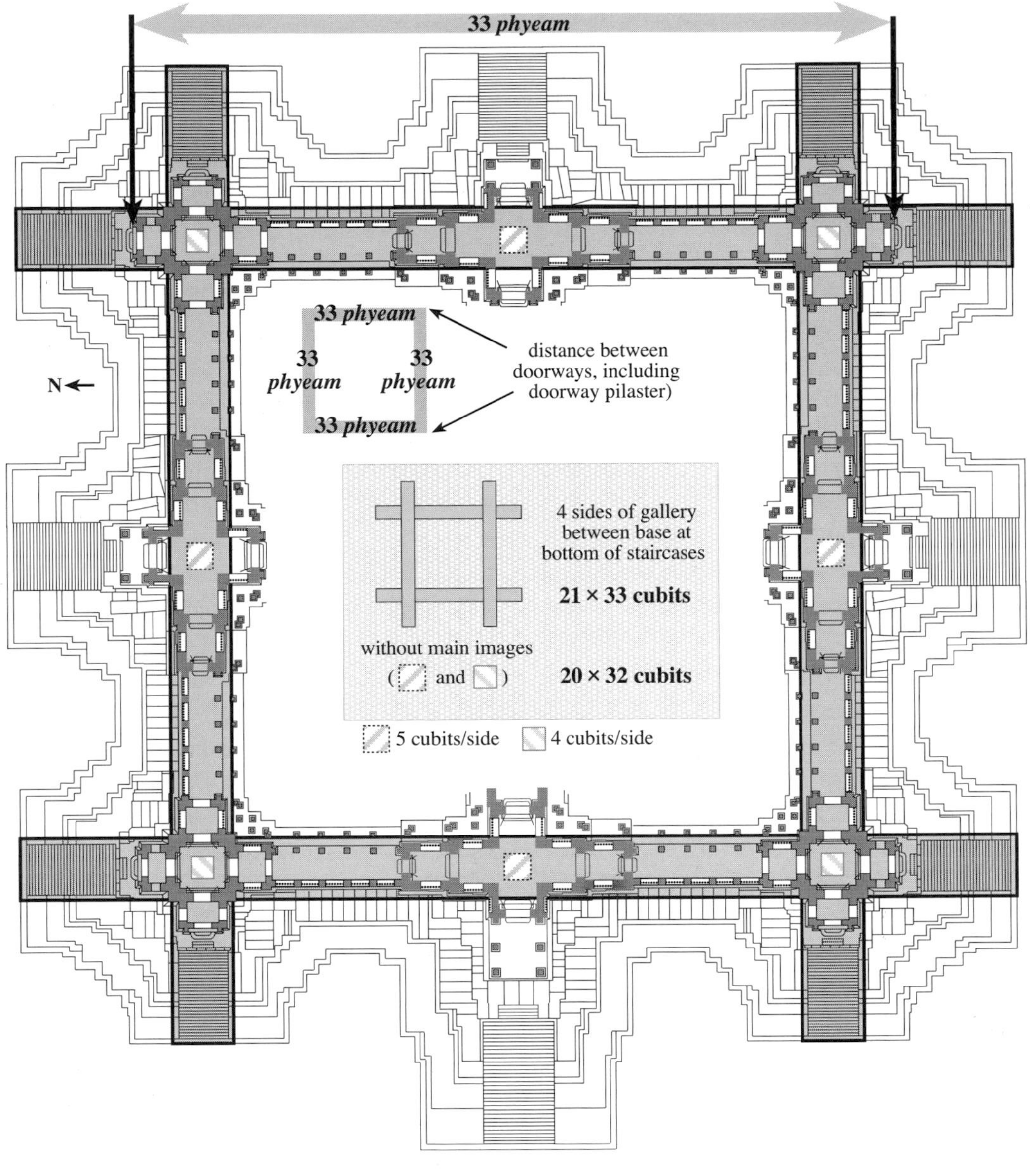

Fig. 8.16. First gallery, lengths along the perimeter.

As on several other occasions, when the main images are subtracted from a total length (of the four sides of the gallery here), the result describes the lesser deities, 20 or 32 in number. When the images are included, the totals change to 21 and 33. Once again, the perimeter and the images together define a supreme deity. The 33-*phyeam* length between opposite doorways on each side of the gallery conveys the same kind of definition for the images inside, although in this instance there are no numerically significant totals when the images are excluded. (See Appendix A, Table 8.5.)

The most encompassing 32-unit measurements on the upper level of Angkor Wat are all along the periphery which exactly corresponds to the location of the 32 gods in the mandala. The sides of the gallery are a multiple of 32 or 33 units, depending on whether or not the main images are included in the distance (Fig. 8.16).[11] When 21 appears now as a multiple, as in 21 × 33, it matches 21 × 24 in the circumference (Fig. 8.12). The same four axial entrances produce the same 21-unit total when seen in conjunction with the periphery of the gallery. There are also 32 chambers around the gallery, and 33 steps in the northern or southern axial staircases (both long and short staircases on each side, together). On this level, the periphery is usually defined in terms of 20 and 32 if the images in the axial chambers are not included in the measurement, but 21 and 33 when they are included (Figs. 8.10, 8.12–13, 8.16–17). Both 21 and 33 connect the occurrences of 32 in the perimeter to a supreme Viṣṇu.

Other than the periphery, there are only two types of measurements which include the number 32. In one type, 32 is an axial length for the entrances or central tower (Figs. 8.9c and 8.17).[12] But when that axial length occurs, it never occurs without a 45-unit counterpart. For example, there are 32 cubits that lead up to the central Viṣṇu

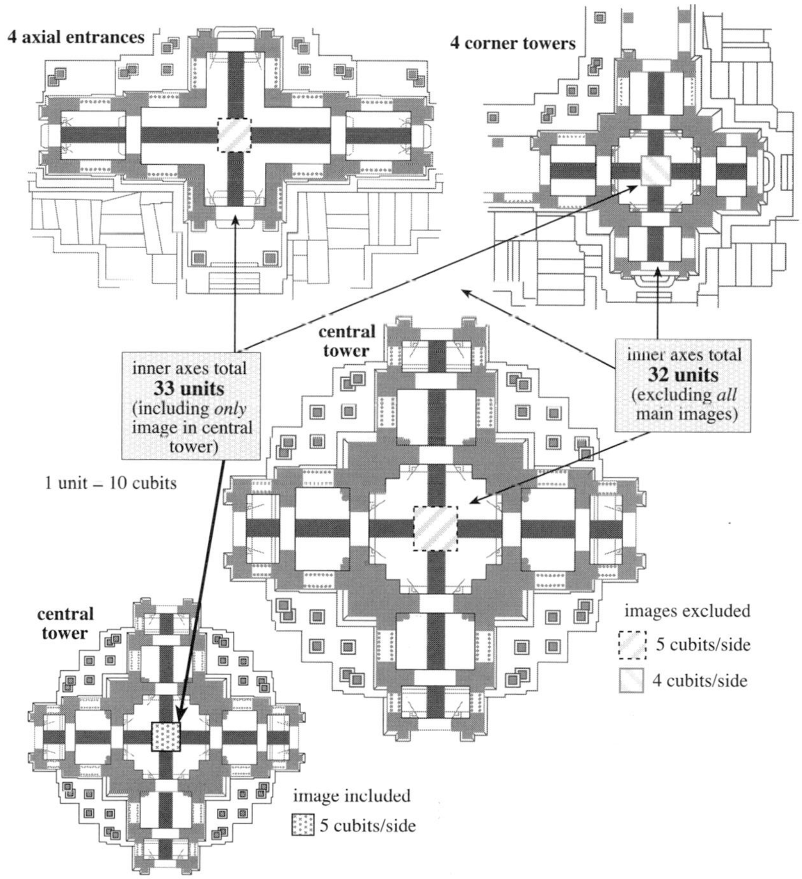

Fig. 8.17. First gallery, inner axes of central tower and all entrances together.

Whereas the measurements that join the entrances to the circumference of the gallery describe both of these architectural aspects as a supreme deity (Figs. 8.12 and 8.16), the inner axes of all the chambers in the gallery clarify that point. When seen as a set, the inner axes refer to the 32 gods of the mandala without Brahmā at their center—if the main images are all excluded. However, by including only the central Viṣṇu, that total for the interior of the chambers comes to 33 units. The alternation of 32/33 in this instance places the main image of Viṣṇu above the others in the gallery. (See Appendix A, Table 8.5.)

image but they lie within a 45-cubit total (Fig. 8.9a and c).[13] There are 32 units in the inner axes of the entrances and towers (Fig. 8.17) but most of these are included within a 45-unit total for the full outer axes' lengths (Fig. 8.18).[14] One type of 32-unit measurement, then, defines the axial lengths of the entrances on this level within a larger, encompassing 45-unit total. Once again, the 32 gods are joined to a supreme Viṣṇu.

The second type of 32/32-unit measurement occurs only once, as the height of the central tower with or without the Viṣṇu image (Fig. 8.19).[15] In this instance the 32/33 units are included within a larger, 108-cubit measurement which extends above and below the main sanctuary, putting 32 in association with 108 again. Since the 28-cubit height of the sanctuary is also a part of the 32-*phyeam* vertical extension of the tower, the number 32 is connected to the lunar constellations as well. Just as the focus of the central, western

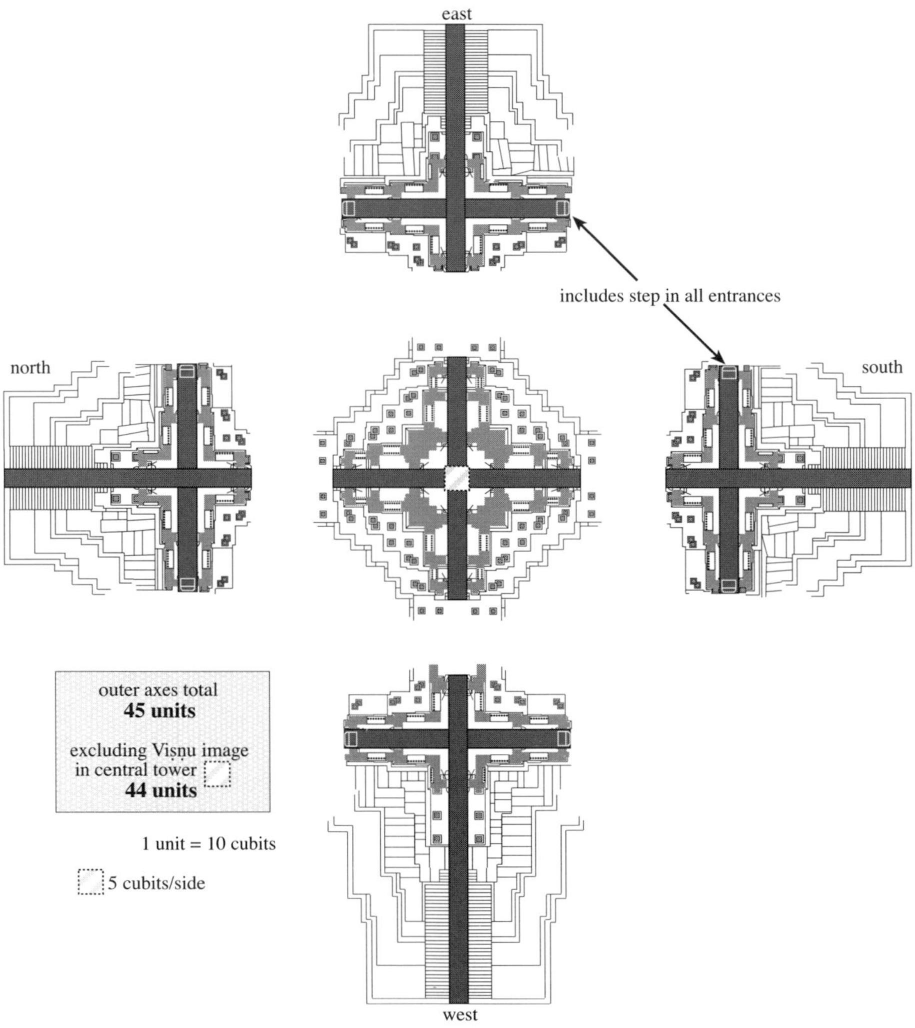

Fig. 8.18. First gallery, outer axes of central tower and axial entrances together.

In a pattern similar to that of the inner axes of the chambers in the gallery (Fig. 8.17), there is a 45-unit total for the outer axes of the central tower and of the axial entrances combined. By eliminating the central image of Viṣṇu, the total changes to 44 units. Once again, the central Viṣṇu is characterized as a supreme deity with a higher standing than the surrounding images. (See Appendix A, Table 8.6.)

path through Angkor Wat—with its 32-unit repetitions—is the Viṣṇu image in the central tower, so is Viṣṇu the focus of 32 on the upper level.

In summary, we see that the numbers 32/33 on the upper elevation are primarily joined to the periphery and secondarily define the axes of the entrances but only within a broader, 45-unit boundary. In the one case they describe the border of the mandala, and in the other they are shown as only one component in a full mandala, subsumed under the main image of Viṣṇu (45). Nothing could be more accurate or more in accord with the meaning of the mandala and the role of Viṣṇu on this level.

If we look again at the role of 44/45, there is only one instance in which it does not directly include the central Viṣṇu. The circumference of the gallery in combination with the inner axes of the northern, southern, eastern, or western axial entrances is 45 units (Fig. 8.20).[16] The 45-unit

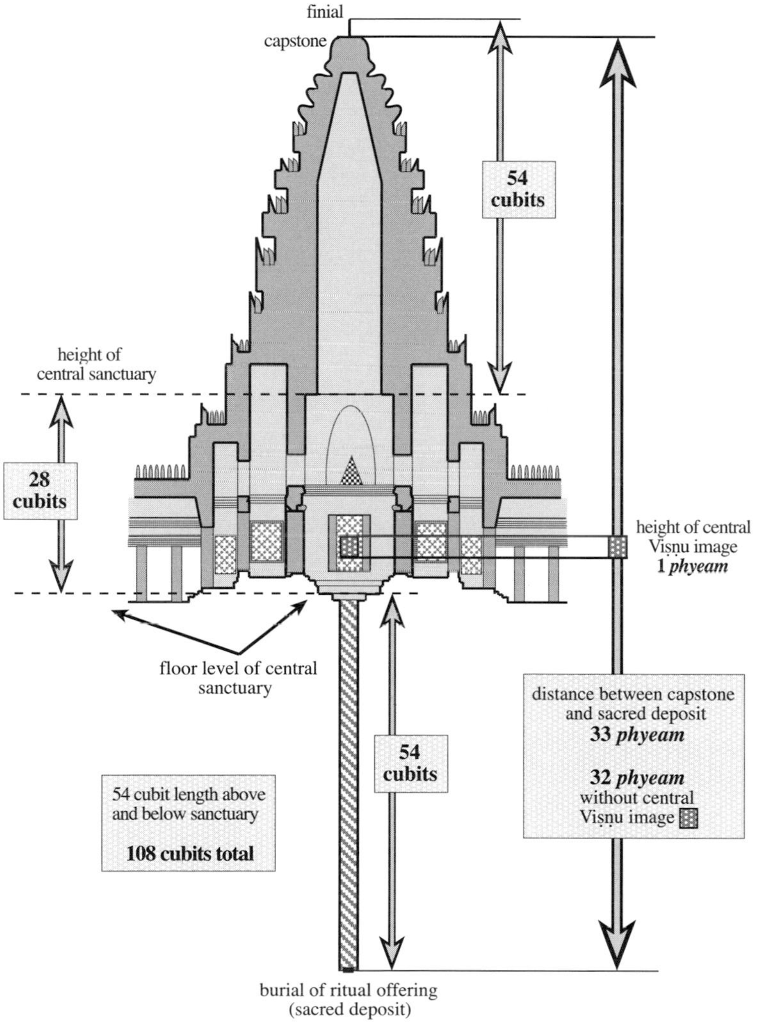

Fig. 8.19. Central tower, vertical measurements.

The vertical axis of the central tower defines the image of Viṣṇu in three different ways: he is at the center of the mandala of gods (32/33); he is between the *devas* and *asuras* (54/54); and he is at the center of 28 constellations that revolve around him in the night sky. The latter measurement brings him into the visible celestial sphere that is also partially defined by the 32 gods as 28 constellations and 4 directional deities. The 54/54 division embraces the solar movement involved in the solstice and equinox definitions of Viṣṇu at the temple, not to mention references to the coronation of the king. From a certain perspective, then, these three celestial and divine locations of Viṣṇu are not disconnected from our terrestrial world. (See Appendix A, Table 8.7.)

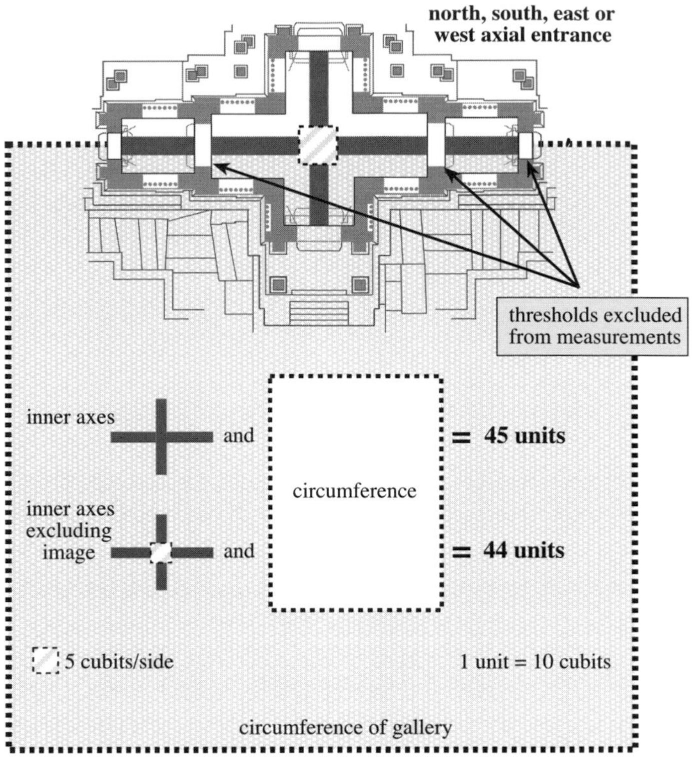

Fig. 8.20. First gallery, circumference and inner axes of each cardinal entrance.

Once more we find the circumference of the gallery defining a supreme deity in conjunction with an axial entrance. In this case, the two together total 45 units but only 44 if the main image in the entrance is excluded. Although in a new format, this particular expression of divinity embodies the same concept found in the 21- and 33-unit circumference and perimeter lengths (Figs. 8.12 and 8.16). (See Appendix A, Table 8.6.)

circumference in union with the axial entrances is in agreement with the twice-repeated 21-unit total when the axial images and periphery of the gallery are joined together. In these three different numerical marriages to the perimeter of the gallery (21, 21, and 45) the four axial entrances as one set assume the status of a supreme deity (Figs. 8.12, 8.16, and 8.20).

THE NUMBERS 44/45

In contrast to the preferred distribution of 32-unit numbers around the outermost boundaries of the upper elevation (vertical or horizontal, axes or circumference), the numbers 44/45, with only one exception, always include the central tower and the main image of Viṣṇu (see Appendix A, Table 8.6).

There are five separate types of 44/45-unit measurements on the upper elevation, including the central tower as a forty-fifth unit for the 44 pillars around it (Figs. 8.9a, 8.15, 8.18, and 8.20). But there are almost no examples elsewhere. One notes the 44-unit axes of the second gallery (which do, in the end, originate from the central tower on this elevation); the 44 units in the axes of the side chambers in the third gallery, eastern and western entrances; the 44 Kaurava leaders in the Battle of Kurukṣetra; 44 pillars around the main western entrance of the second gallery; and 44 pillars along the two lateral entrances at the end of the bridge. This sparse dispersion cannot compare with the systematic association of 45 and the central image of Viṣṇu on the upper elevation.

By means of the number 45, Visnu is paid homage as the center of everything that exists. The number refers to him not only as a supreme god, Nārāyaṇa at the heart of a mandala of 44 deities, but as Nārāyaṇa at the center of Angkor Wat, a vast mandala itself. From another perspective he is at the center of the Khmer capital and nation as well, at the center of the earth's axis between the north and south celestial poles, at the center of the solar year, at the center of a religious hierarchy, and as the creator of time and space, at the center of the temporal and phenomenal universe—both the terrestrial and celestial versions. These are the reasons why the number 45 was reserved for Viṣṇu in the central sanctuary. No other image could lay claim to his exalted position as the hub and source of all existence.

THE CENTRAL TOWER

Aside from measurements that praise Viṣṇu as an omnipotent deity, the central tower has several other measurements that locate Viṣṇu precisely in space. In addition to the 32/33-unit and 44-unit measurements mentioned earlier, the tower contains all the modules used at Angkor Wat, except for 19 and 49 (see Appendix A, Table 8.7).

The configuration of the central tower illustrates that the Khmer astronomer-architects knew the earth was a globe floating in space like a "piece of iron suspended between magnets," described in the fourth century by Varāha Mihira, quoted earlier. The 54-unit lengths above and below the sanctuary symbolize the north and south celestial poles, homes of the *devas* and *asuras* (Fig. 8.19). Between these poles, the height of the sanctuary, or "earth," reaches 28 cubits, and its inner, horizontal axes come to nearly 27 cubits total (Fig. 8.21). By means of these two numbers, 27/28, the sanctuary is depicted as representing the celestial ecliptic and

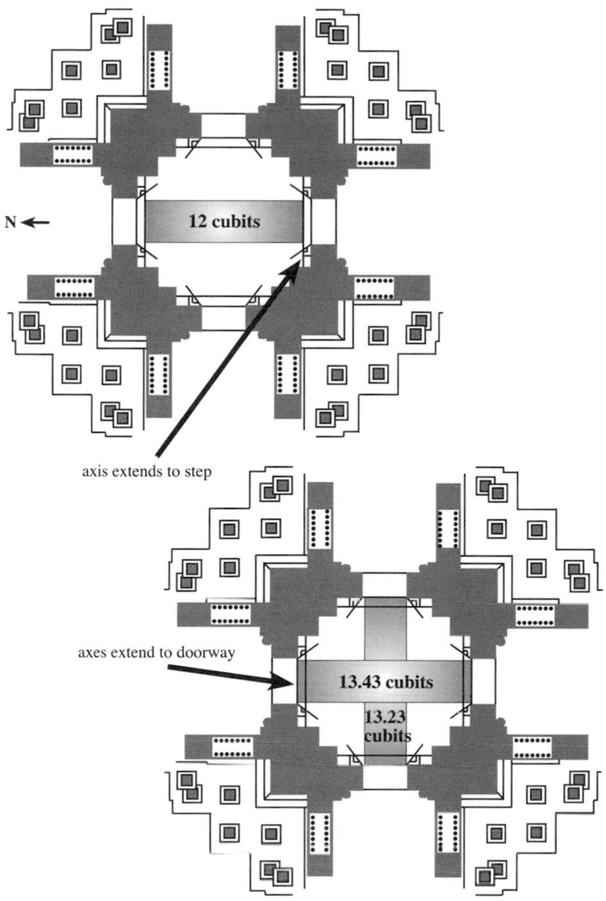

Fig. 8.21. Central tower, main sanctuary.

Two separate measurements in the sanctuary provided a key to unlocking the numerical secrets of Angkor Wat: the 12 cubits between the steps on the north and south, and the 13.43 cubits of the full north–south axis between doorways. In the one instance, a primary numerical definition of the solar Viṣṇu confirmed the correct cubit length; in the other, the distance gave a module used to define Brahmā in the *preau cruciforme* and second gallery. The 13.43 module also opened up the ensuing definition of Brahmā as a nighttime manifestation of Viṣṇu, as well as a deity particularly related to the north celestial pole. Both 12 and 13.43 were indications that astronomy played a major role in the design of the temple. (See Appendix A, Table 8.7.)

its 27/28 constellations. Viṣṇu also occupies a position of an estimated 13.43 degrees on earth, the latitude of his sanctuary at Angkor Wat given in the north–south interior axis. Thus his position on earth, in the sanctuary, and his position in space, surrounded by the ecliptic and the band of constellations, are illustrated at the same time. Other than the coordinates that place Viṣṇu in space, there are 20/21, 32/33, and 44/45-unit numbers in the axes of the tower that praise Viṣṇu's status as the highest deity at Angkor Wat (Figs. 8.9c, d, 8.17, 8.18, and 8.19).[17]

Far below the floor of the sanctuary, two white sapphires and a few gold leaves were once buried slightly underground: the sacred treasure of the temple.[18] From these two precious objects, symbolic of the golden sun and white light of the moon, the temple slowly grew into an organic whole. The fusion of the earthly abode of Viṣṇu in the central sanctuary with the celestial realm of stars and *deva*s, and the origins of the temple itself, is completed in the central tower. But the tower is not an isolated unit. From the vertical axes above and below it to the horizontal axes that cross through it, the central tower is the only place at Angkor Wat that is related to everything else at the temple—including King Sūryavarman.

The central Viṣṇu may have been sculpted to resemble the king. The statue was adorned with the jewelry and clothing of a Khmer monarch by carving these elements onto the stone, a new fashion that began around A.D. 1100. Perhaps this was meant to emulate a former use of real jewelry.

According to a centuries-old tradition, the name of the statue would have been joined to the name of King Sūryavarman. The references in the inscriptions to a portion of divinity in the king, and a "subtle inner self" of the king in the image, raise the interrelationship of god and king to a sublime and transcendent level, beyond the expression of a shared physiognomy or nomenclature alone. Whatever glory accrued to the statue of Viṣṇu in the central tower was shared, in part, by the king.

A UNIQUE NUMERICAL TRAIT

Although we have not discussed it at length, axial, circumference, or perimeter distances such as 19/20, 32, or 44 can define gods in general by excluding the circumambulation space around an image. These distances have alternate measurements of 21, 33, and 45 when they cross through the circumambulation space. The axes of a chamber or tower may measure 33 units, for example, but will measure only 32 if we exclude the 4-cubit axes at the center of the chamber.

The central axes cover the space that is allowed for circumambulation around the image. When the space is subtracted, so is the image. Vertical measurements may be part of this pattern, too, as in the example of the height of the central sanctuary (32 or 33 *phyeam* depending on whether the central Viṣṇu, an estimated 1 *phyeam* in height, is included). This type of manipulation occurs in the other galleries as well, but not as often as here on the upper level. It seems to be a means of emphasizing the difference between an ultimate deity and the lesser gods—an important distinction, especially given the prevalence of the gods and a supreme deity on the upper elevation.

THE NUMBER 108

The number 108 occurs on the upper elevation in a variety of ways. It is the most independent of all numbers because it is not directly connected with the architectural mandala and does not belong to one numerical group alone. It is a factor in the yuga cycles ($4 \times 108 = 432$), it is connected to the lunar month (27 × 4 = 108), and it may refer to the north–south oscillation of both the sun and moon each year (54/54).

In a certain sense, however, the number 108 is in fact connected to the architectural mandala, because time is an expression of the mandala in motion. As the universe revolves, it marks the seconds, days, and years of our celestial and earthbound passage through space. The 12 zodiac signs and 28 constellations in the mandala are not stationary, but they nevertheless provide a grid for measuring the changing position of the sun, moon, and planets. The cycles of planetary, lunar, and solar movement are like visual expressions of time cycles. Moreover, the number 108, as a basic common denominator in all the yuga cycles, is itself a building block of time.[19]

At Angkor Wat, as noted earlier, 108 is arithmetically connected to the gods in the mandala. By means of the 108-cubit unit of measure, the yugas became the 32 *deva*s around the periphery of the mandala and, by extension, were thereby joined to the 28 constellations distributed around the ecliptic and the four planetary deities that are a part of time measurements.

The sacred number 108, in its capacity to transform time into divinity and divinity into time in these two separate instances at Angkor Wat, provides an abstract and profound link between the mandala, the gods, and a difficult concept: the essence of time itself. Its use at Angkor Wat formulates a statement that time and space and divinity are intimately related and ultimately derive from a supreme deity. In this way, 108 introduces the creation of time into the architectural mandala, reaffirming Brahmā's role as the creator of both time and space. Once we understand that the concept of time per se is a part of the mandala (not just in an arithmetic or astronomical role), then the solar and lunar aspects of Angkor Wat are all the more thoroughly integrated with divinity.

Several instances of 108-unit measurements already seen on the topmost level illustrate the variety of meanings inherent in its numerology. For example, 108 defines the position of the central Viṣṇu between the 54 gods above him and the 54 antigods below (Fig. 8.19). This 108-unit component of the vertical axis is met by a 108-*phyeam* introduction along the western axis. In the latter instance, 108 units mark the path from the *nāga* balustrade to the first step up to the central tower.[20] In a similar fashion, the 108-*phyeam* circumambulation paths from the axial entrances to the central Viṣṇu pay homage to the deity as the creator of time, using 108 to adorn the path around Viṣṇu as 108 names adorn his many manifestations (Fig. 8.14). In the 108-unit circumambulation path that enters and exits each corner tower in turn, the lunar aspect of the number may be featured (27 × 4, Fig. 8.11).[21] The number 108 occurs two more times in the corner towers, as their interior axes when images are excluded (Fig. 8.22) and as their full vertical extent (Fig. 8.23).[22]

All of the instances of 108 unit measurements on the upper level of Angkor Wat are connected to the central or corner towers, without exception. The only architectural distinction between towers and axial entrances is the association of the towers with Mount Meru and the deities that reside on the cosmic mountain. Axial entrances cannot visually evoke the home of the gods. Due to that distinction, it might be that the number 108 on the upper level not only incorporates the 54/54 division of *asura*s and *deva*s into Mount Meru iconography, but by so doing brings with it a complex symbolism. The 54/54 divisions at Angkor Wat have referred to the north–south oscillation of the sun and the spring equinox at center stage, the Churning of the Sea of Milk and the *Indrābhiṣeka* of the king, the north and south celestial poles, the reciprocity between the realm of the king and the realm of the gods, the same reciprocity between

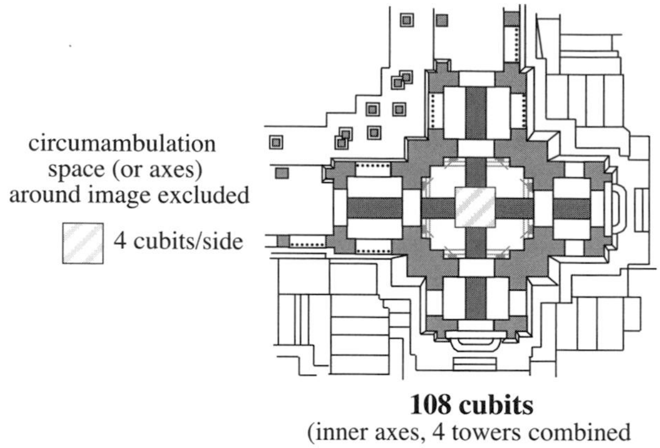

Fig. 8.22. First gallery, inner axes of corner towers as one set.

The corner towers have three important 108-unit measurements, including their inner axes. When seen as a set of four structures, these interior axes total 108 cubits without the image at the center of each tower. We have already seen that a circumambulation around the image, in and out of each tower, also totals 108 cubits (Fig. 8.11). The third repetition of 108 is in the height of the tower (Fig. 8.23). In addition, the number 108 factors into 27 × 4, or one definition of the lunar month in terms of lunar *nakṣatra* and the four quarters of the moon. This latter aspect of 108 coincides with the lunar-related nature of the towers. (See Appendix A, Table 8.8.)

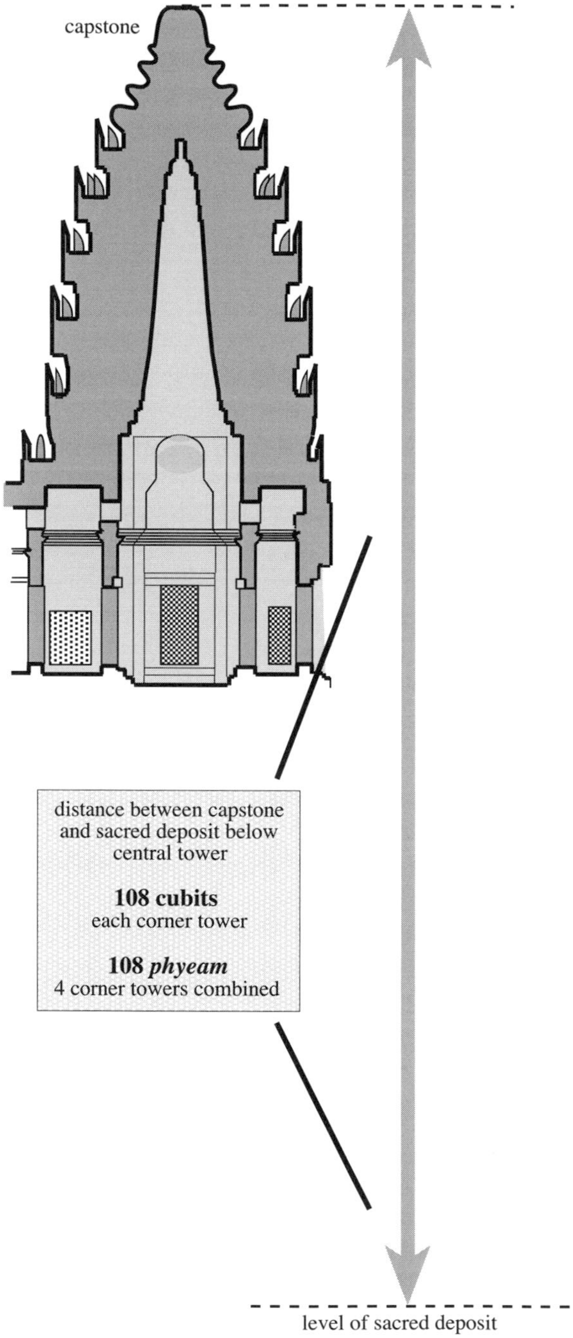

Fig. 8.23. First gallery, vertical axis of corner towers.

The 108-unit vertical measurement of each corner tower numerically reproduces the 108-cubit vertical axis above and below the central sanctuary. Together, all 5 towers on the upper level total 540 cubits in this particular configuration. The length of the western entrance bridge and that of the main western entrances are 540 cubits each. There are 540 *devas* and *asuras* over the bridges into Angkor Thom. The beginning and the end of Angkor Wat share in this unique symbolism that especially honors and exalts the gods and antigods at the north and south celestial poles, and recalls the churning scene itself. (See Appendix A, Table 8.8.)

the realm of the ancestors and that of the gods, and changing the era from the *kali yuga* to the *kṛta yuga*. At the heart and center of the reciprocity and dynamic yin/yang movement of the terrestrial and celestial worlds is Viṣṇu as the creator, the hub, the axis of existence. By placing 108 in association with the central tower, a symbol for the cosmic mountain and its deities, and by placing 108 in association with the surrounding towers as both replicas of Mount Meru in some ways, and as lunar in meaning, the architects have again eulogized Viṣṇu in the highest possible terms.

AN IMAGE OF THE UNIVERSE

When the cosmos expanded outward from Viṣṇu, when the mandala of gods, time, and space was set in motion, a newly created universe emerged from a center that could then be defined in terms of the cosmos around it. When Angkor Wat was completed, this mandala of time and divinity, and its center or creator, was built into the periphery and heart of the temple, making it an image of the universe and its source.

The overlapping definitions of architectural form, mandala design, the northern celestial sphere, and the realm of King Sūryavarman can be summarized in three architectural units:

Central sanctuary: Mount Meru, with 45 gods, the north celestial pole, the center of the mandala, the spring equinox, the axis of the earth, Viṣṇu, Brahmā, and King Sūryavarman

Circumferences: the ecliptic, the moon and lunar periodicity, the constellations, the planets, the celestial year, the *kṛta yuga,* the grid of the mandala, the history of King Sūryavarman

Axes: the building blocks of time (60, 108), the yuga cycles, the solar year, the lunar year, historical dates in Sūryavarman's reign, the mandala and its transformation of time, and, finally, the solar year and lunar time cycles from the vantage point of Mount Meru

Within the shared space of each chamber, tower, corridor, and walkway, divinity and the cosmos were joined to royalty and the terrestrial realm. The goal of temple architecture was completely realized but, the achievement of the priests was lost until their work was surveyed and its original measurements and alignments recovered—850 years later.

9

Basic Patterns

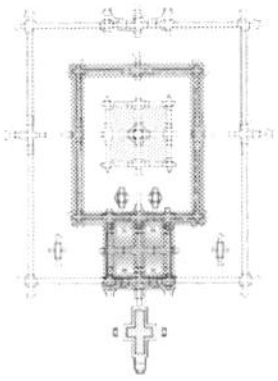

> JUPITER and Saturn are in Leo, Mars is in Capricorn, Mercury and Venus in Aquarius, the sun in Pisces, on a Friday, in the light 15-day period of the month of Phālguna, in the *śāka* year marked by the [9] openings, the number 6, and the [8] forms [869 *śāka* or A.D. 947], he erects here a lingam.[1]

Calendrical values were part of a living cultural context and they invariably emerge in Khmer inscriptions. In this simple one-sentence inscription, two or three words were enough to say that a Śiva lingam was set up (read: in a temple constructed for that purpose), but it took several lines to explain when that happened. The planets' positions in the 12 zodiac signs or in the 27/28 *nakṣatra,* the light or dark half of the lunar month, the solar month, the day of the week, and the year come first by custom—before the main statement. According to tradition, the era date is given "backwards," with the smallest year first and the century last, and spelled out through numerical symbols. The "forms" mean eight because Śiva has eight forms; the "openings" refer to the nine body orifices.

Whether time was expressed in writing or in the galleries and axes of a temple, it was a major component in the quality and efficacy of any ritual. To this culture which understood time as active rather than passive, recording time cycles in sacred architecture, wherever it originated, must have seemed like a very good idea. At Angkor Wat the *vāstupuruṣamaṇḍala* that appears everywhere through temple measurements, and the time cycles that are expressed outright in measurement values together form two means of spatial organization. Their purpose was not simple organization alone, however. They activate the temple in a way similar to the sculpted reliefs. The epic narratives, curling vines and foliage, and *asparases* that inhabit the walls as a symbol of Indra's heaven, all transform blank surfaces into a visually opulent, readable environment. Through measurements, the mandala and time cycles do the same for the ground plan of the temple, and for the empty corridors and chambers. The transformation of space into time and divinity begins at the bridge across the moat.

With the first step onto the western entrance bridge, we encounter a numerical representation of the 32 *devas* that continues around the outer enclosure to the base of the upper elevation and along the entire west–east axis. We are joined by measurement to the *devas* themselves, as unseen companions on the journey into the temple. As we cross into either of these 32-unit representations, several events occur simultaneously: we step onto a *kṛta yuga* distance; we are about to reach the solstice alignment with the end gateways; and we are about to enter the *kali yuga* and then the *tretā yuga*. The 60-unit axes that record how time is measured also start with that first step up to the bridge. The Churning of the Sea of Milk and the *Indrābhiṣeka* of the king appear in the 54/54 split of the columns on the bridge. The latter two events imply a change in time, from the *kali* to the *kṛta yuga*. In one form or another, subdivisions in time provide an orientation into the temple while the 32 gods are omnipresent and inseparable from us, from the time we live in and from the time measured out within the temple.

From the point of view of the 32 *devas*, Nārāyaṇa manifests as Brahmā during the night on Mount Meru or as Viṣṇu during the day. As we have seen, a diurnal and nocturnal setting for the 32 gods occurs repeatedly at Angkor Wat. These omnipresent deities are often found wherever the lunar and solar calendar exists at the temple, especially along the western axis.

1. *The western causeway:* Bracketed by a solar alignment with the central tower on the west and a 12-cubit distance to the cruciform terrace on the east, the causeway also has 12 staircases. Its lunar length and observation points, however, are its dominant motif.
   32 *phyeam* extend between the center of each staircase
   32 balustrade supports extend between each staircase
2. *The libraries:* With all their lunar references (none solar), the libraries share one 32-unit interior axial total.
3. *The cruciform terrace:* The terrace has solar and lunar axes that measure 12, 24, and 27/28 units. These axes are encompassed by one 32-unit axis that runs the entire west–east length of the terrace.
4. *The western entrance and third gallery:* This gallery has lunar references in its circumference, 28 chambers, and the lunar month along its eastern and western facades (27/28, 29.53, 14/15). Its 12 entrances, unique on this level, harmonize with the way in which the solstice and equinox sunlight interacts with the reliefs. The lunar and solar circumference ends in a 32/33-unit passage through the western entrance. Even the dates in the axes are arithmetically related to the 32 gods. The axial preponderance of 32 contrasts with time-related numbers focused around the enclosing corridors.
   32 *phyeam* as a circumambulation path through the western entrance
   32 pillars in front of the western entrance
   33 steps in the western entrance

32 units in the axes:
1021 = 32 × 31.90 cubits
1035 = 32 × 32.34 cubits
1038 = 32 × 32.44 cubits
1048 = 32 × 32.75 cubits
32 false windows, south corridor, west half (king's procession)
33 cubits (women's procession)
32 × 33 cubits, north and south sides of the gallery
32 hells in the panel of heavens and hells
The conjunction of 32 and the four dates along the axes, and the joining of 32/33 to the relief of the king, his ministers, and the women, underscores the presence of the gods in the events of the king's reign. If you did not honor the king's authority while serving him, you would find yourself in the last representation of 32 here.

5. *The* preau cruciforme: The gods are also present in this sector of Angkor Wat with its exceptional connection to the solstice shafts of light and its definition of Brahmā as a nocturnal deity.
   32 *phyeam* as the outermost axes of the central cruciform
   32 pillars radiating outward from the central cruciform in four directions
6. *The walkway to the upper elevation:* This walkway is 32 cubits long, and it stops at the end of a 354-cubit length from the *nāga* balustrade, connects the two lunar libraries, and links the solar upper level to the lunar second gallery.

The 32-unit references on the perimeter and in the entrances of the upper level of Angkor Wat are too many to list again, but they too are in association with the lunar and solar year. As for the second gallery, there are five examples of 32/33-unit measurements that occur exclusively along the circumference, which is lunar.[2]

At Angkor Wat, the 32 omnipresent gods are not only found in time periods, but they provide a deified approach to the Supreme Viṣṇu. They lead us to Viṣṇu from any direction. At the same time, the multiple examples of 32-unit spaces, 32 pillars, 32 windows, and 32 steps contrast with the number of examples of the full total of 44/45 deities. This seems to indicate that when the mandala is considered in its totality, it is inseparable from the supreme deity—and the *totality* of the mandala is not found very often at Angkor Wat.

Six out of ten measurements of 44/45 on the upper elevation are in the central tower, and all but one of them are related to the tower. Other than the topmost elevation and second gallery, there are only four other examples of the numbers 44/45 at the temple. But even they define the concept of Viṣṇu as a supreme deity by means of their architectural or sculptural placement, in addition to their symbolism.[3]

The placement of 44/45 and its rarity in comparison to the omnipresent 32/33-unit measurements agrees with the transition that occurs on the upper elevation. Based on the vertical progression of the axes and the meaning of each gallery in turn, only on the topmost level of Angkor Wat can we see the world from the perspective of Mount Meru and the Supreme Viṣṇu. Therefore, 44/45 would most commonly be found on this level because it fully defines Mount Meru and the Supreme Viṣṇu.

From another viewpoint, the exclusive 44/45-unit central position exists only in terms of its self-created environment. That is to say, the number 45 cannot be a symbol of a supreme deity without the preceding 44 units spatially placed around it. Viṣṇu transformed himself from a nondifferentiated entity into a center when the lotus stalk first emerged from his navel. That began the progression which ended in the symbolism of 44/45 and the creation of time and space.

The central tower at Angkor Wat is the architectural parallel to Viṣṇu at the time of creation. The tower exists as a center only by the placement and definition of the architecture and measurements that surround it. In this analogy, Angkor Wat is also an architectural expression of the universe created by Viṣṇu: the celestial ecliptic, the lunar and solar constellations, the cycles of time, the realm of King Sūryavarman, and the historical dates that surround the central tower are a reflection of the celestial realm created by Viṣṇu. The architects wanted to join that celestial world to Angkor Wat, not just through measurements and reliefs, but though architectural design as well.

Viṣṇu is at the center of the solar year and inside the central tower of Angkor Wat. Both are marked by the spring equinox alignment in March. As the sun moves north and south across the axis of the temple, the axis functions as a horizontal extension of the vertically placed tower. From the very beginning of the bridge, then, we have been approaching Viṣṇu along the spring equinox line, the solar axis of the temple.

Viṣṇu's equinox position was spelled out in the bas-reliefs that have a shaft of light on either side of him during the solstices and show him in full sunlight at the equinox. The central tower, as well as the main entrance tower, have solstice light on either side of them in December and June, and both are illuminated by direct, frontal sunlight on the equinoxes. The opposite is true for Brahmā in the *preau cruciforme.* The temple shows that Viṣṇu (as Brahmā) rules the night as well.

The solar equinox alignment is with the central tower. All of the lunar alignments, however, are with the corner towers, and most of these alignments are with towers in the lunar second gallery. By their architectural stature alone, these towers surpass other chambers in the temple. But the corner towers are subsidiary to the solar central tower in many respects: Viṣṇu in the central tower is both solar and dominant.

The corner towers duplicate the central tower on a smaller scale and are placed below it. The moon is also a duplicate of the sun, but with much less light. Behind the architecture is the concept of an evolving creation, as one divine form recreates itself in a slightly lesser guise in the hierarchy of forms. The essentially solar-related Viṣṇu creates Brahmā (an equal, however), who in turn creates the moon and stars and then favors that expression with his place at the north celestial pole, giving the more honored seat of the daytime manifestation of deity to Viṣṇu himself. During construction, the central tower was created first at Angkor Wat, and then four lesser towers, and from there the rest of the temple evolved downward and outward. Mounds of dirt would have filled the lower pyramid, providing ramps to haul stones to the top. Construction had to proceed from the top down, or not proceed at all. Mandalas are also generated from the center outward and downward. The central deity creates the surrounding deities, often four in number and subsidiary in stature, who then continue the process until the mandala is filled. The very act of creating Angkor Wat, then, mirrors the creation of a mandala and the creation of time and space.

There is one aspect of the temple, however, that seems an exception to the ripple-like effect of mandala creation: the set of six libraries. They are a string of pairs that run along the western axis, and yet their specific location and orientation may ultimately bring them into the center of the mandala. The use of the libraries alternated between the waxing and waning moon. The waxing moon begins in the west and the waning moon in the east. This west–east oscillation regulates the nighttime calendar. In contrast, the north–south oscillation of the sun regulates a daytime calendar. The two types of back-and-forth movement cross each other on a north–south, west–east celestial axis, like the crossing of the axes at Angkor Wat that meet in the central tower in Viṣṇu and Brahmā at the heart of the mandala and hub of creation. Perhaps to harmonize the west–east lunar movement with the north–south solar oscillation, each pair of lunar libraries is internally aligned along a north–south axis. As the moon alternates in size and brightness from west to east, the libraries alternate in use from north to south. They are, therefore, symbolically joined to the center of this cosmic diagram of lunisolar oscillation, to the crossing of north–south and west–east axes in the central tower.

From the perspective of the mandala and architecture together, the subsidiary position of the corner towers mentioned earlier is determined by the location and height of the central tower. As we approach the main sanctuary of the temple along the solar equinox axis, a visit to the corner towers constitutes a departure from the journey to Viṣṇu. Yet from the perspective of the lunisolar calendar, the longer annual time period of the sun and lesser annual period of the moon have to be brought into harmony or time becomes skewed, out of synchrony. It loses its ability to regulate as it loses its definition. In much the same way as a calendar, corner towers or pavilions mark circumference boundaries that in their own circuits spatially describe the cyclical periodicity of lunar time in particular. The solar central tower generates axes that reflect a linear progression of time as we approach along a linear path. Both circumference and axes together define a space that synchronizes the two modes of measuring time, the cyclical and linear, lunar and solar. The visual balance between the central tower and corner towers, and the complementary numerical meaning of the axes and circumferences reflect the practice of bringing these two diverse calendrical systems together. They also reflect a much broader practice of unifying opposites such as dark and light, yin and yang, hot and cold, and even life and death (the living and the ancestors), into one inseparable whole. This is not the mixing of hot and cold water to obtain lukewarm, but the creation of an active dynamic that oscillates between two poles that are recognized as inseparable. In that inseparability arises the much deeper belief of an ultimate unity beyond the superficial polarity. Comparable to the metaphor of creation, this belief finds expression in Viṣṇu in the central tower of Angkor Wat who created Brahmā but is none other than Brahmā. As the solar Viṣṇu and lunar Brahmā regulate day and night, sun and moon, the supreme Nārāyaṇa is forever present as the unseen unity of both.

The axes and circumferences of the temple are therefore grounded in the broader vision of two opposites that interact within an underlying principle of unity. The series of circumference measurements begins with 120 units around the perimeter of the moat, complemented by 60-unit axes. These units refer to the numerical basis for time measurement developed in the Mesopotamian area several millennia before the creation of Angkor Wat. Other than providing the smallest units (12 and 60) as a basis for the time measurements that lie ahead, these two architectural components also provide us with the longest periods of time. If the 120-unit perimeter of Angkor Wat is expressed in cubits it equals three repetitions of the four yuga cycles, or 12,960 cubits. A long journey around the perimeter would end with another, fourth repetition of the yuga cycles all the way to the upper elevation, or 17,280 cubits. Expressed as a single total, this full journey around Angkor Wat and to the upper level along the western axis of the temple is equal to 10 *kṛta yuga* time spans. In this manner, an auspicious shield of protection and augury of good fortune and prosperity directly combines the circumference and axes together. From the largest, most beneficent time cycle, the complementary pair of axes and circumference totals proceed through the temple.

From this point on, we find the lunar year as

a complement to an axial solar year in the outer or fourth enclosure, the *nāga* terrace, and the upper elevation. The *kṛta yuga* in the third gallery defines Sūryavarman's reign as much as the historical dates in the axes. In this instance, it is the king who generates the *kṛta yuga* at his spring equinox inauguration—a terrestrial counterpart of the supreme Viṣṇu who creates all time cycles, especially the solar year at the spring equinox period. After the reign of the king has figuratively ended in this ascension to the upper level, the 49 units in the circumference of the second gallery define the field of a mandala, the same mandala that holds 44 deities along the axes. At the upper level, the lunar circumference (24) is an integral part of the axial entrances. When the axes in all four entrances are included in the circumference measurement the total comes to 21 × 24 cubits. The supreme deity, Indra, and the gods on Mount Meru are thereby joined to this final expression of the lunar year.

Angkor Wat, then, is like a mandala of deities in a field of sculpted stones, stones that are aligned with the sun and moon and time cycles along a west–east and north–south axis. As the mandala generates outward from the central tower to the moat, the stones are animated by measurement patterns and conjunctions with the sun and moon. Rituals kept the temple alive with worship, bringing the ancestors and the sanctuary icons into active union. For in the end, the entire panoply of cosmic architecture was dedicated to ancestor gods in the form of Viṣṇu and Brahmā; or Śiva, Lakṣmī, and others.

The political system of Cambodia was founded on the good relationship between feudal lords and the institution of kingship. By bringing his 19 ministers and his history into the third gallery, King Sūryavarman joined his realm to divinity. His reasons for constructing Angkor Wat, however, must have been as diverse as the multifaceted meanings of the temple itself. As the cosmos was firmly joined to the temple grounds and devout homage given to the gods in every delicate line of bas-relief and in the unseen measurements and alignments, the king never took his vision away from his position, his government, and the exaltation of both at Angkor Wat.

KING SŪRYAVARMAN AND HIS TEMPLE

The role of the king at the temple has its origins in the nature of Viṣṇu and his location in the celestial realm and on Mount Meru. This discussion of the king, therefore, begins with Viṣṇu.

Even though his central position is solar in nuance, when Viṣṇu assumes the role of Nārāyaṇa he can appear in a lunar context as a supreme deity. The 21 cubits at the center of the Battle of Laṅkā, for example, put Viṣṇu at the axis of a 12/12 split in the lunar year, as well as at the axis of the battle scene. Because these 21 cubits are an invisible presence at the center of the battle scene, they were the most accurate means of symbolizing a supreme deity at the heart of a lunar reciprocity—the 12 dark and 12 light halves of the lunar month. So Viṣṇu in this instance is both solar (Rāma was of the solar race of kings) and lunar. King Sūryavarman himself united the solar and lunar races of kings in his own person.

As for the content of this relief, another aspect of Viṣṇu emerges that is more closely related to the king at Angkor Wat. The gods and their enemies, the *asuras*, play out their never-ending battles against the backdrop of an oscillation between the southern and northern solstice positions. Viṣṇu is an arbiter in these battles, or intervenes to balance the odds, so that neither side ever prevails. This equilibrium is symbolized by his place at the spring equinox: halfway between the solstice points of the calendar. The king is at the spring equinox during his *Indrābhiṣeka,* and in that regard he parallels Viṣṇu at the beginning of his reign.

The spring equinox position of Viṣṇu is also symbolized in the central tower of Angkor Wat. Not only is the tower aligned with the sun on that day, but it places Viṣṇu at the center of a vertical axis with the 54 *deva*s above him and the 54 *asura*s below. Viṣṇu is perennially in the middle of these two northern and southern groups of deities. The close identity of the king and the statue of Viṣṇu in the central tower indirectly places the king between the *deva*s and *asura*s as well.

To effect the needed balance between the *deva*s and *asura*s, Viṣṇu incarnates on earth in 10 different avatars, four of which are featured in the bas-reliefs of Angkor Wat: Kūrma, Rāma, Balarāma, and Kṛṣṇa. In the Battle of Laṅkā, when Viṣṇu emerges in the 21 cubits at the axis he is exactly between Rāma and Rāvaṇa, between the *deva*s and *asura*s, as well as between the lunar half-months.

The solstice light that flanks Rāma in this scene, the Pāṇḍava leader in the Kurukṣetra scene, Viṣṇu in the churning scene, and also his *deva* and *asura* forms in that scene—all place him between the two solstices, between the *deva*s and *asura*s again. This time, however, because of the connections between these bas-relief scenes and the history of King Sūryavarman, the figures representing Viṣṇu also allude to the king. Whereas the avatars are full incarnations of the deity on earth, Khmer kings share only in a "portion" *(āṃśa)* of divinity. Sūryavarman shares in the glory and the central position of Viṣṇu by allusion and inference. Once more, the king is indirectly placed between the gods (northern solstice) and antigods (southern solstice).

King Sūryavarman's audience with his ministers and his procession are on the south side of the gallery. In the procession panel Sūryavarman is also at the center, between the past that precedes him and the future that lies ahead. Unlike the central figures of Viṣṇu, however, the king will never directly interact with the sun. He will never have flanking shafts of solstice light on either side of him or receive full equinox light: he is not the same as Viṣṇu. But his realm and his person alternate with the realm of the gods on the north and Indra, respectively.

As the sun moves north and south each year, its diffuse light brightens or dims these two opposite panels. The reciprocity between the divine and human orders is clear. It does not follow the same theme as the antagonism between *deva*s and *asura*s; it follows the division between the two extremes of the sun's path each year. These two realms are also divided by Viṣṇu in the central tower and the spring equinox that runs along the western causeway and up the tower. By allusion and by inference again, the realm of the king and the king himself follow a north–south pattern that is shared by the *deva*s and *asura*s, a pattern that finds its source in a north–south solar division with Viṣṇu and the equinox at the center. At the same time, we find that the king shares in the divinity of Viṣṇu in the central tower, on the highest level literally and philosophically. Viṣṇu also enters into the history of the king's reign in the bas-reliefs and in the dates in the axes of the third gallery. Whether we are looking at the most spiritual aspects of the king's life or the most mundane, Viṣṇu is always present. There is no means of separating King Sūryavarman and Viṣṇu at Angkor Wat.

Although one cannot say the king was an incarnation of Viṣṇu, the image of Viṣṇu in the central sanctuary may have looked like King Sūryavarman and would have been named after the king according to tradition. (We do not know the name of the central statue at Angkor Wat.) The connection between the statue/Viṣṇu and the king is obvious and direct in this case. The near-identity of a central Viṣṇu and King Sūryavarman brings a human, terrestrial dimension to the architecture that rose above each mandala diagram. With Viṣṇu at the center, closely identified with King Sūryavarman, the distinctions between the political-historical realm and the cosmic abode of the gods are considerably lessened.

There are three places along the axis where the king and Viṣṇu seem to be specifically joined. Including the central tower, these are the main western entrance (*Indrābhiṣeka* and 54/54-unit symbolism) and the western entrance to the historically-oriented third gallery. This last location is logical given the gallery's focus on the king and his relationship to divinity. The union of the king and Viṣṇu in each of these three chambers, however, is magnified by the architectural context.

The central western entrance of the temple and the bridge are the closest to the *Indrābhiṣeka* at Angkor Wat, based on the multiplicity of their 54/54-unit measurements. Tied to the spring equinox through Mount Mandara as a pivot, through the axial lintels over the doorways, and through the solar alignments, the main western entrance puts the king, Viṣṇu, the spring equinox, and the beginning of the solar year and the king's reign, all together, in one chamber. At the start of Angkor Wat, therefore, the king shares an equinox space with Viṣṇu that illustrates the beginning of the king's reign, the start of the *kṛta yuga,* and the union of the king and Viṣṇu at the same time.

The *kṛta yuga* circumference in the third gallery is another statement on the king's creation of the golden era. In this second representation, the statue in the main western entrance would be the point of genesis for the circumference measurement. The *kali yuga* implied in the scene of the battle at Kurukṣetra, which started that period of time, is transformed into the *kṛta yuga* by the opposite panel, the scene of the Churning of the Sea of Milk, and the king's *Indrābhiṣeka.* So once again we have a picture of the king banishing the *kali yuga,* starting a perfect era of time, and doing both as he was inaugurated. His possible union with Viṣṇu in the main western entrance, however, now takes place during the context of his entire reign, his whole history. The stories on the walls merge the king and the god together; their union in this historical gallery is grounded by time and place.

When Sūryavarman is joined to Viṣṇu in the central tower, by contrast, it is a union that transcends the sphere he lives in. It takes place in the realm of the gods and at the very top of that realm symbolized by the north celestial pole. The measurements, solar alignment, and placement of the central tower are clear. The king is not simply at Angkor alone: he is elevated to a concurrent, higher location.

This final union with Viṣṇu lies beyond the limits of the sphere that binds the king to the earth and his society. It is the nature of that ineffable union, its strength and its spiritual stature, which transforms Sūryavarman into a king. It was formally acknowledged at his *Indrābhiṣeka* and was sustained thereafter by rituals in the sanctuaries of Angkor Wat.

Looking back on the progression up to each successive level of the temple, then, we see King Sūryavarman everywhere, to one degree or another, except in the second gallery. The difference between the king in the third gallery, where he is shown twice in rare portraiture, and the king in the central tower, where he was joined to the sacred image of Viṣṇu, is significant. It also agrees with the split effected by the second gallery. In his historical third gallery, the king is in his realm, on earth, and symbolically joined to the realm of the *devas*. In the central tower, he is in the realm of the *devas* and symbolically joined to his realm on earth.

In this overview of Angkor Wat, a few patterns seem to have set the broad definition of the temple. The omnipresent 32-unit mandala measurement that occurs everywhere was probably meant to have the same transformative effect as the mandala in the second gallery. As the axes and circumferences rise higher and higher, terrestrial time and the historical era of the king are left behind and, via the mandala again, we reach Mount Meru. And on Mount Meru we are introduced to time, space, and kingship as defined by the gods, on their scale, and from the perspective of a supreme deity.

Even though the various enclosures of the temple are unique and function distinctly from each other, the sacred, celestial realm is never completely separated from our own. References to the king appear right at the first step up to the entrance bridge, and they end in the central tower, the objective of the journey. The king may be emphasized in the third gallery, but he is not confined to its walls.

Similarly, the Supreme Nārāyaṇa, as both Viṣṇu and Brahmā, is represented in the main western entrance of the temple with its position between the solstices and its symbolism of the Churning of the Sea of Milk. Nārāyaṇa will continue to appear in different ways, including the central image in the *preau cruciforme,* until the central tower where the supreme deity was once represented directly in a statue.

This same pattern of recurrence is even more obvious for the sun and moon and their time periods—and for the mandala, as noted. In the end, the temple joins the realm of the gods to the terrestrial world right from the beginning. The supreme deity is present right from the beginning. The king and his world are present, too, right from the beginning. But to function successfully as sacred architecture, the progression up to Viṣṇu in the central tower had to be logical, complete, and in a series of graded stages. Angkor Wat accomplishes this objective in one of the world's outstanding architectural achievements.

Angkor Wat was not constructed in a day, of course, not even by the standards of celestial time. At the Bakheng built in 900 we see a nascent Angkor Wat emerging from its terraces, its original quincunx of towers, and its numerology and ground plan.[4] As noted earlier, the Bakheng has 44 towers around its base that define its five terraces as the heart of Mount Meru and its central image as the highest god. The 60 small towers on the terraces not only allude to the 12 zodiac signs or 12 solar months in a year (12 to a terrace), but there are 20 of the towers on each side. (The corner towers are "shared" by adjacent sides.) The central tower, then, makes a twenty-first unit in relation to the 20 towers, as well as a forty-fifth unit in relation to the towers at the base of the pyramid.

In a similar fashion, when the 12 towers that run along the base on each side of the monument (again the corner towers are shared by adjacent sides) are added to the 20 above, we have a 32-unit introduction to the topmost platform. Thus far these numbers are not new: they have been recognized for several decades now. The numerology does not stop there, however.

Each quadrant of the Bakheng has 15 small towers, 12 large towers at the base, and each was once also marked by a corner tower on the top level, for a total of 27. If we include the central tower, we have an alternate 27/28.

There are 7 steps in the staircase of the top terrace, for a total of 28 steps in all. A total of 28 towers flank the east–west axis, and 28 flank the north–south axis. These straight rows of towers that flank the axes lead right up to the pair of corner towers in a direct line. When these topmost corner towers are added to the axial total, there are 32 towers flanking the north–south axis and 32 flanking the east–west axis. The central tower, then, becomes a thirty-third unit. In other words, we have the 27/28 *nakṣatra* along the axes or placed in a lunar quadrant (four phases of the moon) and transformed into the 32 gods by two corner towers at the top (in the axial progression).

Looking only at the steps themselves, we note that they decrease as the terraces ascend, in the order of 11, 10, 9, 8, and 7 steps in each of four staircases, for a total of 45. Or from the point of view of each side of the monument, there are 44 steps around the first terrace, then 40, 36, 32, and 28 around the second, third, fourth, and fifth terraces, respectively. All of these numbers are related to the architectural mandala, except perhaps for 36. When the staircases are considered in sequence, the first two staircases together have 21 steps and the next three staircases together have 24 steps. There are 24 steps around the topmost platform, 6 steps in each staircase, and 32 steps around the four subsidiary towers (no longer extant). The central tower has 12 steps (not counting the decorative bottom step, which is not in the staircase proper but in front of it), for a total of 44 steps in 20 staircases on the topmost platform. There are 20 staircases that lead up the five terraces (five staircases on four sides). There are four more staircases on the upper platform, and 20 on top of the platform, for a total of 44 staircases at the Bakheng. In fact, the count of steps could be extended to the towers at the base. Since there are 44 towers with four staircases of 2 steps each, the total is 8 steps for each tower, or 352 in all. This is only two steps short of a lunar year.

If the 20 towers on each side of the Bakheng are seen in conjunction with the four subsidiary (and according to the pattern at Angkor Wat) lunar towers at the top, the total is 24. There are also 24 towers on the upper two terraces, and there would have been 24 pillars on the east side of the upper level that once supported a walkway to the central towers. There are also 24 steps on the top platform, as noted. Since this monument was dedicated to Śiva, lunar symbolism is dominant near the upper parts of the temple. Finally, when the 44 towers at the base are added to the 60 small towers on the terraces and the 4 that are on the top platform, the total is 108.

The numerology at the Bakheng may be complemented by the solstice sun as well. When I made a morning visit to the Bakheng during the winter solstice one year, I noticed that shafts of sunlight come through the doors of the central sanctuary. In fact, they precisely frame the northeast and southwest corners of the large, walled pit that is in the center. (This pit is the top of a shaft that descended below the sanctuary.) Although I did not return in the afternoon, it seemed the setting sun would illuminate the opposite northwest and southeast corners of the square pit at that time. In other words, the Bakheng appears to have an orientation to the solstices.

In distant Central Java, there is a temple called Candi Sewu that was constructed in the late eighth and early ninth centuries, antedating the Bakheng by a century or so. Candi Sewu has a cruciform shape with a central sanctuary and four subsidiary and independent axial chambers.[5] It is surrounded by an inner square of 28 subsidiary temples: 12 facing north–south (6/6), 16 east–west. When we add the four chambers around the central image to this number, we find there would have been 32 individual sanctuaries around the center of Candi Sewu.

The inner, 28-temple square is ringed by another that had small temples (also called *candis*): 20 facing north–south (10/10) and 24 facing east–west (12/12). After a large courtyard distinguished by a pair of temples that flank the axes on each side, there are two outer rectangles of smaller temples. The inner rectangle was planned with 40 temples facing east–west (20/20), or 44 if we add in the corner temples. Although these corner temples have no porch, they do mark the ends of the inner rectangle. The inner rectangle was to have a full 80 subsidiary temples, then, and if we add this number to the 28 temples in the inner square around the heart of Sewu, the total is 108.

The outer rectangle has 48 small temples facing east–west (24/24) and 40 facing north–south

(20/20). If we add all the subsidiary temples that face north–south together, they come to 108 total. There are also 108 temples facing east and west if we exclude the central square of 28 temples from the count. Not all of these temples are extant.

Each quadrant formed by the axes has 60 small temples total, for a split of 120/120 on each side of the axes—or 240 in all. Since there are 24 niches in the four subsidiary chambers around the central image, 6 per chamber, the number 24 is not accidental.

An exploration of the numerology at the Bakheng and Candi Sewu could continue in much the same vein. But the objective here is not to analyze Candi Sewu and the Phnom Bakheng, but to illustrate that what happens at Angkor Wat does not happen in isolation. And it does not happen outside a long history of development—perhaps even an international development.

ANGKOR WAT TODAY

Today, in our own reality, one's footsteps echo through empty corridors at Angkor Wat, at least outside the peak tourist season in December and January. Flowers and incense are still placed daily in front of the few remaining statues, but the chambers are not animated by ritual. The stones and corridors seem asleep.

At night during the cooler months, fireflies sparkle across the moat, terrestrial points of light that move in and out of the stars reflected in the water. During the rainy season, monsoon clouds roll across the sky, forming a mottled-gray turbulent canopy over the temple, whose own facade reflects the somber gray of the pending storm. At dusk, warm-hued and rather small cows meander back across the bridge from a lazy day's grazing in the courtyard. They are the last to leave before night settles in. In all respects, the temple seems to partake of the world around it.

But at twilight, the modern world recedes from Angkor Wat as the last stragglers leave with memories of sunset over the western entrances. Reclaimed by the twelfth century again, the temple slowly disappears from view during the encroaching darkness. Brahmā reappears at the north celestial pole. Silence descends, and in the soundless night, time seems to stand still.

APPENDIX A: MEASUREMENTS

Table 2.1. 54-Unit Lengths on the Western Bridge

NUMBER	MEASUREMENT
53.80 *phyeam*	western half of span
53.97 *phyeam*	eastern half of span
53.39 cubits	north–south length between ledges at top of pair of western stairways (Fig. 2.6)
53.97 cubits	north–south length between ledges at top of pair of eastern stairways
538.52 cubits (54 × 10)	length of bridge
538.43 cubits (54 × 10)	length of western entrances at east end of bridge
54/54	columns and balustrade supports on each side of span
54.21 *phyeam*	north–south axes of three sets of staircases combined

Table 3.1. 54/54 Unit Pairs in the Outer Enclosure

NUMBER	MEASUREMENT
54.29 cubits	north lateral entrance, inner axes (Fig. 3.11)
54.11 cubits	south lateral entrance, inner axes (Fig. 3.11)
53.97 *phyeam*	circumambulation path into the central entrance and out of the north lateral entrance (Fig. 3.12)
53.98 *phyeam*	circumambulation path into the central entrance and out of the south lateral entrance (Fig. 3.12)
54.05 *phyeam*	circumambulation path into the north lateral entrance and out of the central entrance (Fig. 3.12)
54.08 *phyeam*	circumambulation path into the south lateral entrance and out of the central entrance (Fig. 3.12)
53.55 *phyeam*	circumambulation path into and out of both lateral chambers combined (26.85 *phyeam* north chamber, 26.98 *phyeam* south chamber, Fig. 3.12)
54.16 cubits	total inner north–south axial lengths for the four side chambers of the central entrance (27.80 cubits each on the north and south, Fig. 3.12)
53.67 cubits	central cruciform axes for the end gateways combined with their central area excluded (Fig. 3.15)
54.74 *phyeam*	corridor length to the central square area of the central entrance on the north (Fig. 3.11)
53.33 *phyeam*	corridor length to the central square area of the central entrance on the south (Fig. 3.11)
56 and 52	number of *pairs* of pillars along the northern (56) and southern (52) corridors of the western entrances
53.94 cubits	total inner axes for the far lateral end chambers in the eastern, northern, and southern entrances combined (Fig. 3.16)

Table 3.2 Mandala Numbers in the Lateral Western Entrances, North and South Combined, Enclosure 4

NUMBER	MEASUREMENT	MEANING
44 pillars	total pillars (Fig. 3.11)	all deities in mandala
28 pillars	total pillars, west facade only (Fig. 3.11)	*nakṣatra*
33 steps	total steps (Fig. 3.11)	32 *deva*s and Brahmā
31.87 *phyeam*	total outer west–east axes (Fig. 3.11)	*deva*s
27.44 *phyeam*	total outer west–east axes excluding central chamber (Fig. 3.11)	*nakṣatra*
26.98 *phyeam*	circumambulation in and out of south entrance (Fig. 3.12)	*nakṣatra*
26.85 *phyeam*	circumambulation in and out of north entrance (Fig. 3.12)	*nakṣatra*
28.09 cubits	north–south axis of side chambers (Fig. 3.12)	*nakṣatra*
48.72 *phyeam*	full length of all three western entrances including doorways into corridors (Fig. 3.12)	49 squares in mandala

Table 3.3 Mandala Numbers in the End Gateways, North and South Combined, Enclosure 4

NUMBER	MEASUREMENT	MEANING
40 (28 + 12) pillars	total pillars (Fig. 3.15b)	*nakṣatra* and *āditya*s
32 pillars	total pillars, west facade only (Fig. 3.15b)	*deva*s
32 windows	total windows, real and false (Fig. 3.15a)	*deva*s
32.38 cubits	length of pavement to west doorway (Fig. 3.15c)	*deva*s
32.74 *phyeam*	circumambulation path to north end chamber, each end gateway (Fig. 3.15a)	*deva*s and Brahmā
32.82 *phyeam*	circumambulation path to south end chamber, each end gateway (Fig. 3.15a)	*deva*s and Brahmā
33.02 cubits	north–south axis, all four end chambers (Fig. 3.15c)	*deva*s and Brahmā
20.08 *phyeam*	central cruciform, inner axes (Fig. 3.15d)	not a mandala number but refers to *deva*s and king

Table 3.4. Mandala Numbers in the Central Western Entrance, Enclosure 4

NUMBER	MEASUREMENT	MEANING
12 steps	total steps in entrance (Fig. 3.11)	solar months, *āditya*s
49 pillars	pillars in front of entrance and side chambers, including porches (Fig. 3.11)	squares in mandala
45 steps	total steps, main entrance and flanking entrances (Fig. 3.11)	total deities in mandala

Table 3.5. Mandala Numbers in the North, South, and East Entrances, Enclosure 4

NUMBER	MEASUREMENT	MEANING
28.20 *phyeam*	circumambulation path into and out of each entrance from outside (Fig. 3.16a)	*nakṣatra*
318.15 cubits (32 × 10)	inner axes, all chambers, all three entrances (Fig. 3.16d)	*deva*s

Table 3.6. Pillared Corridors, Mandala Numbers in the Western Entrances, Enclosure 4

NUMBER	MEASUREMENT	MEANING
32.01 *phyeam*	north corridor, length between opposite doors (Fig. 3.11)	*devas*
30.43 *phyeam*	south corridor, length between opposite doors (Fig. 3.11)	*devas*?

Table 3.7. Lunar Measurements in the North, South, and East Entrances Combined, Enclosure 4

NUMBER	MEASUREMENT	MEANING
24 pillars	total outer pillars (Fig. 3.16)	lunar half-months in 1 year
24 × 3 pillars	total inner pillars (Fig. 3.16)	
24 × 3 windows	windows excluding end chambers	
30 steps	total steps (Fig. 3.16)	lunar month (29.53 days),
28 × 3	total windows (Fig. 3.16)	*nakṣatra,* lunar month, days of lunar visibility
28.20 *phyeam*	circumambulation path into and out of each entrance (Fig. 3.16a)	
270.15 cubits (27 × 10)	long outer axes (along cross-arm) (Fig. 3.16b)	
11.009 × 24 (264.21 cubits)	inner axes, central cruciform chamber and connecting rooms (Fig. 3.16e)	lunar *kāraṇa* (gods), lunar half-months

Table 3.8. Lunar Measurements in the End Gateways, Enclosure 4

NUMBER	MEASUREMENT	MEANING
27 *phyeam*	outer west–east axis (Fig. 3.13e)	*nakṣatra,* lunar month, days of lunar visibility
24 *phyeam*	outer west–east axis without central area (Fig. 3.13d)	lunar half-months in 1 year
24 interior steps	both gateways combined (Fig. 3.13a)	12/12 division of half-months in 1 year (12 steps in each gateway)
27 cubits	inner axes without center of passageway	*nakṣatra,* lunar month, days of lunar visibility

Table 4.1. Lunar Measurements along the Western Causeway (Fig. 4.3)

MEASUREMENT	MEANING AND LOCATION
28.05 × 28.00 cubits	causeway length between *last* step of western entrance and *nāga* balustrade around central galleries sidereal lunar month, days of lunar visibility, number of *nakṣatra*
29.53 × 29.51 cubits	causeway length between *first* step of western entrance and *nāga* balustrade synodic or tropical lunar month
28.22 *phyeam*	distance between facing sides of staircases number of *nakṣatra*
32.04 *phyeam*	distance between center points of staircases number of *devas* on Mount Meru and in mandala
32 balustrade supports	between successive staircases
12 staircases	solar *ādityas*, solar months
5 × 12 (60) steps	5-year lunisolar period

Table 4.2. Lunar Measurements in the Libraries of the Western Causeway, Enclosure 4 (Fig. 4.9)

MEASUREMENT	MEANING AND LOCATION
24 lunar half-months in 1 year:	
24 windows	
24 interior pillars	
23.66 *phyeam*	west–east outer axis, south library
24.11 *phyeam*	west–east outer axis, north library
27/28 *nakṣatra,* days of lunar visibility, sidereal lunar month:	
27 steps	south library
28 steps	north library
27.10 *phyeam*	south library, in-and-out circumambulation
26.92 *phyeam*	north library, in-and-out circumambulation
27.68 cubits	south library, distance to image from base of (north) stairway on causeway side
27.32 cubits	north library, distance to image from base of (south) stairway on causeway side

Table 4.3. The Middle Libraries between Galleries 2 and 3 (Fig. 4.11)

MEASUREMENT	MEANING AND LOCATION
20/21 gods/king/supreme deity:	
21 steps	each library, north stairways (in succession)
21 steps	each library, south stairways
20 steps	each library, west stairways
20 steps	each library, east stairways
20 pillars	each library, total interior and exterior pillars
20.01 cubits	each library, distance between base of structure and image in central chamber
20.004 × 10 cubits	both libraries together, in-and-out circumambulation of central image
19.42 *phyeam*	each library, west–east outer axis
24 windows	both libraries together
24 interior columns	lunar half-months in 1 year

Table 4.4. The Topmost Libraries between Galleries 1 and 2 (Fig. 4.14)

MEASUREMENT	MEANING AND LOCATION
4 phases of moon; 4 mountains, continents, and rivers around Meru:	
4 doorways	
4 interior pillars	
4 porch pillars	
4 blind windows	
12 light and 12 dark half-months in 1 lunar year:	
9 steps + 3 cubits =	each library, units of access
12 units	(no steps on walkway side)
(3 + 3 + 3 steps + 3 cubits)	
28.02 cubits	each library, inner axes between doors
27.02 cubits	each library, inner axes minus ledge by doors
20.96 *phyeam*	each library, in-and-out circumambulation path
10.98 *phyeam*	each library, outer west–east axis (lunar *karāṇa*)
7.19 *phyeam*	each library, outer north–south axis (7-day lunar week, oceans around Meru)

Table 4.5. The Cruciform Terrace (Fig. 4.19)

MEASUREMENT	LOCATION
24 total steps	three staircases combined
24.60 *phyeam*	north–south axis between bases
28 balustrade supports	north and south perimeters
28 balustrade supports	east and west perimeters
27.00 *phyeam* (107. 98 cubits)	west–east axis between first step to intermediary level on the west and porch of third gallery on the east
20.65 *phyeam*	west–east axis between opposite staircase ledges at ends of upper cruciform
20.42 *phyeam*	north–south axis between opposite staircase ledges at intermediary level
32.48 *phyeam*	west–east axis between accolade step on the west and porch of third gallery on the east
54 columns	north and south sides of cruciform
54 columns	west and east sides of cruciform
11.97 *phyeam*	north–south axis between opposite staircase ledges on upper cruciform

Table 4.6. Lunar Measurements in the Eastern and Western Corridors, Gallery 3

MEASUREMENT	LOCATION
27.02 *phyeam*	east corridor, south half (Fig. 4.27)
27.76 *phyeam*	west corridor, south half (Fig. 4.27)
29.54 *phyeam*	east corridor, north half (Fig. 4.27)
29.42 *phyeam*	west corridor, north half (Fig. 4.27)
28.02 × 32 cubits	east and west corridors together (Fig. 4.27)
28 × 11 pillars	east and west corridors together (Fig. 4.27)
28.60 cubits	eastern and western entrances together, axes of forechambers (Fig. 4.28)
29 outer steps	western lateral chambers (lunar month)
30 outer steps	eastern lateral chambers (lunar or solar month)
15 inner steps	eastern and western lateral chambers together (lunar half-month)
43.96 cubits	eastern entrance, axis of side chambers (Fig. 4.28)
43.52 cubits	western entrance, axis of side chambers (Fig. 4.28)

Table 4.7. *Deva* Related Numbers in the Northern and Southern Corridors, Gallery 3

MEASUREMENT	LOCATION
53.74 *phyeam*	north corridor, west half (Fig. 4.27)
53.74 *phyeam*	south corridor, west half (Fig. 4.27)
32 false windows	north corridor, west half (Fig. 4.27)
32 false windows	south corridor, west half (Fig. 4.27)
21 false windows	north corridor, east half (Fig. 4.27)
21 false windows	south corridor, east half (Fig. 4.27)
20.74 cubits	northern and southern entrances together, axes of forechambers (Fig. 4.29)
32 × 32.99 cubits	north and south sides of gallery (Fig. 4.27)
32.98 cubits	northern or southern entrance, axes of side chambers (Fig. 4.29)

Table 7.1. The *Preau Cruciforme*

NUMBER	MEASUREMENT
32 pillars	number of pillars radiating outward from center of each corridor (Fig. 7.11)
320.61 cubits (32 × 10) or 23.87 latitude units	circumambulation path between north lateral entrances, second and third galleries (Fig. 7.13)
322.18 cubits (32 × 10) or 23.99 latitude units	circumambulation path between south lateral entrances, second and third galleries (Fig. 7.13)
32.25 *phyeam*	outer north–south and west–east axes of central section of cruciform (Fig. 7.13)
119.69 cubits (12 × 10)	inner north–south and west–east axes of central cruciform (Fig. 7.13)
27.60 *phyeam*	outer north–south and west–east axes of central cruciform without central area around image (Fig. 7.13)
20.12 latitude units	pathway from south lateral corridor to central image, exiting to second gallery (Fig. 7.15)
20.13 latitude units	pathway from north lateral corridor to central image, exiting to second gallery (Fig. 7.15)
20.01 latitude units	pathway from main entrance in third gallery to central and lateral images, exiting to second gallery (Fig. 7.13)
360.28 *phyeam* or 107.31 latitude units	circumambulation path around *preau cruciforme* (Fig. 7.14)

Table 7.2. The Second Gallery

NUMBER	MEASUREMENT
27 steps	north entrance total (21 main staircase + 6 top staircase)
27 steps	south entrance total
28 steps	east entrance total
27.60 latitude units	in-and-out circumambulation of four corner towers (Fig. 7.22)
26.84 latitude units	in-and-out circumambulation of north, south, and east axial entrances (Fig. 7.23)
19.07 × 28 (533.84 cubits)	east and west sides of gallery between bases of corner towers (Fig. 7.21)
33 × 26.996 (890.88 cubits)	outer axes, all entrances (Fig. 7.24)
21.06 × 29.53 (622.00 cubits)	north and south sides of gallery between bases of corner towers (Fig. 7.21)
33 × 29.55	inner north–south axis, northern and southern entrances, plus circumference of gallery
33 × 29.67 cubits	inner west–east axis, eastern entrance, plus circumference of gallery
33 × 29.66 cubits	inner axes, each of four corner towers, plus circumference of gallery

Table 7.3. Latitude Measurements of the Second Gallery

NUMBER	MEASUREMENT
21.13 latitude units	distance between *nāga* balustrade on the west and first step of western staircase to second level (Fig. 7.25)
21.33 units	in-and-out circumambulation of each lateral entrance on the west and through main western entrance (Fig. 7.26)
26.84 units	in-and-out circumambulation of north, south, and east axial entrances (Fig. 7.23)
27.60 units	in-and-out circumambulation of four corner towers (Fig. 7.22)
44.16 units	axes of gallery excluding axes of central sanctuary

Table 8.1. Axes of the Upper Elevation

NUMBER	MEASUREMENT
366.33 cubits	solar axes of gallery from walkway on west to bases on each side (Fig. 8.7)
368.33 cubits or 27.43 x 13.43 (27/28 latitude units)	axes of gallery base to base (Fig. 8.8)
12 x 28.19 (338.33 cubits)	axes of gallery, base to base, without images (Fig. 8.8)

Table 8.2. Circumambulation Measurements in the Axial Entrances, Upper Elevation (Fig. 8.10)

NUMBER	MEASUREMENT
28 x 10 (279.81 cubits)	in-and-out circumambulation of northern entrance with three circuits of two lateral images
28 x 10 (280.63 cubits)	in-and-out circumambulation of southern entrance with three circuits of two lateral images
28 x 10 (278.59 cubits)	in-and-out circumambulation of eastern entrance with three circuits of two lateral images

Table 8.3. Circumference Measurements of the Upper Elevation

NUMBER	MEASUREMENT
19 x 24 cubits (455.07 cubits)	circumference of gallery (Fig. 8.12)
21 x 24 (504.33 cubits)	circumference of gallery if entrant axis of *each* axial entrance is included (Fig. 8.12)

Table 8.4. Lunar Measurements Leading Up to the Upper Elevation

NUMBER	MEASUREMENT
30 steps	steps in main western staircase (from walkway)
+ 29 steps	steps in main eastern staircase
= 59	(59 days in 2 lunar months, eastern and western staircases combined)
353.65 cubits	distance between *nāga* balustrade and first step at end of walkway to upper elevation

Table 8.5. The Numbers 32/33, Upper Elevation

NUMBER	MEASUREMENT
32 chambers	chambers around gallery
33 chambers	chambers *plus* gallery
32 × 10 (322.27 cubits)	interior axes of all chambers, including central tower, without main images (Fig. 8.14)
33 × 10 (332.27 cubits)	interior axes, all chambers, with Viṣṇu image in central sanctuary and excluding other images (Fig. 8.14)
33 × 21 (689.84 cubits)	sides of upper elevation between projecting bases of corner towers (Fig. 8.15)
32 × 20 (637.84 cubits)	four sides of elevation without main images (Fig. 8.15)
32 × 10 (318.89 cubits)	outer axes of four axial entrances without main images (Fig. 8.13)
33.24 *phyeam*, west side 33.24 *phyeam*, east side 33.16 *phyeam*, north side 33.16 *phyeam*, south side	sides of gallery, between opposite doorways, including door base between pilasters (Fig. 8.15)
33.35 *phyeam*	height of central tower between top of capstone and level of sacred deposit (Fig. 8.16)
32.10 *phyeam*	height of central tower without estimated 5-cubit vertical space of Viṣṇu image (Fig. 8.16)
32.47 cubits	outer west–east axis of central tower without axis of sanctuary (Fig. 8.9)
32.30 cubits	outer north–south axis of central tower without axis of sanctuary (Fig. 8.9)
33 steps	northern axial stairways
33 steps	southern axial stairways
32 pillars	pillars of each axial entrance and in corridor leading to central tower, originally on west side as well
33 pillars	with central tower as final "pillar"

Table 8.6. The Numbers 44/45, Upper Elevation

NUMBER	MEASUREMENT
Each axial entrance plus circumference of gallery (Fig. 8.20):	
45 × 10 (449.53 cubits)	western entrance
45 × 10 (449.49 cubits)	eastern entrance
45 × 10 (449.54 cubits)	northern entrance
45 × 10 (449.49 cubits)	southern entrance
44 × 10	each axial entrance without circumambulation space around image (subtract 10 cubits) (Fig. 8.20)
45 × 10 (450.18 cubits)	outer axes of central tower and four axial entrances together (Fig. 8.18)
44 × 10 (440.18 cubits)	without main image in central tower
45 × 10 (448.68 cubits)	circumambulation up to and around main Viṣṇu image (Fig. 8.15)
45.70 cubits	outer west–east axes of central tower (Fig. 8.9a)
45.58 cubits	outer north–south axes of central tower (Fig. 8.9a)
44 pillars	number of pillars around central tower

Table 8.7. The Central Tower

NUMBER	MEASUREMENT
12 cubits	north–south axis of sanctuary between steps (Fig. 8.21)
13.23 cubits	west–east axis of sanctuary (Fig. 8.21)
13.43 cubits	north–south axis of sanctuary (Fig. 8.21)
20.32 *phyeam*	outer axes of central tower without main image of Viṣṇu as twenty-first unit (Fig. 8.19d)
20 cubits	distance up to main image of Viṣṇu from each side of central tower (Fig. 8.9d)
26.66 cubits	total inner axes of sanctuary (Fig. 8.21)
28.36 cubits	height of central sanctuary, floor to ceiling (Fig. 8.19)
53.85 cubits	vertical distance between floor of sanctuary and sacred deposit (Fig. 8.19)
54.17 cubits	vertical distance between top of finial and ceiling of sanctuary (Fig. 8.19)
54.37 cubits	inner axes, all nine chambers, without central image (Fig. 8.9b)
108.02 cubits	distance above and below sanctuary (Fig. 8.19)

Table 8.8. The Number 108, Upper Elevation

NUMBER	MEASUREMENT
107.39 *phyeam*	in-and-out circumambulation of four corner towers together (Fig. 8.11)
108.70 *phyeam* (south) 108.77 *phyeam* (north) 108.50 *phyeam* (east)	circumambulation of the central Viṣṇu image from three axial entrances (Fig. 8.14)
107.33 cubits	inner axes of all four corner towers without images (Fig. 8.22)
107.75 *phyeam*	combined vertical height of all four towers measured from level of sacred deposit; also average height of each corner tower in cubits (Fig. 8.23)
107.89 *phyeam*	distance between *nāga* balustrade on the west and first step of central tower (no illustration)
108.02 cubits	full vertical distance above and below central sanctuary (Fig. 8.19)

APPENDIX B: THE BAS-RELIEFS OF THE THIRD GALLERY

Table 1. Third Gallery: Numerical Data for Individual Entrances

ENTRANCE	COLUMNS	WINDOWS	STEPS
Western	32 west facade 54 total	36	33 outside 15 inside
Eastern	32 east facade 36 total	34	4 west side 0 east side
Lateral	28 west pair	16	29 outside 10 inside
	20 east pair	16	30 east side 5 west side
	48 total	32 total	
Northern	28 north facade 32 total	30	18
Southern	28 south facade 32 total	30	18
Corner pavilions	52 total (all four pavilions)	32 total (all four pavilions)	29 (each pavilion)

Source: Nafilyan, *Angkor Vat,* pls. 28–30, 53–55, 57–59, and 63.

Table 2. Battle of Kurukṣetra (west wall, south side)

BAS-RELIEFS

5 commanders (riding chariots)	5 commanders and Bhīṣma pierced by arrows	. . . . 31 commanders	Officer above is dying, holding an arrow that has pierced his head; commander-in-chief below is being slain by Pāṇḍava leader wearing a high conical crown; horses pulling chariots have arrows in neck, rider on horse has an arrow through his neck

□ □ □ □ □ □ □ □ □ □ □

—— 1 —————— 2 ———3 — 4 —5 — 6 — 7 — 8 — 9 ——————— 10 (center) ————→

North end of panel

Actual fighting begins, 15 commanders across the top and 17 along the bottom of the panel; 32 major figures in all, counting 3 who are standing in a warlike posture on horseback, not counting ordinary fighters riding horses

□ □ □ □ □ □ □ □ □ □

———11 ——12 —— 13 ——14 —— 15 —— 16 —— 17 —— 18 —— 19 ———

South end of panel

MEASUREMENTS AND NUMERICAL DATA

Length of panel		Divisions in panel	Number of figures
48.35 m	54.74 cubits	north end of panel to back of central chariot	44 Kaurava commanders
111.04 cubits	(23.83 m)		32 Pāṇḍava commanders
27.76 *phyeam*	53.97 cubits	south end of panel to nose of horse pulling chariot	1 Pāṇḍava leader to complete 45th and 33rd unit for both factions
19 bays	(23.50 m)		

□ Pillars across from bas-reliefs (scaled to relief)

——1——2——3—— sequential spaces between pillars (bays)

Source: Finot et al., *Angkor Vat*, pls. 497–515.

Table 3. Procession of King Sūryavarman and His Ministers (south wall, west side)

BAS-RELIEFS

Upper register: .... Seated warriors, trees in background.	Seated Brahmans	Seated king and attendant ministers	Warriors descending mountainside
Lower register: 12 male attendants, one on right is larger, with parasol over his head	Procession of 6 women, carried in litters, headed by a group of 5 large men who hold a scroll-like object in their left hand and have their right hands in the form of allegiance at their chest	3 women succeed each other in palanquins, with many attendants, and also entertainers and dwarfs	2 more women in palanquins; 3 people kneel behind second litter; in front, a man on his knees offers something to the man leading this procession

□ — 1 — □ — 2 — □ — 3 — □ — 4 — □ — 5 — □ — 6 — □ →

(West end of panel)

MAIN PROCESSION — BAS-RELIEFS

Śrī Jayendravarman (Ldau)	Śrī Vīrendrādhipativarman (Chok Bakula)	Śrī Vīrāyudhavarman (Anak Sanjak Kancas Pryak)	Śrī Jayāyudhavarman (Anak Sanjak Mat Gnan)	Śrī Mahīpatīndravarman (Canlattai)	Śrī Raṇavīravarman (Anak Sanjak Vidyāśrama)	Śrī Rājasiṁhavarman (Anak Sanjak Vīrajaya)

□ — 7 — □ — 8 — □ — 9 — □ — 10 — □ — 11 — □ — 12 — □ — 13 — □ →

Śrī Vīrendrādhipativarman (Anak Sanjak Aso Vnyaphlan)	Śrī Narapatīndravarman (Anak Sanjak Anak Cih)	Śrī Śūrādhipativarman (Anak Sanjak Vni Satra)	Long procession of soldiers in much larger scale	Dhananjaya	King Sūryavarman (Paramaviṣṇuloka)	Soldiers ahead of Sūryavarman

□ — 14 — □ — 15 — □ — 16 — □ — 17 — □ — 18 — □ — 19 — □ — 20 — □ — 21 — □ →

Anak Sanjak Trailokyapura	ŚrīVardhana	Escorts of ŚrīVardhana	Śrī Rājendravarman (Anak Sanjak Aso Lnis)	Rājahotar, carried on a hammock	Vraḥ Vleṅ, the sacred fire, preceded by musicians	Entertainers, dancers, jugglers, monkeys, birds in a tree	Archers, people on horseback, carrying parasols

□ — 22 — □ — 23 — □ — 24 — □ — 25 — □ — 26 — □ — 27 — □ — 28 — □ — 29 — □ →

Śrī Pṛthivīnarendra (Anak Sanjak Travan Svay)	Archers	Mahāsenāpati Śrī Vīrendravarman (Anak Sanjak Kavīśvara)	Śrī Siṁhavīravarman	Soldiers	Śrī Jayasiṁhavarman, from Lvo (Lopburi)	Unnamed head of leading contingent (*syam kuk*), an archer with an arrow set in his bow; foot soldiers			
30	31	32	33	34	35	36	37	38	39

MEASUREMENTS AND NUMERICAL DATA

Length of panel	Length of procession of women	Length of procession of ministers
93.60 m	14.05 m	78.92 m (to tail of last elephant)
214.95 cubits 53.74 *phyeam* 39 bays	32.25 cubits 6 bays	45.31 *phyeam* 33 bays
Measurements to left and right of king		Distance between king and west end of panel
46.6 m 107.60 cubits (left) 19 bays	46.75 m 107.35 cubits (right)[a] 19 bays	83.31 m 191.31 cubits (19 × 10)

NUMBERS OF PARASOLS ASSOCIATED WITH FIGURES

1. 17 + 6 in front	Śrī Jayasiṁhavarman
2. 15 + 7 in front	King Sūryavarman
3. 13 + 4 in front	Śrī Rājasiṁhavarman
4. 12 + 6 in front	Śrī Vardhana
5. 11 + 7 in front	Sacred Fire (exact number indistinct)
6. 10 + 5 in front	Dhananjaya
7. 10	Śrī Narapatīndravarman
8. 9	Śrī Jayendravarman
9. 9 + 6 in front	Śrī Vīrendrādhipativarman
10. 9	Śrī Vīrendrādhipativarman (second occurrence)
11. 8	Śrī Jayāyudhavarman
12. 8 + 3 in front	Śrī Śūrādhipativarman
13. 8 + 6 in front	Anak Sanjak Trailokyapura
14. 8 + 6 in front	Śrī Rājendravarman
15. 8 + 7 in front	Leader of *syam kuk*
16. 7 + 5 in front	Śrī Siṁhavarman
17. 7 + 5 in front	Mahāsenāpati Śrī Vīrendravarman
18. 6 + 6 in front	Śrī Raṇavīravarman
19. 6 + 4 in front	Śrī Vīrāyudhavarman
20. 6	Śrī Mahīpatīndravarman
21. 6	Śrī Pṛthivīnarendra
22. 0	Rājahotar[b]

a. Includes king.

b. Perhaps the 11 or more parasols and 7 preceding parasols for the sacred fire indirectly reflect on the importance of the *Rājahotar.* Otherwise, only those of political rank are honored with parasols.

☐ Pillars across from bas-reliefs (scaled to relief)

—— 1 —— 2 —— 3 —— sequential spaces between pillars (bays)

Source: Finot et al., *Angkor Vat*, pls. 522–560.

Table 4. Heavens and Hells (south wall, east side)

BAS-RELIEFS						
Top Register: Procession	2 women	2 men	3 men	2 men	1 woman	2 women 1 man, 1 woman
Middle Register: Procession	1 woman taking leave of attendants	1 woman with litter awaiting her	2 men, 1 woman	2 men	Yama	Dharma and Citragupta opening to hells
Bottom Register: (various hell scenes)						

□ □ □ □ □ □ □ □ □

—— 1 —— 2 —— 3 —— 4 —— 5 —— 6 —— 7 —— 8 —— 9 ⟶

West end of panel

UPPER REGISTER: CELESTIAL PALACES				LOWER REGISTER: 32 HELLS		
1 man	1 woman, 1 man	1 woman, 1 man	1 woman, 1 man	1 woman, 1 man	1 woman, 1 man	1 woman, 1 man
(1) Avīcī	(2) Kṛminicaya (3) Vaitaraṇi Nadī	(4) Kūṭaśalmali (5) Yugma Parvata	(6) Nirucchvāsa	(7) Ucchvāsa (8) Dravattrapu	(9) Taptalākṣāmaya	(10) Asthibhaṅga (11) Krakaccheda

□ □ □ □ □ □ □ □

—— 9 —— 10 —— 11 —— 12 —— 13 —— 14 —— 15 ⟶

1 woman, 1 man	1 woman, 1 man	1 woman, 1 man	1 woman, 1 man	1 woman, 1 man	1 woman, 1 man	1 woman, 1 man
(12) Pūyapūrṇahrada (13) Asṛkpūrṇahrada	(14) Medohrada (15) Tīkṣṇāyastuṇḍa	(16) Aṅgāranicaya (17) Ambarīṣa	(18) Kumbhīpāka (19) Tālavṛkṣavana	(20) Kṣuradhāraparvata (21) Santapana	(22) Sūcimukha (23) Kālasūtra	(24) Mahāpadma (25) Padma

□ □ □ □ □ □ □ □

—— 16 —— 17 —— 18 —— 19 —— 20 —— 21 —— 22 ⟶

1 woman, 1 man	1 woman, 1 man, 1 woman, 1 man, 1 woman		1 man, 1 woman	1 man
(26) Sanjīvana	(27) Name missing (...raka..) (28) Name missing (..kmala..)	(29) Sīta	(30) Sāndratamaḥ (31) Mahāraurava	(32) Raurava

□ □ □ □ □ □

—— 23 —— 24 —— 25 —— 26 —— 27 ——

East end of panel

Length of panel	Distance between Yama and east end of panel	Distance between Dharma and Citragupta and east end of panel	Distance between first celestial palace and west end of panel	Length of panel excluding figures of Yama, Dharma, and Citragupta (3.326 m)
66.05 m 151.68 cubits 37.92 *phyeam* (19/19 = 38) 27 bays	49.97 m (measured from nose of Yama's buffalo) 28.12 *phyeam* 21 bays (including Yama)	46.99 m 107.92 cubits 26.98 *phyeam* 19 bays	20.88 m 11.99 *phyeam* 8 bays	62.724 m 144.04 cubits (12 × 12)

NUMBER OF MAJOR FIGURES

21 figures with palanquins heading toward heavens[a]
(6 women and 8 men in upper register, 3 women and 4 men in middle register)
18 women in celestial palaces
19 men in celestial palaces

a. Inscriptions on the bas-reliefs identify the upper two registers as being the "paths to heaven."

☐ Pillars across from bas-reliefs (scaled to relief)
——1——2——3—— sequential spaces between pillars (bays)

Note: Upper two registers; only figures in palanquins are noted here.
Source: Finot et al., *Angkor Vat*, pls. 574–600.

Table 5. Churning of the Sea of Milk (east wall, south side)

BAS-RELIEFS

Upper register: charioteers
Lower two registers: *asuras* in rows, face toward center (north)

Upper register: large *asura* holding heads of Vāsuki, line of flying celestial maidens (continues throughout panel)
Lower registers: *asuras* pull on Vāsuki; below, Vāsuki in Sea of Milk with aquatic creatures (continues throughout panel)

Asuras pulling on *nāga*

Large *asura*

☐ ☐ ☐ ☐ ☐ ☐
—— 1 —— 2 —— 3 —— 4 —— 5 ——►
South end of panel

Asuras pull on *nāga* | Large *asura* | *Asuras* pull on *nāga* | Kūrma, Mt. Mandara, Viṣṇu, and *deva* | *Devas* pull on *nāga* | Large *deva* | *Devas* pull on *nāga*

☐ ☐ ☐ ☐ ☐ ☐ ☐ ☐ ☐ ☐
—— 6 —— 7 —— 8 —— 9 —— 10 (center) —— 11 —— 12 —— 13 —— 14 ——►

Large *deva* | *Devas* pull on *nāga* | Sugrīva (?) holding tail of Vāsuki | Upper register: *deva* charioteers; Lower two registers: *devas* in rows face toward center (south)

☐ ☐ ☐ ☐ ☐ ☐
—— 15 —— 16 —— 17 —— 18 —— 19 ——
North end of panel

MEASUREMENTS AND NUMERICAL DATA

Length of panel	From south end of panel to Viṣṇu	From north end of panel to Viṣṇu	Distance to Viṣṇu from hood or tail of Vāsuki	Numbers of *devas* and *asuras* (one *asura* is Viṣṇu; one *deva* is Rāhu in disguise)
48.45 m 111.38 cubits 27.85 *phyeam* 19 bays	23.496 m 53.96 cubits	23.69 m 54.40 cubits	36.70 m 21.07 *phyeam*	29, 28, 28 (*devas*), 30, 29, 29 (*asuras*) (pulling on *nāga* between large figures) 1 *deva* on top of Mt. Mandara 3 large *devas* (includes Sugrīva) and 3 large *asuras* 180 total, 89 *devas* and 91 *asuras* 3 "days" for central Mt. Mandara

☐ Pillars across from bas-reliefs (scaled to relief)
——1——2——3—— sequential spaces between pillars (bays)

Source: Finot et al., *Angkor Vat*, pls. 351–369.

Table 6. Battle of Viṣṇu and the *Asuras* (east wall, north side)

BAS-RELIEFS

28 and possibly 29 or more *asuras* on chariots, elephants, felines, and horses, facing center of panel and poised for combat	Viṣṇu on Garuḍa, facing to our left; 5 dying elephants around him, Viṣṇu unusually small in scale	26 to 35 *asuras* on various mounts, facing central Viṣṇu
□ □ □ □ □ □ □ □ □ □ □	□	□ □ □ □ □ □ □ □ □ □ □
—1— 2 — 3 — 4 — 5 — 6 — 7 — 8 — 9 — 10 ——	—11 (center) ——	—12—13—14—15—16—17—18—19—20—21—
South end of panel		North end of panel

MEASUREMENTS AND NUMERICAL DATA

Length of panel	Figural representations
51.45 m	No clear number of *asuras*:
118.15 cubits	between 54 and 64 or more
29.54 *phyeam*	
21 bays	

□ Pillars across from bas-reliefs (scaled to relief)

——1——2——3—— sequential spaces between pillars (bays)

Source: Finot et al., *Angkor Vat*, pls. 374–394.

Table 7. Victory of Kṛṣṇa over Bāṇa (north wall, east side)

BAS-RELIEFS

Soldiers moving westward	Man on elephant	Pradyumna, Kṛṣṇa, Balarāma on Garuḍa	Soldiers	Garuḍa putting out fire, Agni on rhinoceros	Soldiers fighting	Pradyumna, Kṛṣṇa, Balarāma on Garuḍa	Balarāma fighting opponent in a chariot

□ □ □ □ □ □ □ □ □ □ □ □

—— 1 —— 2 —— 3 —— 4 —— 5 —— 6 —7— 8—9 —— 10 —— 11 ——▶

East end of panel

Soldiers fighting	Kṛṣṇa on Garuḍa, holding *cakra,* mace, bow, and arrow	Soldiers fighting	Pradyumna, Kṛṣṇa, Rāma on Garuḍa	Soldiers fighting	Pradyumna, Kṛṣṇa, Balarāma on Garuḍa	Soldiers	The *asura* Bāṇa on a chariot pulled by fierce felines

□ □ □ □ □ □ □ □ □ □ □ □ □

—12—13—14—15 —— 16 —— 17 —— 18 —— 19 —20 —— 21 —— 22 —— 23 ——▶

Soldiers	Pradyumna, Kṛṣṇa, Balarāma on Garuḍa	Kṛṣṇa paying homage to Śiva on Mt. Kailāsa: ascetics in caves, Śiva sits with Pārvatī on top of mountain, Gaṇeśa and Skanda are to his right, looking at Kṛṣṇa	Śiva's seated attendants, *kinnaris*, ascetics

□ □ □ □ □

—— 24 —— 25 —— 26 —— 27 ——

West end of panel

MEASUREMENTS AND NUMERICAL DATA

Length of panel	Figural representations
66.03 m	5 occurrences of 3 figures on Garuḍa
151.64 cubits	1 occurrence each of Kṛṣṇa alone, Agni, Balarāma, Bāṇa, and Śiva
37.91 *phyeam*	
27 bays	

□ Pillars across from bas-reliefs (scaled to relief)

——1——2——3—— sequential spaces between pillars (bays)

Source: Finot et al., *Angkor Vat* , pls. 398–424.

NOTES

ABBREVIATIONS

AA	*Arts Asiatiques*
AARP	*Art and Archaeology Research Papers*
ABIA	*Annual Bibliography of Indian Archaeology*
AO	*Ars Orientalis*
BCAI	*Bulletin de la Commission Archéologique Indochinoise*
BEFEO	*Bulletin de l'École française d'Extrême-Orient*
BSEI	*Bulletin de la Société des Études Indochinoises*
CHM	*Cahiers d'Histoire Mondiale*
IAL	*Indian Arts and Letters*
IC	*Inscriptions du Cambodge*
JA	*Journal Asiatique*
JAOS	*Journal of the American Oriental Society*
JIH	*Journal of Indian History*
JRAS	*Journal of the Royal Asiatic Society*
JSEAH	*Journal of Southeast Asian History*
JSS	*Journal of the Siam Society*
PEFEO	*Publication de l'École française d'Extrême-Orient*

CHAPTER 1

1. According to the *Grand Larousse de la langue française,* vol. 4 (Paris: Librairie Larousse, 1975), the term Indochina was first recorded in 1845. The French began to consolidate their power over Cambodia between 1863 and 1885. On November 9, 1953, Cambodia was granted independence.
2. The site of Oc-eo, near the southern coast of Cambodia, has yielded jewelry, coins, relief images, and inscriptions on seal rings that illustrate an early contact with India. It is difficult to determine exactly how much this contact would have affected the ordinary citizen, however. For more information, one can refer to Mireille Benisti, *Rapports entre le premier art Khmèr et*

l'art Indien, Mémoire Archéologique V (Paris: École française d'Extrême-Orient, 1970).

3. In Long Seam, "Contacts externes des langues mon-khmèr," *BEFEO* 70 (1981): 195–230, there is an annotated bibliography of most linguistic studies of Mon-Khmer up to 1978. The Russian Y. A. Gorgoniev was the leading exponent of an ancient Chinese and Khmer language connection (p. 199). W. Schmidt was the primary advocate for an Austro-Asiatic family group for Khmer (pp. 202–204). Robert Shafer and R. A. D. Forrest see both a Sino-Tibetan and Austro-Asiatic connection to Khmer (p. 213).

   There is a Chinese junk sculpted on a south wall of the Bayon temple, built around 1200, as part of an aquatic scene that is most likely set on the Tonle Sap Lake, or Great Lake, about 1 hour or less on a bumpy road south and west of Angkor.

4. One version of the legend recorded in an inscription from Mi-son in Vietnam, dated to A.D. 648, relates that a Brahman named Kauṇḍiṇya obtained possession of a special javelin from a son of Droṇa. He traveled to Cambodia by boat and threw the javelin into the ground to mark the site of his future capital, the city of Bhavapura. Afterwards, Kauṇḍiṇya married a daughter of the king of the *nāga*s named Somā, who began a royal line of kings. The inscription is translated and recorded by Louis Finot in "Notes d'épigraphie XI: Les inscriptions de Mi-Son (no. III)," *BEFEO* (1904): 923, st. 16–19. There is also a Chinese version of this story going back to the mid-third century that describes a king named Kauṇḍiṇya (Huntian) who was challenged by the queen of Cambodia (the nation of Funan), intent on capturing his ship. He frightened her by shooting an arrow from his magical bow into her ship; she surrendered and married him. The brief story appears in "Le Fou-nan" by Paul Pelliot, *BEFEO* 3 (1903): 254. Eveline Porée-Maspero discusses the importance of a matriarchal transfer of power that traces its origins back to Somā in her "Nouvelle étude sur la *Nāgī* Somā," *JA* 238 (1950): 237–267.

5. The noted French scholar Claude Jacques discusses the relationship of Aninditapura's kings to Kauṇḍiṇya–Somā in "Études d'épigraphie Cambodgienne IX: Sur l'emplacement du royaume d'Aninditapura," *BEFEO* 59 (1972): 195–205. George Coedès, the great *maitre* of Khmer epigraphy and history, thought that Bhavapura was located north of the Tonle Sap Lake (see note 7).

6. A synopsis of the stories related to Kauṇḍiṇya–Somā and their association with the kingdom of Funan and other states is given in Louis Finot, "Sur quelques traditions Indochinoises," *BCAI* 11 (1911): 30–37. Inscriptions concerning the stories are discussed in Laurence Palmer Briggs, *The Ancient Khmer Empire,* Transactions of the American Philosophical Society, n.s., vol. 41, pt. 1 (Philadelphia: American Philosophical Society, 1951), p. 40. George Coedès notes that in A.D. 480 there is a reference to a Funanese king as a "descendant of Kauṇḍiṇya" in the History of the Southern Ch'i; see Coedès, *The Indianized States of Southeast Asia* (Honolulu: East-West Center, 1968), p. 38.

7. Coedès discusses the location of Bhavapura in *Inscriptions du Cambodge* (hereafter *IC*), vol. 6 (1954): 100–106, Inscriptions de Prasat Ampil Rolu'm. The inscription on the north door jamb of this sanctuary is dated between 789 and 797 and says that the "son of Śrī Indrāditya" was "king in the city of Bhavapura" (st. XI). Coedès thinks that Bhavapura must have been located at the site of this inscription, 30 km northwest of Kompong Thom. He also notes that the *-āditya* endings of the three kings mentioned here are identical to the suffixes of the kings of Aninditapura, who were also descended from Kauṇḍiṇya and Somā. This link suggests a connection between these lines of royalty.

8. Jacques, "Aninditapura," pp. 195–199. Jacques' arguments are based on the location and interpretation of the Prasat Sak inscription (2 km from the center of Siem Reap) and its relationship to the 14 other major inscriptions that mention Aninditapura.

9. Zhou Daguan, *Mémoires sur les coutumes du Cambodge de Tcheou Ta-Kouan* (Paris: Librairie d'Amérique et d'Orient, 1951), p. 12. Many other authors have noted the connection between Zhou Daguan's account and the Kauṇḍiṇya–Somā legend.

10. Auguste Barth, *Inscriptions sanskrits du Cambodge,* Académie des Inscriptions et Belles Lettres, Notices et Extraites des Manuscripts de la Bibliothèque Nationale, vol. 27, pt. 1, fasc. 1, Paris (1885): 134, st. A, 13. This

inscription is from Lovek (old capital, on the right bank of the Tonle Sap River) and was written during the reign of Harṣavarman II.

11. This measurement and the 28-unit measurement noted here are discussed in Chapter 2.
12. The moon crosses through 27 or 28 constellations *(nakṣatra)* each month. A synodic lunar month, measured against the moon's position in relation to the stars, is 27.3 days long. The moon is also visible for 27 or 28 days a month, no more and no less. Therefore 27/28—as an alternating pair or individually—both represent a lunar month.
13. Khmer methods of calculating astronomical data are really no different than those found in early Indian texts. For examples one can look at F. Gaspard Faraut, *Astronomie Cambodgienne* (Saigon: F. H. Schneider, 1910). See also H.M. Prince Phetsarath, "Le calendrier lao," *France-Asie* 12 (March–May 1956): 787–814. The Lao and Khmer calendrical reckonings are exactly the same. As an example of the methodology involved, the *horakhoune,* which marks the number of days from the beginning of the era (used in the calendar) to the first civil day of the new year, is calculated by multiplying the date by (292,207 + 373) and dividing by 800. The number 292,207 refers to the days in 800 years, and 373 is the advance of the sun at the beginning of the epoch, expressed as 1/800/day. After this arithmetic process is completed, "1" is added to the result and the remainder is subtracted from 800; the result is then used to calculate the leap years, as well as the mean anomaly of a star. The given totals in these arithmetic processes are like the given totals in the circumferences and axes of Angkor Wat. Working within a set total, one finds subdivisions that include additional information.
14. Three periods of Indian astronomy have been noted by Roger Billard in *L'Astronomie Indienne,* PEFEO 83 (Paris: École française d'Extrême-Orient, 1971), pp. 15–17. The first period Billard describes begins in the tenth to eighth centuries B.C., when astronomy was dedicated to the lunisolar and rituals delineated in the *Jyotiṣavedaṅga.* The 27/28 *nakṣatra* are present, but the planets are very minor. Texts are for divination. The second period, from the third century B.C. to the first century A.D., is influenced by Babylonian astronomy; the *tithi,* one-thirtieth of a synodic revolution of the moon, comes into use. The third period begins in the second century, when the influence of the Greco-Roman world results in the introduction of trigonometry. Billard does not discuss the influence of Babylonian astronomy on the Greco-Roman tradition.
15. Robert Stencel, Fred Gifford, and Eleanor Morón, "Astronomy and Cosmology at Angkor Wat," *Science* 193 (July 23, 1976): 281–287.
16. The dates for the accession and the end of Jayavarman's reign are not wholly certain, despite their general acceptance. In "Aninditapura," pp. 206–213, Claude Jacques notes that references to King Jayavarman occur in the years 770, 781, and 790, before he was made a *cakravartin* on Mount Kulen in 802. Jacques also disputes a translation of "16 years" in the Prasat Sak inscription (K774), arguing that "16" refers to how long the king had been on the throne in 850, the date of the inscription. If Jacques is correct, Jayavarman III assumed power in 834 (850 - 16). He presents his theories in "Études d'épigraphie Cambodgiennes VI: Sur les données chronologiques de la stèle de Tuol Ta Pec (K834)," *BEFEO* 58 (1971): 165–166. This stele had dates and the names of kings scratched out and written over, which has made its subsequent interpretation controversial.
17. See note 3.
18. Franklin E. Huffman et al., *Cambodian System of Writing and Beginning Reader* (New Haven: Yale University Press, 1970), p. 4.
19. Coedès discusses the *sūryavamśa* in "Études Cambodgiennes XII: Le site primitif de Tchen-la," *BEFEO* 18/9 (1918): 1–3, and in "L'inscription de Baksei Camkron," *JA,* 10th ser., 13 (1909): 496. Aside from being the only source of our information on Kambu and Merā, the inscription gives a history of kings at Angkor up to Rājendravarman.
20. Coedès, "Baksei Camkron," pp. 496–497, st. XI: "Honorez Kambu Svāyambhuva doné d'une gloire eminente, dont la célèbre lignée, obtenant l'alliance de la race solaire et de la race lunaire, dissipant les ténèbres de tous les çastras, éclatante, a des impôts légers (ou: des rayons doux) et est accomplie dans les arts (ou: a toutes ses kālas)."

21. Ibid., p. 497.
22. Henri Mouhot, *Voyage dans les royaumes du Siam, de Cambodge, et de Laos* (Paris: Hachette, 1868).
23. Most of our information on the *devarāja* cult is contained in one inscription: that found at Sdok Kak Thom, 25 km northwest of Sisophon in eastern Thailand, near the Khmer border. From the very beginning, the importance of this inscription was fully recognized; no other Khmer inscription has been so widely published, translated, annotated, analyzed, and discussed. A synopsis of its history and translations can be found in George Coedès and Pierre Dupont, "Les stèles de Sdok Kak Thom, Phnom Sandak, et Prah Vihar," *BEFEO* 43 (1943–1946): 56–134. The explanation of the *devarāja* cult given here is based on the Sdok Kak Thom stele and the following studies: Hubert de Mestier du Bourg, "À propos du culte du dieu-roi *(devarāja)* au Cambodge," *CHM* 11/3 (1968): 499–516; Ian W. Mabbett, *"Devarāja," JSEAH* 10 (Sept. 1969): 202–223; and Hermann Kulke, *The Devarāja Cult,* Data Paper 108 (Ithaca: Cornell University, Department of Asian Studies, Southeast Asia Program, 1978); originally published as "Der *Devarāja* Kult, Legitimation und Herrscherapotheose im Angkor Reich," *Saeculum* 25/1 (Munich and Freiburg: Karl Alber, 1974), pp. 24–55. The theory that the *kamrateng jagat ta rāja,* the original Khmer title that was translated as *devarāja,* was an image symbolizing supremacy over all the territorial gods is my own, as is the theory that the image therefore *had* to be worshiped in the capital.
24. As quoted in Briggs, *Ancient Khmer Empire,* p. 176, an inscription from Preah Ngouk, a Buddhist temple site at Angkor, with internal references to the years 802, 1051, and 1066, has this reference. In st. 27, a Senāpati (general) of the king is asked to keep the bounty he has won in battle; he answers: "If I have found grace (in front of you), who are grace itself, [please offer] this bounty to your 'subtle inner self' *(sūkṣmāntarātman),* [in the god] Īśvara who abides in the golden *liṅga,* then my loyalty today will have borne fruit." This not only implies that the "subtle inner self" of the king resides in the lingam, but that it is also identified with the god Śiva.
25. Kamaleswar Bhattacharya, "Les religions brahmaniques dans l'ancien Cambodge," PEFEO 49 (1961): 47, citing Coedès, *IC,* vol. 1 (19—): 202–204, 213–215. Coedès' translation was not available to me in any other source. However, Bhattacharya notes that he improved Coedès' translation because of suggestions by Jean Filliozat. The original does not seem complicated.
26. Coedès, *IC,* vol. 2 (1942): 105, Stele of Tuol Prasat (pp. 97–114).
27. Ibid., p. 93, door jamb inscription of Lobok Srot, dated 781 (pp. 92–94).
28. The relationship between the king's royal pyramid-temple and the city is discussed in my article, "Angkor: Relationships Between the Pyramid-Temple and the City," *AARP* 4 (Dec. 1978): 65–68.
29. When one reads Chinese accounts of Angkor such as that of Zhou Daguan, cited earlier, there is no description of the interior of any monuments or of any sanctuary. Only exterior, distant views are described.
30. Jacques Dumarçay and Bernard-Philippe Groslier, *Le Bayon,* Mémoires archéologiques III–2, 2 vols. (Paris: École française d'Extrême-Orient, 1973); vol. 2, B. P. Groslier, *Inscriptions du temple,* pp. 113–116.
31. Rāmacandra Kaulācāra, *Śilpa Prakāśa,* trans. Alice Boner and Sadāśiva Rath Śarmā (London: Brill, 1966), p. xxiv.
32. Ibid., p. xxxiii.
33. We do not know if there was a previous temple at the site of Angkor Wat. Although there are no signs that this was the case, it would not be unusual to build over an already sacred site. There are layers of laterite paving underneath the Bayon that in certain respects may indicate the presence of an earlier temple. There are also the remains of an older trench around the inner perimeter of Angkor Thom, and there were indications of a wall beneath two of the eastern structures at the Bakheng. The Phimeanakas has an A.D. 910 inscription which indicates that a Viṣṇu temple may previously have occupied that site. Temples built over the remains of previous temples are common outside of Cambodia as well, in Indonesia and Thailand especially.
34. In fact there is no central eastern staircase, and there may never have been. Instead there is an earthen ramp with the stone walls of the staircase frame on each side (a staircase without the stairs). If elephants or chariots were required to approach the central galleries without using the western axis, they would have needed a ramp like this one.

35. Angkor Wat's precise measurements were revealed for the first time in Guy Nafilyan, *Angkor Vat: description graphique du temple,* Mémoire archéologique IV (Paris: École française d'Extrême-Orient, 1969). M. Nafilyan generously provided me with his working plans and drawings with written measurements on them.
36. Ibid., pl. 11. This and the following measurements are written on pl. 11.
37. After basing the .43545 unit on the measurements of Guy Nafilyan, I later found that Georges Trouvé's measurements were slightly different. Nevertheless, since the unit worked so well with the rest of the temple, I did not alter it in any way. In fact, I tried experimentally reducing it to .435, .434, and .436, as well as a range between .4354 and .4356, but none of these variations worked as well with all the measurements of the temple (although some yielded results that were more accurate in some instances). Since the .43545 unit seemed to work the best over the longest distances (4 km and more), I retained it.
38. The 13.41-cubit unit, the latitude of Angkor Wat, and their relationship to the second gallery and Brahmā are discussed in Chapter 7.
39. The Phnom Rung inscription contains most of the information quoted here. It is located about 90 km east-southeast of Korat, in northeastern Thailand. A translation is given by George Coedès, *IC,* vol. 5 (1954): 297–305.
40. Ibid., pp. 300–311. A stele from Phnom Sandak describes several donations of cities and villages to Śrī Vijayendralakṣmī from Jayavarman VI. It equates the queen to Lakṣmī herself and generally praises her beauty and kindness.
41. Louis Finot, "Notes d'épigraphie XIII: L'inscription de Ban That," *BEFEO* 12/2 (1912): 26, st. 28.
42. Coedès, *IC,* vol. 5 (1954): 292, st. 2. "In the year designated by ten, the [three] fires and [five] arrows [1035 *śāka* or A.D. 1113], Śrī Sūryavarman took over the royalty by uniting two [factions]." Coedès supplies the referent for "two" as "kingdoms"; he postulates a division in the territory of Cambodia itself at this point in history, a division ending with the advent of Sūryavarman II. Actually the text cited here does not have a noun, and so we do not know exactly to what the "two" refers. It is possible that the "two" or "double" refers to the two sides of King Sūryavarman's family that were united only in the king himself; he was the only known descendant of the founder of the ruling family on both his mother's and his father's side. If these were the factions to which the "two" refers, then the two families would certainly have been in natural contention for the throne; both sides had viable heirs. Sūryavarman would have presented a good compromise. Whether or not he had defeated Dharanīndravarman in battle, Sūryavarman still was descended from Hiraṇyavarman on both his father's and mother's side of the family.
43. For a full discussion of the lineage and family of both Sūryavarman II and his second cousin, Jayavarman VII, see George Coedès, "Études Cambodgiennes XXIV: Nouvelles données chronologiques et généalogiques sur la dynastie de Mahīdharapura," *BEFEO* 29 (1929): 297–330.
44. Finot, "L'inscription de Ban That," p. 26, st. 33. If there were any doubt that the factions in King Sūryavarman's family were enemies, this inscription dispels it. One is inadvertently reminded of the dead snake dangling from Sūryavarman's hand in the scene of allegiance at Angkor Wat.
45. Coedès, *IC,* vol. 4 (1952): 230–231, st. 108.
46. Finot, "L'inscription de Ban That," p. 27, st. 30–35.
47. Ibid., st. 32. "Two masters" may be another reference to the two factions discussed in note 42—in this case, a reference to the leaders of the factions and also to the paternal and maternal lineages of Sūryavarman.
48. Until recently, historians assumed that Dharanīndravarman II, Jayavarman VII's father, reigned after Sūryavarman. There is no proof for this assertion, but there are several reasons to think that Yaśovarman II ruled from 1150 to 1165 instead of 1160–1165. Bernard-Philippe Groslier first argued for this viewpoint in *Le Bayon, inscriptions du temple,* pp. 141–144. Claude Jacques also agrees with this assessment.
49. An account of King Sūryavarman's military exploits is found in Georges Maspero, *Le Royaume du Champa* (Paris and Brussels: Librairie nationale d'art et d'histoire, 1928), pp. 154–158.
50. Finot, "Les inscriptions de Mi-son," p. 965. The date of the battle is given in the Batau Tablah inscription, a translation of which is found in Étienne Aymonier,

"Première étude sur les inscriptions Tchames," *JA* 17 (Jan./Feb. 1891): 40.

51. The Thommanon has been analyzed by Lan Sunnary in "Étude iconographique du temple khmēr de Thommanon (Dhammananda)," *AA* 25 (1972): 155–198. Sunnary believes the Thommanon is "slightly before Angkor Wat."
52. Jean Boisselier, "Beng Mealea et la chronologie des monuments du style d'Angkor Vat," *BEFEO* 46/1 (1952): 187–226. Boisselier puts the Thommanon first, then Chau Say Tevoda, more or less at the same time as Beng Mealea. He thinks Beng Mealea was started after Angkor Wat but finished earlier (perhaps constructed in honor of Divākarapaṇḍita). Banteay Samré would be last, with parts of this monument close to the Bayon style. The sanctuary of the Bakong he would place as beginning after Banteay Samré. He sees Prasat Khna Kev, Prasat Phan, and Phnom Rung as transitional between the Baphuon style and Angkor Wat. The porch/vestibule of Wat Phu would begin the Angkor Wat style, along with Phimai. The sequence would continue with the Preah Palilay sanctuary close to Beng Mealea and Banteay Samré, Preah Pithu T, the first and second enclosures of Preah Khan of Kompong Svay, Prasat Trapeang Srei, and the *gopura* of Preah Palilay. He believes the entire period of the Angkor Wat style would extend from 1066 to 1177. He also thinks Preah Palilay was begun under Jayavarman VI.
53. George Coedès and Pierre Dupont, "Les stèles de Sdok Kak Thom, Phnom Sandak, et Prah Vihar," *BEFEO* 43 (1943–1946): 145, st. 13–19, and 146, st. 21–28.
54. Ibid., p. 145, st. 9–11.
55. Ibid., p. 154, st. D1–23.
56. Coedès, *IC,* vol. 5, p. 293, st. 18. The line, taken from a stele at Wat Phu dated to the reign of King Sūryavarman, states simply that in 1058 *śāka* (A.D. 1136), a statue of the Vraḥ Śrī Guru was set up at Wat Phu. There could only be one deceased Vraḥ Śrī Guru at this time, and that is Divākara.
57. Ibid., vol. 2 (1942): 126–133, stele of Kuk Trapeang Srok. If Śrī Kavīśvarapaṇḍita was in fact Divākara's grandfather, this is an interesting connection to the king's history. According to this inscription, Kavīśvarapaṇḍita was the "superior" of Śivapāda. At the beginning of his reign, Sūryavarman held a ceremony and began a grandiose procession from a Mount Śivapāda.
58. All of the following information on Divākara is recorded in the steles from Phnom Sandak and Preah Vihear, as translated in Coedès and Dupont, "Les stèles," pp. 145–154. These two steles were dedicated in A.D. 1119 by King Sūryavarman especially to honor Śrī Divākara.

CHAPTER 2

1. The first balustrade pedestal at the beginning of the span does not have a column beneath it because it rests on the stairway base. Rather than accept a total of 53 columns, the architects doubled the final column on the north–south central stairway leading down to the moat, bringing the total to 54.

   A raised ledge extends across the threshold or top of the stairways on all three sides of each end of the bridge. The 54-cubit length is measured between these ledges across the width of the bridge. This distance measures 9.3 cm (23.25 m, or 53.39 cubits) for the western end of the bridge and 9.4 cm (23.5 m, or 53.97 cubits) for the eastern end. In addition, the full north–south axial width of all three perpendicular stairways, measured between their last step on the ground, comes to 94.43 m, or 54.21 *phyeam* (37.77 cm on the plan). The western and eastern stairways together total 56.68 m, or 32.54 *phyeam* (27.67 cm on the plan). The ledges mentioned above are drawn on pl. 94 of Nafilyan. They are raised up about 10–15 cm. from the surface of the bridge.

   The length of the bridge measures 93.8 cm on the plan, or 234.5 m (538.52 cubits). Unlike the western end of the bridge or the ends of the stairways, the eastern border of the bridge does not have an upraised ledge. The flat surface simply stops a little beyond the staircase to the western entrance. The length of the western entrance is shown in Nafilyan, pls. 67–69, 76, and 81. Derived from written measurements, it includes the base of the two gateways on the north and south (which makes a difference of 3.6 m). The exact written measurement was 234.46 m to the projecting base, or 538.43 cubits.

2. For a comparison of the basic elements in the churning story see V. M. Bedekar, "The Legend of the Churning of the Ocean in the Epics and the Purāṇas: A Comparative Study," *Purāṇa* 9/1 (Jan. 1967): 7–61; Asoke Kumar Bhattacharyya, "The Themes of Churning of the Ocean in Indian and Khmer Art," *AA* 6/2 (1959): 121–134; Madeleine Giteau, "Le barattage de l'Océan au Cambodge," *BSEI,* n.s. 26/2 (1951): 141–159; and Horace Hayman Wilson, trans., *Vishṇu Purāṇa,* 5 vols. (London: Trubner, 1864–1870), vol. 1, bk. 7, chap. 9, pp. 146–147, n. 1. The story of the churning event itself is told in the *Vishṇu Purāṇa,* pp. 139–147.
3. Hari Prasad Shastri, trans., *Rāmāyaṇa of Vālmīki,* 3 vols. (London: Shanti Sadan, 1952–1957), vol. 1, p. 92. See also Wilson, *Vishṇu Purāṇa,* vol. 1. After the Churning of the Sea of Milk and the defeat of the *asuras* in battle, "Indra, the chief of the gods, was restored to power."
4. The distance between the south end of the panel and the central Viṣṇu is 23.496 m, or 53.96 cubits; the same distance for the northern half is 23.69 m, or 54.40 cubits. This information was taken from the photographs in Louis Finot, *Angkor Vat,* pt. 3, no. 2, pls. 351–369, and an unnumbered plan at the back of the volume. The measurement for the panel was written on the plan. The measurement for the width of the figure of Viṣṇu, taken between his outstretched arms, was estimated at 1.25 m based on the photographs (and later verified in situ). The procedure for estimating lengths from the photographs in Finot was simple and fairly accurate, however. Each photograph equals the width of one interpillar space. Once that distance is known—it can be taken from plans—the measurements for any figure or place on the photograph can be calculated in meters and centimeters. This technique is useful if one cannot go to Angkor Wat to take the measurements from the relief itself.
5. Lucien Rudaux and G. de Vaucouleurs, *Larousse Encyclopedia of Astronomy,* 2nd ed. (New York: Prometheus Press, 1962), p. 39.
6. Ibid., p. 122.
7. Varāha Mihira, *The Panchasiddhāntikā,* trans. G. Thibauth and Mahāmahopādhyaya Sudhākara Dvivedī (Benares: Medical Hall Press, 1889), p. 69, st. 1, 2, 5, and p. 7, st. 27. This text dates to the sixth century.
8. All accounts of the churning story describe Mount Mandara as the mountain that is uprooted and brought to the shores of the Sea of Milk to serve as the churning pivot. Despite a Khmer tendency to identify Mount Mandara with Mount Meru and the axis of the earth, this is not at all the case according to cosmology. Mount Meru *is* the north–south axis of the earth, and Mandara is not. This point is taken up in Madeleine Giteau, "Le barattage," pp. 145–147, and Kamaleswar Bhattacharya, "Notes d'iconographie khmère," *AA* 4/3 (1957): 211–213. In the cosmology of the Puranas, Indian philosophical and religious treatises written in the first centuries of the Christian era, Mount Mandara is a distinct mountain that lies to the east of Mount Meru, while the *Mahābhārata* also distinguishes Mandara according to its size, color, and inhabitants. Mount Meru would remain stable as the axis of the earth while Mount Mandara gyrates, just as the world's axis remains stable while the sun and moon appear to oscillate. This pattern is illustrated in the churning scene. See also Johannes Adrianus Bernardus van Buitenen, trans. and ed., *The Mahābhārata, Book 1, The Book of the Beginning,* 1 (Chicago and London: University of Chicago Press, 1973), pp. 1–5, Astika, 72 and 73, 15.5–16.5; and the *Vishṇu Purāṇa,* vol. 2 (1865), bk. 1, pp. 110–111, no. 1, and pp. 112–138.
9. Faraut, *Astronomie Cambodgienne,* pp. 17, 26–27, and 97.
10. I made this observation in late December 1991. There are several other winter solstice alignments at the temple. One alignment runs between the porch of the north causeway library and the center of the southwest pavilion in the third gallery. Another alignment goes between the eastern doorway of the northeast tower (on the upper level) and the center of the south lateral entrance on the east side of the second gallery.
11. "Review of *Siamese State Ceremonies: Their History and Function,*" *JIH* 11/3 (Dec. 1932): 401.
12. Shastri, *Rāmāyaṇa,* vol. 1, p. 92: "Indra, after slaying the *asuras*, became king of the *devas* and with the help of the sages began to rule with joy." Naturally, not all ver-

sions of the story of the Churning of the Sea of Milk include this ending, but it does occur in several versions and must have been common knowledge to the Khmer pundits.

13. Arthur Berriedal Keith, trans., *Rigveda Brāhmaṇas: The Aitareya and Kauṣītaki Brāhmaṇas of the Rigveda,* Harvard Oriental Series, 25 (Cambridge: Harvard University Press, 1920), pp. 299–343. Johannes Cornelius Heesterman analyzes the *rājasūya* ceremonies based on the Vedas and the commentaries in the Brāhmaṇas in *The Ancient Indian Royal Consecration* (The Hague: Mouton, 1957). The *rājasūya* may have begun as a new year ritual since its central ceremony, the "*Mahābhiṣeka* of Indra" (the *Indrābhiṣeka,* in other words), "clusters around the new year" (p. 10). In addition to these textual references, there is another reference to the *Indrābhiṣeka* in Julius Eggeling, trans., *Śatapatha Brāhmaṇa,* in *Sacred Books of the East,* ed. F. Max Müller (Oxford: Clarendon Press, 1894), vol. 56, pp. 68–110. The central ceremony, or the consecration itself, also involves a tiger skin, a throne, anointment, and the deities of all the directions (as in the previous texts).
14. Varāha Mihira, *Bṛhat Saṁhitā,* trans. Hendrik Kern, *JRAS,* n.s. 6 (1873): 80.
15. The ceremony is described in Horace G. Quaritch Wales, *Supplementary Notes on Siamese State Ceremonies* (London: Bernard Quaritch, 1971), pp. 14–15. This is a revised translation of the version in his *Siamese State Ceremonies* (London: Bernard Quaritch, 1931), pp. 121–123. The suggested date of the *Kot Monthianbān,* the source for information on the performance of the *Indrābhiṣeka,* is the fifteenth century, according to David K. Wyatt, "The Thai 'Kata Maṇḍiarapāla' and Malacca," *JSS* 55/2 (1967): 279–286. Other references to the *Indrābhiṣeka* in Southeast Asia are discussed by Forrest McGill in "The Art and Architecture of King Prāsātthōng of Ayutthayā (1629–1656)" (Ph.D. dissertation, University of Michigan, 1977), p. 85, n. 114. Hiram Woodward, Jr., also draws attention to a possible *Indrābhiṣeka* performed for King Kyanzittha of Burma (r. ca. 1084–1113) in "Tantric Buddhism at Angkor Thom," *AO* 12 (1981): 63 and n. 65.
16. George Coedès, "Études Cambodgiennes," *BEFEO* 32/1 (1932): 74. A discussion of the *Indrābhiṣeka* follows on pp. 74–76. The English here is my translation of Coedès.
17. Varāha Mihira, *Bṛhat Saṁhitā,* p. 80.
18. Groslier, *Le Bayon, inscriptions du temple,* vol. 2, p. 171. My translation.
19. George Coedès agrees with Moura and Aymonier in identifying this figure as Indra (Coedès, "Les bas-reliefs," p. 175). Indra, as king of the *devas*, should be located at the top and center of Mount Meru, the home of the gods. Insofar as Mandara and Meru are interchangeable in Khmer depictions, Indra is then in his appropriate place.
20. Scholars have not reached a consensus on the identity of Bali and Sugrīva. Although some believe that these two figures are Rāvaṇa and Hanuman, no one offers any "proof" for an opinion. The only such evidence that can be given here is the predominance of the theme of kingship, coronation, and kings in the scene itself, something that was not suspected earlier.
21. The measurements for the bridge were taken from Nafilyan, *Angkor Vat,* pl. 84. Written measurements were not available. Each half of the span measures 37.40 cm on the plan, or 93.50 m on the ground, including the balustrades. The elevation shows a width of 1 mm, or .25 m on the ground, for the balustrade base (between the balustrade and the bare surface of the bridge). Thus the length of each half of the span is closer to 94.00 m, or 215.88 cubits, if measured from the wall surface. The western half of the bridge appears possibly 30 cm or so shorter than the eastern half. Taking that discrepancy into consideration, there would be 215.19 cubits in the length of the eastern half of the bridge, making the total of both halves of the span 431.07 cubits. There are 53.97 *phyeam* in 215.88 cubits.
22. Among the many good explanations of these time cycles, one may refer to Wilson, *Vishṇu Purāṇa,* vol. 1, pp. 44–54, and the *Matsya Purāṇam,* trans. A Talukdar of Oudh, in *The Sacred Books of the Hindus,* ed. Major B. D. Bose, 17/1–2 (New York: AMS Press, 1974), pt. 2, pp. 36–47 and 128–129.
23. The distance is approximately 751.54 m, or 1725.89 cubits, based on written measurements and pls. 11, 28, 69, and 84 of Nafilyan, *Angkor Vat.* The distance from

the center of the western entrance, second enclosure, to the center of the western entrance, fourth enclosure, is 490.958 m according to written figures. The rest of the distance was calculated from a combination of plans and written measurements.

24. This distance covers a total of 562.61 m, or 1292.02 cubits. Although it is 4 cubits short of an ideal 1296, it is close enough to indicate a *tretā yuga,* especially given the context of the other three yuga periods that begin on the bridge. Measurements here were based on written figures.
25. The balustrade that encircles the central three galleries opens up in front of all the major entrances. In doing so, it extends a few meters toward the visitor as one enters. In fact, the balustrade extends toward the western causeway for the space of two supports, beyond the double corner support. The distance between the center of each successive balustrade support is 1.43 m according to pl. 60 of Nafilyan, *Angkor Vat.* Thus the distance between the *nāga* balustrade around the central three galleries and the point at which its extension ends on the causeway is 2.86 m. That is to say, the balustrade that encircles the center of Angkor Wat would extend approximately 3 m westward. At that point, it turns toward the causeway and intersects it on each side. The distance between the first step of the western entrance to Angkor Wat and the point at which the balustrade intersects the causeway is 376.59 m, or 864.83 cubits. Causeway lengths are explained in Chapter 4.
26. Van Buitenen, trans. and ed., *The Mahābhārata, Book 4, The Book of Virata; Book 5, The Book of the Effort,* vol. 2 (Chicago and London: University of Chicago Press, 1978), pp. 5–54, *The Coming of the Lord, con't.,* p. 430, 130.15–.20.
27. These citations come from the following source: Coedès, *IC,* vol. 4, various pages. Starting at p. 23, st. 8, the inscription is from Sambor Prei Kuk, group N, outer enclosure, east door, south jamb; p. 227, st. 77, Prasat Srung stele inscription, side C, from the southwest corner of Angkor Thom, and in vol. 5, p. 322, st. 14, Wat Sla Ku stele inscription, side B. Other inscriptions that describe the Khmer ruler as initiating the *kṛta yuga* or eliminating the *kali yuga* can be found in the following volumes of *Inscriptions du Cambodge:* vol. 2, p. 174, st. 16, Phimeanakas; vol. 3, p. 82, st. 4, Kok Samrong; vol. 4, p. 11, st. 14, Sambor Prei Kuk; vol. 7, p. 181, st. 4, Prasat Beng stele; and Louis Finot, "Inscriptions d'Angkor," *BEFEO* 25/3–4 (1926): 402, st. 6, Mangalartha.
28. The lengths were taken from Nafilyan, pl. 2, and written measurements. The distances in meters are 376.96 on the north and 375.71 on the south.
29. Ibid. The southern distance is 564.43 m; the northern is 563.28 m.
30. Ibid. The lengths are 374.10 m between the doorway to the southern entrance and the base of the upper elevation and 376.58 m for the comparable distance on the north. Each of these distances would be doubled for a round trip, bringing the total in cubits to 1718.22 and 1729.61, respectively. Because the upper elevation is displaced about 1.5 m south of the axis of Angkor Wat, the southern distance is shorter.
31. Ibid., pls. 2, 11, and 14. The distance is 756.95 m, or 1738.32 cubits, measured to the base of the great western staircase. The base was chosen as a terminus because it marks the end of a 32-cubit space between the two *kṛta yuga* lengths along the west–east axis, as explained in the text.
32. Ibid., pl. 28. In contrast to a previously published measurement by the author (as Eleanor Morón) in "Configurations of Time and Space at Angkor Wat," *Studies in Indo-Asian Art and Culture* 5 (Dec. 1977): 219, no. 5, a remeasurement at the site showed a distance of 45 ft 2 in. between the doorway to the second gallery and the base of the upper elevation. This converts to 13.77 m, or 31.62 cubits. The base is 17½ in. wide, and the step under the walkway 15½ in. wide, or 83.8 cm for both (1.93 cubits).
33. The description of Meru given here was taken from William M. McGovern, *A Manual of Buddhist Philosophy* (Lucknow: Oriental Reprinters, 1976), pp. 64–70, the realms of the gods, and pp. 51–56, a geography of Meru. Many other texts describe Mount Meru, but this text has the advantage of summarizing the cosmology in direct, easy-to-read terminology. I have adopted the totals of 24 and 28 accepted by the Mahayanists, since these correspond more readily to

Khmer iconography. Some texts, however, stipulate 27 and even 26 as a total for the god realms.

34. The four directions: East: Dhṛtarāṣṭra, king of the *gandharvas*; West: Virūpākṣa, king of the *nāgas*; South: Virūḍhaka, king of the *kumbhāṇḍas*; and North: Vaiśravaṇa or Kubera, king of the *yakṣas*.
35. The *vāstupuruṣamaṇḍala* is fully discussed in Kramrisch, *The Hindu Temple,* vol. 1, pp. 29–39 and 79–97.
36. The 28 *nakṣatra,* their deities, and the Western equivalents are:

1. Kṛttikā	Agni	Alcyone	Pleiades
2. Rohiṇī	Prajāpati	Aldebaran	Taurus
3. Mṣgaśīrsā	Soma	Orionis	Orion
4. Ārdrā	Rudra	Betelgeuse	Orion
5. Punarvasu	Aditi	Pollux	Gemini
6. Puṣya	Bṛhaspati	Cancrii	Cancer
7. Āśreṣā	Sarpa	Hydrae	Cancer
8. Maghā	Pitris	Regulus	Leo
9. Pūrvaphālgunī	Bhaga	Zosma	Leo
10. Uttaraphālgunī	Aryamā	Denebola	Leo
11. Hastā	Savitā	465 Corvii	Crow
12. Citrā	Tvaṣṭa	Spica	Virgo
13. Svātī	Vāyu	Arcturus	Virgo
14. Viśākhā	Indrāgni	559 Librae	Libra
15. Anurādhā	Mitra	597 Scorpionis	Scorpio
16. Jyeṣṭhā	Indra	Antares	Scorpio
17. Mūlam	Nirṛti	652 Scorpionis	Scorpio
18. Pūrvāṣādhā	Āpah	687 Sagittarii	Sagittarius
19. Uttaraṣādhā	Viśvadeva	706 Sagittarii	Sagittarius
20. Abhijit	Dakāa	Vega	Capricorn
21. Śrāvaṇa	Viṣṇu	Altair	Aquila
22. Śatabhiṣāk	Varuṇa	864 Aquarii	Aquarius
23. Dhaniṣthā	Vasu	Delphinis	Aquarius
24. Pūrvabhadrapāda	Aja-ekapāda	Markab	Pegasus
25. Uttarabhadrapāda	Ahi-Budhna	Andromedae	Pegasus
26. Revatī	Pūṣa	Piscium	Pisces
27. Aśvinī	Aśvinau	b. Arietis	Aries
28. Bharaṇī	Yama	a. Muscae	Muscae

One listing for the 12 *ādityas* is:

Dhakṣa	Rudra	Varuṇa	Sūrya
Mitra	Bhaga	Vivasvān	Pūṣan
Aryaman	Savitṛ	Tvaṣṭṛ	Viṣṇu

Variants in this list may include Śakra or Indra, Āṃṣa, and several others. The 12 *ādityas* are not generally discussed in books on Indian astronomy, but their correspondence to the 12 zodiac signs is clear: both sets of 12 define the length of a solar year. How the sets are related and the history of their relationship lies outside the research objectives in this study.

The solar months themselves go by another set of names that is nothing more than the names of the lunar half-months, chosen in a regular pattern to cover a 12-month period:

1. Caitra	7. Āśvina
2. Vaiśākha	8. Kārttika
3. Jyeṣṭhā	9. Mārgaśīrṣa
4. Aṣādhā	10. Pauṣa
5. Śrāvaṇa	11. Māgha
6. Bhadrapāda	12. Phālguna

Information on the *nakṣatra, ādityas*, and solar months was taken from: Alain Danielou, *Hindu Polytheism* (New York: Bollingen Foundation, 1964), pp. 112–127 (*ādityas*); Jitendra Nath Banerjea, *The Development of Hindu Iconography* (Calcutta: University of Calcutta, 1956), pp. 309–311 (*ādityas*); S. B. Roy, *Prehistoric Lunar Astronomy* (New Delhi: Institute of Chronology, 1976), pp. 52–55 (*nakṣatra* tables); J. B. Biot, *Études sur l'astronomie Indienne et sur l'astronomie Chinoise* (Paris: Albert Blanchard, 1969 reprint), facing p. 136 (chart of zodiac signs, stars, and *nakṣatra*); and McGovern, *A Manual of Buddhist Philosophy,* p. 44 (solar months).

37. Kramrisch, *The Hindu Temple,* p. 91.
38. Based on written measurements and pl. II of Nafilyan, *Angkor Vat,* the axis that runs west to east measures 1522.26 m, including, of course, the projecting staircase to the bridge on the west. That equals 3495.83 cubits, or 32.27 units of 108 cubits each.
39. There are no written measurements for the north–south axis, but 1300 m is the generally stated length. This figure coincides with the plans in Nafilyan, *Angkor Vat.* That length is 2985.42 cubits.
40. In this measurement, the west–east and north–south axes were just doubled to give an approximate perimeter. Since the 108-cubit unit is so large, this approximation lies between 119 and 121, still easily indicative of 120.
41. Note 13 mentioned that in Heesterman, *The Ancient*

Indian Royal Consecration, p. 10, the central *abhiṣeka*s of Indra and the king "cluster around the new year."

CHAPTER 3

1. Robert Brown, *Researches into the Primitive Constellations of the Greeks, Phoenicians, and Babylonians* (London and Oxford: Williams & Norgate, 1899; Ann Arbor: University Microfilms, 1979), vol. 2, pp. 112–113. The Sumer-Akkadian name for Aquila, Idkhu, refers both to the constellation and to Altair. Examples from a cuneiform tablet are given to illustrate that Idkhu had to be near the ecliptic.
2. Ibid., vol. 1, pp. 45–46.
3. The material in this segment is taken from Brown, *Primitive Constellations,* vol. 2, pp. 195–201.
4. I remember reading somewhere an accounting of the *kāla* head as a possible representation of Leo in relation to Indonesian art. That account connected the *makara* to Capricorn, suggesting that the Leo–Capricorn stellar orientation determined the *kāla-makara* composition. I do not know how or when the word "*kāla*" originated as a description of this head. A common term in Southeast Asian art, it means "time."
5. The length of a sidereal lunar month is 27.32166 days, according to the *Larousse Encyclopedia of Astronomy,* p. 148.
6. Brown, *Primitive Constellations,* vol. 2, chap. 11, pp. 59–105. The Assyro-Babylonian list of lunar constellations, 30 or 31 in all, was compiled in the third millennium B.C.
7. George Rusby Kaye, "The *Nakshatra* and Precession," *IA* (Feb. 1921): 44–48.
8. *Larousse Encyclopedia of Astronomy,* p. 148. The length of the synodic lunar month is 29.530588 days.
9. Sankar Balakrishna Dikshit, trans. R. V. Vaidya, *Bhāratīya Jyotish Śāstra,* Pt. 1: *History of Astronomy During the Vedic and Vedāṅga Periods* (Delhi: Manager of Publications, Civil Lines, 1969), p. 27.
10. It is recognized here that the standing, four-armed Viṣṇu also has 24 variant forms, created by the maximum combinations of his four attributes. Although this is one of the iconographic realities of Viṣṇu, it does not outweigh the predominant lunar associations of the number 24. In fact, it may be one way to *connect* Viṣṇu to the lunar months, not the other way around.
11. Brown, *Primitive Constellations,* vol. 1, pp. 332–333.
12. Ibid., vol. 2, pp. 1–3.
13. Ibid., vol. 1, pp. 333–335. On these pages Brown also discusses the Indian system of yugas. He thinks the celestial periods that begin with 12,000 years for the *kali yuga* in the time period of the gods are based on the original 120 degrees in a circle.
14. Ibid., p. 325.
15. George Coedès, "L'origine du cycle des douze animaux au Cambodge," *T'oung Pao* 31 (1935): 315–329. The names of the 12 animals are the same in China and in Cambodia. Coedès thinks the 12 animals were introduced before the eleventh century. The 10-year cycle used with the 12 animals may have come into use in the thirteenth century, he postulates. Based on the information in the measurements of Angkor Wat, it would appear that the system of 12 and 10 was in use before the twelfth century, at least. The Chinese system is explained in most good Chinese–English dictionaries. The 12 terrestrial "branches" are joined with the 10 celestial "stems." The 12 branches correspond to the 12 zodiac signs, the 12 periods of the day, and the 12 animals:

11–1 A.M.	Rat	Aries
1–3	Ox	Taurus
3–5	Tiger	Gemini
5–7	Rabbit	Cancer
7–9	Dragon	Leo
9–11	Snake	Virgo
11–1 P.M.	Horse	Libra
1–3	Sheep	Scorpio
3–5	Monkey	Sagittarius
5–7	Cock	Capricorn
7–9	Dog	Aquarius
9–11	Boar	Pisces

16. Dikshit, *Bhāratīya Jyotish Śāstra,* pt. 1, p. 15: "In the *Vedāṅga Jyotiṣa* (ca. 400 B.C.) the *yuga* is taken to be a cycle of five years. The names of these years are *Saṃvatsara, Parivatsara, Idāvatsara, Anuvatsara,* and *Idvatsara.* Although these names do not occur in the *Vedāṅga Jyotiṣa* itself, there is no doubt that these were the names of the years, inasmuch as they occur in the

Vedas." The exact number of lunar months in the 5-year period is 62 (synodic).

17. William Soothill's *Dictionary of Chinese Buddhist Terms* (Taipei: Ch'eng-wen, 1960), p. 23a, lists these 20 *devas* and gives their Chinese equivalent names. The guardians of the directions are in the group of 20, as well as Skanda, Sūrya, Candra, and various others, including Hāritī, Sarasvatī, and Lakṣmī. The 20 gods on the north wall of the third gallery, however, are all male.
18. Billard, "L'Astronomie Indienne," pp. 84–85, notes that Āryabhaṭa was the first astronomer to record yuga cycles of 1,080,000 years each. If equal yuga periods were current at the same time as the *Mahābhārata,* which describes the degeneration of the yugas and emphasizes their inequality (but does not refer to their length in years), then perhaps the original astronomical yugas belonged to a different system. Otherwise it is difficult to understand why the yugas would be unequal in the literary tradition and equal in the astronomical tradition. In any case, by the time both traditions were in effect at Angkor, the four yugas are considered to be a staggered time sequence.
19. Jean Filliozat was the first to remark on the 108 towers that surround Phnom Bakheng (A.D. 900) at Angkor, and he gives a good overview of the number 108 in "Le symbolisme du monument du Phnom Bakheng," *BEFEO* 44/2 (1954): 527–544.
20. Brown, *Primitive Constellations,* vol. 1, p. 12.
21. The architect Guy Nafilyan, surveyor of Angkor Wat in the early 1960s, believes that these towers were never fully constructed (pers. comm.).
22. The measurements for the western entrances are based on written figures and pls. 67–69 of Nafilyan, *Angkor Vat.* Written measurements give a longer length to the axes of the two lateral entrances: .10 m longer for the south entrance and .20 m longer for the north (cf. pl. 69). With regard to the north–south axial lengths of the side chambers, their measurements are 11.79 m for each north–south set of antechambers, according to written figures. That is 27.08 cubits for each set, or 54.16 cubits total. The length of the corridors, at 54 *phyeam* each, is measured up to the central square area of the main western entrance chamber. That entrance is 37.5 m long, based on written figures. The square central area of the chamber measures 4.6 m north–south, as well as west–east, or 2.64 *phyeam* on a side. It is somewhat larger than the normal size of 3 or 4 m on a side.

    Additional measurements for the western entrances are shown in my dissertation, "Angkor Wat: Meaning Through Measurement" (University of Michigan, 1985), pp. 104–105. All the measurements for the end gateways are based on written figures. They can be compared to pls. 76 and 81 of Nafilyan, *Angkor Vat.* The pair of end chambers for each northern, southern, and eastern entrance measures 3.91 and 3.92 m. (See pl. 85 of Nafilyan.)
23. Rāmacandra Kaulācāra, *Śilpa Prakāśa,* p. xxxiii.
24. The lengths of the corridors are 55.75 m on the north and 53.00 m on the south, according to written figures and pl. 68 of Nafilyan, *Angkor Vat.* It should be noted that one interpillar space has been inexplicably deleted in pl. 67. According to pl. 68 and Finot, *Angkor Vat,* pt. 1, no. 1, pls. 6 and 11, there are 27 and not 26 interpillar spaces along the northern corridor. The length for the northern corridor on pl. 67 should therefore be 2 m longer, to account for the missing space. That brings the length of the northern corridor to 55.75 m.
25. Stencel, Gifford, and Morón, "Astronomy and Cosmology," pp. 281–283.
26. Giteau, "Le barattage," pp. 145–146.
27. The measurements for the lateral entrances are based on written figures and pl. 69 of Nafilyan, *Angkor Vat.* In reference to the west–east axis, the written measurement for the outer west–east axis of the south lateral entrance is 27.86 m (63.98 cubits) and for the north entrance 27.64 m (63.48 cubits). Both of these distances are slightly longer than those shown on pl. 69. The square central area of the chamber is 3.8 m west–east for the south entrance and 3.9 m west–east for the north. The connecting antechambers have only one axis that marks their length. (They are not cruciform in shape.) The written measurements for all four rooms add up to 12.23 m, or 28.09 cubits. The full length of all three entrances is 84.86 m, based on written figures. Plate 69 shows a somewhat shorter length (84.12 m).

The measurements for the end gateways are based on written figures; for comparison see pls. 76 and 81 in Nafilyan. Their circumambulation routes are 57.03 m for the path through the north end chamber and 57.17 m through the south end chamber.

The northern, southern, and eastern entrances are identical, and their measurements are given in Nafilyan, pl. 85. The outer north–south axis measures 30.02 m, or 68.94 cubits, for each entrance. The west–east axis is 39.17 m for each entrance. Written measurements give the axes of the central cruciform chamber as 11.17 m north–south and 15.11 m west–east, for a total of 26.28 m. The two side chambers measure 6.00 m (west) and 6.07 m (east). For all three central chambers, the inner axial total is 38.35 m, or 88.07 cubits, which comes to 264.21 cubits for all three entrances. The pair of end chambers for each entrance measures 3.91 and 3.92 m. It should be noted that one pillar in front of the central western entrance, to the right, was never built. Because of that one missing pillar, the full total for the number of pillars in front of the main entrance and its side chambers is 49. Also because of that omission, the total in front of the entrance is 31 and not 32. Pillars at the end of the facade of a chamber are quite often doubled. One of the pair supports the roof over one chamber, and the other supports the roof over the next. Therefore, when counting pillars, it is important to note with which part of the facade they are physically connected.

28. This information and more on the *kāraṇa* can be found in the *Sūrya Siddhānta,* trans. Ebenezer Burgess (Varanasi and Delhi: Indological Book House, 1977), pp. 106–107; and in Dikshit, *Bhāratīya Jyotish Śāstra,* p. 98.
29. This figure is based on the written measurements of Guy Nafilyan. The circumference around the enclosure is 3689.70 m and the west–east inner axis of the main western entrance is 14.8 m for a total of 3704.52 m, or 8507.33 cubits (354.3671 × 24.007).
30. The western entrance is 37.5 m long, or 86.12 cubits (31.53 *phyeam*). The circumambulation path would circuit the main image three times at 5 cubits on a side (60 cubits total) and then move to the right or left to go around the image (5 cubits more) in order to exit from the opposite door. The total comes to 151.12 cubits. The lateral towers have circuits of 107.98 cubits on the south and 107.48 cubits on the north. The distance is given in note 24 above and can be measured from pls. 67–69 in Nafilyan, *Angkor Vat.* When the in-and-out circuits of the lateral entrances are added to the path through the main entrance, the result is 366.58 cubits.
31. These figures are based on the written measurements of Guy Nafilyan. The axes are measured between the bottom step of the staircase up to the main western entrance and the base of the entrances on the north, south, and east. That total comes to 1911.45 m, or 4389.60 cubits (365.24 × 12.02).

CHAPTER 4

1. Stencel, Gifford, and Morón, "Astronomy and Cosmology," pp. 283–284.
2. The causeway length was calculated at 341.95 m, based on a combination of written measurements and measurements from plans in Nafilyan, *Angkor Vat.* A complete explanation of the derivation of causeway measurements is given in my dissertation, "Angkor Wat," chap. 4, n. 1. The full length of the causeway, from the last step out of the western entrance up to the *nāga* balustrade (but not including the balustrade), is 341.95 m, or 785.28 cubits (28.00 × 28.05). The length of the western entrance is 37.5 m, based on written figures and pl. 69 of Nafilyan. That gives 379.45 m or 871.40 cubits (29.53 × 29.51) for the length of the causeway from the first step up to the western entrance.

   There are six equal divisions between and including the stairway on the west and the intersecting balustrade on the east, a length of 334.78 m, or 55.80 m per division (32.04 *phyeam*). The stairways measure 6.64 m in width, based on written measurements and pl. 69 of Nafilyan. That measurement includes the base around the projecting staircase. According to these figures, there would be 49.16 m or 28.22 *phyeam* between successive staircases, measured base to base.
3. The oldest example of a 5-year yuga period occurs in 36 verses of the *Ṛgveda,* as explained in David Pingree, "Jyotiḥśāstra," in *A History of Indian Literature*

(Wiesbaden: Otto Harrassowitz, 1981), p. 9. The cycle is also noted in Dikshit, *Bhāratīya Jyotish Śāstra,* p. 15, as mentioned in chap. 3, note 16.

The 5-year cycle and its possible representation at Phnom Bakheng was first noted by Jean Filliozat in his long discussion of the numerical symbolism of Bakheng's 108 towers, divided into segments of 32/33 and 44/45, like many of the measurements of Angkor Wat. See "Le symbolisme du monument de Phnom Bakheng," p. 530.

4. Stencel, Gifford, and Morón, "Astronomy and Cosmology," p. 281. The text should be corrected to read the northern (not the southern) stairway. The International Video Network in California filmed the spring equinox alignment in March 1995 for a Reader's Digest series on ancient civilizations.
5. More than 150 years later, the Chinese traveler Zhou Daguan does not mention spring equinox festivities, nor does he place the Cambodian New Year in March. He records it as falling in the tenth month of the Chinese calendar (November). This time of year would coincide with the change in the course of the Tonle Sap River and with the annual water festival, which he also does not mention. For these reasons, I suspect he confused the celebration of the new year with the November water festival.
6. In December 1994, I measured the axes of the terrace between the base of the north, south, and east staircases up to the third gallery and from the bottom of the first step of the cruciform terrace on the west to the outer edge of the *nāga* balustrade that crosses the causeway. These were the only segments of the axes for which I had no written measurements. The result came to 1418.66 cubits, or 354.67 *phyeam.* Although I was not interested in taking the circumference measurements at the time, twice the axes (minus the outcropping staircases) would give the circumference of the terrace. Based on my notes, it appears that the west side of the terrace extends about 3 m forward, the north 1.02 m (almost no stairway there), the east 9.17 m (long ramp), and the south 1.45 m. This leaves an approximate total of 675.72 cubits, or 24 × 28.15. Even allowing for a leeway of several meters up or down from this approximation, the total would still be in the range of 24 × 27 or 28.
7. George Coedès offers more evidence for this function in "Études Cambodgiennes VI: Des édicules appelés 'bibliothèques,'" *BEFEO* 11 (1922): 405–406. He notes that the term *"pustakāśrama"* ("book-*āśram*"), used in an inscription on a small building at Prasat Khan, literally defines the building's function. As Coedès explains, the word *"āśram"* is vaguely used in Khmer epigraphy, and the word "structure" or "building" seems a better translation than "monastery" or "hermitage" in many instances.
8. Coedès, *IC,* vol. 3 (1951): 24, n. 2
9. The following inscriptions recorded in George Coedès, *Inscriptions du Cambodge,* all refer to laborers, donations, and work performed during the two separate halves of the lunar month:

   vol. 2 (1942):
   Basak stele, mid-tenth century, p. 56.
   vol. 3 (1951):
   Wat Baset, 1036, p. 9, st. 13–20, and 1042, pp. 21–22, st. 35–59, and p. 24, st. 64–66 and n. 2
   Phnom Kanva, mid-tenth century, p. 75, st. 38–43
   Prasat Ta An, second half tenth century, p. 78, st. 11–15
   Prasat Khtom, first half eleventh century, p. 114, st. 32
   Trapang Don On, 1129, p. 188, st. 17–18, 20, 22–23; p. 190, st. 12–14; p. 191, st. 20–33, 35–38
   vol. 4 (1952):
   Wat Damnak, eleventh century, p. 165, st. 26–29
   Samrong, 1094, p. 195, st. 32–40; p. 196, st. 40–44, 48–50; p. 200, st. 19–26; p. 203, st. 59–63; p. 205, st. 13–15
   vol. 5 (1953):
   Prasat Tasar Sdam, early tenth century, p. 91
   Tuol Kul, 968, p. 149, st. 23–30
   Prasat Trapang Rung, 1002 or 1012, p. 199, st. 6–9
   Prasat Ampil, 1002, p. 210, st. 1–7
   vol. 6 (1954):
   Shong An, 922, p. 112, st. 12–30 and 3–25
   Tuk Shum stele, 949, p. 119, 122, st. B 1–10 left and B 1–10 right
   Prasat Neak Buos, tenth century, p. 155, st. 5–25
   Kok Rosei stele, 949–987, p. 178, st. 12–15
   Prasat Thnal Shuk, tenth century, p. 190, st. 10–14
   Prasat Tnot Shum, early eleventh century, p. 222, st. 19–21

Kampeng Nai, 1042, p. 252, st. 1–11; p. 253, st. 16–17, 22–24
Wat Baset, 1082, p. 292, st. 62–63
Nom Van, 1082, p. 298, st. 1–24; p. 299, st. 1–25
vol. 7 (1964):
Preah Vihear Kuk stele, 912, p. 22, st. 4
Trapang Don Mas stele, 1025, p. 117, st. 11–19
Prasat Beng, 1008, p. 187, st. 3–5

10. Ibid., vol. 3 (1951): 21–22, st. 39–40.
11. Julius Eggeling, trans., *Śatapatha Brāhmaṇa,* in *The Sacred Books of the East,* ed. Max Müller, vol. 12 (Oxford: Clarendon Press, 1882), pp. 2 and 289.
12. The measurements for the causeway libraries are based on written figures and on pl. 98 (south library) and pl. 103 (north library) in Nafilyan, *Angkor Vat.* The exact axial measurements are 23.66 *phyeam* for the southern library and 24.11 *phyeam* for the northern. The north–south axes for the same libraries measure 14.94 *phyeam* and 15.11 *phyeam,* respectively. Those numbers are close to a lunar half-month, which averages 14.77 days.

    The measurements for the circumambulation pathways are 13.5 m (7.55 *phyeam*) from the base to the center of the south library, and 13.00 m (7.46 *phyeam*) from the base to the center of the north library, according to written figures and pls. 98 and 103 of Nafilyan. The circuit around the central image is 5 cubits on a side, or 1.25 *phyeam* per side. This gives 27.10 *phyeam* for the southern library and 26.92 for the northern library. This calculation was mistakenly given a larger total in my dissertation, "Angkor Wat," chap. 4, n. 18

    The measurement in cubits up to the image in each library covers the distance between the base (the outermost physical point of the library) and the circumambulation path around the image. This distance does not go past that boundary. Based on this measurement pattern, it is likely that no one was supposed to set foot inside the path around the image. At any rate, the pedestal itself would come close to occupying the area of the circuit around the image.
13. All measurements for the middle set of libraries are based on written figures and pl. 92 of Nafilyan. The west–east axes come to 19.42 *phyeam* and the north–south axes measure 11.31 *phyeam.*
14. See Filliozat, "Le symbolisme du monument du Phnom Bakheng," for a general elucidation of this concept throughout.
15. All the measurements for the last set of libraries were taken from written measurements and Nafilyan, *Angkor Vat,* pl. 90. The inner axes measure 1 cubit less if a small indentation by each doorway (a kind of ledge or step across the interior front of the door) is excluded. The outer axes include the base, which is presently covered by the raised walkway connecting the libraries. The circumambulation path is measured from the slight elevation where the walkway joins the library and again includes three circuits of the main image at 5 cubits or 1.25 *phyeam* on a side. For more information on the *karāṇa* one can consult the *Sūrya Siddhānta,* trans. Ebenezer Burgess, pp. 106–107, and Dikshit, *Bhāratīya Jyotish Śāstra,* p. 98.
16. The measurements for the inner axes of all the libraries are based on written figures and on pls. 90, 93, 98, and 108 in Nafilyan, *Angkor Vat.*
17. The measurements for the cruciform terrace were primarily based on written figures and can be compared to those in pls. 3 and 37 of Nafilyan, *Angkor Vat.* The number of columns along the basic symmetrical section of the cruciform terrace includes the columns that extend alongside the porch of the third gallery. Their number can be derived from pl. 37 of Nafilyan and pls. 57, 69, and 72 of Finot et al., *Angkor Vat,* pt. 1, no. 1. It should be remembered that the double corner columns are counted as two columns, once for each direction.
18. Specifically, the entrant axis (not counting any overlap with the circumference line) of the two corner pavilions on the west (together), of the two pavilions on the east (together), of each set of lateral chambers, and of each axial chamber make an approximate *kṛta yuga* length in combination with the circumference. The measurements range from 1715.24 at the lower end of the scale (east axial entrance) to 1730.27 at the higher end of the scale (western and eastern corner pavilions). The circumferences at Angkor Wat are calculated as the distance around the gallery (down the center of its corridors) plus the interior, perpendicular axis (usually west–east) of the main western entrance to the gallery. The length of 1728.40 cubits is based on written mea-

surements and can be compared against pls. 11 and 28 of Nafilyan.

The exact cubit measurements for the main chambers in conjunction with the circumference are:

Western entrance	1728.40
Eastern entrance	1715.24
Northern entrance	1727.34
Southern entrance	1727.34
Pair of western corner pavilions	1730.27
Pair of eastern corner pavilions	1730.27
Pair of western lateral entrances	1728.60
Pair of eastern lateral entrances	1728.74

These measurements include the interior, entrant axis of each chamber (with no overlap with the cirumference included) plus the circumference of the gallery. Their lengths are based on written figures but can be compared to pls. 11, 28, 53, 57, and 63 of Nafilyan, *Angkor Vat.* Not only the lateral entrances are paired for a *kṛta yuga* length—which is logical since they are "twin" structures—but also the corner pavilions. Their pairing of two on the east and two on the west is consistent for other measurement patterns as well. It is also consistent with the fact that the two pavilions on the west are sculpted with bas-reliefs and the two on the east are not. The eastern entrance and circumference length seems too short for a *kṛta yuga* distance.

19. Nafilyan, *Angkor Vat,* pls. 2, 11, 53, and written figures. In previous calculations (Morón, "Configurations," pp. 226–228, nn. 18–19), this distance was measured from the bottom step. As determined later, however, all outer measurements should be taken from the outermost section of any structure—which in this case is the base and not the last step of the staircase. The southern distance once again falls short of an ideal 1728 cubits because the center of the temple is displaced southward by 1.72 m (making the south side 6 cubits shorter and the north 6 cubits longer). Adjustments appear to have been made in the borders of the moat to accommodate these discrepancies and arrive at a distance as close to 1728 as possible.

20. These circuits can be calculated from Nafilyan, *Angkor Vat,* pls. 28 and 57. For the lateral entrances, the circumambulation totals come to 26.62 *phyeam* (13.60 m to the center of the north entrance) and 26.51 *phyeam* (13.51 m to the center of the south entrance) for the two lateral entrances on the west and 27.18 *phyeam* (14.09 m to the center of the north entrance) and 27.32 *phyeam* (14.20 m to the center of the south entrance) for the two lateral entrances on the east. The total for all four lateral entrances is 107.62 *phyeam.*

For the three axial entrances, the measurements can be compared to those in Nafilyan, pls. 53 and 57. The exact figures were 37.96 *phyeam* each for the northern and southern entrances (23.43 m to the center) and 32.34 *phyeam* for the eastern entrance (18.5 m to the center), for a total of 108.16 *phyeam.* The circumambulation path always begins at the base of an entrance and, like the lateral entrances, is 4 cubits on a side. In the case of the eastern entrance, there is no stairway on the outside of the structure to the east. Consequently, the circumambulation path is measured from the edge of the porch on the east, that is, the outermost eastern point of the entrance. In the case of the corner pavilions, one can consult Nafilyan's pl. 63 for the measurements. As each pavilion is identical, only one detailed plan is given. There is a slight discrepancy between the two sides of the southwest corner pavilion, taken as a model for all four pavilions: when the slightly longer side is used, the result is 107.51 *phyeam* (13.83 m to the center of each of the four pavilions); when the shorter side of the pavilion is used, the result is 107.15 *phyeam* (13.69 m to the center of each pavilion). A median figure would be 107.33 *phyeam.* This route is also 4 cubits on each side of the circumambulation path, or 16 cubits for one circuit and 48 cubits for three circuits. (Three circuits is the rule in this type of circumambulation.)

21. These axes are measured from the eastern end of the eastern entrance. The present study accepts the dimensions of the gallery exactly as they are, without postulating a hypothetical length for the missing staircase at the main eastern entrance (see Morón, "Configurations," pp. 237–238, n. 32). The axes come to 214.7 m north–south and 241.89 m west–east, for a total of 456.59 m, or 1048.55 cubits.

22. This measurement simply excludes the western entrance porch, which is 6.05 m between the step in front of the door to the gallery (to a forechamber) and

the bottom of the steps on the porch. The length was derived from pl. 28 of Nafilyan, *Angkor Vat.*

23. The axes of the central sanctuary were obtained from the written measurements of Georges Trouvé on an unpublished plan of the sanctuary in the possession of Guy Nafilyan. The west–east axis, at 5.76 m (5.85 m for the north–south axis), is slightly shorter than the same axis shown on pl. 22 of Nafilyan, *Angkor Vat.*
24. George Coedès, "Études Cambodgiennes," *BEFEO* 43 (1943–1946): 1–8.
25. These distances were primarily obtained from written measurements. The distance between the outer enclosing wall and the southern, inner border of the moat was estimated at 39.5 m from pl. 2 of Nafilyan, *Angkor Vat.* There are 405.33 m between the center of the central sanctuary and the wall around the fourth enclosure, for a total of 444.83 m, or 1021.54 cubits. Similarly, the distance to the northern, inner border of the moat was 452.27 m, or 1038.62 cubits. This latter distance was divided between the written measurement of 408.77 m (between the sanctuary and the outer wall) and 43.5 m (between the wall and the moat) obtained from pl. 2. There seem to be no comparable, significant distances along the west–east axis (center of central sanctuary to inner border of moat). Examining the southern distance to the moat in situ proved to be no help at all. The border of the moat is in disrepair and mostly buried, as on the north as well. Therefore, only surveyors working with the remains along these borders, as in the case of Nafilyan and his team, could come close to establishing this distance.
26. This suggestion changes the theory first proposed in my dissertation: that 1048 was the year of the *Indrābhiṣeka.* This does not seem likely because the reliefs and an inscription at the Bayon argue strongly for the *Indrābhiṣeka* of King Jayavarman VII during the year he came to power (1181). This would indicate that Khmer kings did not postpone their consecration. In any case, 13 years seems too long a period to wait to ritually consecrate the king, but not too long a period for the installation of the Viṣṇu image in the central sanctuary. For these reasons, the theory in the dissertation was changed.
27. "Still very young, at the end of his studies, he fulfilled the desire of the royal dignity of his family while [the family was?] still under the dependence of two masters, like the nectar in Rāhu." See Louis Finot, "Notes d'épigraphie XIII: L'inscription de Ban That, *BEFEO* 12/2 (1912): 27, st. 32.
28. The Phnom Rung inscription describes the end of one's studies as coming at the age of 16. See Coedès, *IC,* vol. 5, pp. 297–305.
29. The stele in the Musée Guimet has 17 images across and 15 figures in each row. The Guimet stele is published in Pierre Dupont, *Catalogue des Collections Indochinoises* (Paris: Musées Nationaux, 1934), p. 95. The entry accords it a provenance of Prah Khan of Kompong Svay and mentions 255 images on a side (1020 total). I was mistaken in my discussion of the Guimet stele in my dissertation: the missing small figures of Viṣṇu are simply due to a breakage in the stone; there is no doubt that there were originally 1020.
30. The stele in the Conservation is 38 in. high (87–89 cm) and 15 in. across (37.5 cm) on its two wider sides (A and C) and 11¾ in. across (29 cm) on the narrower sides (B and D). There are 17 registers of 17 figures each on sides A and C, with 17 registers and 13 figures in each on the narrow sides B and D. Both this example (6906/N79) and another stele (N100) in the Conservation have tenons at the bottom set into a base. This second stele is the one with 960 figures on it.
31. The Luang Prabang stele is published in Louis Finot, "Recherches sur la literature Laotienne," *BEFEO* 17/5 (1917):172, and in Paul Levy, "Les traces de l'introduction du Bouddhisme à Luang Prabang," *BEFEO* 40/2 (1940): pl. xxxix. Finot says there are 18 rows on each side, I see only 17. There are 11 figures in each row. More small figures are inside the tympana frames at the top, but it is hard to discern how many. The pleated *sampots* on the Viṣṇu figures would date the stele to the end of the ninth century.
32. The measurements for the height of the drop-off are taken from Nafilyan, p. 58 and estimated at 1.5 m in situ.
33. The steps and windows in this entrance do not add up to a calendrically or cosmologically significant total. Like the other chambers here, its inner axes and outer axes have no numerically meaningful totals. Even the

108-*phyeam* circumambulation path through this entrance and the combined northern and southern entrances could not have been realized on the east because there is no staircase to start the circumambulation. The circuit exists in theory, but not in practice.

34. Maspero, *Royaume du Champa,* p. 155.
35. These dimensions are discussed in note 21 above. They come to 1293.16 cubits.
36. If the lateral chambers are included, there are 54 pillars in front of all three western entrances together.
37. Originally, it appeared as though the total number of steps and windows in this gallery was significant. But on closer inspection, this is not the case. As in other galleries, the architects seemed more interested in entrance sets or pairs, rather than a gallery total.
38. The written measurements for each section of the corridors in the third gallery are given in Finot et al., *Angkor Vat,* pt. 3, nos. 2 and 3, in the plans at the back of each book. The exact distances are 27.82 and 27.76 *phyeam* for the southern halves of the eastern and western corridors, respectively, and 29.54 and 29.42 *phyeam* for the northern halves of those corridors. The full length of the eastern and western corridors together was derived from written figures and can be compared to measurements in Nafilyan, *Angkor Vat,* pls. 11 and 63. The exact figures are 195.25 m for the eastern side of the gallery and 195.15 m for the western side. Together they equal 390.40 m, or 896.54 cubits (32 × 28.02).

    The axes of the forechambers for the main western and eastern entrances are based on written measurements and can be compared to the measurements in pls. 28 and 57 of Nafilyan. They come to 15.62 cubits (written measurement, 16.8 m) for the forechambers of the western entrance and 12.98 cubits (5.65 m) for the eastern, for a total of 28.60 cubits. The side chambers of the western entrance total 43.52 cubits; those of the eastern entrance, 43.96 cubits. The written measurements were 18.95 and 19.14 m, respectively.

    The total number of pillars on the eastern and western sides of the gallery is 308. All the pillars around each corner pavilion are included in the count for the west and east, even the pillars on the northern or southern side of the pavilions. Thus the entire pavilion is understood as "belonging" to either the western or eastern side of the gallery.
39. The written measurements for these corridors are in Finot et al., *Angkor Vat,* pt. 3, nos. 2 and 3, the plans at the back of each book. The western half of the northern and southern corridors comes to 93.60 m in each case, or 53.74 *phyeam*. The eastern half of both corridors is 66.03 m or 37.91 *phyeam* (north side) and 66.05 m or 37.92 *phyeam* (south side). Each side of the gallery, north and south, measures exactly 229.82 m, for a total of 459.64 m or 1055.55 cubits (32 × 32.99). See Nafilyan, *Angkor Vat,* pls. 11 and 63. The two forechambers total 9.03 m, or 20.74 cubits, and the two side chambers (for each entrance) total 14.36 m, or 32.98 cubits. These figures were based on written measurements. The plans show slightly longer axes (pls. 28, 53, and 57). Further numerical data are given in Appendix A, Table 1 which illustrates additional lunar-related numbers on the west and east.
40. The lateral chambers have significant axes when seen together as a set, but it is worthwhile noting the absence of any inner and outer axial measurements and the absence of measurements related to the corner pavilions. This would mean that the architects wanted to emphasize the 108-unit paths into and out of the chambers on this level, even at the expense of giving up significant outer and inner axial lengths. Circumambulation measurements were apparently more important than axial measurements in this gallery.

CHAPTER 5

1. Faraut, *Astronomie Cambodgienne,* pp. 24–26.
2. The Kurukṣetra panel is illustrated in Finot et al., *Angkor Vat,* pt. 3, no. 3, pls. 497–521.
3. I have recounted these figures in situ several times, and there are 43 larger protagonists, not the 44 I stated in my dissertation. The count in the dissertation was taken from the photographs in Finot et al., *Angkor Vat.*
4. Coedès, "Nouvelles données chronologiques," pp. 297–330. Coedès thinks that the kingdom was divided. Although that is quite possible, Sūryavarman united two separate branches of his family in himself, since both his father and mother were descended from the

same king, through different queens. One assumes that there was a division in the family since there was a battle between Sūryavarman and Dharanīndravarman, something inconceivable without political antagonism.

5. Van Buitenen, *The Mahābhārata,* bk. 1, p. 32, v. 9, refers to the battle at Kurukṣetra as inaugurating the *kali yuga.*
6. Specifically there are 54.7 cubits between the northern or left end of the Kurukṣetra panel and the back of the chariot in which the two central figures are mounted and fighting. There are 53.95 cubits between the nose of the horse pulling the central chariot and the southern or right end of the panel. All measurements of the Kurukṣetra panel were derived from Finot et al., *Angkor Vat,* pt. 3, no. 3, pls. 497–515, and the foldout plan at the back of the volume, with written measurements. The long panels were divided into sections by the width of the interpillar spaces. Once the length of each interpillar space was determined from the total length of the panel, the percentage of space covered with major figures was calculated using a ruler. Measurements were taken from the furthest edge of a figure, whether determined by an outstretched arm or the ends of decorative sashes. Based on the precise measurements, markers may have originally been drawn on the walls to show exactly how far the boundaries of significantly placed figures could extend. As far as markers are concerned, one notes that during the time of the winter solstice, the wheels of most of the chariots are alongside the shadows of the pillars on the wall. They are generally just emerging from the shadow.
7. I reserved photography on this panel for the day of the solstice and the following 4 days. Intense rain began on June 20 in the evening, however, and the next 4 days were completely clouded over. This inclement weather, due to typhoon Koryn, negated the possibility of a summer solstice shot.
8. The southwest corner pavilion is completely illustrated in Finot et al., *Angkor Vat,* pt. 3, no. 1, pls. 287–319. The "entrance" to these pavilions (southwest and northwest) is considered here to be the doorway used in a counterclockwise circumambulation of the gallery. That entrance would be the eastern doorway for the northwest pavilion and the northern doorway for the southwest pavilion.
9. See Madeleine Giteau, "Une representation de la Bhikṣāṭanamūrti de Çiva à Angkor Vat," *AA* 11/1 (1966): 131–132, and Sandra Collins, "The Lizard-Portal Motif: Its Meaning and Function" (master's thesis, University of Michigan, 1976). The figure in question seems to be wearing a type of conical miter common to Viṣṇu or Kṛṣṇa at Angkor Wat. Therefore, the final interpretation of the scene is yet to be decided.
10. The procession panel is fully illustrated in Finot et al., *Angkor Vat,* pt. 3, no. 3, pls. 522–573.
11. Ibid., pls. 522–560, and the plan at the back of the volume, with written measurements.
12. The inscriptions are noted in Coedès, "Les bas-reliefs d'Angkor Vat," p. 202 and nn. 1 and 2.
13. Coedès, "Études Cambodgiennes IX: Le serment des fonctionnaires de Sūryavarman I," *BEFEO* 13 (1913): 11–17, and *IC,* vol. 3, pp. 205–216.
14. Aymonier, *Le Cambodge,* vol. 3, p. 251. Coedès comments that the word for "gathering" can be translated as "sent down" or "cause to descend," as explained in "Les bas-reliefs," pp. 201–202. He translates the inscription as "S.M. le roi Parama Viṣṇuloka, au moment ou il reside sur le mont Śivapāda pour faire descendre l'armée," and in Khmer, "Samtac Vraḥ Pāda Kamrateng an Parama Viṣṇuloka na stac nan vnaṃ Śivapāda pi pan cuh vala." Based on the story of King Sūryavarman's rise to power, Aymonier's translation of "gathering" the troops is also appropriate. In the end, because double entendres are the rule rather than the exception in Khmer epigraphy, both "gathering" and "sent down" could have been intended, with no contradiction. The troops would have to gather on the mountain before being sent down to form the procession.
15. The names of the ministers are given in Appendix B, Table 3. Additional information concerning their regions or titles can be found in Aymonier, *Le Cambodge,* vol. 3, pp. 253–264; Finot et al., *Angkor Vat,* pt. 3, no. 3, pls. 522–573; and Coedès, "Les bas-reliefs," pp. 201–203. The reading for the Anak Sanjak Trailokyapura, just in front of King Sūryavarman, was not available to Aymonier or Coedès in 1911. By 1932, however, Coedès was able to decipher the name and recorded it in the plates of *Angkor Vat.* In this work

Coedès transcribed the name of the minister just behind Śrī Jayasiṁhavarman, the third from the front of the procession, as Śrī Siṁhavīrāvarman. One wonders if the name should be Śrī Vīrāsiṁhavarman, the minister who is handing King Sūryavarman a scroll in the scene of allegiance. That minister is not recorded in the inscriptions for the procession.

16. The effaced inscription was first noticed by a Russian visitor who lamented the lack of protection against vandalism and reported the desecration to the authorities. Unfortunately, I cannot find the original reference to the missing inscription in the most likely texts. My memory of the source, it seems, has been equally effaced.
17. This measurement was derived from Finot et al., *Angkor Vat,* pt. 3, no. 3, pls. 522–526, and the plan at the back of the volume. It does not include the figure of the king and was calculated with a ruler, using the size of the photograph and percentages. Given the great lengths and my lack of surveying knowledge and equipment, these distances could not be verified in situ.
18. Eggeling, *Śatapatha Brāhmaṇa,* vol. 12, pt. 1, p. 289.
19. While similarities and a certain reciprocity do exist between the two long northern and southern panels, any attempt to pair off *devas* and ministers fails completely (Appendix B, Table 8). Often minor *devas* correspond to important ministers; often major *devas* have no minister opposite them. One can only conclude, then, that the order in each sequence was established independently.

    The ministers in King Sūryavarman's procession do not align with any specific numerical divisions with the exception of one: Śrī Jayasiṁhavarman, who is just behind the *"syam kuk"* at the beginning of the procession and is marked by 17 parasols, an unusually high number (Appendix B, Table 3). It is possible that the *"syam kuk"* troops were slightly discounted, as their chief is not named. If they were considered to be a kind of forerunner, Śrī Jayasiṁhavarman with his 17 parasols may signal the true beginning of the procession.
20. The central western entrance in the outer enclosure is 37.5 m long, based on written figures. The square central area of the chamber measures 4.5 m north–south, as well as west–east, or 2.64 *phyeam* on a side. It is somewhat larger than the normal size of 3–4 m on a side. All the measurements of the northern and southern gateways in the outer enclosure, western side, are based on written figures. They can be compared to pls. 76 and 81 in Nafilyan, *Angkor Vat.* For the northern and southern entrances in the third gallery, the central area of its main chamber, delineated by its corners, is 3.40 m along its north–south axis. The outer north–south axis measures 36.57 m for a total of 83.98 cubits, or 21.00 *phyeam.* When the 3.40 m of the central area is discounted, the alternate axial measurement is 19.05 *phyeam.* These lengths were based on written measurements and can be compared to pl. 53 of Nafilyan, *Angkor Vat.*
21. The panel of heavens and hells is illustrated in Finot et al., *Angkor Vat,* pt. 3, no. 3, pls. 574–608.
22. The 32 hells are not always the same. They are listed in M. Roeske, "L'enfer Cambodgien d'après le Trai Phum (Tri Bhūmi), les Trois Mondes," *JA,* 11th ser., no. 4 (1914): 587–606, and described in George Coedès and C. Archaimbault, *Les Trois Mondes (Trai Bhūmi Braḥ Ravan),* PEFEO 89 (Paris: École française d'Extrême-Orient, 1973). Coedès briefly summarizes the "Three Worlds" in "The *Traibhūmikakatha,* Buddhist Cosmology and Treatise on Ethics," *East and West* 4 (Jan. 1957): 349–352. According to Roeske, the hells in the Khmer *Trai Phūm* text correspond more closely to the so-called Southern Buddhist schools (Hinayana) and the hells at Angkor Wat correspond to those in the Northern Buddhist schools (Mahayana). The hells at Angkor Wat that also occur in the *Trai Phūm* are Avīci, Kṛminicaya, Vaitaraṇīnadī, Kūṭaśalmalī, Yugmaparvata, Tīkṣṇāyastuṇḍa, Aṅgāranicaya, Kumbhīpāka, Kālasūtra, Sītā, Mahāraurava, and Raurava.
23. Aymonier, *Le Cambodge,* vol. 3, p. 266.
24. Ibid., p. 267. The three central figures are identified by inscriptions that read: "Vraḥ Yama," "Vraḥ Dharma" (another form of Yama), and "Vraḥ Citragupta" (the scribe who records good and bad karma).
25. The measurements for the panel of heavens and hells were taken from Finot et al., *Angkor Vat,* pt. 3, no. 3, pls. 574-600, and the plan at the back of that volume.
26. There are six courtly women in the top register, and

one in the bottom register, on their way to judgment and the heavens and hells; they are riding in special palanquins. Two additional women are apparently taking leave of their servants. There are eight men in the top register and four in the lower register, also in special palanquins. Thus 21 major figures precede the scene of heavens and hells.

27. Coedès, "Les bas-reliefs," pp. 204–207.
28. The panel of the churning scene is illustrated in Finot et al., *Angkor Vat,* pt. 3, no. 2, pls. 351–373.
29. Sometimes this figure is identified as Rāvaṇa. Since Bali, the king of the *asuras*, is part of the story, however, and since he is the king of one-half of the figures in this panel, one assumes he should be present. At the same time, Rāvaṇa on the south end and Sugrīva on the north end would make a good pair. Both are primary antagonists in the Rāmāyaṇa.
30. Brown, *Primitive Constellations,* vol. 2, pp. 28–29. This information comes from the stone of Nabukudurra-utsur I.

CHAPTER 6

1. Coedès, "La date d'exécution des deux bas-reliefs tardifs d'Angkor Vat," *JA* 250/2 (1962): 235–248. The two inscriptions are translated on pp. 237–238. There was some difficulty in reading the names, but the identifications are clear and they fit historical circumstances. The word "panels" was supplied by Coedès, as the inscription only says "had not yet finished two." In "Notes sur les bas-reliefs tardifs d'Angkor Vat," *JA* 250/2 (1962): 244–248, Jean Boisselier suggests there were tracings on the walls before the bas-reliefs were "finished" in the sixteenth century, based on the wording of Coedès' translation. "Not yet finished" refers to the work of Ang Chan, however, not an earlier king.
2. Finot et al., *Angkor Vat,* pt. 3, no. 2, pls. 374–397, illustrates this panel.
3. Boisselier, in "Notes sur les bas-reliefs," pp. 244–248, proposes that the style of art at Ayutthaya in the sixteenth century influenced the style of these late bas-reliefs at Angkor Wat.
4. Ibid., pls. 398–428.
5. Wilson, *Vishṇu Purāṇa,* vol. 5, p. 120.
6. There are six separate depictions of Garuḍa as a mount for Kṛṣṇa, Balarāma, and Pradyumna, but none of their measurements from either end of the panel show a consistent system. There is a possible 54-cubit measurement up to and including Garuḍa in the tenth interpillar space of the corridor, but this is the one exception in the six representations. Neither the *asura* Bāṇa nor Śiva himself show a significant measurement from either end of the panel. Śiva does appear in the twenty-seventh and final interpillar space, and Garuḍa with his three riders faces Bāṇa in the twenty-first interpillar space of the corridor, but these occurrences are too random to suggest a knowledge of the previous numerical systems in the gallery. Besides, once the large monuments were no longer being built, from the thirteenth century onward, and once the religion changed to Hinayana Buddhism, there is no reason to believe the architectural systems that contained the keys to temple building were preserved.
7. The Battle of *Devas* and *Asuras* is illustrated in Finot et al., *Angkor Vat,* pt. 3, no. 2, pls. 429–470.
8. Bryant Tuckerman, *Planetary, Lunar, and Solar Positions A.D. 2 to A.D. 1649 at Five-Day and Ten-Day Intervals* (Philadelphia: American Philosophical Society, 1964), vol. 2, pp. 574–581.
9. The scenes in the northwest corner pavilion are illustrated in Finot et al., *Angkor Vat,* pt. 3, no. 1, pls. 320–350.
10. Wilson, *Vishṇu Purāṇa,* vol. 5, pp. 87–92.
11. Shastri, *Rāmāyaṇa,* vol. 1, bk. 1, chap. 67, pp. 127–128. In the Indian version, Rāma breaks his bow. The meaning of this relief is specifically discussed in Finot, "Notes d'archéologie Cambodgienne II: Deux bas-reliefs d'Angkor Vat, tir à l'arc," *BCAI* 12 (1912): 191–193. The interpretation offered here is taken from Finot.
12. Ibid., chaps. 15–16, pp. 28–29.
13. Ibid., vol. 3, bk. 6, chaps. 123–125, pp. 346–351. In fact, the relief itself seems to have places for only two figures, one on each side of Rāma, or possibly three additional figures at the most. Since all of the figures except for Rāma are effaced, it is difficult to determine the original number.
14. This interpretation of the scene seems the most logical

based on the visual evidence. Coedès thinks that the scene describes the fight with the demon Kabandha ("Les bas-reliefs," pp. 188–189). This reading is doubtful, however, because Kabandha has a face on his stomach, and the stomach of the demon is not shown in the relief. Coedès may have read the giant head on the shoulders of Virādha as the "stomach" of Kabandha.

15. Most of this explanation of the planetary sequence was taken from my article, "Configurations," pp. 228–234.
16. In July 1131, Altair was 29.332 degrees north of the ecliptic. Professor Antonio Guarnieri of the Geodesics School at the Universidad del Zulia, Maracaibo, Venezuela, kindly agreed to do the calculations in this section during my stay in Maracaibo.
17. Louis Malleret, "Contribution à l'étude du thème des neuf divinités dans la sculpture du Cambodge et du Champa," *AA* 7/3 (1960): 205–230.
18. The intent here is to understand why the Cambodians associated these particular deities with the nine planets. These figures are not the planets as represented in a typical *navagraha* relief from India. Rather, they are regents, or deities connected to the planets. In India there are many different associations of deities to planets, not one unified system. Thus the Indian tradition is not helpful in this case. In one example of the unique Cambodian expression of these deities, Agni is shown riding on a rhinoceros—which never occurs in India.
19. Varāha Mihira, "The *Bṛhat Saṅhita,*" translated by Hendrik Kern, *JRAS,* n.s., vol. 5 (1872): chap. 16, pp. 233–234. In this section of the *Bṛhat Saṅhitā,* the dominant character of every planet is amply illustrated by a list of objects and kinds of people that fall under the aegis or rule of each planet.
20. Edward T. C. Werner, *A Dictionary of Chinese Mythology* (New York: Julian Press, 1961), p. 314. Mercury is called *shui-xing,* and is also the god of winter. He is known as the "Black Ruler."
21. Mihira, *The Brihajjātakam,* chap. 2, p. 57, verse 19 and note. This is only one of many listings that place Venus in the northern quarter.
22. Werner, *Chinese Mythology,* p. 543. Venus is called *jin-xing* and is the god of autumn. He is known as the "White Ruler."
23. Van Buitenen, *The Mahābhārata,* bks. 4 and 5, p. 405: "Under the constellations of the Foot of the Stool, with Śukra (Venus) as Lord of Riches, Śukra bestows on men the wealth that they have earned with their thoughts." The text goes on to name Śukra as one of the guardians of treasures.
24. George Coedès, "Études Cambodgiennes X: L'inscription de Prasat Pram," *BEFEO* 13/6 (1913): 24, n. 2.
25. The importance of the *dikpālaka* or directional guardians in the Khmer *navagraha* sequences is discussed by Kamaleswar Bhattacharya in "Notes d'iconographie Khmère, XI, Les *navagraha* et les 'neuf divinités,' " *AA* 10/1 (1964): 91–94.
26. Tuckerman, *Planetary, Lunar, and Solar Positions,* vol. 2, p. 583. In these tables the planets are arranged in increasing degrees of longitude. That is to say, Venus with a longitude of 102.10 would rise in the east before the sun, with a longitude of 136.50.
27. The measurements of this relief are derived from Finot et al., *Angkor Vat,* pt. 3, no. 2, pls. 471–479, and the plan at the back of the volume. Illustrations of the Battle of Laṅkā are also found in pls. 471–496. I took the 21-cubit measurement at the center of the panel in June 1993. The distance extends outward from the tip of the hand of Hanuman to the hooves of the dragonlike coursers pulling Rāvaṇa's chariot. If there is any discrepancy at all, it is only about a centimeter or so.
28. At this point it should be noted again that in the Battle of Kurukṣetra, the Kuru army, "bad" in connotation, is on the north side of the relief while the Pāṇḍava forces are on the south. The only explanation I have for this anomaly is that the Pāṇḍus are about to retrieve their rightful territory from the hands of the Kurus, who are considered "usurpers" of sorts. Therefore, the Pāṇḍu leader and his army will soon wrest control of the "north" from the Kaurava forces, who do not belong there.
29. The derivation of the measurements in the Kurukṣetra panel is explained in chap. 5, note 6.

CHAPTER 7

1. The latitude of the west–east axis of Angkor Wat was determined from the "Carte archéologique de la

region d'Angkor" annexed to the article by Pierre Paris, "L'importance rituelle du nord-est et ses applications en Indo-Chine," *BEFEO* 41/2 (1941): facing p. 333. The latitude and longitude degrees are marked on the map in the French system of 100 degrees for a right angle. Every .10 degree is noted. The latitude of the west–east axis is somewhat south of 14.90 degrees, estimated here at 14.897 degrees or 13°24'26" in the system of 360 degrees to a circle. The angle of 13.41 degrees would not have been difficult for the Khmer astronomers to calculate. As noted earlier, there are more than a dozen separate angles at Angkor Wat that are in alignment with the movements of the sun and moon. These angles had to be calculated. In addition, the precise measurements for the solar and lunar calendars in evidence in a variety of distances at Angkor Wat would require the ability to calculate angles during the course of stellar and planetary observation.

2. The written measurements for the outer axes are 26.405 m north–south and 29.77 m west–east (129.01 cubits), including the width of the bottom decorative step (*accolade* step in French, a low step similar in outline to a curving bracket, mentioned earlier in discussions on measurement boundaries). The central square area between and including the pillars measures 4.10 m west–east and 4.00 m north–south (18.60 cubits), or 3.14 m and 3.13 m for the same distances between pillars. These measurements can be compared to Nafilyan's pl. 28. These outer axes are determined by the doorways and lintels and the special steps that were put into the corridors.
3. The inner axes are 27.99 m west–east (64.28 cubits) and 24.13 m north–south (55.41 cubits). The total is about .5 m shorter than the measurements on Nafilyan's pl. 28.
4. According to written measurements, the distance between the base of the northern lateral entrance to the third gallery on the west, and the opposite base to the northern lateral entrance of the second gallery on the east, is 71.68 m, or 164.61 cubits. With three circuits of each of three images, plus 12 cubits for the detour around each image to get back to the center line of the path, the total is 320.61 cubits. The corresponding southern route is 72.365 m, or 166.184 cubits. When the extra 12 cubits and the three circuits of the images are added, the total is 322.18 cubits. These measurements can be compared to those on pl. 28 of Nafilyan, *Angkor Vat*.
5. This pathway begins on the west with the first step into the main western entrance of the third gallery. It continues to the left (or right) around the *preau cruciforme,* through the western entrances of the second gallery, back through the cruciform, and out the western entrance of the third gallery again. This circuit includes three circumambulations of each image along the way. Based on written measurements, there are 196.07 m around the center of the *preau cruciforme,* or 450.27 cubits. The two images in the central western entrances have circuits of 5 cubits on a side; the four images in the corner entrance chambers and the eleven images in the connecting chambers and the corridors also have circuits of 4 cubits on a side. When the distance for going around an image and back to the center of the circumambulation path is included (a total of 53 cubits), the full sum comes to 1441.10 cubits, or 360.28 *phyeam*. That includes the distance into and out of the western entrance to the third gallery (42.6 m), measured from and returning to the last step of its western staircase. In fact, this route is very simple and probably quicker to follow than to describe.
6. The measurements for the circumambulation paths through the *preau cruciforme* are based on written figures. They can be compared to pl. 28 of Nafilyan. The written measurements were 53.205 m (122.184 cubits) for the distance from the beginning of the south lateral corridor to the exit to the central western entrance of the second gallery. A total of 148 cubits would be added for the three circuits of each image, making 270.184 cubits in all, or 20.12 latitude units. The total for the same route from the beginning of the northern corridor is 53.28 m (122.356 cubits) plus the 148 cubits for the circuits of the three images, for 270.356 cubits (20.13 latitude units). Another of these 20-unit paths is the most comprehensive pathway through the center of the cruciform in that it connects the three images at the center. A visitor would enter via the main west–east corridor; at the intersection, go north–south to each lateral image; and after returning

to the center, exit to the second gallery through the main west–east corridor again. The north–south arm measures 11.50 m between the centers of each flanking image, or 26.41 cubits. Anyone working this out with a diagram will see that the 2 cubits between the center of the image and the circumambulation path must be considered. The distance out to a lateral image is 2 cubits shorter going and 2 cubits shorter returning because one does not walk to the center of the image and then circuit it. That total of 4 cubits is compensated by the extra 2 cubits needed to walk around to the front of the central image of the triad. At any rate, the total is 268.68 cubits (20.01 latitude units). The exit toward the east is 14.7 m to the center of the *preau cruciforme* and 14.48 m up to the path around the central image. Its opposite (western) distance is 14.67 m plus .4 m for the low decorative step. These measurements vary slightly from those of Nafilyan's pl. 28 (by about .3 m, or less than a cubit).

7. I first observed and photographed this phenomenon at the end of December 1992 and returned to Angkor to study the summer solstice effects in June 1993.
8. Stencel, Gifford, and Morón, "Astronomy and Cosmology," p. 283. The top of the northeast corner tower marks a 5-degree alignment with the northern gateway of the western entrance to the temple and the second projection along the causeway. There are also three 5-degree sighting angles between the top of the southeast corner tower, the southern gateway of the main western entrance, and the third and fourth projections along the causeway. There are two 5-degree angles between the top of the southwest corner tower, the main western entrance to the temple, and the first projection along the causeway, and a 19-degree alignment with the western steps of the cruciform terrace.
9. The east and west sides of the gallery between the protruding bases of the four corner towers are paired for one total and the north and south sides are paired for another total. The measurements were taken from Nafilyan, pls. 11 and 50.
10. Using measurements from pl. 50 of Nafilyan, *Angkor Vat,* one finds that there would be 370.67 cubits in an in-and-out circumambulation of all four corner towers, making three circuits of each image at 4 cubits on a side. The towers average 9.725 m from their base up to the path around the image, according to pl. 50. Written measurements for the corner towers were not available. Although the distance of 370.67 cubits may have some significance in itself, or in relation to the three eastern entrances, it is not clear in what manner.

   The eastern entrance measures 16.46 m from its outer base up to the circumambulation path around its central image. The southern entrance measures 15.304 m for the same distance, and the northern entrance is 15.37 m. Traveling in and out doubles that distance, for a total of 94.37 m (216.48 cubits, 54.12 *phyeam*). These measurements are based on written figures and can be compared to pls. 43 and 46 of Nafilyan. When the images are circumambulated three times, at 4 cubits on a side, the result is 48 × 3, or an additional 144, for a total of 360.52 cubits. This total is also expressed here in the "latitude" unit of 13.43 cubits. Even though it is equivalent to one celestial year in the basic unit of a cubit, the celestial year does not seem to fit in with the other measurement of 370 cubits for the same path in the corner towers. Perhaps a 360-unit and 27-unit distance were meant to be placed together to emphasize the relationship between the lunar month and celestial time (discussed below).

   Outer axial measurements extend from base to base on the outside and from the outer side of the doorway for opposite sides opening onto a corridor. For the main western entrance of the gallery, the outer axes cover its porch on the east, including the width of the balustrade. The measurements are based on written figures and can be compared to pls. 28, 43, 46, and 50 in Nafilyan. They are:

   Eastern entrance: 57.83 m (33.20 *phyeam*)
   Northern entrance: 47.65 m (27.36 *phyeam*)
   Southern entrance: 47.40 m (27.21 *phyeam*)
   Three western entrances: 111.77 m (64.17 *phyeam*)
   Four corner towers: 123.28 m (70.78 *phyeam*)

   In the examples of the eastern, northern, and southern entrances, the outer axes are significant on their own.
11. The distance of 21.13 latitude units (123.57 m) between the *nāga* balustrade and the first step of the stairway to the second gallery is derived from written measurements and Nafilyan, pls. 11, 28, and 37. A dis-

tance of 12 cubits lies between the base of the balustrade and the first step up the cruciform terrace. I measured that distance in 1991 and 1992.

12. The southern lateral entrance measured 9.88 m (22.69 cubits) up to the path around the image; the northern lateral entrance was 9.73 m (22.35 cubits) for the same distance for a total of 45.38 cubits and 44.7 cubits round-trip. The central entrance is 15.4 m between its bottom step on the west and the outer edge of the eastern doorway. The total comes to 286.43 cubits or 21.33 latitude units, including all the circumambulations of the images.
13. The length of the axes of the second gallery is 269.87 m, based on written figures. This length can be compared to the measurements on pls. 11, 28, 43, and 46 of Nafilyan.
14. Nafilyan, pls. 11 and 28. The circumference length is 418.53 m plus 8.25 m for the west–east inner axis of the main western entrance.
15. Unlike all the other galleries at Angkor Wat, every sector of the corridors in this gallery has doors that can close it off. Because of this distinction, each of the sections marked by doors along the periphery of the gallery is counted as a chamber. The doors are an indication that images may once have been installed in each of the 49 sections. From the point of view of historical evolution, these corridors at Angkor Wat and elsewhere had antecedents in the form of separate, long buildings that eventually came to be joined into a rectangular gallery. The rooms in this gallery, then, remind one of these original separate buildings with their distinct, individual, interior spaces.
16. The distance around the gallery is 418.53 m (961.14 cubits), based on the written measurements of Nafilyan's pl. 11. The inner, north–south axis of the northern or southern entrance (8.25 m or 18.95 cubits) in conjunction with the circumference comes to 977.90 cubits or 20 × 48.90 cubits. The axial length can be compared to that on pl. 46 of Nafilyan.

    The eastern entrance (8.28 m, west–east interior axis or 19.02 cubits), in conjunction with the circumference, comes to 980.16 or 20 × 49.008 cubits, based on written figures and Nafilyan, pl. 43.

    Both inner axes of the corner towers up to the circumference are 7.00 m or 16.08 cubits. This gives a total of 977.22 (20 × 48.86) cubits for each corner tower in conjunction with the circumference of the gallery. The corner tower axes are based on written figures and Nafilyan, p. 50.

CHAPTER 8

1. The axes of the gallery measure 83.17 m west–east and 77.19 m north–south, based on written figures except for the lengths of the stairways. These lengths were taken from pl. 14 of Nafilyan, *Angkor Vat*. The total is 160.36 m, or 368.26 cubits, between the bases on all four sides. If the west–east axis is measured to the walkway, that length is 2 cubits shorter, since the base and the first step on the west (a total of 2 cubits) are excluded. Written measurements give slightly longer axes for the upper level. Nafilyan's pl. 14 defines the axes as closer to 365 cubits. A slight adjustment was made when the last step and base were measured in situ, for a total of 368.33 cubits between the base on all four sides. The image in the central sanctuary occupies 10 cubits of that space; the axial total for the main images in the northern, southern, western, and eastern axial entrances is 20 cubits. Therefore, 30 cubits are deducted from the axes when the circumambulation space around the images is eliminated, for a total of 338.33 cubits. The main western and eastern entrances have 30 and 29 steps, respectively. The easternmost entrance on the north (the northeast corner tower, north facade) also appears to have 27 and not 28 steps.
2. There is an average of 91.31 days between equinox and solstice points, but that amount varies from one part of the year to another. The written measurements for the outer axes of the central tower give a slightly longer length than the measurements taken from pl. 22 of Nafilyan. Written measurements record 39.75 m as the axes, or 22.82 *phyeam*.
3. The distance to and from the circumambulation path around the main image in the southern entrance is 27.43 m; in the northern entrance, 27.02 m; in the eastern entrance, 26.12 m. For all three entrances together, the totals are 180 cubits for three circuits of

the images and 185.00 cubits (80.56 m) for the distance up to the circuit around each image and back down to the base of the gallery.

4. The length of the circumambulation route for each of the entrances was based on written measurements. These routes are:

Northern entrance:	121.84 m, 279.80 cubits
Southern entrance:	122.20 m, 280.63 cubits
Eastern entrance:	121.31 m, 278.59 cubits
Total:	365.35 m (839.02 cubits or 209.76 *phyeam*)

5. The lengths for each individual entrance are given in note 4 above.
6. Measurements are based on written figures and Nafilyan, pl. 25.
7. Because each axial chamber is identical on this level, all of the solar-related central images inside must have had the same standing in relation to each other. As the story of the measurements on this level unfolds, that fact becomes more and more obvious. Thus one can calculate the circumference as usual by adding in the west–east axis of the entrance chamber on the west—or adding in the main axis of all four axial chambers, since they are identical. According to Nafilyan, pl. 11, the circumference of the gallery is 191.09 m, or 438.83 cubits. According to written measurements, each axial entrance has an entrant axis of:

Eastern entrance:	7.12 m
Western entrance:	7.07 m
Northern entrance:	7.14 m
Southern entrance:	7.19 m
Total:	28.52 m (65.50 cubits)

8. This length was derived from pls. 11, 14, and 28 of Nafilyan and written measurements.
9. The written figures for the outer axes of the four axial entrances are:

Western entrance:	44.13 m
Eastern entrance:	37.72 m
Northern entrance:	36.56 m
Southern entrance:	37.87 m
Total:	156.28 m (358.89 cubits)

10. The full length of the circumambulation of the central Viṣṇu image from the west is 195.38 m based on written measurements except for the length of the staircase of the western entrance. The path starts at the bottom of the western staircase to the upper elevation. After climbing the steps, we circuit each image in the western entrance three times and then enter the central tower to circuit the image in the large chamber just before the central sanctuary three times, then we circuit the main Viṣṇu image three times. After that, the path ends as we step down the last step out of the central tower on the west. This is the only numerically significant circumambulation path around the central Viṣṇu, approaching from the west, that I could find. The pathway for the axial approaches to the central Viṣṇu is the same as that on the western side of the gallery. The lengths of the pathways are based on written measurements except for the main staircases in the axial entrances, whose lengths are derived from pl. 14. The lengths of the pathways are:

Northern entrance:	189.45 m
Southern entrance:	189.35 m
Eastern entrance:	188.98 m

11. The measurements between the bases on each side of the gallery are based on pls. 11 and 28 and written figures.

West side:	75.59 m
East side:	75.19 m
North side:	74.91 m
South side:	74.70 m
Total:	300.39 m (689.84 cubits)

The length of the sides of the gallery between door pilasters is based on pl. 14 and written figures.

West side:	57.89 m
East side:	57.89 m
North side:	57.76 m
South side:	57.75 m

12. The measurements for the upper elevation of Angkor Wat are based on written figures and the following plans in Nafilyan, *Angkor Vat:*
    - pl. 11: written measurements for circumference
    - pl. 12: height of floor levels from surface of western causeway
    - pl. 14: plan of upper elevation
    - pl. 22: plan of central sanctuary
    - pl. 24: height of central tower
    - pl. 25: plan of southwest corner tower

pl. 27: height of southwest corner tower
pl. 28: western entrances to third and second galleries and walkway to upper level
pl. 37: length of cruciform terrace, south facade

The inner axes for the corner towers were estimated from pl. 24. That plan shows the variations in axial lengths:

Northwest corner tower:	15.70 m
Northeast corner tower:	15.17 m
Southwest corner tower:	15.07 m
Southeast corner tower:	14.73 m
Total:	60.67 m
	(139.33 cubits)

The inner axes for the four directional entrances, based on written figures, are:

Western entrance:	21.85 m
Eastern entrance:	21.80 m
Northern entrance:	21.94 m
Southern entrance:	21.75 m
Total:	87.34 m
	(200.57 cubits)

The inner axes for the central tower, based on pl. 22 and written figures, are 28.03 m, or 64.37 cubits. The total of all the foregoing chambers is 322.27 cubits.

13. The west–east outer axis of the central tower measures 19.90 m, or 45.70 cubits, and the inner west–east axis of the sanctuary is 13.23 cubits, giving 32.47 cubits west–east without the sanctuary.

The north–south outer axis of the tower is 19.825 m, or 45.43 cubits, and the inner north–south axis of the sanctuary is 13.43 cubits for a total of 32.00 cubits north–south without the sanctuary. These figures are based in written measurements and pl. 22 of Nafilyan, *Angkor Vat*. The written measurements for the outer axes of the central tower give a slightly longer length in each case than the measurements taken from Nafilyan. Written measurements record a total of 39.75 m as the axes. That figure comes to 22.82 *phyeam*. When the west–east and north–south axes of the main Viṣṇu image (2.5 *phyeam*) are subtracted from that total, the result is 20.32 *phyeam* without the image.

14. The length of the outer axes of the four axial entrances, based on written figures is given in note 9; the outer axes of the central tower are discussed in note 13. The inner axes of each of these entrances and of the tower are given in note 12.

15. The height of the central tower, based on written figures and pl. 24, is 58.08 m, or 33.35 *phyeam,* between the top of the capstone and the level of the sacred deposit. The measurements for the vertical divisions in the central tower are based on pl. 24 of Nafilyan and written figures. There is 23.45 m. (53.85 cubits) between the top of the shaft under the central tower and the level of the sacred deposit (written measurements). The distance between the top of the capstone and the point at which the square sanctuary turns into a round tower is 22.28 m, or 51.17 cubits (pl. 24). That point is suggested as the height of the sanctuary because of the physical change from a square format to the round tower. Any interior wooden ceiling has long since disappeared. The height of the sanctuary, measured between the top of the shaft and the top of its square walls, is 11.95 m, or 28.36 cubits. It is estimated that the finial that was once inserted into the central hole of the capstone (1 cubit in depth) was 4 cubits long and rose for 3 cubits over the top of the capstone. The vertical measurements of the tower, from top to bottom, would then be 54.17, 28.36, and 53.85 cubits.

16. The inner axes are measured between thresholds (doorways). In the case of the side chambers, there are only two doorways, so only the long axis is measured. It is as though the axis in these chambers were a continuation of the axis in the central chamber. For the combination of the inner axes and the circumference, the measurements were based on written figures. The procedure was to subtract the width of the thresholds along the circumference from the circumference and then add the inner axis perpendicular to the circumference. The result is a combination of full inner axial measurements and the circumference of the gallery up to that entrance. The circumference is 191.09 m (n. 7). The lengths subtracted for the thresholds were 2.41 m for the southern entrance, 2.5 m for the northern entrance, 2.56 m for the western entrance, and 2.48 m for the eastern entrance.

17. The 20-unit distances are taken from the written measurements of Trouvé and pl. 22 of Nafilyan. They are

measured between the bottom of the exterior step and the circumambulation path around the image. The distances are:

West side:	20.33 cubits
East side:	20.19 cubits
North side:	20.36 cubits
South side:	19.98 cubits

The written measurements specifically for the inner axes of the central sanctuary were not available in the remaining records of Nafilyan. Plate 22 of *Angkor Vat* shows slightly larger inner axes for the sanctuary than the written figures of Trouvé. Because of these minor discrepancies, measurements for the axial lengths of the sanctuary may vary. For example, the outer axes derived from Nafilyan's written figures and the plan of the sanctuary are 91.29 cubits, as noted earlier. If the written figures of Trouvé are used, the axes would be closer to 90.86 cubits.

18. In 1935 Georges Trouvé supervised the final, successful attempt to retrieve the sacred deposit of the temple. The shaft was filled with water and it took about 8 months to get to the bottom and pull up the two stones that hid the deposit between them: a cavity about 12 cm deep in the bottom stone contained two white sapphires and two gold leaves. The leaves bore impressions from two other leaves, then missing. This was one of the very rare times in the history of work at Angkor that a sacred deposit was uncovered. The story is told in Georges Trouvé, "Chronique," *BEFEO* 35 (1935): 483–486, and in George Coedès, "Discovery of the Sacred Deposit," pp. 43–47.
19. In his book *L'astronomie Indienne,* Roger Billard discusses the fact that the astronomer Āryabhaṭa calculated equal yuga periods of 1,080,000 years. Billard believes that these four equal periods antedated the four unequal periods as we know them from later texts. If he is right, then the importance of the number 108 to the yuga cycles is even more evident.
20. This measurement is based on written figures and pls. 11, 14, and 28 of Nafilyan. The distance between the *nāga* balustrade and the cruciform terrace was estimated at 12 cubits based on photographs and measurements which include that area.
21. The northwest, northeast, and southwest corner towers show a distance of 12.83 m up to the circumambulation path around the main image. That distance is 13.23 m for the southeast tower. The total, going in and out of all four towers, is 103.44 m (237.55 cubits), and the three circuits of all four images equal 192 cubits. Together, the full in-and-out circumambulation is 429.55 cubits, or 107.39 *phyeam*. These figures are based on pl. 14 of Nafilyan.
22. The measurements of the inner axes of the corner towers are given in note 12 above. The measurement without the images is 8 cubits less for each tower (the axes of the circumambulation space around the image), or 32 cubits less for all four towers.

    The length for the full vertical height of the corner towers was based on written measurements and on pls. 12 and 27 of Nafilyan. The heights are:

Northwest tower:	47.05 m
Northeast tower:	46.96 m
Southwest tower:	46.81 m
Southeast tower:	46.85 m
Total:	187.67 m (107.75 *phyeam*)

In Morón, "Configurations," pp. 248–249, n. 55, the measurements for the distance between the floors of the corner towers and the level of the sacred deposit were too long by .18 m. The level of the causeway was given as 1.44 m aboveground, whereas it is closer to 1.26 m. This new figure is derived from calculations of the ground levels of Nafilyan and Trouvé, the level of the top of the shaft of the central sanctuary, and the height of the deposit stone and depth of the cavity in the deposit stone.

CHAPTER 9

1. Coedès, "Études Cambodgiennes X: L'inscription de Prasat Pram," *BEFEO* 13/6 (1913): 24. I once asked Roger Billard if the planets were listed in the order of their appearance in the sky, in the order of the constellations, or in the order of the days of the week. He checked his database and said their order varies. There was no set rule.
2. These examples are listed in Chapter 7. Most are either circumference measurements or in conjunction with entrances along the circumference.

3. One occurrence is in the axes of the side chambers to the east and west entrances in the third gallery. There are 44 Kaurava leaders in the Battle of Kurukṣetra, 44 pillars around the northern and southern lateral entrances on the west side of the fourth enclosure, 44 pillars around the main western entrance of the second gallery, and the axes of that gallery are 44 latitude units in length. These lengths were discussed in the preceding chapter.
4. There is much more information about the Bakheng than can be cited here. The numbers of steps, staircases, and towers and other aspects of the ground plan and elevation were obtained in situ, but more easily and less expensively, from the plans in Jacques Dumarçay, *Le Phnom Bakheng,* Mémoires Archéologiques VII (Paris: École française d'Extrême-Orient, 1971).
5. Data on the towers and architecture of Candi Sewu were obtained from Jacques Dumarçay, *Candi Sewu et l'Architecture Buddhique du Centre de Java* (Paris: École française d'Extrême-Orient, 1981). I am indebted to the work of a student, Jan Mrazek, for much of the numerical analysis of Candi Sewu.

BIBLIOGRAPHY

Angkor: L'Art Khmèr au Cambodge et en Thaïlande. Dossiers Histoire et Archéologie 125, March 1988.

Aung-Thwin, Michael. "Divinity, Spirit, and Human Conceptions of Classical Burmese Kingship." In *Centers, Symbols, and Hierarchies: Essays on the Classical States of Southeast Asia.* Edited by Lorraine Gesick. New Haven: Yale University, Southeast Asia Studies, 1983.

Aymonier, Étienne. "Première étude sur les inscriptions Tchames." *JA* 17 (Jan./Feb. 1891): 5–86.

———. *Le Cambodge.* Vol. 1: *Le Royaume actuel.* Vol. 2: *Les Provinces Siamoises.* Vol. 3: *Le Groupe d'Angkor et l'histoire.* Paris: G. Van Oest, 1901–1903.

Banerjea, Jitendra Nath. *The Development of Hindu Iconography.* Calcutta: University of Calcutta, 1956.

Barth, Auguste. *Inscriptions sanskrits du Cambodge.* Vol. 27, pt. 1, fasc. 1. Paris: Académie des Inscriptions et Belles Lettres, Notices et Extraites des Manuscripts de la Bibliothèque Nationale, 1885.

Bedekar, V. M. "The Legend of the Churning of the Ocean in the Epics and the Purāṇas: A Comparative Study." *Purāṇa* 9/1 (Jan. 1967): 7–61.

Benisti, Mireille. *Rapports entre le premier art Khmèr et l'art Indien.* Mémoire Archéologique V. Paris: École française d'Extrême-Orient, 1970.

Bergaigne, Abel. "L'Ancien royaume de Campa." *JA* 11 (Jan. 1888): 5–105.

Le Bhagavata Purāṇa. Translated by Eugene Burnouf. 5 vols. Paris: Imprimerie Royale, 1840–1898.

Bhattacharyya, Asoke Kumar. "The Themes of Churning of the Ocean in Indian and Khmer Art." *AA* 6/2 (1959): 121–134.

Bhattacharya, Kamaleswar. "Notes d'iconographie khmère." *AA* 4/3 (1957): 211–213.

———. "Note sur le Śivapāda." *JA* 252/3 (1964): 379–382.

———. "Notes d'iconographie Khmère, XI, Les *navagraha* et les 'neuf divinités.'" *AA* 10/1 (1964): 91–94.

Billard, Roger. *L'astronomie Indienne.* PEFEO 83. Paris: École française d'Extrême-Orient, 1971.

Biot, J. B. *Études sur l'astronomie Indienne et sur l'astronomie Chinoise.* Paris: Albert Blanchard, 1969. Reprint.

Boisselier, Jean. "Beng Mealea et la chronologie des monuments du style d'Angkor Vat." *BEFEO* 46/1 (1952): 187–226.

———. "Notes sur les bas-reliefs tardifs d'Angkor Vat." *JA* 250/2 (1962): 244–248.

———. *Manuel d'archéologie d'Extrême-Orient, Asie du Sud-Est.* Pt. 1, vol. 1: *Le Cambodge.* Paris: A. & J. Picard, 1966.

Boner, Alice, and Sadāṣiva Rath Śarmā. *New Light on the Sun Temple of Koṇāraka.* Varanasi: Chowkhamba Sanskrit Series Office, 1972.

Bosch, F. D. K. "Notes archéologiques IV: Le temple d'Angkor Vat." *BEFEO* 32 (1932): 7–21.

Boulbet, J., and Bruno Dagens. "Les Sites archéologiques de la region du Bhnam Gulen (Phnom Kulen)." *AA* 27, Special Issue, 1973.

Briggs, Lawrence Palmer. *The Ancient Khmer Empire.* Transactions of the American Philosophical Society, n.s., vol. 41, pt. 1. Philadelphia: American Philosophical Society, 1951.

Brown, Robert. *Researches into the Primitive Constellations of the Greeks, Phoenicians, and Babylonians.* 2 vols. London and Oxford: Williams & Norgate, 1899; Ann Arbor: University Microfilms, 1979.

"Carte archéologique d'Angkor." *BEFEO* 37/2 (1937): 64 and pl. 110.

"Carte archéologique de la region d'Angkor." *BEFEO* 41/2 (1941): facing p. 333.

Coedès, George. "L'inscription de Baksei Camkron." *JA,* 10th ser., 13 (1909): 496–510.

———. "Les bas-reliefs d'Angkor Vat." *BCAI* 11 (1911): 170–220.

———. "Études Cambodgiennes IX: Le serment des fonctionnaires de Sūryavarman I." *BEFEO* 13 (1913): 11–17.

———. "Études Cambodgiennes X: L'inscription de Prasat Pram." *BEFEO* 13/6 (1913): 17–26.

———. "Études Cambodgiennes XII: Le site primitif de Tchen-la. *BEFEO* 18/9 (1918): 1–3.

———. "Études Cambodgiennes VI: Des édicules appelés 'bibliothèques.'" *BEFEO* 22 (1922): 405–406.

———. "Études Cambodgiennes XXIV: Nouvelles données chronologiques et genéalogiques sur la dynastie de Mahīdharapura." *BEFEO* 29 (1929): 297–330.

———. "Études Cambodgiennes." *BEFEO* 32/1 (1932): 71–112.

———. "Angkor Vat, temple ou tombeau?" *BEFEO* 33 (1933): 303–309.

———. "Discovery of the Sacred Deposit of Angkor Wat." *ABIA* 10 (1935): 43–47.

———. *Inscriptions du Cambodge.* 8 vols. Paris: École française d'Extrême-Orient, 1942–1966.

———. "L'origine du cycle des douze animoux au Cambodge." *T'oung Pao* 31 (1935): 315–329.

———. "Études Cambodgiennes." *BEFEO* 43 (1943–1946): 1–8.

———. "The *Traibhūmikakatha,* Buddhist Cosmology and Treatise on Ethics." *East and West* 4 (Jan. 1957): 349–352.

———. "La date d'exécution des deux bas-reliefs tardifs d'Angkor Vat." *JA* 250/2 (1962): 235–243.

———. *The Indianized States of Southeast Asia.* Edited by Walter F. Vella. Translated by Susan Brown. Honolulu: East-West Center Press, 1968.

Coedès, George, and C. Archaimbault. *Les Trois Mondes (Trai Bhūmi Braḥ Rvan).* PEFEO 89. Paris: École française d'Extrême-Orient, 1973.

Coedès, George, and Pierre Dupont. "Les stèles de Sdok Kak Thom, Phnom Sandak, et Prah Vihar." *BEFEO* 43 (1943–1946): 57–154.

Collins, Sandra. "The Lizard-Portal Motif: Its Meaning and Function." Master's thesis, University of Michigan, 1976.

Condiminas, George, et al. *Disciplines Croisées: Hommage à Bernard-Philippe Groslier.* Paris: Éditions de l'École des Hautes Études en Sciences Sociales, 1992.

Dagens, Bruno. *Mayamata.* Pt. 1. Pondicherry: Institut Français d'Indologie, 1970.

Danielou, Alain. *Hindu Polytheism.* New York: Bollingen Foundation, 1964.

de Mestier du Bourg, Hubert. "La Première moitié du XIe siècle au Cambodge." *JA* 258/3–4 (1970): 281–314.

Dikshit, Sankar Balakrishna. *Bhāratīya Jyotish Śāstra* (History of Indian astronomy). 2 vols. Translated by R. V. Vaidya. Delhi: Manager of Publications, Civil Line, 1969.

Originally published as *Bhāratīya Jyotish Śāstracha Prachin Ani Arvachin Itihas,* 1896.

Dumarçay, Jacques. *Le Phnom Bakheng.* Mémoires archéologiques VII. Paris: École française d'Extrême-Orient, 1971.

———. *Candi Sewu et l'Architecture Buddhique du Centre de Java.* Paris: École française d'Extrême-Orient, 1981.

———. *Documents Graphiques de la Conservation d'Angkor, 1963–1973;* Paul Courbin, *La Fouille de Sras Srang.* Collection de Textes et Documents sur l'Indochine 17. Paris: École française d'Extrême-Orient, 1988.

Dumarçay, Jacques, and Bernard-Philippe Groslier. *Le Bayon.* Mémoires archéologiques III–2. 2 vols. Paris: École française d'Extrême-Orient, 1973.

Dupont, Pierre. *Catalogue des Collections Indochinoises.* Paris: Musées Nationaux, 1934.

Faraut, F. Gaspard. *Astronomie Cambodgienne.* Saigon: F. H. Schneider, 1910.

Filliozat, Jean. "Le symbolisme du monument de Phnom Bakheng." *BEFEO* 44/2 (1954): 527–544.

———. "Le Temple de Hari dans le Harivarsa." *AA* 8/3 (1961): 195–202.

Finot, Louis. "Notes d'epigraphie XI: Les inscriptions de Mi-Son." *BEFEO* 4 (1904): 897–977.

———. "Sur quelques traditions Indochinoises." *BCAI* 11 (1911): 30–37.

———. "Notes d'archéologie Cambodgienne I: Nouvelles inscriptions Cambodgiens." *BCAI* 12 (1912): 183–189.

———. "Notes d'archéologie Cambodgienne II: Deux bas-reliefs d'Angkor Vat, tir à l'arc." *BCAI* 12 (1912): 191–193.

———. "Notes d'épigraphie XIII: L'inscription de Ban That." *BEFEO* 12/2 (1912): 1–27.

———. "Recherches sur la literature Laotienne." *BEFEO* 17/5 (1917): 171–172.

Finot, Louis, Victor Goloubew, and George Coedès. *Le Temple d'Angkor Vat.* Mémoires archéologiques II. 3 pts. Paris: G. Van Oest, 1929–1932.

Giteau, Madeleine. "Le barattage de l'Océan au Cambodge." *BSEI,* n.s. 26/2 (1951): 141–159.

———. "Une representation de la Bhikṣāṭanamūrti de Çiva à Angkor Vat." *AA* 11/1 (1966): 131–138.

———. *Angkor, un peuple—un art.* Paris: Bibliothèque des Arts, 1976.

Heesterman, Johannes Cornelius. *The Ancient Indian Royal Consecration.* The Hague: Mouton, 1957.

Jacques, Claude. "Études d'épigraphie Cambodgiennes VI: Sur les données chronologiques de la stèle de Tuol Ta Pec (K834)." *BEFEO* 58 (1971): 165–166.

———. "Études d'épigraphie Cambodgienne IX: Sur l'emplacement du royaume d'Aninditapura." *BEFEO* 59 (1972): 195–205.

———. *Angkor.* Paris: Borbas, 1990.

Kaye, George Rusby. "The *Nakṣatra* and Precession." *IA* (Feb. 1921): 44–48.

Kaulācāra, Rāmacandra. *Śilpa Prakāśa.* Translated by Alice Boner. Leiden: E. J. Brill, 1969.

Kemp, Jeremy. *Aspects of Siamese Kingship in the Seventeenth Century.* Bangkok: Social Science Association Press of Thailand, 1969.

Kramrisch, Stella. *The Hindu Temple.* 2 vols. Calcutta: University of Calcutta, 1946.

Le Clere, Adhemard. "La Fête des eaux à Phnom Penh." *BEFEO* 4/1–2 (1904): 120–130.

The Mahābhārata, Books 1–5. Translated by Johannes Adriannus Bernardus van Buitenen. Chicago and London: University of Chicago Press, 1973–1978.

Malleret, Louis. "Contribution à l'étude du thème des neuf divinités dans la sculpture du Cambodge et du Champa." *AA* 7/3 (1960): 205–230.

Mannikka, Eleanor. "Angkor: Relationships Between the Pyramid-Temple and the City." *AARP* 4 (Dec. 1978): 65–68.

———. "Angkor Wat: Meaning through Measurement." Ph.D. dissertation, University of Michigan, 1985.

———. "The Battle of Laṅkā at Angkor Wat: A Visual Metaphor." In *The Legend of Rāma: Artistic Visions.* Edited by Vidya Dehejia. Bombay: Marg, 1994.

Marchal, Henri. *Guide archéologique aux temples d'Angkor.* Paris and Brussels: G. Van Oest, 1928.

Markel, Stephan. *Origins of the Indian Planetary Deities.* Studies in Asian Thought and Religion, vol. 16. Lewiston, N.Y.: Mellen, 1995.

Maspero, Georges. *Le Royaume du Champa.* Paris and Brussels: Librairie nationale d'art et d'histoire, 1928.

Matsya Purāṇam. Translated by A Talukdar of Oudh. *The Sacred Books of the Hindus.* Edited by Major B. D. Bose. Vol. 17. New York: AMS Press, 1974. Originally published in 1916.

Mazzeo, Donatella, and Chiara Silvi Antonini. *Monuments of Civilization: Ancient Cambodia.* London: Cassell, 1978.

McGill, Forrest. "The Art and Architecture of the Reign of King Prāsātthōng of Ayutthayā (1629–1656)." Ph.D. dissertation, University of Michigan, 1977.

McGovern, William. *A Manual of Buddhist Philosophy.* Lucknow: Oriental Reprinters, 1976.

Meister, Michael W. "*Maṇḍala* and Practice in Nāgara Architecture in North India." *JAOS* 99/2 (1979): 204–219.

———. "Muṇḍeśvari: Ambiguity and Certainty in the Analysis of a Temple Plan." In *Kalādarṣana.* Edited by Joanna G. Williams. New Delhi: Oxford and IBH, 1981.

Mitra, Debala. "A Study of Some *Graha* Images of India and Their Possible Bearing on the *Nava-devas* of Cambodia." *Journal of the Asiatic Society of Calcutta* 7:1–2 (1965): 13–37.

Morón, Eleanor. "Configurations of Time and Space at Angkor Wat." *Studies in Indo-Asian Art and Culture* 5 (Dec. 1977): 217–261.

Mouhot, Henri. *Voyage dans les royaumes du Siam, de Cambodge, et de Laos.* Paris: Hachette, 1868.

Mus, Paul. "Angkor in the Time of Jayavarman VII." *IAL,* n.s. 11/2 (1937): 65–75.

Nafilyan, Guy. *Angkor Vat: description graphique du temple.* Mémoire archéologique IV. Paris: École française d'Extrême-Orient, 1969.

Neugebauer, Otto, and David Pingree. *The Pañcasiddhāntikā of Varahāmihira.* 2 vols. Historisk-Filosofiske Skrifter, no. 6:1:1–2. Copenhagen: Danske Videnskabernes Selskab, 1970–71.

Parmentier, Henri. *L'Art khmèr classique: monuments du quadrant nord-est.* PEFEO 29. Paris: École française d'Extrême-Orient, 1930.

———. *Angkor: Guide.* Saigon: A. Portail, 1955.

Pichard, P. "Note sur quelques ouvrages inachevés à Pimai et à Panom Rung." *Sinlapa lae bōrānkkadi nai Prathēt That (Art and Archaeology in Thailand)* 1. Bangkok: Fine Arts Department, 1974.

Pingree, David. "On the Greek Origin of the Indian Planetary Model Employing a Double Epicycle." *Journal for the History of Astronomy* 2 (1971): 80–85.

———. "The Mesopotamian Origin of Early Indian Mathematical Astronomy." *Journal for the History of Astronomy* 4 (1973): 1–12.

———. "The Recovery of Greek Astronomy from India." *Journal for the History of Astronomy* 7 (1976): 109–123.

———. "History of Mathematical Astronomy in India." *Dictionary of Scientific Biography* 15 (1978): 533–633.

———. Trans. and ed. *The Yavanajātaka of Sphujidhvaja.* 2 vols. Harvard Oriental Series, no. 48. Cambridge: Harvard University Press, 1978.

———. "Jyotiḥśāstra." In *A History of Indian Literature.* Wiesbaden: Otto Harrassowitz, 1981.

Poree-Maspero, Eveline. "Nouvelle étude sur la *Nāgī* Somā." *JA* 238 (1950): 237–267.

———. "Notes sur les particularités du culte chez les Cambodgiens." *BEFEO* 44/2 (1954): 619–641.

Przyluski, Jean. "Pradakśiṇa et prasavya en Indochine." In *Sonderdruck aus Festschrift fur M. Winternitz zum Siebzigsten Geburtstag.* Edited by Otto Harrassowitz. Leipzig: Otto Harrassowitz, 1933.

Rāmāyaṇa of Vālmikī. Translated by Hari Prasad Shastri. 3 vols. London: Shanti Sanda, 1952–1957.

"Review of *Siamese State Ceremonies: Their History and Function.*" *JIH* 11/3 (Dec. 1932): 401.

Rigveda Brāhmanas: The Aitareya and Kauṣītaki Brāhmaṇas of the Rigveda. Translated by Arthur Berriedal Keith. Harvard Oriental Series, 25. Cambridge: Harvard University Press, 1920.

Roeske, M. "L'enfer Cambodgien d'après le Trai Phum (Tri Bhūmi), les Trois Mondes." *JA,* 11th ser., 4 (1914): 587–606.

Roy, S. B. *Prehistoric Lunar Astronomy.* New Delhi: Institute of Chronology, 1976.

Rudaux, Lucien, and G. de Vaucouleurs. *Larousse Encyclopedia of Astronomy.* 2nd ed. New York: Prometheus Press, 1962.

Sastri, T. S. Kuppanna. "Some Misinterpretations and Omissions by Thibaut and Sudhakara Dvivedi in the Pañcasiddhāntikā of Varāhamihira." *Vishveshvaranand Indological Journal* 11 (1973): 107–118.

Śatapatha Brāhmaṇa. Translated by Julius Eggeling. *Sacred Books of the East.* Edited by F. Max Müller. Vols. 12 and 56. Oxford: Clarendon Press, 1882–1884.

Spink, Walter. "Ajanta Chronology: Politics and Patronage." In *Kalādarśana*. Edited by Joanna G. Williams. New Delhi: Oxford and IBH, 1981.

Stencel, Robert, Fred Gifford, and Eleanor Morón. "Astronomy and Cosmology at Angkor Wat." *Science* 193 (1976): 281–287.

Stern, Philippe. "Diversité et rythme des fondations royales Khmères." *BEFEO* 44/2 (1954): 649–687.

Stierlin, Henri. *Angkor.* Fribourg: Office du Livre, 1970.

Sunnary, Lan. "Étude iconographique du temple khmèr de Thommanon (Dhammananda)." *AA* 25 (1972): 155–198.

Sūrya Siddhānta. Translated by Ebenezer Burgess. Varanasi and Delhi: Indological Book House, 1977. Originally published in 1860.

Trouvé, Georges. "Chronique." *BEFEO* 35 (1935): 483–486.

Tuckerman, Bryant. *Planetary, Lunar, and Solar Positions A.D. 2 to A.D. 1649 at Five-Day and Ten-Day Intervals.* 2 vols. Philadelphia: American Philosophical Society, 1964.

Varāha, Mihira. *Bṛhat Saṁhitā*. Translated by Hendrik Kern. *JRAS,* n.s. 5 (1872): 231–28 and n.s. 6 (1873): 36–91.

———. *The Panchasiddhāntikā*. Translated by G. Thibaut and Mahāmahōpadhyāya Sudhākara Dvivedī. Benares: Medical Hall Press, 1889.

———. *The Brihajjātakam of Varāha Mihira*. Translated by Swami Vijnanananda (Hari Prasanna Chaterjee). *Sacred Books of the Hindus.* Edited by Major B. D. Bose. New York: AMS Press, 1974. Originally published in 1912.

Vishṇu Purāṇa. Translated by Horace Hayman Wilson. 5 vols. London: Trubner, 1864–1870.

Wales, Horace G. Quaritch. *Siamese State Ceremonies.* London: Bernard Quaritch, 1931.

———. *Supplementary Notes on Siamese State Ceremonies.* London: Bernard Quaritch, 1971.

Werner, Edward T. C. *A Dictionary of Chinese Mythology.* New York: Julian Press, 1961.

Woodward, Hiram. "Tantric Buddhism at Angkor Thom." *AO* 12 (1981): 57–67.

Wyatt, David K. "The Thai 'Kata Maṇḍiarapāla' and Malacca." *JSS* 55/2 (1967): 279–286.

Yano, Michio. "Knowledge of Astronomy in Sanskrit Texts of Architecture (Orientation Methods in the *Īśanaśivagurudevapaddhati*)." *Indo-Iranian Journal* 29:1 (1986): 17–29.

Zhou Daguan. *Mémoires sur les coutumes du Cambodge de Tcheou Ta-Kouan*. Translated by Paul Pelliot. Paris: Librairie d'Amérique et d'Orient, 1951.

INDEX

Note: Italicized numbers refer to the illustrations.